CABBAGE AND CAVIAR

FOODS AND NATIONS is a new series from Reaktion that explores the history – and geography – of food. Books in the series reveal the hidden history behind the food eaten today in different countries and regions of the world, telling the story of how food production and consumption developed, and how they were influenced by the culinary practices of other places and peoples. Each book in the Foods and Nations series offers fascinating insights into the distinct flavours of a country and its culture.

Cabbage and Caviar

A History of Food
in Russia

Alison K. Smith

REAKTION BOOKS

Published by Reaktion Books Ltd
Unit 32, Waterside
44–48 Wharf Road
London N1 7UX, UK
www.reaktionbooks.co.uk

First published 2021
Copyright © Alison K. Smith 2021

Printed and bound in India by Replika Press Pvt. Ltd

A catalogue record for this book is available from the British Library

ISBN 978 1 78914 364 5

CONTENTS

A NOTE ON TRANSLITERATION AND TRANSLATION

Transliterations from Cyrillic in the text use a simplified version of the Library of Congress system, omitting hard and soft signs and diacritics. Hard and soft signs are included in transliterations in the References and Bibliography. Some Russian words and names have come regularly into use in English with spellings that do not follow these rules (blini, borscht, rouble, soviet, Mikoyan, Yeltsin) or by using English equivalents (Peter the Great instead of Petr the Great); I use the familiar English versions. All translations from Russian and French are my own unless otherwise noted. Quotations from English-language sources retain original spellings and punctuation.

Two men drinking tea, with samovar, mid- to late 19th century,
photograph by William Carrick and John MacGregor.

INTRODUCTION
Let Us Begin with Soup

In 1837, the same year that the great Russian poet Alexander Pushkin was killed in a duel, a man named Vladimir Burnashev published two new entries in a rather different field of literature: books for children. Burnashev had begun his career as a journalist earlier in the decade, publishing descriptions of Russian industrialists in the newspaper the *Northern Bee*, one of the most widely read periodicals in the empire. He would go on to edit the journal of the Russian Free Economic Society, to publish several cookbooks, to write his memoirs, and at the end of his life to write stories for a mass peasant audience. In the middle of the 1830s, however, he turned to children's literature. In a series of books (and writing under a pseudonym), Burnashev introduced his young readers to the Russian Empire, to world geography and, of all things, to economics. His was a capacious understanding of economics, encompassing not just trade and manufacturing, not just agriculture, but also home economics. And part of the home economy, Burnashev made clear, was the kitchen and all of the good things that came out of it.

'Let us begin with soup,' he began, because soups were among the most important of Russian dishes:

> There are various kinds of soups; soup made of bouillon has
> as its most important base a good piece of good beef, which
> is boiled in water, and then this water is called bouillon;
> in it one can put groats, greens, forcemeat, quenelles, or
> sometimes *pelmeni*, as one desires. And do you know what
> *pelmeni* are? They are a Siberian dish, and nothing other than
> small dumplings made of beef, which are not fried, but instead
> boiled in soup. Milk soup is made from scalded milk with some

Everyone in Russia ate bread, from peasants to nobles. This print, one of a number showing different street vendors in the 19th century, shows a man carrying a tray laden with large, round loaves of what was almost certainly sour, rye bread – perhaps the quintessential Russian food.

sort of grain or noodles; noodles are mixed up flour and egg, making a thick dough, which, having been rolled out with a pin, is cut into thin strips. Pea soup is made of boiled big peas; for taste, one adds pork to this soup, and sprinkles on *grenki*, that is, white bread fried until dry.[1]

What a set of possibilities to begin a meal! A simple bouillon, a more complicated pea soup, even dumplings.

Elsewhere in the text, Burnashev turned not just to descriptions of foods but also to instructions for how foods were made. In particular, although soup came first, bread was close behind: it was, as he put it, 'the principal basis of our food'. Burnashev gave instructions for making bread, although instructions that were unlikely to bring his would-be child bakers much success. While he gave specific instructions as to how long to bake bread for (up to three hours for the largest loaves), he forgot to mention any leavening agent among the ingredients.[2] Or rather, he forgot to explain how to make Russian sour bread rise – via the remnants of dough left over in the mixing bowl, which served as a starter for the next batch. (In this he was not alone. Another book from the following year began a description of bread baking with the statement that 'the leavening of dough for breads from rye flour is known to everyone who makes them', hardly useful advice for someone new to bread-baking.³)

In the middle of his description of specific foods, Burnashev shifted gears entirely and described 'Russian cuisine' as a particular cuisine within the context of other European cuisines:

> The table that is kept here in Russia in all houses is a mixture of the most refined French table with the most elegant of all others, from German, English and Russian, because at one and the same dinner you eat *botvinia*, and then a French soup to warm the stomach, then an English beef steak, Italian macaroni, a German sweet salad for the roast and so on and so on. In general, every nation has its preferred foods. Let's look at them quickly. Almost every people has its favourite national dish: the Turk, the Greek, the Persian, the Georgian, the Armenian, the Arab do not sit at their carpet that serves as a table without pilaf . . . the Englishman always eats roast beef and beefsteaks . . . the Italian adores macaroni, vermicelli and a particular kind of bread called polenta. The German particularly admires blood sausage, beer soup and goose with a stuffing of shredded cabbage and with apples.⁴

Burnashev included a specifically Russian dish in this description of the Russian table – *botvinia* was a cold soup based on the lightly fermented drink *kvas* with beetroot, greens and fish – but he was also suggesting that the normal way of eating, at least among a certain undefined stratum of society, was harder to define as purely 'Russian'. At the same time, however, even here he made clear the idea that different peoples had different particular foods.

Russian tables of the moderately elite might welcome foods from many lands, but there were also 'national Russian dishes'. Burnashev's description of them came elsewhere:

> National Russian dishes are *shchi*, instead of soup, thick buckwheat *kasha* with fat or butter, *kulebiaka*, *okroshka*, *botvinia*, suckling pig with horseradish, sour cabbage, *kvas* of various sorts and *sbiten*; and for *Maslenitsa* blini, especially *krasnye* [literally 'beautiful' but here meaning of wheat flour]

or buckwheat. Here is everything that the not-made-delicate Russian prefers to the delicacy and exquisiteness of the French table, which is not infrequently very dangerous for the stomach and always hard on the wallet.[5]

What were all these dishes? *Shchi* was cabbage soup, and *kasha* was porridge, usually cooked from buckwheat groats. A *kulebiaka* was a particular kind of baked savoury pie filled with fish (and one that found fame outside Russia as *coulibiac*). *Okroshka* and *botvinia* were both cold soups based on *kvas*, usually described as a sour, slightly fermented drink brewed from bread. *Sbiten* was a hot, spiced drink and blini were small, yeast-raised pancakes of wheat or buckwheat flour eaten in huge quantities during the pre-Lent festival of *Maslenitsa*. Burnashev portrayed these foods as simpler in preparation, as heartier and more filling, and as cheaper, as well, in comparison to the French cuisine that already stood for refinement.

This image of the tough Russian stomach opposed to French refine-ment also appeared in another section, in Burnashev's description of the mechanisms of cooking. He contrasted the modern 'English' stove, capable of cooking the 'renowned and delicate sauces and fricassees . . . which have been brought to us by foreigners and now gratify our educated taste', with the traditional Russian stove, which 'had not changed since the time that thrifty housewives and even noble *boyarinas* themselves still cooked and worked in the kitchen'. That stove prepared true Russian foods:

> they cooked tasty *pokhlebki*, roasted fatty geese, pheasants,
> turkeys, baked *pirogi*, made mead and cordials . . . Our
> predecessors were not delicate gourmands: they loved
> only to be filled, and were satisfied with *shchi* with salted
> meat or beef, with *salnik*, with various roasts, with *pirogi*,
> blini, and *karavai*.[6]

Here Burnashev includes a few new foods – a *pokhlebka* was a soup, but a heartier one than the bouillon-based ones of French cuisine; a *salnik* was an organ-meat dumpling wrapped in caul fat; *pirogi* were filled pies or turnovers of some sort; and *karavai* were decorated breads, sometimes with a filling, usually made of an enriched dough and often associated with celebrations and festivities. Again, Burnashev portrays Russian cuisine as something hearty, filling and comparatively simple (though not all of these dishes were actually that easy to prepare).

All of these descriptions were meant to describe the world of Russia's small but growing reading public – probably not the world of the wealthiest of Russia's nobles, but the world of small-scale serf-owners on their estates and of merchants and bureaucrats in Russia's towns. Even the description of the 'Russian stove' emphasized that this is what a '*boyarina*' might have prepared. In another children's book published that same year, Burnashev described something different: the 'table of the Russian common man', by which he meant the Russian peasant, and particularly the Russian serf. This description was related, but distinctly different:

> he eats a lot and loves healthy, nutritious and simple food: bread, meat, *shchi* or another kind of hot soup and *kasha*; on holidays *pirogi*; during fasts fish and mushrooms. That is the

Mushrooms were and are one of the most characteristic foods on the Russian table. This illustration from a 17th-century traveller's account shows several varieties, including *smorchki* (morels) (2), *rizhiki* (milk caps) (3) and *masleniki* (butter mushrooms) (6).

normal food in winter; at other times of the year he uses a lot of turnips, radishes, carrots, onions, cucumbers, all sorts of garden vegetables. Onion, *kvas*, bread and salt – those are the elements from which the poorest peasant prepares a quantity of different dishes.[7]

Soups, bread, *kasha* and *pirogi* – all were part of both descriptions of Russian food. Elite tables were influenced by foreign goods, and here Burnashev describes other influences on the Russian food of the common folk: the time of year and the religious calendar with its fasts. Both affected how and what Russians ate, giving a certain kind of abundance in summer and a certain kind of restriction in fasting periods. Furthermore, Burnashev went on to note, Russia's peasants and workers also ate in a different manner than did its more elite subjects. Rather than sitting to table at defined times, the Russian peasant 'generally worries about neither the time nor the place of his breakfasts or dinners. He eats where he happens to be and at that time that he feels a need to do so.' As a result, Russia's towns were places where there were not only 'pubs or simple taverns for the people' but

> hundreds of vendors walk the streets or stand near the bridges with foods and drinks, depending on the time of year . . . They sell: rich white bread, buns, pretzels, hot *pirogi* with various fillings, blini, *studen*, *kisel*, cooked fish, caviar, salted mushrooms, cucumbers, baked eggs, vegetables and so on. To drink, in winter they carry aromatic *sbiten*, in huge copper urns swathed in white linen; in summer *kvas*, or berry mead, a rather tasty drink, foaming in big glass flasks. The Russian loves to treat himself, and he finds dessert, too, on every street. Various *prianiki*, nuts, carob pods, raisins, fresh berries and apples, or cooked pears, cherries and so on are sold on trays by passing vendors.[8]

This description moves beyond the 'simple' foods that the 'poorest peasant' might eat, with its wheaten loaves and caviar. Many of the same foods appear here – blini, *sbiten* and *kvas* – as well as a few new ones. *Studen* was aspic, and *kisel* was fruit juice thickened with starch. *Prianiki* were spice cakes.

Burnashev's description of Russian food is a very idiosyncratic vision of what was normal or common; a surprisingly lengthy disquisition on puff pastry is probably the most glaring example, but it is also hard not to wonder if he was just listing his favourite soups rather than those that were the most common. But even given his own personal spin on things, there is a lot in his description that echoes other accounts from his own time and from times much closer to our own. Soup, particularly *shchi*, was the alpha and bread, particularly sour rye bread, was the omega. *Kasha*, usually buckwheat, was nearly as common. Although the puff pastries, creams and jellies of his description were hardly common foods at his time, other delights – spice cakes, berries, dried fruits and nuts – were, he claimed, treats within reach of more of the population.

This is perhaps the most important element of Burnashev's description of Russian food. Often when people think of Russian food, two opposing images are likely to come to mind. One is an image of poverty and dearth: at best meagre portions of potatoes or porridge, at worst mass famine. The second is an image of abundance and even excess built on lack of freedom: in one era tsars and nobles drinking champagne and eating caviar, this luxury made possible by the service of dozens upon dozens, if not thousands upon thousands, of serfs; in a later era Party elites enjoying access to all manner of abundance in special stores while outside the masses stood in long queues for bread and potatoes.

These two images are of long standing. After August von Haxthausen visited the Russian Empire in 1843, the account he wrote of his travels

This photograph of a banquet from the Soviet-era cookbook *The Book of Tasty and Healthy Food* shows a kind of abundance out of reach for most of the Soviet population, with wines aplenty, bowls of fruit, dishes of caviar, even a roast suckling pig.

Opposite to the groaning tables of the Russian and later Soviet elites was the simpler meal of the Russian peasant. Here, a group of peasants sit around a small table, with a bowl probably of *shchi* – cabbage soup – a loaf of bread, and a mug of water, beer or *kvas*.

became hugely influential in Russia and abroad. It is best known for his comments on the peasant commune, a structure he believed marked Russian peasant life as distinctly different from places to the west and which were taken by some Russians themselves and developed into a rationale for a Russian brand of socialism. He also commented on food, both the food that was served to him in elite houses and that eaten by the Russian peasant. He depicted a stark difference between the two. On the one hand, there was his description of his dinner at a model landowner's home:

> immediately before it coffee and liqueurs were handed round – a Russian custom, borrowed perhaps from Sweden, where also before dinner are presented several liqueurs, with something piquant to stimulate the appetite, as cheese, caviar, herring, etc., which you eat standing, and afterwards sit down at table. Our dinner was in other respects in Western style, as is the case in all good Russian houses; but the national dishes and drinks, the *pirogi*, the *kvas*, and at the close the *nalivki* [flavoured liquors or cordials], were not wanting.[9]

This was a dinner of abundance and good taste, where Russian and foreign foods and practices were more or less seamlessly brought together to create a pleasant experience for the visitor. Rather different was Haxthausen's description of what the Russian peasant ate. In his telling, it consisted above all

> of bread; potatoes are unknown in most districts; cabbage is the only vegetable which is much used. Animal food, milk, and butter are little eaten. In the army each soldier receives two pounds and a half of bread daily, beside groats, etc. A healthy Russian peasant cannot subsist without three pounds; in the harvest he eats five pounds, and in White Russia even as much as seven pounds. If women, old people, and children are counted, one pound and a half must be reckoned for each individual of the population.[10]

This was not an account of starvation, but it was an account of restraint (or even constraint). His was a description of two very different worlds of eating: a luxurious one for the elite, a monotonous one for the peasant.

Although there were of course exceptions, similar visions of two different worlds of food – one of abundance and luxury, one of poverty and dearth – were common to travel accounts of tsarist Russia. Elite houses were home to 'hospitable boards, loaded with choice and dainty viands, and generous, rare wines, the best and most expensive that the fields of France, Spain, and Germany could furnish' even in provincial towns.[11] The 'common people', however, suffered from a 'general poverty of their aliment', eating 'toadstools stewed in train oil and cabbage soup a few degrees worse than sauer krout'.[12] Even a time of widespread constraint – Lent – manifested differently in these two worlds. One French visitor described the common people's diet during fasts as consisting of only 'bread, onion, oil and mushrooms', while the elite had access to 'cauliflower, asparagus, fresh cucumbers, peas, green beans'.[13]

Visions of two different worlds of Russian food, one of abundance, one of limitations, continued through the Soviet era. Robert Robinson, a Jamaican-born American machinist who moved to the Soviet Union in the 1930s, described 'shoddy and drab' food stores in Moscow, where 'there were bare shelves throughout the food section, except for the jars of mustard which I had figured by now were the only thing in regular supply anywhere, and loaves of black bread.' At least initially, however, he had access as a 'foreign specialist' to elite shops where there were more things to buy. Later in the text he described the kind of feast that could be had if one enjoyed particular kinds of access to special shops: 'we feasted: boiled ham, sausage,

This picture from a late 19th-century illustrated journal depicts the contrast between wealth and poverty that has consistently been a part of the story of food in Russia. Titled 'in front of the sweetshop', the illustration shows a woman dressed plainly and with a humble basket standing in front of a display of decorated boxes filled with sweets, longing for a treat she cannot have.

salmon, veal, sardines, cheese, pickled cucumbers, tomatoes, red and black caviar. We drank champagne, red and white wines, vodka, and assorted soft drinks. There were also cakes and candy and tea from a samovar.'[14]

In many ways, these differences mapped on to a perceived issue with Russian society more generally: that it lacked a middle class. One English traveller from the early nineteenth century described it thus: 'Russia contains but two classes of people, the nobles and the slaves.'[15] Another specifically noted that the lack of a middle class was particularly a problem in realms like cuisine: 'unfortunately, there is no middle class,' he noted, 'who, in other countries, contribute so essentially to the progress of civilization in general, and to the cultivation of the domestic duties and virtues more particularly.'[16] Nor were foreign travellers the only ones who saw things this way: the early nineteenth-century Russian statistician Konstantin Arsenev stated that 'Russia has very little of a middle class (tiers-etat),' and went on to estimate the ratio of people who might count as members of a middle class to the entire population as a mere one out of every twenty-five people.[17] The concern over the lack of a middle class re-emerged in the post-Soviet era, particularly on the part of foreign experts who saw the presence of a middle class as essential to political and economic stability and increasing democracy.

Of course, these images are incomplete. There were tables groaning with good things, whether at the time of Ivan the Terrible, of Catherine the Great or of Leonid Brezhnev, and there were (and are) also many who contented themselves with endless meals of bread and cabbage soup or a plate of buckwheat *kasha*, but there were also people whose lives (and meals) were somewhere in between. Burnashev may have been overemphasizing the wonders of the street vendors. Even so, there was something to his vision of a broad world of Russian food, from linen-covered tables where household serfs served the finest game and champagne to street vendors hawking spice cakes and *shiten* to cottages where cabbage soup and *kasha* more or less filled peasant stomachs. All of these together made up the world of Russian food and Russian cooking.

Even this broad view of what makes up Russian cooking, though, hides a complication. One of the most challenging tasks for the historian of Russia, particularly for the historian trying to cover more than a millennium of its history, is defining what 'Russia' and therefore 'Russian' meant at any particular point. 'Russia' is shorthand for a series of different states with different names and different boundaries. The borders of the contemporary Russian Federation reach from the Baltic and Black Seas in the west to the Pacific Ocean in the east; from the Arctic Ocean in the north to the Caspian Sea and the Sea of Japan in the south. At its greatest extent the Russian Empire at various times reached further west through Finland, Estonia, Latvia, Lithuania, Poland, Belarus, Ukraine and Moldova; further south through Georgia, Azerbaijan, Armenia, Kazakhstan, Turkmenistan, Uzbekistan, Kyrgyzstan and Tadzhikistan, and further east through Alaska. In earlier years, it was more geographically constrained. The earliest state formations associated with Russia centred along the corridor from the Baltic to the Black Sea; the origins of Russia proper were slightly further east and north, along the Dvina river and the northern reaches of the Volga river and its tributaries.

Histories of Russia usually begin in a place that is now no longer entirely part of Russia – Kyivan Rus. Along the Dnieper and Volkhov rivers, from the city of Novgorod to the city of Kyiv, a multitude of different 'tribes' settled and fought. These were largely East Slavic groups, with some Iranian and Finnic influence, as well. Early settlements were driven from the rich soils of the steppe by wave after wave of attack; life further north was harsher and more restricted when it came to agriculture, but richer when it came to foods of the forest. In 862 CE, according to the earliest chronicles, these separate tribes were more or less united under the rule of a Varangian (Viking) prince named Riurik. The Kyivan Rusian state led by Riurik's descendants reached its apogee in the eleventh century. In 988 the ruler of Kyiv, Grand Prince Vladimir, declared his lands to be part of the larger Orthodox Christian world. Not only did Orthodoxy bring a certain unity, it also brought both occasions to celebrate and an everyday world of frequent fasts that in the end fitted the limits of Russia's forested agricultural world remarkably well. When Kyiv was sacked by the Mongols in 1240, any hope of maintaining unity was destroyed along with the city itself. For more than two centuries, the various principalities of Rus were separately subject to the demands of the part of the Mongol Empire known as the Qipchaq Khanate.

That changed when one principality, Moscow, began to expand its influence. When Kyiv fell, the principality of Moscow was still relatively young (founded in 1147) and relatively obscure (located on the Moskva river, a tributary of the Oka, itself a tributary of the Volga). It had some clever princes, though, who leveraged their relationship with the church and with the khanate to their advantage. Moscow became the holder of the patent, the right to collect taxes for the khanate, and the home of the Metropolitan, the leader of the Russian branch of the Orthodox church. It grew in prestige and wealth, and once the khanate itself began to fade, Moscow began to expand. By the beginning of the 1500s Moscow was no longer a tiny provincial power but the centre of a huge state spreading north to the Arctic, west to the Baltic and east to the northern Urals. This new Muscovite state is in many ways the origin state of contemporary Russia. By this point, too, and for all its successes and expansion, the Muscovite world was also regularly subject to one of the great challenges to its food system: famine, most dramatically as part of its 'Time of Troubles' at the beginning of the seventeenth century.

Despite such times of trouble, Muscovy continued to expand during the sixteenth and seventeenth centuries. Its expansion up to this point had been, according to later ideologues, at least, the 'gathering of the Russian lands'. That is, the separate states Moscow had annexed through diplomacy or through war had all been in principle Russian, which meant Orthodox, and primarily settled and ruled by Russians. In practice, though, the situation was already more complicated than that, because these different 'Russian' lands had developed in different ways, and furthermore many non-Russians lived on these lands, particularly in the Baltic and in the

Arctic and sub-Arctic. Later in the sixteenth century, the profusion of non-Russian populations under Muscovite rule exploded as the state's borders crept out in nearly all directions. Ivan IV (the Terrible) (r. 1533–84) took on some of the successor states of the Qipchaq Khanate in the 1550s, annexing first Kazan and then Astrakhan, thereby extending his realm along the entire Volga. Then, starting in the 1580s, Muscovite influence began to spread ever further to the east, less according to any grand state plan than pushed by economic adventurers and the fur trade. Traders followed by Muscovite administration quickly travelled east via the vast network of rivers that spread through Siberia, reaching the Pacific by the end of the 1630s and founding Okhotsk, Russia's first Pacific port, in 1647. Muscovite expansion in Siberia disrupted existing relationships among the vast region's Indigenous population. Some allied with the Muscovites, some fought them off. In the end, Russian firepower triumphed.

Although Muscovy's eastward expansion seemed bounded only by the ocean (at least until the move to Alaska in the late eighteenth century), there were different geopolitical limits in other directions. Its border had crept south along the Volga, but to the east and west it remained further to the north. The Crimean Khanate, supported by the Ottoman Empire, made the European steppe a place of danger for settlers. The Silk Roads still made Central Asia a vibrant space with connections to east and west, not open to the relatively easy expansion that had allowed the rapid expansion through Siberia to the north. Cossacks, though, found a place in these regions between the growing Muscovite state to the north and the various powers to the south. They settled along river valleys: the Dnieper, the Don, the Yaik.

When Peter I (the Great) came to the throne at the very end of the seventeenth century (r. 1682–1725), he began a process of more conscious, active efforts to engage with 'the West'. Kyivan Rus had been part of the larger Christian world, with marriage ties linking its royal family to those of Sweden, France and even (possibly) England. The increasing division between the Eastern and Western churches, as well as the devastation of the Mongol invasion, curtailed those ties. They never completely disappeared: Novgorod continued to trade out through the Baltic, eventually becoming an outpost of the Hanseatic League, and Italian architects designed some of the Moscow Kremlin's churches built at the end of the fifteenth century. Those ties were weaker and more constrained than in the past, however. As a result, when British merchant explorers seeking the northeast passage instead stumbled upon a northern sea route to Muscovy during the reign

ПЕТРЬ I IМПЕРАТОРЬ ИСАМОДЕРЖЕЦЬ ВСЕРОССИСКИІ.

Although historians now emphasize the ways that Peter the Great built on changes already happening in Russia rather than creating everything anew, his reign still marks a dividing point between an older 'traditional' world and a new one. Simply put, Russia's nobles and to a certain extent its townspeople more broadly came to dress differently, to play a different role in the economy, military and state, and, of course, to eat and drink differently. This woodblock print from later in the 18th century hints at the ways that Peter was a man who bridged a past world (of such prints) and a new world (of Western clothing and – though not pictured here – Western foods and drinks).

of Ivan the Terrible, they helped begin a new era in Russia's relationship with the wider world. More and more foreign merchants came to Muscovy, as did foreign military experts, but they were supposed to stay in their suburbs, not mix with the wider population, both out of fear of religious contamination and out of an effort to protect Russia's own merchants from foreign competition.

Under Peter I, things changed, bringing in by (almost) all accounts a new era of Russian history. He fought a lengthy war against Sweden to retake access to the Baltic Sea and moved his capital to St Petersburg, his new port city in his new lands. He became no longer simply the tsar of Muscovy but the emperor of the Russian Empire. Peter travelled to Western Europe, 'incognito' in order to avoid the strictures of diplomatic protocol, and variously persuaded, encouraged and forced his elites, in particular, to take on elements of Western European fashion and habits. In large part as a result of this, one of the great stories of Russia's eighteenth and nineteenth centuries came to be the contestation between Westernizers – who believed that Russia's future ought to look to ever greater ties with Europe – and Slavophiles – who rued Peter's new orientation and instead argued for a return to pre-Petrine forms. They went by different names over the centuries but similar tensions between outward-looking reform and inward-looking tradition remained a constant. Foodways were part of this contest. New agricultural practices, new crops, new imports, all began to alter the ways in which people ate. As in changes to language or to clothing, the elite were most affected, but some changes impacted on the population more widely.

The imperial era ushered in by Peter I was a time of opulence and serfdom, when the empire continued to expand and the bureaucratic autocracy continued to evolve. The steppe border had been largely stabilized in the middle of the seventeenth century; both Peter and his immediate successors tried to move it further south, but Catherine II (the Great) (r. 1762–96) was the leader to do it. Her acquisition of this 'New Russia' brought the empire down to the wide northern coast of the Black Sea and Crimea just as her participation in the partitions of Poland dramatically altered Russia's western border. During the nineteenth century, smaller but important new acquisitions in the west (Finland and Moldova) were followed by a lengthy battle to pacify the Caucasus and then rapid movement further south in Central Asia and along the Pacific coast, as the Russian Empire took advantage of political destabilization caused in part by other European imperial activities.

Autocracy and serfdom underlay everything. All of Russia's peasants were constrained in their mobility, and the half of them that were privately owned serfs were not entirely in control of their own labour, as well. Even after serfdom was abolished in 1861, the constraints on mobility remained, somewhat ameliorated by a system of internal passports that dated back to the reign of Peter I. Peasant labour paid for elite culture; peasant bodies fought the empire's wars. Some of Russia's rulers believed in the radical possibility of the autocracy to enlighten and to reform society from above in everything from the clothes they wore to the economic activities they engaged in to the plants they sowed. But particularly in the later nineteenth century, they also came to defend the autocracy qua autocracy with force against an increasingly educated and in some cases radicalized society that demanded more of a role in its own governance and future. Rather than focusing on their potential for reform, the reigns of Alexander III (1881–94) and Nicholas II (1894–1917) instead pushed an increasingly chauvinistic version of Russian nationalism as their unifying mythology. It failed.

The crisis of the late imperial Russian state was also presaged and perhaps even caused by larger issues in the world of food. A massive famine in the early 1890s – the first such extensive famine since the Time of Troubles almost three centuries before – signalled a failure in the stability of the autocracy. And then, in February 1917, a women's protest about bread sparked the series of protests that toppled the tsarist state. The tsarist state collapsed, but the empire did not; or at least, most of its briefly separate parts were reassembled into the new Soviet Union only five years later. Many forces contributed to the collapse of the autocracy, not least of which was the stress of the First World War. The success of the Bolshevik party in founding a new Soviet state was based in its own organizational capabilities – and its willingness to extend and expand the use of violence – as well as on the failure of any other single group to unify an opposition.

The Soviet experience brought significant change: some traumatic, some more rhetorical than real. The Soviet state had even more radical goals for top-down reformation of society than had the most ardent Enlightener of the imperial era. They wanted to create a unified, classless society by both raising the status of the masses and by eliminating the status of the elites – sometimes by eliminating their privileges, sometimes by eliminating the elites themselves. The 1930s under Stalin's leadership saw the harshest phases of this restructuring, with collectivization and purges combining to exile or eliminate millions. Famines were part of this Soviet world, as well, in massive waves following the revolution and civil war, following collectivization and following the Second World War. The Soviet state also set out to remake the world of Soviet food – which incorporated but went beyond 'Russian' food – in other ways, from how it was produced to where it was consumed to what exactly it was. Not all of these planned changes were made real in the lives of most of the Soviet population, but some were.

The trauma of and eventual victory in the Second World War killed millions more, both civilians and military personnel. It also gave a new

This staged photograph of peasants at table from the late 19th century shows the juxtaposition of old and new found in the Russian countryside in this time of change. One peasant wears a jaunty hat and leather boots, another plays a balalaika; the table shows off a samovar, a tea set and small glasses, into which a boy is pouring what is probably vodka. But this is set against a dirt street and a thatched roof – though on a cottage with glass windows.

As more and more people flocked to Russia's towns, feeding them became an even more
pressing issue than it had in the late tsarist period. In this 1919 watercolour by Ivan
Vladimirov, people line up outside a 'communal canteen', while others are so hungry
they sit and eat their meals right outside its door. The faded poster on the wall of the
canteen hints at what the building once was – it promises a ball and dancing.

origin point for post-war reconstruction. The post-war Soviet Union could
be viewed not as recovering from the excesses of the 1930s, but instead
as carrying its military victory back into the effort of recovery from a
devastating war. Immediately after the war, living standards had plum-
meted; first recovery from the war and later the attainment of a certain
level of general prosperity beyond pre-war levels in the Brezhnev era was
a slow process. This relative prosperity did not mean general abundance,
nor did it mean the total end of political repression and state control, of
course, but particularly after Stalin's death in 1953 there was a 'Thaw', as
the Khrushchev era came to be known.

By the end of the Brezhnev era and the onset of the Gorbachev era,
however, cracks were beginning to show. The now very educated population
chafed at the limits of its ability to be heard. Separatist movements in many
of the national republics began to speak more loudly and to gather more
adherents. And the briefly fulfilled promise of a general level of material
prosperity began to collapse as the Soviet Union's supply problems came
to the forefront. Shortages affected many aspects of everyday life, not least
of all in the food supply in both countryside and town. Early Soviet economic growth, which was real and striking, had been accomplished at the

expense of the peasantry. Once Khrushchev and Brezhnev shifted policy to ameliorate the status of the Soviet Union's rural population, that source of 'easy' (although deadly for the rural population itself) growth was gone.

Everything collapsed in 1991. Gorbachev's policies of glasnost and perestroika were efforts to rebuild the Soviet economy and to relax some of the constraints on society. The latter outpaced the former, leading perhaps to an inevitable collision. But in the end, the real collapse of the Soviet Union occurred because of the assertion of sovereign control on the part of its national republics. Not least among them was the RSFSR – the Russian Soviet Federated Socialist Republic – itself. Its charismatic president, Boris Yeltsin, became one of the strongest voices against the reassertion of hardline Communist Party control during the failed coup of August 1991; in its aftermath, he became the leader of a new Russian Federation, by far the largest of the fifteen successor states of the Soviet Union.

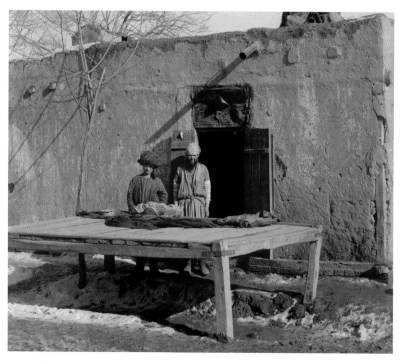

As the old core of Muscovy expanded first through Russian lands, later into Siberia, the Baltics, Poland, Belarus, Ukraine, the Caucasus and eventually Central Asia, different food traditions entered the wider empire. Some stayed regional, while others eventually became part of a pan-Imperial (or particularly pan-Soviet) world of eating. This photograph taken in Central Asia in the early 20th century shows two men standing at a table covered with round flatbreads. Variations on this kind of flatbread are still common in grocery stores and markets around Russia today.

The new Russian Federation faced enormous challenges, not least of which was figuring out what it meant to be Russia without its larger empire. That is too simple a way to put it, of course. The very idea that this was the Russian 'Federation' recognized the many other peoples who had long lived and continue to live across the broad Eurasian landmass. In addition, one legacy of the Soviet era, in particular, was not just population movement that left sizable Russian minorities in the various successor states and sizable non-Russian minorities in the Russian Federation but also the creation of a pan-Soviet culture, heavily based on Russian culture, to be sure, but reaching out to incorporate the wider Soviet world. Figuring out the new Russia played out against a backdrop of extreme economic and political instability in the 1990s. Since his emergence as president (then prime minister, and then president again), the government of Vladimir Putin has actively tried to solve the question of Russia as much as it has asserted increased political control, and at least for a while benefitted from global commodities trends to help stabilize its economy.

Furthermore, the legacy of the Soviet past continued to affect eating after 1991. The Russian Federation had to build a new economy and a new culture out of the remnants of the Soviet state. Food supply lines, already stretched by the end of the Gorbachev era, were further disrupted. A new wave of foreign products and foods caused a different kind of disruption, as eating patterns evolved to incorporate some of the new. Out of all of this change, a newly vibrant world of Russian food has emerged in the early twenty-first century, a world that follows older traditions as much by a willingness to incorporate new things as in its desire to preserve older patterns.

This long history of shifting borders was not only a reflection of larger geopolitical issues but had at times a significant effect on the everyday lives of people across this huge expanse of Eurasia, including on the ways in which they ate. Russian culinary practices spread along with Russians through Siberia, for example, uprooting or at least altering indigenous practices. Differences remained, of course. The Russian practice for tea drinking, for example, involves perhaps sugar, *varenye* (fruit preserves) or lemon – but never milk. One of the Indigenous peoples of Siberia, the Buriats, however, consider milk (or even more traditionally, other forms of animal fat) to be a necessary accompaniment, a distinction in practice that still holds true.[18]

Other culinary traditions from the wider Russian Empire have had significant influence on Russian eating and drinking. In the middle of the nineteenth century, two fermented dairy products from Russia's empire began to receive new attention in part for their perceived health benefits: *kumys*, fermented mare's milk from Russia's new Central Asian territories, and *kefir*, another fermented milk, usually now cow, this one from the Caucasus. Taking a *kumys* cure became fashionable in the late nineteenth century, and *kefir* was available through apothecaries by the 1880s; or, if one was travelling in Crimea and went to the resort town of Evpatoriia, the hairdressing establishment run by Mr Teodor also sold *kumys* and *kefir*! In the twentieth century, *kefir* in particular began to be produced in large quantities and to appear on grocery shelves and now has been listed among the fermented, probiotic superfoods.[19]

Other foods or even entire cuisines from the empire also came to play important roles in Russian cooking. In the 1830s and 1840s, some of the first major Russian cookbook authors began to include recipes from the empire, usually described as being part of the 'Asiatic table'. In a cookbook from 1837, Gerasim Stepanov, for example, claimed to be the first Russian author to write about such things. He included recipes for *shashlik* (grilled meat on a skewer) and *plov* (highly seasoned rice cooked in a large pan with meat and vegetables) from the empire's Central Asian and Caucasian lands, and also 'Polish *shchi*' – hardly 'Asiatic' but also distinct (in part because the recipe called for a surprising ingredient: Dutch cheese!).[20] By the beginning of the twentieth century, another major cuisine began to appear in Russian cookbooks: Georgian food. A. I. Nikishova's 1928 cookbook included recipes for *chakhokhbili* (a chicken stew) and two different preparations of lamb 'Georgian-style'.[21] In part because Stalin (whose birth name was the Georgian Dzhugashvili) wanted the food of his childhood available in Moscow (and probably in part because it is delicious) Georgian food came to the Soviet capital and Georgian restaurants to towns across Russia.[22] As other people moved around the Soviet Union, too, they brought their foods with them: Armenian, Tatar, Uzbek and, of course, Russian.[23]

The distinctions of empire are particularly fraught along Russia's western border, fraught not only geopolitically but culinarily. The many peoples there – Ukrainians, Belarusians, Poles, Jews and also Russians – have overlapping culinary traditions, rich in soups and dumplings distinguished by slight differences in preparation and by different names. Cabbage soup is *shchi* in Russian, *kapusniak* in Ukrainian, *kapusta* in Belarusian and Polish. Dumplings vary more: the tiny Siberian/Russian *pelmeni*, filled with meat; the larger Ukrainian *vareniki*, filled with potato, cabbage, cheese or cherries; the Polish *pierogi*, as varied as the *vareniki* in their possible fillings. Perhaps no food reflects the

Georgian Food

Of all the foods to come into Russia through its empire, Georgian food is by far the most popular, for the good reason that it is utterly delicious. What is now the Republic of Georgia became part of the Russian Empire in several stages beginning in the 1780s. Georgia lies at the eastern end of the Black Sea, and its annexation was in part geopolitical manoeuvring between the Russian Empire, the Ottoman Empire and Persia. Its cuisine is in some ways reminiscent of Persian or Turkish cuisine (a love of pomegranate seeds and garlic, for example), but is also clearly distinct. For one, ground walnuts are a common ingredient. There are herbs both fresh and dried that are particular to Georgian cuisine, as well, like dried marigold leaves instead of saffron, or *tsitsmat*, a peppery green. Georgian food stayed a mostly regional cuisine until the early Soviet era, when Georgian Bolsheviks now in Moscow (like Stalin) wanted the tastes of their home. The Aragvi became one of the best known of Moscow's restaurants, and a few other Georgian restaurants followed. In recent years, Georgian cuisine has seen an explosion of popularity, with stand-alone restaurants and chains popping up.

challenges of the border as much as borscht, however, in part because its Ukrainian origins have been largely obscured. Instead, it has taken on the mantle of the quintessential 'Russian' soup, much to the consternation of culinary purists both Russian and Ukrainian. When the Russian culinary historian Maksim Syrnikov asked younger Russians to name traditional Russian foods, he noted: 'what they named was horrible: borscht, which is Ukrainian, and potatoes, which are an American plant.'[24] Nor are contemporary Russians alone in associating borscht with Russia. It shows up in cookbook titles, in humorous essays and even – in a version based on red cabbage, not beetroot – in restaurants in Hong Kong, where it is known as 'Russian soup'.[25]

Despite all of these potential sources of difference and confusion, there are some commonalities that form the core of Russian cuisine – foods and drinks consumed today that have long histories, discussed in Chapter One.

Georgia is a mountainous country, and as a result its various regions developed related but distinct cultural (and culinary) traditions, which makes it incredibly difficult to summarize its rich and varied cuisine. Two foods are perhaps most famous. One, *khachapuri*, is a cheese-filled bread, but that bland description does not capture the salty, oozy, rich joy of eating it. There are regional variations on *khachapuri*, as well – Adjarian, with an egg yolk sitting on top in a pool of melted cheese and butter is the most famous. *Khinkali* are steamed dumplings usually filled with meat, but also now often with mushrooms or vegetables. They have a characteristic shape: flat on the bottom and pleated around the sides, with the pleats gathered in a tight, dense handle at the top, left behind after eating in part to help the diner keep track of how many she has eaten! *Lobio* is a warm bean stew, *pkhali* a salad of cooked vegetables – beetroot or spinach or green beans are particularly common – mashed together with garlic, ground walnuts and herbs. Aubergine dishes abound. *Chakhokhbili* is a savoury, herb-inflected chicken stew, and *satsivi* a cold chicken dish topped with a ground walnut sauce.

In part those commonalities are due to certain long-term environmental and technological constraints, discussed in Chapter Two (as are some of the ways in which shifting borders started to change those constraints, allowing for new practices or foods to become somehow 'traditional'). In addition, beyond the complications of defining Russian cuisine as a concept, there is a much broader story of the role that food, and sometimes the lack of food, played in Russian society. That broader story unfolds in the remaining chapters, starting with what we know about the eating habits of the first Slavic settlers of the northern forests and ending with recent developments caused by the wave of sanctions and countersanctions that specifically targeted foodways. Overall, the history of food in Russia is one of abundance, of dearth, of variety, of simplicity, of continuities, but perhaps above all of change.

ONE

The Elements of Russian Cuisine

The canteen at the Russian State Library in Moscow, still commonly known as the Leninka, is always busy. The library, located only steps from the tourist entrance to the Kremlin and all its treasures, holds nearly 50 million items, making it the fifth largest library in the world. Entering the library, past the cloakroom and guard, the reader has two choices. She can walk up the grand staircase that leads to the reading rooms and the books, or can turn left and follow a narrow path around the cloakroom to a staircase. There she can again choose up to the books or down to the basement and the canteen.

If she chooses down to the canteen, she will enter it through an outer 'buffet', where coffee, tea, bottled water, soft drinks and sweet or savoury snacks can serve as a quick break. The canteen proper is a large, bright, clean space, with wooden tables well spaced. A giant urn of boiling water sits in one corner, waiting for users to fill their cups. It is also a sign of the role that the library and its canteen serve in the lives of some of the giant city's poorer residents: a place of refuge and warmth, with endless hot water to fill and refill a cup with a teabag brought from home over the course of a day.

Most of the customers at the canteen pass through it more quickly. If the reader arrives at the lunch hour, the queue can be long; wait until later, and a few particularly popular items may be sold out. No matter the time, she takes a tray and glances at the daily menu always posted at the end of the service counter. Everyone looks at the menu, considers, possibly consults with other people in line, but usually decides only when faced with the food itself. First of all is a cold case filled with small plates of salads. These are not leafy green salads, but different composed salads. Some are simple: shredded cooked beetroot with a bit of mayonnaise and cheese on top, or quick soured cabbage. Some are more complicated mixes, of vegetables, sometimes meats, sometimes rice or potato, in vinegar or mayonnaise-based dressings. Their names are sometimes obvious lists of ingredients, but often are more abstract: salad 'Olivier', 'Springtime', 'Capitol'. These are names with meaning if you grew up in the Soviet and then post-Soviet world of canteens and cookbooks. Fortunately for those who did not, the Leninka canteen uses labels with ingredient lists to help parse the meaning of these names.

The salads are self-service, but the next phase of the canteen experience involves a conversation. 'What will you have for a first [course]?' the person (usually but not always a woman) behind the counter asks. 'And for a second?' she follows. 'First' really means soup. There are always two or three soups, no matter the time of year. *Shchi* (cabbage soup), borscht (beetroot soup), *rassolnik* (a sour soup that usually involves pickled cucumbers) and *ukha* (fish soup) are joined by chicken noodle soup, pea soup, mushroom soup, vegetable purees and occasionally the spicy Georgian *kharcho*. Often there is an additional question that follows: 'With sour cream?' Almost everyone says yes.

Second courses are even more varied. There is almost always some sort of *kotlet* (cutlet), not a cut of meat but instead a patty of minced meat held together with breadcrumbs and eggs, often with herbs, either pan-fried or baked. A couple of fish options and something with poultry, perhaps liver or a cut of pork. They are baked, stewed or served with a particular sauce. If the reader orders one of these options, she will then be asked 'And for a garnish?' That means, does she want buckwheat *kasha*, or noodles, or potatoes, mashed or roasted, or vegetables as a side dish. The thrifty will sometimes ask for just a plate of *kasha* with a spoonful of the sauce from one of the meat dishes. There are a couple of other options in frequent rotation that often go without a garnish: *plov*, spiced rice with meat and vegetables, or *lenivye golubtsy*, 'lazy' cabbage rolls, which just means that the ground meat and onions and rice that normally go into cabbage rolls are mixed up and baked with chopped cabbage.

Sitting on top of the canteen's food-service counter is an array of baked goods to which the reader can help herself. There is sliced bread, dark sour rye and white, and also plate after plate piled high with *pirozhki*. These are yeasted buns filled with different things: cabbage, mushroom, egg and green onion, chicken, liver, rice, apple, dried apricot, cherry. The reader can help herself to a drink, too, although there is a difference between what is available in the canteen and the buffet. The buffet has coffee and bottled drinks. In the canteen there is only tea or glasses of *kompot*: a kind of sweetened fruit juice often made by boiling dried fruit, with bits of fruit at the bottom of the glass.

The pattern of this canteen is repeated all over Russia and even beyond, in former Soviet countries. Salad, first course of soup, second course of meat and a side, an array of filled rolls and bread – all appear in similar canteens both within institutions and along city streets. This might not be all that remarkable it if were not for the way in which this pattern echoes much earlier descriptions not just of individual foods but of the way meals were constructed. The first printed Russian cookbooks, which date back to the end of the eighteenth century, were as much concerned with presenting an order of dishes common to the eating patterns of their readers' households as they were with any individual Russian dish. The order that came to be standard is essentially the same as the order of foods presented in this typical post-Soviet Russian cafeteria: a cold dish, a soup, a stew or roast and a filled pastry. There were differences; the cold dish was often a cold meat or fish dish, not a salad; salads, if they appeared, came with the roast. The soup course could also be labelled a 'hot dish'

A meal at the Russian State Library canteen: a salad of sliced radishes, no first course of soup (a somewhat sacrilegious choice!), *plov* – spiced rice with meat and vegetables, a Central Asian addition to the Soviet and now Russian menu – with a side of aubergine and peppers, also more akin to dishes from the Caucasus than to the old Russian heartland, and a sweet roll with cinnamon as a treat to end the meal.

This menu from a dinner in St Petersburg in 1899 features a mixture of 'Russian' and foreign foods, organized more or less according to the meal order that had been standardized more than a century earlier: a soup, in this case featuring the Russian fish sterlet, *rasstegai* (a small oblong pie with an open filling), a cold dish of Rouen duckling, several hot dishes and a sweet to end it all.

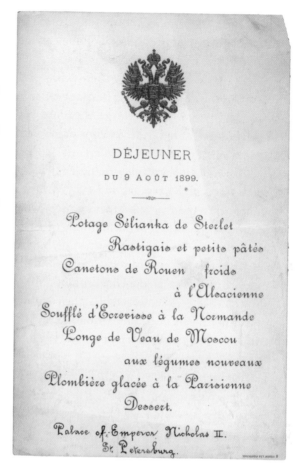

DÉJEUNER

DU 9 AOÛT 1899.

Potage Sélianka de Sterlet

Rastigais et petits pâtés

Canetons de Rouen froids

à l'Alsacienne

Soufflé d'Écrevisse à la Normande

Longe de Veau de Moscou

aux légumes nouveaux

Plombière glacée à la Parisienne

Dessert.

Palace of Emperor Nicholas II.
St. Petersburg.

course, although soups were the norm. Overall, though, the pattern is remarkably consistent.

Nor were cookbooks presenting unrealistic ideals: this basic description mapped on to actual meals. In wealthy households, meals might include multiples of some of these courses, but the outline remained. A detailed proposal for a new restaurant from 1797 listed its most expensive menu as including a cold dish, a 'soup or *shchi*', a sauced meat dish, a roast and a filled pastry. It cost 1 rouble. Eliminating one of the meat dishes brought the meal down to 75 kopeks; three courses cost 50 kopeks; two cost 25 kopeks.[1] In the middle of the nineteenth century, the array of foods at taverns and restaurants was similar:

The usual dinner supplied for three-quarters of a rouble (half a crown) consists of soup, with a pie of mince-meat, or minced vegetables, an *entrée*, roast meat, and some kind of sweet. That, too, may be considered the kind of dinner which persons of moderate means have every day at home.[2]

Or, there was this description of a Russian dinner from 1805:

> I will just give a brief sketch of a Russian dinner, which is seldom later than three o'clock: upon a side-board in the drawing-room is always placed a table filled with fish, meats, and sausages salted, pickled, and smoked, bread and butter, and liqueurs; these airy nothings are mere running footmen of the dinner, which is in the following order: a cold dish, generally of sturgeon or some other fish, precedes, followed by soup, a number of made dishes, a profusion of roast and boiled meats, amongst which the Ukraine beef is distinguishable, and abundance of excellent vegetables; then pastry, and a desert of very fine melons, and sour flavourless wall fruit; the table is covered with a variety of wines, and excellent ale and beer. The master of the house or a cook carves, and slices of every dish are handed round to the guests. One of the most gratifying things that I always saw upon the table, was a large vase of ice broken into small pieces, with which the guest cools his wine and beer.[3]

In some ways, holding on to this organization of a meal was a way of preserving the Russian table in the face of all sorts of new foods. One of the first cookbooks to lay out this organization was Vasilii Levshin's multi-volume *Cooking, Serving, Confectionery-making and Distilling Dictionary*.[4] Its longer title, which included 'Russian Cooking' as only one cuisine among a whole series of other national cuisines, suggested that the world he was describing was undergoing radical change in the kinds of foods eaten by its hypothetical readers. Levshin even claimed that Russian cooking was being forgotten among the elite, at least, pushed out by foreign dishes. As a result, thinking through the Russian meal course by course, as laid out by Levshin and as standardized by twentieth- and twenty-first-century practice, becomes one of the best ways to describe and define Russian cuisine.

TO BEGIN: *ZAKUSKI*

First, there is one Russian culinary tradition that appears explicitly neither in eighteenth-century cookbooks nor in twenty-first-century cafeterias, but which has been frequently mentioned by travellers to Russia starting at least in the late eighteenth century. This was what has come to be known as the *zakuski* table: an array of bits and bites, usually salty or smoked, to consume with a quick drink. The late eighteenth-century Russian writer Ivan Boltin described the practice as a rebuttal to what he believed was an incorrect description by the French traveller Leclerc. Leclerc had written that 'to awaken the appetite [Russians] eat a little bread with salt, turnips or radishes and such, and then drink vodka or spirits.' This was turned upside down, Boltin claimed:

> A quarter of an hour or so before dinner, we drink vodka or
> spirits; but we snack, that is, eat the aforesaid things in pieces,
> after drinking vodka, not before; and this habit is the same
> everywhere in Russia. In some homes, particularly in the
> countryside, they serve as an appetizer not only turnips, but
> many other things like it, such as ham or smoked goose, smoked
> sausage, dried chicken or game, salted fish, herring or anchovies,
> butter, cheese, pretzels and such; and in such a case one can
> consider it a meal; but always vodka is drunk beforehand.[5]

In other words, Boltin believed that Leclerc was not inaccurate in his statement that there was a tradition of pre-dinner snacks and drinks, only in his description of the order of eating and drinking.

Boltin likely found this troubling because it was an example of what he saw as Leclerc's lack of attention and care, but it also implied something else. In the middle of the nineteenth century, a number of British travellers were particularly struck by the fact that Russians drank their vodka or wine, and ate their cheese, before their dinner and not after. One, Henry Sutherland Edwards, noted that the opposite practices of the English and the Russian could lead to cross-cultural confusion – and excessive consumption, as well, as each encouraged the other to drink at a different point in the meal.[6] Another described his surprise at how well the custom went:

> though I certainly never before *began* dinner with cheese and
> brandy, I felt bound to do as the others did, and truth compels
> me to declare that I did not find my appetite any the worse for

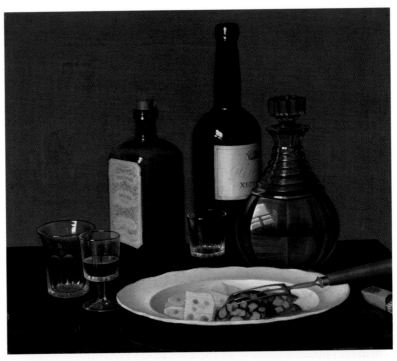

This still-life by a little-known artist named Volkov could just as easily be titled *zakuski*, for it portrays the kind of food and drink often laid out as a prequel to the main meal. A plate with sausage and cheese, and several bottles of alcohol – the bottle in the middle is labelled 'sherry', the square one appears to hold red wine or a red cordial, and the green flask might hold vodka. All were potentially part of the *zakuski* ritual – as was a smoke, indicated by the box of matches lying by the plate.

it. In fact, there is no saying, until he has tried, what a man can, or cannot, do in this world.[7]

The tradition continued into the Soviet era, and continued to lead some travellers to overindulge. Charles Thayer, an American helping to open the new U.S. embassy in Moscow in the 1930s, also enjoyed the *zakuski* tradition – even a bit too much, he admitted. At one point he supplied some of the alcohol for a party thrown by an actor acquaintance. Along with the booze, there was 'every available *zakuski* in Moscow: hard-boiled eggs, ham, red caviar, black caviar, cucumbers, radishes, sardines, herrings and huge stacks of white and black bread, and even butter'.[8]

Charles William Vane, Marquess of Londonderry, wrote of the practice in his description of his northern European travels in the 1830s. Unlike some others, he found it to be a problem, but for a particular reason:

Before the dinner, there is universally a sort of luncheon in an anteroom for the gentlemen, by way of giving a craving to the stomach and sharpening the appetite. At this no ladies appear. It consists generally of caviar, (so renowned in this country for its perfection,) anchovies, dried salt salmon, cheese, and articles of similar description, with liqueurs, cognac, eau de vie, &c. This custom would be more honoured in the breach than in the observance, as the gentlemen return to the room where the ladies are assembled, eating these unsavoury morsels, and talking to the fair sex, as if wholly unconscious of the disagreeable odour that arises from them. I condemn the practice, decidedly. It affords no society, it cannot be wholesome; the exciting food could be served round (if desired) when all are at table; but this ambulant eating with greasy fingers, and then parading with unwashed mouths amongst the fair sex, do not correspond with the general gallantry of the Russians.[9]

Londonderry emphasized the social aspects of eating, and the ways in which this practice was part of the world of men, not of women (and was perhaps even actively unpleasant for elite women). There is definitely something to this idea. Account books from the first half of the nineteenth century belonging to one noble family, the Golokhvastovs, show most kitchen expenses recorded in kitchen account books. But some expenses related to food were kept instead as part of the account books associated with the male head of the household, Dmitry Pavlovich Golokhvastov, himself. Wine purchases are here (bottles upon bottles!) and books and journals, too. Also included is a note of purchases made for 'dinner on 29 July 1841'. The purchases were not for the meal itself, but rather for its dessert (mostly fruit – but lots of it: cherries and watermelon and melon and twenty plums and fifteen peaches and 3 *funty* of grapes) and its start: the *zakuski* array. The plan was to purchase a container of sardines, a half-*funt* of parmesan, Italian ham, sausage, olives (according to a separate note, two shops were out of stuffed olives, so whoever was making the purchases had to go to a third) and caviar (½ a *funt*).[10]

It was not precisely the foods involved that made this Russian, for some of the elements of the *zakuski* table, particularly the cheese, were decidedly not traditionally Russian, but rather the entirety of the practice. At least, for the most part, it was not the foods – except for caviar. As the Briton George Augustus Sala put it, 'that by me abhorred, by others adored, condiment, caviare: caviare simple, in little yellow hooped kegs: caviare spread on bread and butter: caviare artfully introduced between layers of pastry'.[11] There is perhaps no other food that is as closely linked with images of extravagance and opulence, and perhaps no other food so closely associated with Russia. It finds its way into the titles of memoirs and books on history (including this one), perhaps particularly of the Soviet era, where its association with luxury struck many as an especially dramatic contrast with the larger world of shortages or terror: *Caviar and Commissars, Caviar for Breakfast, Bears in the Caviar*.[12]

Although now 'caviar' encompasses many varieties, the caviar that most stands for luxury and for Russia is the roe collected from several different sturgeons, the huge bottom-dwelling river fish common to the Volga and other rivers flowing through Russia's steppe, some swimming out into the Caspian and Black seas. Cossacks and other settlers along the rivers depended on the flesh of the sturgeon for their sustenance and also on their other products that required more processing and were valuable enough to bring an income: *viziga*, the dried spinal cord of the sturgeon, was cooked into pies or soup; their bladders produced isinglass, used in

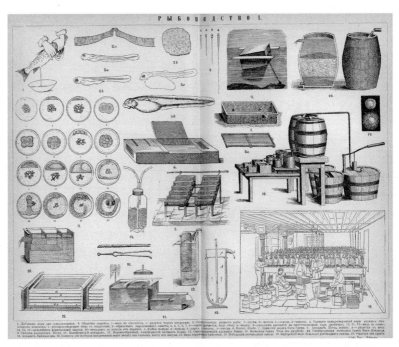

Caviar (and fish farming more generally) became big business by the end of the nineteenth century. The illustration above shows some of the technologies in place for cultivating fish and harvesting caviar.

beer and wine production and as a thickener for jellies. And, of course, there was caviar. The largest female beluga ever recorded, caught in the early nineteenth century, weighed 1,143 kilograms (2,520 lb) – and 408 kilograms (900 lb) of her weight was roe. Even an average beluga could yield a hundred or more kilograms of roe, immediately processed by caviar makers. They separate out the tiny eggs, rinse them and mix with salt. The longer the caviar has to sit or travel, the more salt is added and the more salt is absorbed.

Caviar was mostly locally consumed until the end of the eighteenth century. At that time Catherine II annexed the whole northern coast of the Black Sea, thereby pacifying the southern steppe and making it a potential source of greater profit. It is also when a Greek merchant adventurer, Ioannis Varvarkis, managed to make himself known to Catherine, ended up with exclusive fishing rights out of Astrakhan and then figured out how to package caviar in order to export it. Other countries eventually challenged or overcame Russia when it came to the export market, and became greater international suppliers of caviar itself. Even so, the association of caviar with Russia and its nobility remained an essential part of its mystique.[13]

COLD DISHES AND SALADS

A Russian meal proper moved on from the *zakuski* table to a defined series of courses. The usual beginning, as presented in everything from eighteenth-century cookbooks and tavern menus to post-Soviet canteen displays, was a cold dish of some sort. In the eighteenth and nineteenth centuries, these openers were usually cold meat or fish dishes; in the Soviet and post-Soviet world, they came usually to be salads – often composed salads of cooked vegetables and sometimes with meat.

As Katerina Avdeeva, whose cookbooks became bestsellers in the middle of the nineteenth century, put it, the cold dishes of her time were 'simple'. She listed twelve options: chicken, turkey, wildfowl, goose or duck and tongue were boiled, cut into pieces and served cold, usually with a sprinkling of chopped egg, pickled cucumber or slices of lemon. Suckling pig was also boiled, cut up, chilled and served with grated horseradish mixed with sour cream. *Buzhenina* was a fresh ham, cleaned, scored and baked; 'whoever wishes may spike it with garlic.' It was served cold with horseradish, mustard, vinegar or lemon juice. Cured ham (*vetchina*) could be boiled, but Avdeeva recommended instead baking it in a thick rye-flour

Okroshka began as a dish to use up leftover cooked meat. Initially served more as a salad, now *okroshka* is a cold soup that uses *kvas* as a base.

crust, to be removed before serving the ham. Cow's feet could be boiled into *studen* (aspic), and a sheep's head and feet could be cooked and served in a similar way. Tripe, too, was served in aspic. Finally there was *okroshka*, not so simple but very thrifty. It took leftover cooked meat and mixed it with onion, dill, cucumbers and eggs, and then doused the whole with *kvas*.[14] These were the cold dishes that Avdeeva included in her section on 'the Russian table'; she also included other cold dishes as part of her 'general table'. They were for the most part nearly the same cold meats, but with slightly more complicated sauces made from peas, from cauliflower, from cabbage.

Avdeeva also gave a recipe for a cold dish called *vinegret* (vinaigrette). Like *okroshka*, it started with leftover meat. This time, however, the meat was mixed with cooked potato, beetroot and cucumbers (either fresh or salted). All was topped with a dressing of vinegar, mustard, olive oil and salt.[15] In many ways, this recipe presages the kinds of cold starters that came to the fore in the twentieth century – salads. During the Soviet era, salads, sometimes with meat but more often featuring vegetables or starches, became the more normal way to open a meal. The *Book of Tasty and Healthy Food* – the ultimate Soviet culinary authority, released in multiple editions from the 1930s to beyond the end of the Soviet Union – listed mostly very simple salads of vegetables in dressing. There was a 'salad of raw vegetables' of cucumbers, carrots, turnips and radishes mixed with sour cream; salads of blanched or preserved cabbage, or of cooked beetroot or potatoes. There were slightly more complicated salads with meat and mayonnaise, or with fish and potatoes. And there was also now a salad called *vinegret*, which came to be a standard: potatoes, beetroot, carrots, cucumbers, sometimes canned peas and onion, in a dressing of oil, vinegar and salt (in other words, much like Avdeeva's version, but without the meat). There were also other cold dishes that harked back to the meat-based cold dishes of the pre-revolutionary era: marinated fish or herring and particularly *studen*.[16]

The real shift in the world of Soviet salads, however, came in the Brezhnev era of the late 1960s and early 1970s. Then, named prepared salads started to appear, some initially associated with particular places but which soon spread out into the wider culinary world. The salads often featured mayonnaise – not a new ingredient, but one increasingly produced not at home but industrially for sale in shops. Two of the most famous are layered salads that also featured another not new but newly prominent product: canned fish. After the Second World War, the Soviet Union put significant resources into expanding its fishing fleet; as a result, its yearly catch rose, as did consumption. In salad 'Mimosa', canned fish is layered with chopped boiled potatoes, hard-boiled eggs separated into whites and yolks, cooked carrots and mayonnaise. Finely chopped hard-boiled yolks make up the top layer, giving the salad its name: the yolks mimic mimosa

Vinegret had its origins as a way to use up leftover meat; now it is a familiar salad that starts many a meal, combining beetroot, peas and other vegetables in a simple vinaigrette dressing.

flowers. Another salad, *seld pod shuboi* – literally herring under a fur coat – is similar, but uses herring instead of other canned fish and adds a layer of grated cooked beetroot under the topping of mayonnaise and chopped egg yolk. The beetroot bleeds into the mayonnaise, making the salad one of the most vibrantly coloured parts of the Russian table.[17]

As a First: Soups

Vladimir Burnashev began his description of Russian foods with soup, and that is as it should be, for soups are central to the Russian table. The transliterated word *sup* was in use by the eighteenth century, but it layered onto other older words for soups. There were specific soups with their own words: *shchi* (cabbage soup), borscht (beetroot soup), *rassolnik* (a sour vegetable soup), *botvinia* (a sour, cold soup) and *ukha* (fish soup). Or there was a *pokhlebka*, a more general term for soup, probably largely vegetable-based. Cookbooks might indicate that they had recipes for both *shchi* and soup, or even separate them into their own sections. Soups, and particularly *shchi*, figured in peasant aphorisms: '*shchi* and porridge, that's our food'; 'what's a wife if she can't make *shchi*?'

Above all, the homely cabbage soup that is *shchi* was and is the quintessence of Russian dishes. It was, as Ivan Boltin put it at the end of the eighteenth century, 'from the most elite to the last peasant eaten nearly daily with the difference that it is made better among the rich and worse among the poor'.[18] A mid-nineteenth-century British traveller also described its importance across the social spectrum:

> *Shchee* is made out of beef, cabbage, parsley, carrots, salt and 'English pepper;' and is the most thoroughly national of all the Russian soups. Peasants, soldiers, merchants, and nobles eat this soup. Indeed, the peasant seldom takes any other, though there is frequently this important difference between his *shchee* and that of his betters – in the former, the important item of beef is omitted. However, at the Moscow 'fabrics,' of which I visited about a dozen, the daily food of the workmen was very good, consisting of *shchee* with beef in it, black bread and *casha* (the meal of buck-wheat) moistened with oil. We may here remark, that black bread is eaten by all classes, particularly with the *shchee*: even in the best houses white and black, or white and brown, bread are put together on the table.[19]

For the poor, *shchi* was little more than the 'cabbage broth' one traveller described with some disgust.[20] According to one of the first Russian ethnographers, Ivan Snegirev, *shchi* was usually prepared from the chopped, fermented cabbage every peasant household stored each autumn. It was usually eaten 'empty', that is, without meat; meat was added only on holidays. Instead, to make the everyday meatless *shchi* thicker, it was 'sprinkled with flour' and served with either a dollop of hempseed oil or of sour cream, depending on whether it was a fast day or one on which meat and dairy were allowed.[21] In some areas, 'grey' *shchi* was the norm: this was the most frugal form of the soup, made from the cabbage's outer leaves and trimmings.[22] Even today, the *shchi* served in restaurants or cafeterias or in homes can be little more than cabbage and a bit of onion and carrot boiled in water or possibly bouillon. The dollop of sour cream added to each soup bowl is what gives it body.

There were also much more luxurious variations that made *shchi* a food consumed on the tables of the wealthy, too. Recipe books aimed at more elite audiences, for example, gave instructions to cook the cabbage with beef, with ham, with pork or even with 'pork, beef, ham, a goose and two chickens'.[23] One culinary advisor recommended what he called 'double *shchi*': *shchi* cooked once, then put through a sieve and used as the liquid for a second cooking.[24] *Shchi* was also part of winter travels – travellers would bring along frozen *shchi* and reheat it along the way. According to an anonymous memoirist, 'the old lady from the steppe', in the early nineteenth century a noble family travelling from their estate to Moscow in the winter would bring along

> frozen *shchi*, prepared with sour cabbage, and with beef,
> mutton, goose, duck, turkey, chicken; all of this together
> was frozen, and at stops, that is in villages, where we fed
> the horses during the day or where we stopped for the night,
> we would hack off a piece of the frozen mass and heat it in
> a peasant stove. Each of us would choose for ourself the piece
> of meat we wanted from the *shchi*.[25]

Although strictly speaking borscht – vegetable soup with beetroot as its main ingredient – is the national soup of Ukraine, not of Russia, it also became ubiquitous in Russian cooking. It was part of Russian diets at least by the end of the eighteenth century. One of the first Russian cookbook writers, Sergei Drukovtsov, included a recipe for borscht in his *Cooking*

There is nothing as truly Russian as *shchi*, cabbage soup usually made from sour, fermented cabbage.

Notes from 1779.[26] In the 1820s, the noble Vorontsov household in Moscow regularly served borscht (possibly to clerks, not to their elite guests, but it was at least still in common use there). Kitchen registers note purchases of 'beetroot for borscht' or 'sour cream for borscht'.[27]

In her bestselling cookbooks from the 1840s, Katerina Avdeeva included both a recipe for borscht as a Lenten soup and a recipe for 'Little Russian' (as Ukrainian was then known) borscht in a separate section of 'various dishes that have come into use among Russians'. By the end of the nineteenth century, borscht had nearly switched positions with *shchi*. Although the early editions of Elena Molokhovets's *Gift to Young Housewives* listed *shchi* before recipes for 'Little Russian' and 'Polish' borscht, her later cookbooks listed borscht (without a foreign qualifier) before *shchi*; in the Soviet era, so did the *Book of Tasty and Healthy Food*. In the twentieth century, too, borscht was often removed from its Ukrainian roots; in the 1930s, 'proletarian borscht' found its way onto tables; later, 'Moscow borscht' – which included, above all, many, many varieties of meat – did so as well.[28]

These two are the most well-known 'Russian' soups, but there are other common ones, as well. *Ukha*, fish soup, is one of the oldest. Originally the word was used for meat soups more generally, but by the end of the seventeenth century it came to refer exclusively to soups made of fish, particularly the freshwater river fish common to Russia. *Ukha* could be very simple. Elena Molokhovets gave a recipe for *ukha* of ruff or gudgeon that called for two ingredients if the fish was still alive: only fish and potatoes; if the fish was 'asleep', she recommended adding a bay leaf, peppercorns 'and even root vegetables: one carrot, one parsley root, 1–2 onions'.[29] More often *ukha* was prepared with several varieties of fish. One recipe called for carp, perch, ruff and gudgeon; others suggested using 'small fish' to make a bouillon as a base to cook sturgeon.

Some of the other Russian soups were characterized by a particular sourness. Two related soups, *rassolnik* and *solianka*, used pickles and pickle brine to add tang. Drawing a line between the two is difficult; in contemporary Russian cuisine they look distinctly different, but in nineteenth-century recipes their differences are less clear; all involved pickled/salted cucumbers, possibly brine, some other vegetables, though often not many, and usually meat or fish. Another sour soup, *botvinia*, became another symbol of Russian cooking in the nineteenth century, in particular, perhaps because it encompassed several traits: it contained sour *kvas* or its effervescent variation *kislye shchi*, the quite common (at least among the elite) fish and beetroot greens. It was also served cold, a trait, noted by some, that was a unique part of Russian summer cuisine, necessitated by the summer heats.[30] One list of national treasures included it as Russia's greatest culinary particularity: 'Russian *botvinia*, English

Although borscht originated in Ukraine, it has become synonymous with Russia, perhaps because of its vibrant colour – it seems a brilliant contrast to the bread, porridge and potatoes that make up so much of Russian cuisine.

engravings, German sauerkraut, Italian ice cream, these are the concoctions which in other countries they can only imitate.'[31]

For travellers, in particular, *botvinia* came to be seen as among the most absolutely foreign foods they encountered; it stood for the oddities of Russian cuisine. The English visitor Richard Southwell Bourke, for example, wrote of his surprise at the 'very good looking green soup, called "*badvinieh*" (I'll not answer for the correctness of the name)', which turned out to be

> an iced mixture of salmon, parsley, pickled cucumbers and vinegar, instead of what I expected it to be, good hot pea soup! It was not nice, so I with difficulty swallowed the first mouthful, and put down my spoon with so serious a face, that it caused great merriment to all near me.[32]

Botvinia was the bane of more than one foreigner's existence in Russia. Another Englishman described it as 'kvass, (the vehicle,) kislistchi, salt-fish, craw-fish, spinage, salt-cucumbers, and onions. These form a mixture (a mixture with a vengeance!) which is used and served up with a piece of ice in the middle'.[33] For those a bit more adventurous, though, the soup could be a summer treat; another Englishman noted that 'some of our party gave unmistakeable signs of enjoying it' – although he apparently did not![34]

AND FOR A SECOND DISH?

Entrées – usually called 'second dishes' now – overall have a much less distinctly 'Russian' character than some of the region's soups and salads, perhaps in part because they were not part of the regular meals of the peasant masses of Russia's history. By most accounts, Russia's peasants ate mainly soup, bread and porridge; multi-course meals were not for them. There had always been an elite who ate better, or at least more, of course, but that elite's meals did not create particularly renowned dishes. As in many other parts of Europe, roasts and braised meats were the norm. There was perhaps a bit more of a tendency to use particular condiments like horseradish, mustard or garlic, or to add pickled or fermented cucumbers, mushrooms or cabbage to the braise, or to use buckwheat *kasha* as a stuffing, than in some other areas. Some early travellers reported feasting on roast swans as a particular Russian extravagance and oddity, as well.

For the most part, however, there were no dramatically distinct entrées on the Russian table.

This general world of roasts and braises, plus additions from French, German and English cookery, remained the norm through the nineteenth century. Nineteenth-century cookbooks give variations on braised or stewed beef, or roast meats of all sorts, for the bulk of their second courses. In Katerina Avdeeva's list of foods of the 'Russian table', recipes for 'second' dishes are mostly a series of instructions for how to roast different meats: geese and ducks, turkey, chicken, suckling pig, lamb, game, veal, beef, mutton, tongue, cow's udder and sheep's or cow's intestines stuffed with buckwheat *kasha* – by far the most distinct of these possible 'roasts'. Most were simply roasted or baked, some gave suggestions for a stuffing, usually of chopped hard-boiled eggs, some suggested adding buckwheat or other *kasha* to the roasting pan. In other sections of her cookbook Avdeeva listed further meat dishes, including stews, 'sauces' (which at this point usually meant a dish of meat and vegetables cooked together) and fricassees. Things had not changed much by the end of the century. At that point, Elena Molokhovets's cookbooks – which used the terms 'first' for soups and 'second' for entrées – still most of all listed recipes for stewed or braised beef and roasted meats and fish.

The Russian table did have one significant difference from some of those of Western Europe, in particular. Even in cookbooks aimed at a middling or elite audience, who unlike peasants could afford to purchase meat if they so wished, authors like Avdeeva and Molokhovets included large numbers of vegetarian main dishes. The reason was simple: Orthodoxy, which had strict dietary rules for what foods were allowed when. Devout Orthodox abstained from meat (and dairy and eggs) not just during Lent but several days a week throughout the year. As a result, their cookbooks featured recipes not only for Lenten *shchi* or borscht (no dollop of sour cream at the end, for those) but for heartier dishes like 'sauce of cabbage', which was actually a head of cabbage stuffed with buckwheat and baked, 'lentil sauce' or 'mushroom cutlets'. But they also included recipes that were vegetable-based but not Lent-appropriate because of their use of milk, eggs or small amounts of meat. That meant baked or roasted pumpkin, vegetables in milk sauce or a main-dish version of *solianka*, which here layered sour fermented cabbage with meat or fish and pickled cucumbers and mushrooms.

This part of the meal was particularly affected by the Soviet era. Then, the creation of the concept of *obshchestvennoe pitanie* or *obshchepit*

Lenten Foods

The act of fasting is intended both to remind Orthodox faithful of their duty to lead a modest life and to remember particular moments in the life of Christ. Avoiding all animal products, including milk, butter and cheese, was supposed to be not quite a kind of penance, but a definite process of giving up something pleasurable. In general, it brought many frugal meals, particularly for Russia's peasant population. By the eighteenth and nineteenth centuries, members of the elite were looking for ways to eat according to the rules, but still with a fair degree of pleasure. One culinary author described the three bases of Lenten cooking as vegetable oil, mushrooms and onions, though he went on to include pepper and bay leaves as two additional 'necessities of Lenten cookery' because they added so much flavour. The author also went on to give a recipe for sterlet in champagne sauce that was in principle Lenten, but hardly a hardship. Even non-fish dishes could be quite luxurious. Another culinary author gave instructions for how to make 'Lenten cream': essentially nuts finely ground and mixed with water. It was used to make *kotlety* of mushrooms and chestnuts, or a dish based on truffles. This author also suggested that any Lenten food was improved by 'the addition of English soys [sauces], under the names of Harvey Sauce and Coratsch' but not of others on the market, for 'there are many kinds of them, and not all of them are good.'[35]

(literally 'social nutrition'), as well as a more regimented approach to cookbook writing, meant that a set array of foods became standardized as part of a Soviet cuisine that owed much to the Russian table. In areas like soups, not too much changed: *shchi* and borscht and *rassolnik* all continued. But 'second' courses did see a bigger change, in part because they were relatively undefined before.

Perhaps the most common 'second' course to come out of this period that is clearly related to Russian foods from before the revolution is the *kotlet*. The *kotlet* is not a particular cut of meat. Instead, it is a patty of minced meat or possibly vegetables mixed with egg and often starch of some kind, perhaps with some seasoning as well, often lightly breaded and pan-fried. Earlier authors like Molokhovets included various kinds of *kotlety* in their cookbooks, although at that point they were as often vegetable based. One French traveller even commented on the general prevalence of something that seems to be the *kotlet*: 'I was served again that abominable cabbage soup, in which swims a piece of beef; then, the obligatory cucumber, and an equally invariable plate of meatballs.'[36]

In the Soviet era, the *kotlet* came to take precedence over whole roast pieces of meat. It was economical and could be made so as to stretch out a small portion of meat with breadcrumbs or other starch, and it made tougher cuts more palatable. It was also a challenge. In 1933, a contributor to the journal *Obshchestvennoe pitanie* described 'the history of the battle for mince [ground meat]'. The problem was that 'transporting mince is dangerous', which meant that it could not be produced in factories and brought to market. The greatest attempts of Soviet scientists had still not fixed this problem, the contributor sadly concluded. With the coming of more reliable refrigeration after the Second World War, however, mince became a more regular part of the world of Russian food. By 1954, the *Book of Tasty and Healthy Food* claimed that ground meat was now available to all, but still only from shops with proper cooling mechanisms, where it was prepared on site, and not from factories, the ultimate goal.[37]

In addition, second courses are where the greatest expansion of the Russian table to include foods from the wider Soviet Union – the former Russian empire – took place. Already in the 1945 edition of the *Book of Tasty and Healthy Food*, basic stews are joined by goulash, moussaka, *shashlik* (shish-kebab), *chakhokhbili* (a chicken stew from Georgia) and *plov* (spiced rice and meat). Then, in the 1954 edition, even more new things join in. *Kotlety* are accompanied by schnitzel. *Golubtsy* (stuffed cabbage rolls, often associated with Ukraine) are partnered with goulash and dolma. The larger Soviet world began to amalgamate into a single, unified Soviet cuisine. That cuisine was predominantly Russian, but reached well beyond it, as well.

Breads, Porridge, Dumplings and Pirogi

Bread, *kasha*, dumplings, pies: all of these grain-based foods were and are central to the Russian table, whether as staples of life or as treats for holidays and festivals (or, eventually, treats for every day). Grain-based foods played different roles for different people. They could be nearly entire meals, even entire diets: at the beginning of the twentieth century, peasants in European Russia got almost two-thirds of their daily calories from grains.[38] Or they were 'garnishes' or 'third courses' to more elaborate meals eaten by people of higher social status and greater wealth. In some ways these foods transcended association with Russia itself – most of Eurasia ate different kinds of bread or porridge or pies or dumplings. What marked some of these foods as distinctly Russian, though, was ingredients and technique.

Bread was simply the dominant food of the Russian people. Bread (*khleb*) and salt (*sol*) together formed the symbol of hospitality (*khlebosolstvo*). Folk sayings emphasized bread's importance: 'Bread and water – that's peasant food', 'what makes a man sated and strong, if not bread?'[39] Bread also reached across the divide of wealth: the rich and the poor alike ate it, although as one nineteenth-century author put it, only the rich could think about different ways of making bread, while the poor had to think of the basic task of finding enough.[40]

True Russian bread had two characteristics: it was made of rye and it was sour, sour to the point of unpalatability for those who were not used to it. As the British traveller Robert Pinkerton put it in the 1830s:

> Rye-bread is in common use throughout the whole empire.
> It is daily upon the table of the peasant and the prince; and
> every family bakes it for their own consumption. It is usually
> well leavened; and possesses a degree of acidity, which,
> to the stranger, is not at first agreeable, but is considered
> indispensable to suit the peculiar taste of the Russian. The
> loaves are round, from eighteen to twenty-four inches in
> diameter, and six or seven inches thick. This rye-bread,
> commonly called *tschernoi hleb* (black bread), is the staple
> support of the common people. With three pounds of this
> bread, an ounce of salt to strew on it, and a can of quass, the
> labouring man performs the hardest work, and the soldier
> goes through the greatest fatigue, without murmuring.
> In general, they prefer rye to wheaten bread, because they
> affirm the former to be more nourishing. Very little white
> bread is yet in use among the people or in the army.[41]

For the most part, Pinkerton was right. Everyone ate some rye bread, and peasants in particular ate large amounts of it; it was sour, and it was usually baked in huge round loaves. When a seventeenth-century monk from Antioch travelled to Muscovy, he saw loaves of rye bread 'looking like a large mill-stone' and carried by 'four or five men'. He and his companions also found themselves repulsed by the bread: 'we, however, could not eat it at all ... [it] was as sour as vinegar, both to taste and smell.'[42] A nineteenth-century author gave cooking times for loaves of bread weighing as much as 12 *funty*, or nearly 5 kilograms/11 lb (such a loaf took three hours to bake).[43] Baking loaves of this size made sense given how much people ate. In the middle of the nineteenth century, Russian soldiers received daily bread allotments that amounted to about 1.25 kilograms (2¾ lb) a day – and they perhaps ate less bread than their peasant fellows, for they received an allotment of meat, as well.[44] On the other hand, such large loaves could be difficult to cook through. One Russian author described an unfortunate encounter with bread in a peasant cottage in the 1840s: 'my God, what was this for bread! The whole mass was grey and undercooked; my teeth stuck in it like mud!'[45]

Rye bread was dunked in soup or eaten alongside other foods, or, perhaps most often, it was eaten on its own. Butter was a luxurious condiment; salt a common one. Peasants working in the fields sometimes also made a concoction known as *tiuria* from it, dousing a chunk of (probably stale) rye bread with *kvas* or water, adding hempseed oil and sprinkling it with onions.[46] It was the kind of hearty, calorie-rich food that kept them labouring through the short, intense growing season. Late in the Soviet era, *tiuria* emerged from semi-obscurity in the writing of Viliam Pokhlebkin, a popular culinary historian and cooking columnist. According to him, *tiuria* was a national soup like *shchi* and *botvinia*. Other culinary writers, though, believed that its disappearance from contemporary tables was nothing but a good thing and a sign of the country's increased prosperity.[47]

There was a traditional Russian version of white, wheaten bread known as a *kalach*, but it was bread for holidays, not the true everyday Russian bread. It was still seen as a particular speciality of Moscow in the middle of the nineteenth century. One English traveller was advised to try it, and found it good: 'it is made in the shape of a flat hand-basket, and, when eaten hot with lots of butter, reminds an English stomach of a married muffin and crumpet.' It was such a Moscow speciality that 'a fellow-traveller on the railroad told us that whenever he went to Moscow in the winter he took back to St. Petersburg a supply of this bread, hanging it out of the window to freeze.'[48] Another traveller noted that there were 'upwards of ninety establishments that bake nothing else' in Moscow, and that 'when the emperor [Nicholas I] presented his son, the crown prince who was born here, to the citizens, he called him "his Moscow kalatch".[49]

Eventually, however, white, wheaten bread became more common. Foreign master bakers came to the country starting in the eighteenth century and began selling other kinds of wheaten breads. One traveller through Siberia in the middle of the nineteenth century noted that

> Bakers are in great force in Irkutsk, many of them Germans. *Frantsooski khleb* (French bread) is all the rage in Siberia, and this sign is adopted by all the bakers indiscriminately. The 'French bread' is simply white bread made into rolls. It is very good, and being unobtainable in the country villages, travellers carry a supply with them from one town to another.[50]

In the twentieth century, wheat bread became more and more common. Despite this, the sour rye loaf is still the proper carrier of Russianness, the proper accompaniment to *shchi* or borscht, and still present at most meals.

Kasha – porridge – was the other major staple of the Russian table. '*Kasha* is our mother' went a folk saying.[51] In the opening scenes of Tolstoy's *Anna Karenina*, the bon vivant and man about town Stiva Oblonsky and his friend, the very earnest Nikolai Levin, go to a restaurant for dinner. Stiva spends his journey there coming up with a menu, only to have it thrown into disarray when a waiter tells him the restaurant has just received fresh oysters from Flensburg. He wants the oysters, of course, but needs to construct a different menu to accompany them. Levin, however, wants none of this. 'I'd like *shchi* and *kasha*,' he says, glumly, 'but there's none of that here.' Ah, the waiter asks, 'you'd like to order *kasha à la russe*?' (In the end, Levin happily eats the grander meal that Stiva orders, his principles overcome by the tastiness of the meal.)

Although there are many kinds of *kasha* eaten in Russia – oat, farina, millet, rice – just as rye bread is the true Russian bread, buckwheat is the true Russian *kasha*. As one agricultural writer put it in the nineteenth century, 'there is no other country on earth where so much buckwheat is sown and buckwheat groats used and *kasha* cooked and blini baked . . . buckwheat is for the Russian what potatoes are to the Irish and the Germans.'[52] And as Vladimir Odoevskii, a nineteenth-century nobleman who masqueraded as a culinary author under the pseudonym Doctor Puf, put it, 'all other *kashas* are before our common, aromatic, well-steamed buckwheat *kasha* like a candle before the sun!'[53]

Initially buckwheat *kasha* was cooked in a clay pot in the oven. Katerina Avdeeva advised filling the pot a bit more than halfway up with buckwheat, adding salt and boiling water, stirring it together and placing it in the oven. Once the *kasha* thickened, the pot could be turned upside down and left in the oven to brown slightly. *Kasha* was served with butter or oil, or – once it had cooled – with milk.[54] As cooking implements changed, so too did the process of making *kasha*. At the end of the nineteenth century Molokhovets was still giving recipes for *kasha* baked in the oven, but in the Soviet era *kasha* moved to the stovetop – at least for the most part. The *Book of Tasty and Healthy Food* recommended starting *kasha* on top of the stove and then moving it into the oven.

Russians also often ate (and in one case, still often eat) two other grain-based dishes that demonstrate frugality. One is *tolokno*. To make it, oats (or less often barley) were soaked in water, then dried out and finely ground. The resulting meal could be consumed without further cooking, making it a food associated with peasants at work. It was, according to a writer in the 1840s,

Some foods, like *tolokno*, were particularly consumed on the go – by soldiers in camps or by peasants in fields, as in this photograph from the early 20th century. Here, peasants are taking a break from their labours in the field – they may not be eating *tolokno*, but there is a kettle there, perhaps ready to rehydrate the oat powder for a quick, hot meal.

the principal condiment of the peasant table, a necessary
food for the peasant when he is on the road . . . *tolokno* is
sprinkled on *shchi*, *tolokno* is cooked with oil like a porridge,
but most often of all, in summer during the heavy work season,
particularly at harvest time and during the haying, *tolokno* is
eaten or drunk, mixed with *kvas* and wort, and with a garnish
of sour cream and green onions.[55]

It was a particular favourite in some old northern provinces of European
Russia; peasants from there were supposedly called *tolokonniki* because of
their love of the stuff.[56]

In the 1830s, the ethnographer Snegirev reported that seventeenth-
century travellers to Muscovy had been shocked that the strong Russian
soldier could possibly fight so well when eating something as basic as
tolokno; in their minds, this was all the more shocking because *tolokno* was
not even cooked! That was exactly the point, he noted, quoting another
peasant as saying: '*tolokno* is a quick food: mix it up and it's ready for the
mouth.'[57] It was not only seventeenth-century foreigners who wondered
in amazement that *tolokno* could support hard labour. One anonymous
Russian author opined that 'seeing the labour of the agriculturalist it is
impossible to imagine properly how human strength may carry such pro-
longed and incessant exercise, and it is made completely improbable when
you see what the worker eats': bread and *tolokno*.[58]

Although *tolokno* is no longer common, another dish born of frugality
is still both common and a treat: *kisel*. At base, *kisel* is simply liquid thickened with starch. Initially, it was a way of capturing and consuming the
starchy water left over after boiling oats or bran; later, it took advantage of
industrially produced potato or corn starch. In its most basic form, oats or
bran and water were boiled not to make porridge but to thicken the water
with starch. This could be a meal in and of itself; Avdeeva even advised *kisel*
made from bran as a possible alternative to *kasha* as a food for servants.[59]
Alternatively, fruit, either dried or fresh, could be added to the mixture,
resulting in a slightly sweet, thick liquid. This was a favourite both as a
pleasure – 'happiness is *kisel* and beer' – and as something healthy – 'with
kisel you don't ruin your stomach' and '*kisel* brings no harm to the teeth.'[60]
Kisel also had a particular advantage on Lenten days: its creamy consistency
was something otherwise hard to get without dairy, egg or animal fat.

Tolokno and *kisel* were born of frugality (even if one also became a
treat); their opposite, in many ways, were the numerous filled pies and

The sweet treat *kisel* uses potato or other starch to thicken cooked fruit juices; it can be made thin enough to drink or thick enough to eat with a spoon.

dumplings common not only to Russian but to Siberian and other East Slavic cooking: *pelmeni, pirogi, vatrushki, kulebiaka, vareniki.* Some of these were frugal, in a way, for they took small amounts of meat or other special fillings and stretched them out with a dough to be baked or boiled or fried (or, in the case of *kundiumy,* baked and then steamed). Others became luxurious displays, both in their fillings and in their decorations.

Boiled dumplings came in two major forms, and developed in two different ways. *Pelmeni* are small meat-filled dumplings twisted up somewhat like tortellini. This shape may give them their name, which is thought to derive from the Komi or Udmurt word *pel*, or ear.[61] That linguistic origin says something about the origins of the dumplings themselves – the Komi and Udmurt are both Finnic peoples who live in the very far northeast of European Russia – but its uncertainty also reflects the fact that the exact origins of *pelmeni* are unclear. At the very beginning of the nineteenth century one Russian journalist described them as an unfamiliar, natively Tatar dish, common around the city of Kazan – a long way east of Moscow, but still only on the Volga.[62] More often, *pelmeni* are associated with a place yet further east: Siberia. Katerina Avdeeva, herself a native of Siberia, called them 'Siberian' *pelmeni* when she included them as one element of the Russian table. This is the description that stuck; when a later cookbook author, Ignatii Radetskii, included them in his gastronomically inflected cookbook, he called them *petits patés à la sibirienne*.[63] Part of what made them Siberian is the story of how they were kept: made in bulk in the autumn, then frozen in bags or boxes outside the house all winter long, to be enjoyed at will. In the Soviet (and now post-Soviet) era, this part of the story of *pelmeni* made them perfect for new goals of mechanization and developing freezing technologies; *pelmeni* stands were joined by bags of *pelmeni* available at frozen food counters.

Vareniki came from the other side of the empire: Ukraine. These boiled dumplings were often half-moon shaped, rather than little twisted-up dumplings, and filled with a wide variety of usually vegetarian fillings: cabbage, mushrooms, *tvorog* (curds), cherries or other fruits. Avdeeva lists a recipe for *vareniki* filled with *tvorog* among 'foods that have come into use by Russians'. By the end of the nineteenth century Molokhovets's cookbook gives many more varieties. Like *pelmeni*, *vareniki* fitted in well with the rise

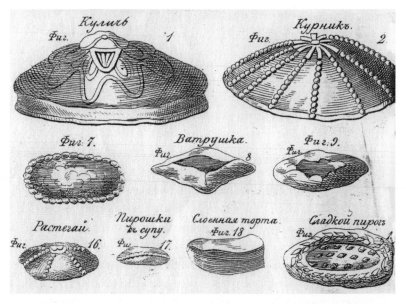

These illustrations from Katerina Avdeeva's mid-19th-century cookbook show off some of the many, many filled pastries that appeared on the Russian table. In the first figure a decorated *kulich* and *kurnik* take pride of place (the *kurnik* was filled with chicken, the *kulich* by many other possibilities). In the second row differently shaped *vatrushki* have open tops to show off their fillings. The third row features a series of different options: a *rasstegai* noted for its round shape, 'small *pirogi* for soup', a puff-pastry tart and a 'sweet *pirog*', here highly decorated.

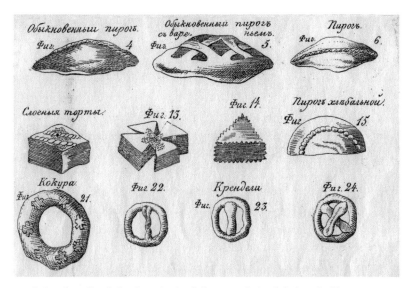

Avdeeva's cookbook also showed off a whole series of other baked goods. The top row shows a series of 'ordinary *pirogi*', the middle one filled with jam (these shapes are still seen in display cases around Russia). The second row shows different varieties of tarts made from puff pastry, and at the end another *pirog*. The bottom row suggests several shapes for krendely, a pretzel-like bread.

of packaged and mechanically produced foods. Although restaurants may still offer them made by hand, freezer cases make them an easy fast meal.

Possibly even more than dumplings, filled pastries and *pirogi* were a regular part of holiday meals for some, and everyday meals for the wealthy. The satiric culinary author Doctor Puf called Russians 'true laganovores', making up the word from the Latin *laganum*, or pie.[64] Pies – *pirogi* or, for smaller ones, *pirozhki* – were baked from yeast-risen wheat dough, filled with meat, with cabbage or mushrooms or potatoes, with fruit, with eggs and onions, then folded over and closed before baking or frying. *Vatrushki* used the same sort of dough, but were baked open with the filling on top; *tvorog* is the most common filling, but fruit or preserves can also serve as a treat.

The most spectacular of the *pirogi*, though, was the *kulebiaka*. As Katerina Avdeeva put it, it was 'in general the favourite dish of people of all statuses', and could be 'served for breakfast, or at the dinner table, in some places before the hot dish, when it is served with *botvinia*, and sometimes with the hot dish or after it'.[65] It was essentially simply a large pastry with a rich, yeasted dough, filled with either an entire fish or fillets of fish and some additional filling: more fish, mushrooms, *viziga*, thin crêpes, rice. It was usually long and oblong, to echo the shape of the fish, and could be highly decorated. The *kulebiaka* also made its way outside Russia as *coulibiac*, a dish the American food writer Craig Claiborne declared to be 'the world's greatest dish'.[66]

THE FESTIVE TABLE

Although dishes like the *kulebiaka* were probably not everyday foods even for the elite, any of these could in principle be served up at any time. Some baked goods, however, were prepared and eaten only, or at least predominately, on particular festive occasions. Wedding feasts, for example, usually featured a particular form of rich, highly decorated bread known as the *karavai* (sometimes *korovai*). Made with a dough enriched with butter, eggs and/or sour cream, and decorated with swirls, braids and figures, it was a true celebration treat. It turns up in descriptions of the weddings of Russian tsars. When Vasilii III married Elena Glinskaia in 1526, the wedding ceremonies involved multiple *karavai* carried in processions or served at table; the breads also appeared at the multiple weddings of his son, Ivan the Terrible.[67] The process of baking the *karavai* was woven into many pre-wedding and wedding ceremonies of Russian peasants, as well.

Other distinct treats were associated with the most important religious celebration of the Orthodox world: Easter. Before Easter, and before the Great Lent that preceded it, Russians celebrated their version of a carnival: *Maslenitsa. Maslenitsa* is usually translated as 'butter week': *maslo* is the term for butter or oil, and this pre-fasting celebration luxuriated in it. Not in any form, though; instead, it savoured one particular dish: blini (singular: blin). Everyone stuffed themselves with blini during *Maslenitsa*; as an English traveller recounted,

> there are blinnies at lunch and blinnies at dinner, whilst the lower classes do nothing but regale on them all the day long. 'Well, Grushia,' I once said to a servant, 'and how many have you had to-day?' 'Thirty-four, Madame; but I am going to have some more.'[68]

Another agreed that they were 'a very tempting form of food', 'a sort of scone, a cross between a pancake and a crumpet, eaten with fresh butter and caviare'.[69]

The proper blini of butter week were no simple pan-fried treat. There are many variations on blini, essentially just a pancake, but according to

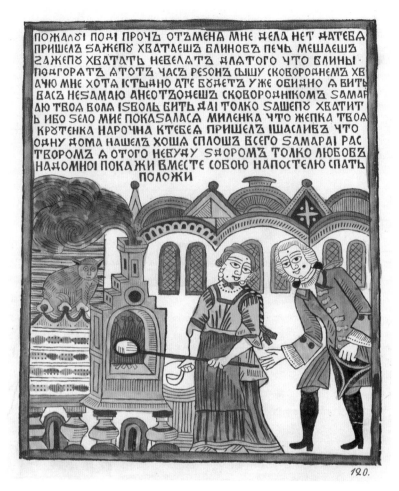

ПОЖАЛУI ПОДI ПРОЧЪ ОТЪМЕНА МНЕ ДЕЛА НЕТ' ДАТЕБА
ПРИШЕЛЪ ЗАЖЕПУ ХВАТАЕШЪ БЛИНОВЪ ПЕЧЬ МЕШАЕШЪ
ЗАЖЕПУ ХВАТАТЬ НЕВЕЛАТЪ ДЛАТОГО ЧТО БЛИНЫ
ПОДГОРАТЪ АТОТЪ ЧАСЪ РЕЗОНЪ СЫШУ СКОВОРОДНЕМЪ ХВ
АЧЮ МНЕ ХОТА IСТЬЯНО ДТЕ БУДЕТЪ УЖЕ ОБИДНО А БИТЬ
ВАСЪ НЕЗАМАЮ ДНЕОТЪОДНЕШЪ СКОВОРОДНИКОМЪ SАМАР
АЮ ТВОА ВОЛА IЗВОЛЬ БИТЬ ДАI ТОЛКО SАШЕПУ ХВАТИТ
Ь ИБО SЕЛО МНЕ ПОКАSАЛАСА МИЛЕНКА ЧТО ЖЕПКА ТВОА
КРУТЕНКА НАРОЧНА КТЕБЕА ПРИШЕЛЪ IШАСЛИВЪ ЧТО
ОДНУ ДОМА НАШЕЛЪ ХОША СПЛОШЪ ВСЕГО SАМАРАI РАС
ТВОРОМЪ А ОТОГО НЕБУДУ SДОРОМЪ ТОЛКО ЛЮБОВЪ
НАДОМНОI ПОКАЖИ ВМЕСТЕ СОБОЮ НАПОСТЕЛЮ СПАТЬ
ПОЛОЖИ

120.

The small, raised pancakes known as blini were the special treat of *Maslenitsa*, sometimes
translated as butter week – the carnival before Great Lent. Blini were originally baked in
the Russian stove in small pans made just for the purpose, as depicted in this 18th-century
woodcut print. The *blinishchitsa*, or blini maker, also holds a small ladle to scoop out the batter
for the blini directly into the hot pan. The print shows baking, but the text is a risqué one
about the baker warding off the untoward advances of the 'gentleman'.

Doctor Puf, 'the true, indigenous Russian blini are buckwheat blini; all
other blini are futile and vain desires to approximate buckwheat blini.'[70]
They were yeast-risen, requiring pre-planning (which of course everyone
anticipated during the holiday). Special blini pans helped keep them their
characteristic small round shape. Nor were they simple to make. 'The first
blin is for the fire,' went a folk proverb, recognizing that the first pancake
usually stuck to the pan and came out wrong. The verb used for cooking
blini is 'to bake', as they were originally cooked in the oven, though pan

frying on a stovetop became the norm. They were supposed to be so light and fluffy that one author advised eating them without the use of cutlery, for even the touch of a knife would cause them to deflate. Their usual accompaniments also added to the luxury of the festivities, for they were eaten with sour cream, with butter, or with caviar.[71]

Blini became a treat beyond *Maslenitsa*, eaten with sweet things for breakfast or with salty things for *zakuski*. So too did other kinds of blini, prepared with different kinds of flour and different kinds of leavening. By the end of the nineteenth century Molokhovets was giving recipes for raised blini leavened either with yeast or with soda and also for *blinchiki*: larger, thinner, unleavened blini, essentially crêpes. They, in particular, have come to stand in for a kind of essential Russian cuisine. At the contemporary fast-food chain Teremok, servers – who still call their customers by traditional terms of respect – serve thin, crêpe-like blini or buckwheat *kasha* filled or topped with things either traditional (cabbage, *tvorog*, mushrooms) or not (ham and cheese).

After the deprivation of Lent, Easter was again a time to enjoy the things that had not been allowed: not just meat, but especially dairy products and eggs. Two treats – *kulich* and *paskha* – were the special foods of Easter. As one traveller put it, Easter was a time when

bread and a kind of conical cake made of curds, both
consecrated beforehand, and hard-boiled eggs dyed mostly

When served with caviar and sour cream, as here, or with other savoury or sweet toppings,
small blini like these make a perfect, delicious single bite.

These two Easter postcards by Elizaveta Bem put the culinary delights of the holiday at their centre. In one the Easter *paskha* – in which *tvorog*, or farmer's cheese, was mixed with additional dairy, sugar and dried fruits and shaped into a pyramid with its top cut off – takes pride of place alongside a bowl of dyed eggs. In the other, it is joined by a tall, cylindrical *kulich* and also what is probably a filled *pirog*, or large pie.

red, will be found even in the lowliest of cottages, while the tables of the higher and middle classes groan also with viands and refreshments of a more solid kind.[72]

Kulich was a rich yeast bread, not necessarily particularly sweet, though often spiced or studded with raisins. What made it *kulich* in particular was its decoration, always with a cross. *Paskha*, meanwhile, emphasized the dairy products that had been skipped during Lent. It was basically *tvorog* – farmer's cheese – mixed together with sour cream, butter, sugar and sometimes raisins or dried fruit. It could be eaten uncooked, or mixed with eggs and baked. In either case, it had a particular shape: a sort of four-sided pyramid with its top cut off.

These Easter treats could be part of celebrations that were quite spectacular. In April 1827 the noble Vorontsov household made a number of special purchases 'for cooking for the holiday'. They included *tvorog* and sour cream; cinnamon, cloves, raisins and sugar; turkey, a suckling pig, a pair of chickens; herbs, lettuce, horseradish and 10 *funty* (about 4 kilograms/8¾ lb) of butter; a purchased *kulich*; and 250 eggs, mostly for dying and handing out, not for cooking.[73] The meal celebrated all that had been gone without during Lent.

Sweet treats were not and are not only eaten at particular celebrations, of course. Nineteenth-century authors believed that Russians were particularly fond of sour and salty tastes, but the modern visitor to Russia would probably think that an average Russian has a sweet tooth, instead. Grocery shops will usually have an entire aisle or two given over to confectionery, and emigré grocery shops stock perhaps even more than ones in Russia itself. The particular sweet treats of childhood call even to those who have left their homes. Moscow and St Petersburg have rival confectionery factories, still called by their Soviet-era names: Red October in Moscow, Krupskaia (named after Lenin's wife Nadezhda) in Petersburg. The Red October factory lies on the Moskva river, nearly directly across from the Kremlin itself; it dates to before the revolution, when it was called the Einem chocolate company before being nationalized. They, along with others, produce bars of chocolate, small individual chocolates wrapped in cellophane and of course elaborate display boxes to give as gifts.

Cookbooks were filled with recipes for sweet foods as soon as they started to appear in the late eighteenth century, but most of these were clear imports. They have names transliterated from foreign languages: waffles, biscuits, plum pudding. In addition, there were sweet versions of the dumplings and *pirogi* and *kasha* and *kisel* that were more traditionally Russian. *Pirogi* and *vareniki* were often filled with fruit, *kasha* could be cooked with raisins or pumpkin or strawberry juice and *kisel* often used fruit juice as its base. Russian fruit preserves, *varenye*, thinner in consistency than the jams and jellies common in Western Europe, were sources of pleasure, as well, spooned onto *tvorog* or swirled into tea. Russia also has its version of a light, fried doughnut, called either *pyshki* or *ponchiki*.

The town of Tula is known for many things, including metalworks that produced both armaments and samovars. It also is one of the claimants to the origins of the *prianik*, a dry spiced cake baked in at times elaborately carved moulds. This monument in the centre of Tula is in honour of the 'Tula spice cake, known since 1685'.

The former name is particularly associated with St Petersburg, and *pyshki* get their name from their airy texture.

Another particular treat is the *prianik*, or spice cake, and it is a mightily contested one! Several Russian regions vie for the honour of being the original home of the *prianik*. Driving into one of them, Tula province, you see stalls all along the road offering the celebrated 'Tula *prianik*' for sale. *Prianiki* are known not only for their spicy flavour but for their elaborate decoration, created by baking them in carved moulds. They can feature abstract designs or figures or words, and range in size from small circles to large rectangles.

DRINKS (AND DRUNKENNESS)

Of course, the Russian table featured not only foods but drinks, some of which have their origins outside Russia but have been such a part of Russian culture that it is impossible to leave them out. Tea went along with treats like the *prianik* – Tula may have laid claim to the *prianik* in part because it is also the home of the samovar, essential to Russian tea-drinking. Vodka went with festivities (for good and for ill). *Kvas* was the everyday drink of the Russian peasant and the Russian noble, and the basis for many Russian dishes. This world of drink cannot be separated from the world of food.

The most essentially Russian drink is not vodka but *kvas*. 'Even bad *kvas* is better than good water,' went a peasant saying.[74] *Kvas* is a lightly fermented but very low-alcohol beverage brewed from rye bread, usually making use of stale bits and pieces. Molokhovets gave a recipe for *kvas* brewed in a day, where rye bread scraps were first covered with boiling water and allowed to sit. The strained-off liquid that resulted was mixed with yeast, sugar or molasses and half a lemon (definitely not traditional!) and allowed to sit. That mixture was then strained, put into bottles and corked. Other recipes suggested longer soaking or brewing times or slightly different ingredients, but this was the basic idea of the drink.

Everyone in Russia drank *kvas*, and almost every foreigner was troubled by it. One of the first to describe it, the Englishman Giles Fletcher, described it as 'water turned out of his wittes, with a little branne meashed with it'.[75] A couple of centuries later, an American described it as 'the most depressing sour beverage ever invented'.[76] In the nineteenth century, some Russian commentators declared in dismay that it was growing unfashionable:

> The art of brewing good *kvas* – that purely Russian, national drink – is unfortunately little by little losing itself and disappears with each new generation. Here is not the place to look at the reasons for that; but let them call me a *kvas*-patriot, for I remember with pleasure the ancient anecdote of the visiting foreigner, who, not joking, believed that in Russia, if someone ordered *kvas*, then everyone in the room with him would immediately shout out: and me, and me, and me. That was a good time! But today? In many Petersburg houses there are found old-timers of the capital for whom the taste of *kvas* is unknown since birth.[77]

Kvas was the refreshingly (or to some, off-puttingly) sour drink brewed from rye bread that everyone drank.

This was almost certainly an overstatement. One traveller from nearly the same time recounted something rather different. 'Quass was to be had if asked for, but this is avoided in company, as beer is amongst some of the "soi-disant" select in England,' he noted. But he went on: 'I have, however, seen many exceptions to this in Russia; and sometimes sat next to a Countess, who regularly emptied a decanter of this execrable beverage.'[78]

Furthermore, some Russian medical writers viewed *kvas* as an absolute necessity of life for Russia's peasants in particular, because it made their otherwise rough diet more nutritious. In the early 1890s, Doctor I. M. Iakovlev, a member of a public health commission, made this argument forcefully:

> The Russian common people, who primarily consume plant and starchy food, are vegetarians . . . At one and the same time with crude vegetable food the Russian man always consumes *kvas*, as well. *Kvas*, as a drink, likewise enters into the composition of

Street vendors often sold *kvas* in Russian towns. In this photo from 1931, a vendor has two kinds of cold drink for sale depending on the consumer's taste: the sour *kvas* and the sweet berry drink *mors*.

many Russian dishes and soups. Everyone knows that vegetable and starchy foods contain in themselves a mass of indigestible things. By adding *kvas* to crude plant foods containing difficult to digest cellulose, Russian people nonetheless possess healthy digestive organs and rarely suffer from digestive complaints.[79]

Kvas was, in other words, both a necessity in Russian culture and a necessity for Russian stomachs and health – an argument that presaged many contemporary discussions of the positive role that fermented foods and probiotics play in the human diet.[80]

A related beverage, and common at least before the twentieth century, was *kislye shchi*. This was simply an effervescent form of *kvas*, brewed in much the same way but with extra fermentation to make it sparkle. This might be achieved by adding a raisin or two to each bottle, giving it more sugar for the yeast to eat and thereby produce gas. *Kislye shchi* was not the same kind of everyday drink, for it required more careful brewing and preserving, but it was found everywhere and like *kvas* was an essential ingredient of many soups. Unlike *kvas*, which survived the Soviet era, *kislye shchi* did not. A 1927 guide to making 'refreshing fruit drinks' at home included a recipe for *kislye shchi*, but already described it as 'ancient'.[81] After that, it simply fades from view.

Although *kvas* is the most Russian of drinks, it is not the best known; instead, the first thing that comes to nearly anyone's mind when they think of Russian food and drink is vodka. And vodka was, indeed, important for cultural, social and fiscal reasons. Eventually vodka distilling (which used rye, not potatoes, as is commonly thought) and particularly the state monopoly on vodka became, as one early nineteenth-century author put it, 'the most wide and useful part of the Russian state economy. Grain alcohol or vodka is the favourite drink of the common Russian people, and equally an unsurpassed source of great State profits.'[82] As the ethnographer Snegirev put it, vodka 'strengthens the body of the Russian, warms his blood in cold, wind and rain, raises his spirits in bad times; therefore he drinks it in happiness and in sorrow'.[83] Although in the nineteenth century commentators worried that vodka production might divert too much grain and cause famine, in the eighteenth, at least in some regions, it was as much a way to use up excess grain production as anything.[84]

Vodka came into the Russian world early, but not as early as drinks like beer or mead. The word appeared no earlier than the fourteenth century, and probably sometime after that; alcohol distilled rather than brewed from grain certainly existed, and was called *khlebnoe vino*. The term *vino* continued to be used to refer not only to wine (which it could also mean) but to vodka – something that can be very confusing when reading old documents. When exactly vodka proper developed is still uncertain – possibly as early as the twelfth century CE, but more likely sometime in the late fifteenth or sixteenth century. It was definitely present in the sixteenth century, but only widespread and well established in the seventeenth.[85] From that point on, though, it has played a central role in festivities, at feasts and in taverns and bars. Above all, at least through the nineteenth century, vodka consumption was a communal or collective act of celebration; particularly in villages, vodka was part of the normal celebration of religious festivals and of marriages or baptisms. Everyday consumption was not the norm, but regular consumption at festival times was – and furthermore, often amounted to what would normally be called overconsumption.[86]

Boris Kustodiev, *Moscow Tavern*, 1916, oil on canvas. Tea drinking became an important part of Russian sociability. Here, a group of men sit around a table at a *kharchevnia* – an eating and drinking establishment for a non-elite clientele – drinking tea together. Later, communal tea drinking signalled a break from work in Soviet-era offices.

There is also an even longer history of brewing beer and mead in Russia. Buckets used to brew beer are found in archaeological digs dating back to the medieval era, as are traces of hops.[87] In the nineteenth century, the ethnographer and collector of peasant sayings Ivan Snegirev noted that 'before Russians became acquainted with vodka ... they drank strong cellared mead, dark beer ... they called drunkenness *khmelem* [hop-drunk].'[88] Peasants brewed beer not as an everyday drink – that was *kvas* – but for holidays and celebrations. In the early nineteenth century, one source said that 'almost every peasant brews it in his home from rye flour.'[89] Snegirev described the excellent beer brewed on his great-grandfather's estate in Izmailovo near Moscow during the eighteenth century: 'Ivan Savvich had a household serf, Kalina Kuzmich, who brewed excellent beer ... his beer was savoury, clear, tasty and healthy ... there were three sorts: *grandfather, father, son* [*dedushka, batiushka, synok*] depending on the degree of their strength.'[90]

Mead went along with beekeeping, something common in northern, forested, Russia. Mead could be brewed simply or with hops, to make a drink of varying taste and varying degrees of alcoholic content. It was known in the Russian lands as far back as the tenth century and continues to be produced (although now as something self-consciously old-fashioned).⁹¹ Writing in the seventeenth century, Adam Olearius claimed that Muscovites drank *kvas* or mead above all other drinks; 'persons of quality' might also drink beer or wine, but mead was the preferred drink. In particular, he noted, they made meads flavoured with cherries or berries; the mead 'that they make with Rasp-berries is the most pleasant of any'. It was, he noted, often further flavoured by 'a little bag of Cinnamon, and grains of Paradise, with some few Cloves'.⁹² Of course, these spices all came into Muscovy from afar, hinting at the ways that this 'traditional' drink was already being transformed.

Possibly even more common than mead was another drink based on honey: *sbiten.* This was a hot, spiced drink, not alcoholic but warming in another way. One traveller described it as a drink that

> consists of pot-herbs, ginger, pepper, and honey, boiled up
> together, and drunk like tea, which it much resembles in
> colour. It is a very ancient Russian beverage, and was formerly
> used by all classes: now its use is restricted to the common
> people; and it is sold in the streets of Moscow and Petersburg
> by the *izbitenchiki* [*sbiten*-sellers], who carry it about boiling
> hot, and deal it out in tumblers, as the people require it. This
> is a refreshing warm drink, which is very appropriate to the
> condition of the poor peasantry coming to market in severe
> frosts and stormy weather.⁹³

On top of these were all sorts of other drinks, alcoholic and not, made from fruits or honey: *mors* (berry juice); 'mead white, red, cranberry and cherry; various *nalivki* [cordials], like cherry, apple, pear, mountain ash, raspberry, blueberry, currant and others; and still yet *berezovitsa* [birch-brew], which it is possible to prepare such that it very closely resembles champagne'.⁹⁴ These drinks were widely varied, and impressed some visitors. Paul of Aleppo described a meal at a convent when his group was served with

> mead of various kinds, and a vast variety of other drinks . . .
> We were astonished every time we observed the excellence
> of the flavour and the richness of these drinks, used by the
> principal persons here, and made of cherries, apples, and
> many other things of which we know not the names.⁹⁵

Now too there is the non-alcoholic *kompot*: fruit, dried or fresh, mixed with sugar and water and left to soak and infuse the sweet liquid with its taste.

For all that it is not indigenous to Russia, and for all that it has only come into truly widespread use in the last 150 years, tea is now another everyday drink and an essential part of the world of Russian food. One writer claimed that already in the early nineteenth century it was 'necessary in Russia, almost like air'.[96] Another stated that the tea widely available in Russia was recognized to be of significantly higher quality than the tea found in other European countries, noting particularly that it was better than that found in England.[97] In 1860, a newspaper correspondent in Kazan claimed that tea was second only to bread and salt as a demand in Russia.[98] Those statements slightly overstate the case, but tea did have a long history in Russia and was already well-established if not yet entirely common. With Russia's connection to Central Asia and China re-established with the annexation of Siberia through the seventeenth century, tea caravans became an important part of the Russian economy. Tea moved to major trading centres, and from there out into the wider elite and also peasant world.

Perhaps particularly when combined with the technological development of the samovar, not just the commodity of tea but the entire experience of tea drinking – *chaepitie* – became a central part of Russian life. Whether it is in the image of a pre-revolutionary merchant wife sitting at a well-laden table with fruits and pastries and a samovar (and a cat!), or in the image of co-workers in a Soviet office or factory pooling resources for a tea break, it is central to the ways in which the Russian table is part of Russian culture more generally. 'Almost always', a nineteenth-century journalist opined, 'one should not drink tea alone, somewhere in a corner, holding a cup in one's hand, but sit around a table set for tea in a family way, with conversation, and that is exactly the principle and priceless perfection of tea.'[99]

SOME OF THESE FOODS and drinks have persisted with remarkable consistency over a millennium; others have faded in importance, sometimes returning with a turn of fashion, sometimes largely disappearing. All have also been influenced by larger social, economic and even political changes. Russian food developed in a particular place that is now only a fraction of the Russian Federation, let alone the even larger former Russian Empire.

It was altered by the expansion of that empire into new, often more fertile, lands and by interaction with new peoples. Changes in the social composition of Russia – the development of serfdom, Peter the Great's turn to the West as a cultural touchstone, the levelling effects of the Soviet experiment – have also affected Russian food in part by creating different worlds of food eaten by different members of that society. Political decisions have both altered society and aimed to alter people's eating habits in more basic ways by encouraging certain crops or by establishing new norms of eating standards. At times, as well, both war and political actions have had terrible consequences in the form of hunger and famine, both inextricable parts of the history of food in Russia.

TWO

Environment, Agriculture and Technology

Russia is a country of extremes. It is by far the largest country in the world: the modern Russian Federation is nearly as big as Canada and the United States taken together, and the Soviet Union at its peak was nearly as big as all of North America. The Trans-Siberian Railway still takes seven days to make its way from Moscow to Vladivostok on the Pacific. It is a country of immense variety in its peoples and in its environment. There are over a hundred languages spoken in the Russian Federation, reflecting the long history of imperial expansion by the tsars and the movement of peoples, forced and not, in the Soviet era. The environment ranges from the Arctic tundra to the taiga to the wide-open steppe. And it is a definitively northern country: around two-thirds of its immense lands are defined as permafrost.

All of this has implications for the history of Russia and, in particular, for the history of food in Russia. Although the effects of the natural environment are sometimes overdrawn by historians or theorists looking to explain everything about Russia in the most obvious way, there is one area where they almost cannot be overstated: food. Russia's environment is one of certain kinds of riches, but also of significant limitations that had particular implications for how it was able to feed itself. The world of food that developed in these lands therefore reflected both the starkness of the agricultural world and the ways that people figured out how to live and prosper despite its frequent difficulty.

ENVIRONMENT AND AGRICULTURE

Many histories of Russia begin with a description of its harsh environment and vast expanse. To begin thinking about the origins of Russian cooking, we need to move back at least from that vast expanse, although not from

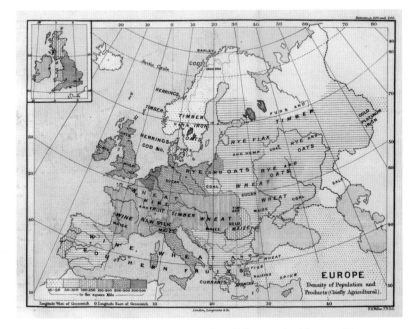

Russia had a distinctly different agricultural world from much of the rest of Europe;
the oldest regions of Russia lay north of the areas in which wheat could be easily cultivated;
it was instead a land of rye, oats, hemp and flax.

the harsh environment. The origins of the people who came to be known
as Russians were somewhere more temperate; archaeological and linguistic
evidence about the origins of the Slavs suggest that they were somewhere
along the Danube or Vistula rivers in Eastern/Central Europe. Over a
millennium or two, wave after wave of invaders – Scythians, Goths, Huns,
Avars, Khazars, among many others – scattered the Slavs to the south,
north, east and west. As they moved apart, they began to differentiate in
language, religion and culture, although echoes remain of their common
past. The Slavs in the Balkans were different from those to their north and
west, who were yet again different from those to their east.

The East Slavs, who would eventually further differentiate into distinct Russian, Ukrainian and Belarusian peoples ('Russia Great, Little and
White', to use a seventeenth-century term), were not initially a unified
whole but instead a cluster of separate 'tribes' living between the Baltic Sea
in the north and the Black Sea in the south. They tended to cluster around
rivers: the Dnieper, the Dvina, the Volkhov. Most of their settlements
were, furthermore, in the northern parts of these lands, from around what
is now Kyiv up to the Baltic. The reason was simple: further south lay the
steppe, which was wide and open and therefore vulnerable to attack. Many

of the waves of invaders came from the steppe, only to settle there and then themselves be attacked by the next wave. The northern lands were covered with forests that gave some protection to its inhabitants.

The downside of the forested lands, however, was that they were not well suited to agriculture. Or at least, they were not well suited to long-term agriculture. The soils of the Russian north were by and large of poor quality, thin and grey, unlike the rich black earth of the steppe. And, of course, the north meant cold, long, dark winters paired with short, intense summers. But none of this meant that the area was entirely inhospitable. In fact, one early eighteenth-century writer even claimed that

> the Genial heat & vigor of Nature being restrained by the Cold
> of the Winter, does not spend it self in vain during that Season,
> and that the Snow whilst it Lies on the ground keeps the
> Natural Productions of the Earth Warm, and free from Injury,
> and that when It goes of, it Impregnates the Earth with such
> quaintitys of Nitre, and drenches it so throughly that the Corn
> is immediatly Sown and presently after ready to be reaped.[1]

That may have been something of an exaggeration (this was an unusually positive view of Russia's agricultural potential in its northern reaches), but there were many ways in which the early inhabitants could thrive. The poor soils could be mitigated, at least for a while. Early inhabitants farmed in areas cleared of trees and brush; the trees became shelter, the brush and smaller branches were burned in situ and then ploughed into the ground, their ashes fertilizing the soil. This slash and burn technique worked well, leading to dramatic yields on sown grains. But it also only worked well for a few years, after which point a family, or more likely a community, would move on elsewhere into the forest to start again.

Of course, that was one of the beauties of the forest: it was vast, and the population was small. At least at first, there was no need to compete over agricultural land. There was always another place to move, and moving might also disrupt the regular pattern of raids and attack from outside forces. As both society and economy developed and became more compli-cated, though, that freedom to move began to fade, as individual peasants found themselves increasingly bound to the land. There were ways around that, too. Although some writers continued to complain that Russian peasants were shockingly unwilling to invest in fertilizing their lands well into the nineteenth century, there were efforts to preserve the fertility of agricultural lands. A three-field system began to develop, by which peasant lands were divided into one field planted with a spring crop (that is, planted in spring and harvested in autumn), a second with a winter crop (planted in late autumn and harvested the following year) and the third kept fallow. By rotating through these crops, the land was not exhausted, and agricultural returns remained meagre but relatively secure. It also helped with the labour cycle. Getting a head start on the year's planting in autumn helped spread the agricultural year's labour through more of the short summer.

This three-field system was well established, it seems, by the sixteenth century and continued as the major agricultural system for centuries. This agricultural world had implications for crops, as well, and therefore for the kinds of foods that Russians most often ate. The usual winter crop came to be rye: winter rye, which sprouted briefly before the hard frosts, then came on again quickly in the short spring. Rye also helped guard the earth against the harsh winter; its roots reached down and held the soil in place when the winds blew. Spring crops were more varied. In medieval Novgorod, barley and millet were the most common spring crops; later and in other areas, oats and buckwheat were also common.[2] Wheat was known, and has been preserved to be dug up at archaeological sites, but was less predictable. Flax and hemp gave both fibre for clothing and seeds for oil.

Peasant lands were held by the entire community and divided into small strips allotted to individual households. In the nineteenth century, some Russian intellectuals championed this system, and particularly one version of it, the repartitional land commune, as an indigenous form of socialism. In the repartitional commune, the lands were reallotted to households every few years to reflect the current size of each household: if one gained more people, it got more land to support it; if another lost family members, its allotment was reduced accordingly. The goal was that every household be able to sustain itself. Not every village was organized like this, and particularly in the north, work off the land was also an important part of the household budget. There were villages in the north where nearly the entire adult male population spent most of the year away, working at trades in towns.

Eventually, although probably not until centuries after the first Slavs moved into the forests, there was vegetable gardening, too, both in the country and in the towns. Cabbage and root vegetables like turnips, parsnips, carrots, radishes, onions and in some areas beetroot were the main vegetable crops. Cucumbers also became a normal food at some point, although exactly when is unclear. Their cultivation was constrained by geography: residents of the far north had less success at cultivating cucumbers and at times even cabbages. Nonetheless, by the eighteenth and nineteenth centuries, both Russians and foreigners thought of Russians as particular lovers of vegetables, above all of cabbage and of cucumber. As the British clergyman and traveller William Tooke put it in his account of Russian food, 'the consumption [of cabbage] in all possible forms, but chiefly as sour-kraut, is immense; and for the greatest part of the year supplies a daily dish to the lower classes.'[3] Katerina Avdeeva described the cabbage as the 'native food of the Russian people'.[4]

Cabbage was above all a vegetable preserved for the winter through fermentation, but cucumbers were, by many accounts, eaten raw nearly year-round. In the seventeenth century, Paul of Aleppo described a yearly competition among the gardeners of Moscow to produce the first cucumbers of the year, which were always presented first of all to the tsar in hopes of a reward.[5] Tooke, writing about the late eighteenth century, claimed that cucumbers were 'frequently eaten raw by the common people, with whom they almost everywhere supply the place of a salad'.[6] Nor were they just food for the 'common' people: in the early nineteenth century the noble Golokhvastov family bought cucumbers nearly every day in winter and spring, according to their kitchen accounts (and were probably supplying themselves with cucumbers at other times of the year).

Other vegetables varied much more, largely due to climate. Root vegetables – onions, garlic, carrots, beetroot, turnips, parsnips – grew reasonably widely, but in Russia's north even these could fail. Perhaps in reaction to the climate, Russian elites came to demand more and more vegetables out of season, leading to the development of hothouse gardening. A French visitor at the beginning of the nineteenth century claimed that the inhabitants of St Petersburg 'are not content, like in Paris, with that which the sun and the season furnish'. Furthermore, he noted, 'the preserved cabbage, the dried peas and the various grains that form the principle diet of the people are not a great part of the middling table,' let alone that of the elite. 'Year round,' he claimed, 'the industrious Russian gardener brings to the houses of the townspeople green vegetables, the produce of his beds: spinach, cauliflower, leafy greens and root vegetables of all kinds for soups and entrées.'[7]

As a result, more and more once-exotic foods were coming into the realm of the everyday (at least for some):

In the neighbourhood of Moscow, vegetables are raised in
greater abundance than at St. Petersburg, and the fruits possess

a richer and more delicate flavour. Both the climate and soil, in this middle tract, are more favourable to vegetation than in the more northern latitudes of the country. Melons, peaches, pine-apples, &c. are very plentiful, besides apples and pears of a most delicate flavour. All the varieties of woodland berries, are very common. The gooseberry alone seems to reach the least perfection. The most delicate fruits are all reared under glass. Hot-houses are remarkably numerous and extensive. It is not unusual to see them, of several hundred feet in length. Dwarf cherry-trees, &c. are planted in pots, and in the season of bearing fruit, they are placed on the tables of the nobles, and the company regale themselves with fruit from the tree. The potatoes are in general round and small, and do not appear to be cultivated with so much assiduity as some other vegetables, particularly cucumbers and garlick. These seem to be the chief food of the poor people. The heaps of cucumbers and garlick exposed to sale in different parts of the street, are almost incredible, and far exceeds the quantity of potatoes or turnips. A peculiar small yellow turnip with a smooth shining rind is very common; also a small apple, which when ripe, becomes semi-transparent; but which, when removed to another climate, loses this peculiar character.[8]

Nor was this only a function of professional market gardeners. Some nobles also produced this kind of variety. In 1801, the following seeds were purchased in Moscow to be planted in the garden at Andreevskoe, an estate in Vladimir province belonging to the Vorontsov family:

Yellow large-head lettuce	Onion
Leaf lettuce	Celery
Early cabbage	Winter endive
Artichokes	Sugar peas
Cabbage 'Slavianka'	Basil
Shag tobacco (*makhorka*)	Marjoram
Late and early cauliflower	Romaine lettuce
Red cabbage	Turnips
Green savoy cabbage	Parsley
Kohlrabi	Chicory[9]
Broccoli	

This variety shrank in some ways and expanded in others during the Soviet era. There was still cabbage; there were still cucumbers; there were still carrots and onions. Some foods largely disappeared: endive and lettuce and artichokes and asparagus, all features of nineteenth-century cookbooks, were gone other than in elite restaurants and in the pages of cookbooks. But at the same time, there were some vegetables that came to appear more regularly: tomatoes, peppers, aubergines and pumpkin, in particular. And, of course, there was the potato, barely consumed through the middle of the nineteenth century, a bit more common by its end, and increasingly important through the first half of the twentieth century.

In fact, of all innovations in agriculture, the gradual introduction of the potato came to have the most dramatic effect on Russian cooking. Potatoes were known by the end of the seventeenth century, but had not moved much beyond a curiosity even by the end of the eighteenth. According to an article from 1758, in St Petersburg, at least, potatoes had come into use through the English, although 'here they are not as big as they grow in England.' The author was not sure whether that was due to methods of cultivation or climate; he only knew that he hoped that their cultivation would soon spread, bringing with it 'great use to Russia'. The author also described how to eat potatoes: 'it is possible to grind them into flour, to bake bread from them, to cook porridge, to make dumplings, pastries, starch and spirits.'[10] This was actually one of the major problems with introducing the potato to European diets – coming to terms with the potato as the potato itself, not as an ingredient for an already known food like bread or porridge.

Catherine II tried to encourage the cultivation of potatoes. In 1765 her Senate released a decree giving 'instructions for the cultivation of *zemlianye iabloki* [a literal translation of the French *pommes de terres*], called *potetes* (*kartofel*)'.[11] In other words, the decree had not yet quite decided on which term for potato would become the norm – a translation from French, or a transliteration from English or German. In the end, it was the German *Kartoffel* that won out. Peasant superstition may have played a role. Through at least the middle of the nineteenth century, a perpetual problem facing potato promoters was that peasants were simply uninterested in eating potatoes. According to many, this was not so much a matter of taste as it was a matter of superstition. V. O. Kliuchevskii, writing in the 1860s, claimed that some peasants believed the potato was 'the devil's apple', because 'a potato grows with a head and eyes, like a person, and therefore he who eats a potato eats a human soul.'[12] A French writer reported that some peasants believed that potatoes were the fruit of the devil, for the 'apple of the earth' was the apple with which Eve tempted Adam.[13] Emphasizing the German term instead of the French might have helped counter such superstitions.

Eventually, something worked to get people to take up the potato. Cookbooks are not necessarily a reliable guide to what people actually ate, but the couple of potato recipes that Avdeeva included in her cookbooks of the 1830s–40s – exactly when a big push to increase potato cultivation also took place – were swamped by many more, even in early editions of Elena Molokhovets's cookbooks in the 1860s. Her later cookbooks included recipes like: 'potato kasha or purée with beef or pork cracklings', 'potato baked with pork, ham or salt beef' and 'potato cutlets with mushroom sauce'. By the middle of the twentieth century, potatoes had found their place on Russian tables even more. A 1968 ethnographic description of Russian peasants and workers noted that vegetables in general were an important part of the Russian diet, but that 'the first place in quantity of consumption is taken by the potato, comprising an essential part of the food ration not only in the country but in the city.'[14] Whether as a *garnir* – a garnish, a side dish – or baked or otherwise cooked into a filling meal, the potato had become a normal ingredient beyond its usefulness as part of a Lenten meal.

The Riches of the Forests

Although the forested lands placed limits on agricultural development, from the earliest years of East Slavic inhabitation the forests were also the source of other riches. Furs are the most notable, just as they would continue to be the most well-known Russian export for centuries. Despite their popularity, they were never the only major source of Russian wealth, whether for export or for domestic use. Instead, the same forests that gave shelter and protection also provided many different sorts of abundance: game, nuts and berries, mushrooms, honey. 'The forest feeds us,' went a folk saying; one still repeated by Russians going off into the woods in search of mushrooms, berries or the sustaining feel of green space.[15]

Russians hunted for sustenance, for sport and for protection. The forests were filled with animals, though not all were suitable for eating. Some descriptions of the dietary practices of the earliest East Slavs suggest that hunting was a major part of the food culture above all; others that it was something enjoyed only by the elite and not by the majority of the population, who found their sustenance in agriculture and in animal

This woodcut print shows a hunter taking on a bear – although it comes from much later than the story Vladimir Monomakh told about his exploits, it reflects the ways that hunting was both a part of the world of food and an activity fraught with real danger.

husbandry. Archaeological evidence, at least, has tended to lead to the conclusion that hunting for food existed, but on a much smaller scale than some have argued. In archaeological digs across northern Russia, bones from domesticated animals outnumber those of wild animals significantly, making up between two-thirds and three-quarters of material.[16]

There were good reasons for hunting not to be a large-scale, general occupation. For one thing, in the earliest Kyivan era, princes displayed their power by establishing their own hunting grounds: the *Tale of Bygone Years*, the chronicle of early Rus, notes the presence of different princes' hunting grounds and their at times violent efforts to maintain them. In addition, there was the question of which animals lived in the forests and how they could be hunted. Large game like bears and wolves and elk almost by necessity had to be the prey of big hunting parties, not of a few villagers. It was dangerous sport, not an everyday pastime of the peasant. In his *Testament* to his successors, Vladimir Monomakh, perhaps the last Kyivan Grand Prince to serve as a real authority throughout his lands, told of his love for the hunt and of the many accidents that befell him. 'I have made a practice of hunting a hundred times a year with all my strength, and without harm,' he wrote. Or, mostly without harm: he also admitted (or boasted) that during his hunting expeditions

> two bisons tossed me and my horse on their horns, a stag once gored me, one elk stamped upon me, while another gored me, a boar once tore my sword from my thigh, a bear on one occasion bit my kneecap, and another wild beast jumped on my flank and threw my horse with me. But God preserved me unharmed.[17]

Still, even in early times, hunting brought in some supplementary food. Wild fowl and hares, beavers and squirrels, all might be consumed as well as at times hunted for their pelts. Excavations from Novgorod show significant numbers of bones from elk and hares of different varieties. Beaver bones are there, too, with marks that suggest that they were butchered for their meat rather than merely skinned for their furs.[18] This situation largely continued, with big game the sport of the elite and smaller fowl and mammals an occasional source of sustenance for the wider population. As that human population grew, it also came to place strains on the wild animals of the forests, leading to controls on hunting.

In some cases, laws affirmed that individuals had the right to hunt animals on their own lands or using hides or blinds they had built. The *Ulozhenie* of 1649, which codified the existing law in Muscovy, stated that bird hides were the possession of those who built them on their own land. Using someone else's legally built bird hide was punishable by a payment of damages. Spoiling someone else's hide by 'smear[ing] it with tar, or garlic, or anything else, and thereby driv[ing] away the birds from that blind [hide]' or stealing nets used to hunt certain birds was an even greater offence. Theft was punished with a fine, but spoiling a hide brought a punishment of 'beat[ing] mercilessly with bastinadoes so that he and other such will henceforth learn not to do that'.[19]

Other laws came to place more general restrictions on hunting. In the later seventeenth and eighteenth centuries, various laws outlawed hunting of certain animals or in certain ways or within a certain distance of St Petersburg or Moscow. In the early nineteenth century, laws explicitly tried to counteract overhunting of wild fowl. In 1827, a decree prohibited the hunting or trapping of wild fowl during their laying season. It was apparently enough of a success that a decade later the wild fowl numbers had increased such that their market price fell.[20] Soon thereafter, two great portrayals of hunters signalled ways in which hunting had moved more fully into the realm of sport. Ivan Turgenev's collection of short stories, often translated as *A Sportsman's Sketches*, follows a Russian nobleman and hunter as he wanders around the countryside in search of sport, chatting with the many peasants he meets along the way. Then, the nineteenth-century Realist artist Vasily Perov produced what has become the most iconic image of hunting in Russia: an image of three hunters at rest, sharing a meal of black bread, a cucumber and a hard-boiled egg, one apparently telling the others a story and another smoking a hand-rolled cigarette as a dog guards their catch – a pair of fowl and a hare.

Forests were also filled with things to gather. It is nearly impossible to trace the use of these kinds of forest products in the earliest years of the Russian lands – the small and the everyday did not make their way into the chronicles, nor into the scattered records of merchants; the fragility of the products of the forest do not necessarily show up in archaeological digs. There are bits of evidence. Excavations in Novgorod have shown remnants of hazelnuts, wild strawberries, wild raspberries, apples, sour cherries and bilberries dating back to the medieval period.[21] Later writers described the many other riches that Russian peasants and others found in the forests. Bitter greens like nettles, sorrel, dandelion and orach were among the first signs of spring and the first new, fresh foods to make their way into the cooking pot. Next came berries of all sorts, which grew wild in the forest. Particularly in the far north, berries were the major source of fruit (and, like sorrel, of vitamin C).

Gathering berries also eventually became a source of profit. One English visitor described the variety and excellence of the berries available in the country:

> Immense quantities of strawberries and raspberries grow
> wild in Russia, also red and black currants are frequently met
> with in the woods. In the northern provinces there is a kind

of yellow fruit, in shape like a mulberry, called maroshca [cloudberry], which makes an excellent preserve, and is also used medicinally as a remedy for the dropsy. Various wild berries, such as cranberries, bilberries, &c., abound in the forests, and numberless species of mushrooms; of all these they make preserves and pickles, which they use in the long winter-season as a substitute for fresh vegetables. The peasant-women and children gather them in great quantities and carry them about for sale, by which means they obtain a little money for the winter.[22]

Berries were a treat when fresh and more precious when preserved for later consumption. Even fresh, they were often cooked into foods that took their sweetness and extended its reach. Berry *kisel* was and continues to be a particular treat; berries could become fillings for *pirogi* or the basis of the drinks *mors* or *kompot*. Today, berries are still a part of the change of the seasons. In spring and summer, men and women stand by the entrances to the underground stations of Moscow and St Petersburg, offering plastic cups filled with fresh berries for sale. Some may be imports made to look like local produce, but others are clearly truly local.

Nuts were also probably collected from early years, although there is only scant archaeological evidence in Novgorod archaeological sites. Although some later travel writers claimed that the average Russian man ate large quantities of nuts – in 1799 William Tooke stated that 'as in all the towns and villages wherever we go, we see the common people eating nuts by way of pastime, we may thence form a conclusion of the vast consumption of them'[23] – most nut trees did not grow in the northern reaches of European Russia. Some (hazelnuts, in particular) did, and trade brought in others, like walnuts, whose shells have also been found in Novgorod digs. Later in the nineteenth century the consumption of pine nuts and pine-nut oil became known as a Siberian speciality; women spent autumn and winter evenings cracking open pine nuts. They used their teeth to crack the shells, which, ethnographers reported, led to crooked or broken smiles.[24]

Perhaps most importantly, Russian forests were the source of mushrooms, which played a central role on the Russian table. Mushrooms were by almost all accounts a commonly consumed food for Russians, both due to their ubiquity and to the role they played in fast-day meals. One Russian journalist from the mid-nineteenth century called them 'almost the most necessary food'.[25] William Coxe noted that he

Gathering berries was and is an important spring and summer activity in Russia – in this photograph from the early 20th century, peasant girls show off plates of berries they probably gathered in the forests near their home on the Sheksna river in the Russian north.

seldom entered a cottage without seeing great abundance of them; and in passing through the markets, I was often astonished at the prodigious quantity exposed for sale: their variety was no less remarkable than their number; they were of many colours, amongst which I particularly noticed white, black, brown, yellow, green, and pink.[26]

Another visitor was also both amazed and impressed by the variety and savouriness of Russia's mushrooms:

Pickled mushrooms . . . kept often in huge glass jars, sometimes in immense barrels, while rather revolting to look at, are most worthy of a moment's attention. How we had rejoiced, while staying at certain houses here, whenever mushrooms were introduced at dinner; they were food fit for an emperor, and were served out without stint. In England the mere mention of mushrooms brings up the idea of a wealthy gourmand making researches in theoretical gastronomy to please an over-indulged

Just as mushrooms are a characteristic food in Russia, mushroom gathering is a characteristic practice. Everyone from peasants to members of the imperial family collected mushrooms, although of course for very different reasons; Romanovs might pick mushrooms as a lark, but peasants relied on mushrooms to consume themselves or to sell.

palate; but in Russia, while equally good, they are in such
prodigious quantities as to form a great part of the food of the
whole people. And a most important part, for here is one of
the quickest-growing of all vegetables – some species rise out
of the ground one day, increase, come to perfection, and again
decay and disappear before the next day has arrived – and yet,
if plucked at the right instant, there is in it a mass of firmer
and more meat-like food than any plant of the whole kitchen-
garden can show . . . An accurate return of the total quantity of
these plants annually consumed in Russia would be a startling
and important document, but is not likely to be procured, for
the greater part is eaten by the same peasants who gather them,
and who, besides feasting on them all through the season,
pickle, salt, and dry them on strings against the winter period;
when fried with a little hemp oil, and eaten with rye bread,
they supply well the place of animal food; but if, with a little
more art they be fried in sunflower oil, then there are some
'mushroom cutlets' which look and taste very much like the
same preparation of chicken.[27]

Particularly important were several subcategories of mushrooms.
Ryzhiki, gruzdy and *volnushki* were varieties of milk caps. These were mushrooms with caps up to 15 centimetres (6 in.) across that were eaten either
fresh (though always cooked) or preserved with salt or by drying. The *belyi
grib*, literally a 'white mushroom', and the *maslianik* were varieties of boletus that could grow even larger. The largest were dried; the smallest might
be marinated and preserved. Chanterelles, morels and champignons were
also common. Different mushrooms appeared at different times of the
year; some were then preserved. Samuel Collins, an Englishman living in
Moscow in the 1660s, described the cartloads of mushrooms brought into
the city every year, mostly preserved in brine. He also described the different mushrooms that appeared at different times of year. The first, appearing
in April or May, were something he called Honeycomb Mushrooms, which
'adorn great mens tables, and carry a good price', as well as *smorchki*, which
were 'put into pyes and pottage'. Next came *ryzhiki*, which 'break forth in
one night' and were 'a lesser sort of Mushrooms'. Later came the *gruzdy*,
'the greatest of mushrooms, an hand breadth, like a Cow-tripe thick and
white, whilst raw very juycy; the Russians correct it (as they do Sea-lettice)
with brine, else they will inflame the chops and throat.'[28]

The preference for mushrooms was extensive, and in a way that struck some as particularly Slavic. 'Nowhere do they use as many mushrooms and as often as in Russia and in Poland,' one Russian culinary author wrote. 'It is strange that the Swedes and Finns do not use mushrooms at all in their food, although it seems that the less the earth gives grain, the more one should look to other means of sustenance.'[29] Hunting mushrooms became more than just a peasant pursuit, as well. Members of the Romanov dynasty went mushroom gathering at the beginning of the twentieth century; in one such instance, Nicholas II's mother and sister were out for a drive, asked to stop by the side of the road, and went mushrooming for a quarter of an hour.[30] In the Soviet Union, urban dwellers descended on dachas and even city parks in search of mushrooms during the mushroom season. Even today, Russians reportedly gather more than 150,000 tons of mushrooms (and 375,000 tons of berries) each year.[31]

Finally, there was honey, an important product initially of the forests. Beekeepers did not build separate, freestanding beehives, but instead laid claim to trees filled with hives. *Bortniki* were men who moved through the forest checking on the trees that they had claimed and harvesting their honey and wax.[32] Both were hugely important; wax was a source of light and useful as a preservative. Honey was the major source of sweetness, used in drinks like *shiten*, used to create alcohol in mead, used to preserve fruits.

Trees filled with beehives were valuable, and their value was recognized in law. In the seventeenth century, Muscovite laws gave stiff penalties to those found guilty of ruining another person's beehive trees. For ruining such a tree by 'cutting the roots or setting fire to it', a fine of up to 3 roubles could be collected. If someone tried to remove the hives and honey from a beehive tree (presumably to get the bees to settle in a tree on his own property), he faced a fine of 1½ roubles to cover the cost of the bees. If he both ruined a tree and scooped out its honey, he faced a fine of 6 roubles.[33] These laws probably took such honey theft so seriously because this was around the time when honey and wax were gaining extra value. Honey and particularly wax became valuable commodities of international trade, especially to English buyers: in the Volga region, honey might be worth 1 rouble per *pud*, but wax could sell for 9 roubles a *pud*.[34]

By the seventeenth century, beekeeping had come out of the forest, at least to some extent. Instead, building and maintaining domestic beehives became part of the larger agricultural world of peasants in much of the Russian lands. Some villages or estates came to specialize in beekeeping. Crown estates became home to apiaries with hundreds of hives, and private estates could rival them in size (of course both crown and private estates could also be much smaller).[35] In the Soviet era, honey lost its role as a primary sweetener when sugar beet production and processing made sugar more affordable – the culinary author Viliam Pokhlebkin even advised his readers to use sugar instead of honey in the preparation of traditional recipes because of its ubiquity.[36] But honey never went away, and has if anything become more popular in the post-Soviet era, championed by figures like the former mayor of Moscow, Yuri Luzhkov (mayor 1992–2010). Beekeepers now bring their wares from all over Russia to large honey markets, where they tout the health benefits of honeys produced from bees visiting certain flowers.[37]

THE EFFECT OF EMPIRE

The replacement of honey by sugar from sugar beet was made possible in large part by Muscovy and then Russia's expansion south through the steppe. Already in the seventeenth century the border of the settled, Moscow-based Russian world with the unsettled and dangerous steppe had begun to move south. Both the construction of extended fortified lines and the waning power of the raiding Crimean Tatars and other forces came to provide some degree of security for more permanent settlement. Laws strove to encourage settlement in the region, as well, allowing people to move there when they might otherwise not have been free to do so. In the eighteenth century, Catherine II completed the move south in European Russia, extending her domains down to the northern shore of the Black Sea and (more or less) to the Caucasus.

These new lands were radically different in their agricultural potential. The black soil – *chernozem* – of the region gave startlingly good returns and the more southern and therefore milder environment allowed different crops to mature. Rye continued to be both a principal crop and an important part of the culinary world in Russia. When the priest Paul of Aleppo travelled from the border 'Cossack lands' to Muscovy proper in the middle of the seventeenth century, just as this southern expansion was beginning, he noted that rye made the bread 'they like better than the white; and when the Voivodes used to send presents to our Lord the Patriarch, they always presented this black [rye] bread first, by reason of the esteem in which it is held among them; and afterwards the white'.[38] Eventually, though, agriculture in these relatively southern reaches turned more often to wheat. It also turned to producing for export, something that Russia's earlier production of rye had largely not allowed – or rather, for which it had not found a market. By the end of the nineteenth century, though, Russia was the second largest exporter of grain, primarily of wheat, in the world.

In addition, this move south allowed for other kinds of vegetables and fruits to grow. While in the very far north fruit trees failed to thrive, here apples, pears, plums and peaches all became sources of food for the household and for the market. Cucumbers grew more freely, and eventually tomatoes, peppers, pumpkins and aubergines all came into regular cultivation in kitchen and market gardens. Watermelon and other melons became not exotic fruits but normal ones. These new products (or more widely available products) began to make their way onto the general Russian table more and more. Already at the beginning of the sixteenth century, the traveller Sigismund von Herberstein claimed that Russians were particularly clever in their cultivation of melons.[39] By the early twenty-first century, melon stands popped up in Russian cities every autumn, selling the products of the southern reaches of Russia to eager northern consumers.

Over and over again, foods from elsewhere entered Russia by trade, and over and over again, Russian agronomists sought to produce some of them domestically. In the early 19th century they tried to introduce potatoes, of course, but also quinoa. In the Soviet era, an agricultural station in Georgia even produced avocados.

Some of the new territories of the Russian Empire were home to another sort of production that the imperial and then Soviet state wanted to develop: grapes and winemaking. The Kingdom of Georgia, which came into the Russian Empire at the very end of the eighteenth century, is possibly the original home of winemaking, and Georgian wines are still sold for top rouble in Moscow and St Petersburg. Movement onto the steppe and particularly into Crimea and Moldova (then known as Bessarabia) also brought possibilities for winemaking. Noble entrepreneurs (or sometimes just noble dilettantes) started vineyards on their estates and, in some areas, new colonists from European wine regions began to produce wine in the empire.[40] In the Soviet era, winemaking took on new political importance. Stalin had a taste for the Georgian wines of his homeland, but came to enjoy other Soviet wines, as well. A focus on increasing production for the sake of making this luxury available in principle (though never in practice) to all workers caused certain problems for the wine industry, forcing it at times to choose quantity over quality. Even so, Soviet wines competed (and occasionally won prizes) at international wine tastings, and 'Soviet champagne' became and remains part of the celebratory world of the larger post-Soviet world.[41]

The movement south also made possible the eventual rise of sugar beet production at the end of the nineteenth century. The technology to extract sugar from sugar beet was one of the last great industrial innovations of the eighteenth century, and one eagerly adopted by those European states that had a hankering for sweetness but had not seized tropical colonies where they could cultivate sugar cane. Russia was one of them. Starting with Alexander I (r. 1801–25), Russian leaders actively supported the development of a sugar beet industry, but through the middle of the nineteenth century it had only limited success. Some Russian serf-owners began to cultivate sugar beet and to produce sugar in the central agricultural zone. But the explosion of sugar production that came to Russia by the beginning of the twentieth century – from 70,414 tons in 1860–61, to 777,129 tons in 1897 and 1,120,878 tons in 1917 – was based outside of that older Russian zone, in what is now Ukraine and the border region in the southern steppe. There, larger sugar concerns took advantage of technological advances and the better agricultural conditions to create a new source of sweetness for Russia and beyond.[42]

Rivers and Transportation

Russia's geography had another feature that affected the Russian table: rivers. Early Russian settlement clustered along rivers, which gave transport, energy and sustenance. In particular, many varieties of freshwater fish, from the enormous sturgeon to the small gudgeon and perch, made their home in the networks of rivers that spread through not only European Russia but Siberia. Russians began to exploit these riches early. The birch-bark charters of medieval Novgorod speak often of fish and fishing, and archaeological excavations have uncovered both fishing equipment and fish bones of all sorts. Archaeologists have identified bones from sturgeon, eel, whitefish, pike, bream, blue bream, chub, ide, roach, silver bream, rudd, chekon, catfish, perch, zander and ruffe.[43]

The great rivers – the Volga, the Don, the Dnieper – were particularly abundant in the larger river fish. These rivers and their particular fish became essential parts of the Russian world of eating. In the mid-nineteenth century, the traveller Henry Sutherland Edwards described *ukha* as 'the most celebrated of the Russian fish-soups'. 'The best kind is made from sterlet,' he continued, 'a rich oily, yellow-fleshed, but at the same time exceedingly delicate fish; in form something between an eel and a whiting. The sterlet is caught in the Volga, and will not live in the water of any other river.'[44] The Volga was the queen of the rivers; as one eighteenth-century scientific traveller claimed, 'I do not think that there is any river in Europe as rich in fish.'[45] Another traveller said the same of the Don: 'the fishes caught in it are too numerous to be mentioned, as perhaps there is no river in the world which presents a greater variety, or in greater perfection.'[46] He went on to list at least some of them:

> Among the principal are the *beluga*, the common sturgeon, the sterlet, sudak [carp], trout, Prussian carp, tench, pike, perch, water-tortoises, and crawfish of an enormous size, some of which are as large as lobsters. The last are caught in great abundance, by sinking small nets, about six inches in diameter, baited with pieces of salt fish. They sold at the rate of twopence (English) per hundred, and in some seasons of the year the same number may be had for half that sum. The beluga is the largest eatable fish known . . . Strahlenberg relates, that he saw a beluga fifty-six feet long, and near eighteen feet thick. In the Don they seldom exceed twelve feet in length. In shape, this fish very much resembles the sturgeon.[47]

Russian peasants developed all sorts of technologies to catch the fish of the country's great rivers. Here, traps strung across a large river aim to catch the mighty sturgeon (top), and a weir allows a man to catch smaller fish (above).

Russians caught fish through different methods, but most of all in fish weirs or in nets stretched across rivers. As a result, fishing was often a group activity, not only something practised by a lone fisherman out on the banks of a river. Rights to specific fishing spots were jealously guarded; Cossacks came to be among those with special rights to fish in particular rivers. In some areas fishing became above all a commercial activity, although it was also a consistent source of sustenance for many who plied it. (And, perhaps again, for those who continue to head out with fishing pole in hand – 'no fishing' signs on major bridges in the centre of major towns be damned.)

The geography of Russia, however it was defined, had one other feature that had a consistent impact on its food history: its size. Its enormity (and variety) had both positive and negative impacts. One positive effect was that Russia was big enough that even serious bad harvests were usually (although catastrophically not always) localized enough to avoid mass, countrywide famine. Almost always, somewhere in the empire, there was enough grain. There were exceptions, times when famine conditions reached shocking proportions – particularly quite recently in Russian history. Still, for the most part Russia's rulers were able to count on its size as a guard against the worst of famine.

In some areas, fishing became a major local industry. Here workers load ships with barrels of codfish near Arkhangelsk, a port in northern European Russia founded in the late 16th century and still an important centre of trade three centuries later.

At the same time, however, Russia's size also made moving things around it extremely difficult. There were moments when these problems were felt particularly acutely. When Peter the Great founded St Petersburg in a swamp at the very edge of his realm, getting food to his new capital required real effort.[48] Even that was still within the world of European Russia, and not too far from ancient Russian cities like Novgorod. When Russians began to move through Siberia developing the fur trade, feeding that trade became a major concern, for among the Russian *promyshlenniki* (fur traders) there were no agriculturists and little interest in eating as the Indigenous population did.[49]

For much of its history Russia's relatively sparse transportation infrastructure limited the ability to move supplies from place to place. Rivers were the most important methods of moving goods – barges often dragged by people moved along all its rivers bringing supplies. The Volga boatmen of the famed song were actually Volga barge haulers. Roads were hard to maintain over the distances required, and particularly bad during the spring thaw and the autumn rains. Only with the rise of the railways did things start to improve, although the network was also riddled with inefficiencies when it came to getting goods to the people who needed them. When famine hit Russia in the late nineteenth century – a startling, disturbing moment that suggested something was truly wrong with the country – some authors placed blame in part on the failures of the transportation system.[50]

On the other hand, there were a few features that helped. The river network was extensive and brought together not only disparate parts of European Russia but of the wide expanse of Siberia. The Volga ran from a source only around 320 kilometres (200 mi.) from St Petersburg and the Baltic all the way to the Caspian Sea in an indirect route. Its tributaries (and tributaries of tributaries) connected even more of these old, central Russian lands. In addition, Russia's cold was a surprising benefit when it came to transportation. It allowed for remarkably efficient movement of goods on sleds. A visitor from Aleppo in the seventeenth century was amazed by what could be transported on such sleds with relatively little effort: 'the immense loads of agricultural produce, and the huge stones transported by these carriages, excited our surprise; for that which one horse draws here could not be drawn by twenty horses in our country.'[51] Nor was he alone. Guy Miège, who took part in an English embassy to Muscovy in the 1660s, was also amazed by the speed of travel in winter, and also by the barges that brought huge quantities of provisions from place to place along the network of rivers at other times of the year.[52]

The train network that began to grow in the nineteenth century of course helped to increase transportation opportunities, but again the vast scale of Russia and its relatively sparsely settled population limited its impact. As a result, even as the train network grew, rivers were still central to transportation. In the 1860s, an English traveller described a sight near the Kremlin at the centre of Moscow:

> the narrow river which, like a silver stream, flowed gracefully at our feet, dotted with its hundreds of great lighters filled with bread, corn, and merchandize, from the interior, far, far away,

Railways

The Russian Empire was a little slower than some of its Western European counterparts to turn to the railway; its first railway, running only the short distance between St Petersburg and its palace suburb Tsarskoe Selo, opened in 1837. The first major line, from St Petersburg to Moscow, opened only in 1851. Once it and then others did, however, food became part of the story of the journey. One English traveller in the early 1860s found the train between St Petersburg and Moscow to be much more comfortable than train travel at home. The trip between the two capitals took twenty hours, largely in order to accommodate long stops for meals, and due to the fact that 'the Buffet interest is very strong on this line.'[53] That meant that travellers were very, even excessively, well fed: as another traveller put it, at every platform he found 'men with trays of tumblers, supported by a belt from the shoulder, each containing a little sugar and the lemon slice, and well-polished samovar in their hands, [who] moved about serving out glasses of tea'. The tea at the station was 'truly refreshing', and he and his company 'made it a point of honour to partake of the tea also as often as it was offered'.[54] Later authors also commended the refreshments available on Russia's railways, even as they stretched out to Siberia. 'I am enthusiastic about these Russian refreshment-rooms,' concluded one British traveller about his trip to Siberia in 1901.[55]

and waiting here, protected by mat roofs from the hot sun of summer, til disposed of.[56]

At the same time, railways did begin to take on more of the burden of transportation, first within European Russia, then reaching out through Siberia.

TECHNOLOGIES: COOKING AND PRESERVING

The Russian table was also influenced by technologies of food processing. Given the short growing season and long, cold winters of much of the Russian land, preserving food for storage was a necessity. So too was a need for warmth, which had an effect on the ways in which Russians developed stoves. Both of these influenced the kinds of foods Russians ate – centuries ago and still today.

Above all, there was the Russian stove, or *pech* – the heart of the peasant cottage.[57] The Russian stove in its relatively modern form, large and box-like, became widespread in Russian lands in the sixteenth century; earlier stoves were probably of similar size but different shape, rounded instead of squared off.[58] It served two purposes: first, it gave warmth, something desperately needed in the Russian winter. According to one English traveller, it did so extremely well. For him, 'a Russian petch or stove is one of the greatest luxuries of civilized life that can be found in cold climates.'[59] Second, it cooked and preserved food. Already in the early nineteenth century many elite Russians were encouraging the adoption of new, modern, foreign stove technology – the 'English' stove with a flat cooking surface on top that Vladimir Burnashev had linked to 'renowned and delicate sauces and fricassees' – to replace the Russian stove. Others thought such a change unlikely on the grounds that it would be impossible to replace completely the stoves that were then 'in use by just about the whole 60 million subjects of Russia', and also that 'the Russian is used to his oven – it is a necessity of his national life.'[60]

The single most noteworthy thing about the Russian stove was its size: it was huge. The large structure of brick or stone plastered with clay took up somewhere between one-sixth and one-quarter of the floor space of an average peasant cottage.[61] It stood as tall as a person, and the broad flat space on its top often served as a place to rest or sleep in the coldest days of winter. The stove had several compartments. At its bottom was an open space, where firewood could be stored (to warm and be dried out by the

This illustration of a post house shows the large Russian stove on the left, with several pots placed in its front cooking area, and several women warming themselves on top of the main heating compartment.

heat above) and even small livestock be kept to protect them from the cold when needed. Above that was the main business of the stove, divided into two compartments. At the back was the fire itself, burning hot and heating the entire structure. At the front was the workspace, an open area for cooking, where heat could be regulated by placing pots in different areas, closer or further away from the flames. The early stoves had no chimneys in order to preserve every last bit of heat for the people inside. Such chimney-less stoves were still in use through the nineteenth century. Although by that point the 'black' or 'smoky' cottage was seen as a sign of particular poverty, backwardness and lack of proper hygiene, peasants still preferred them because of their greater warmth; one author estimated that seven-eighths of the heating power of the stove was lost through the chimney.[62]

These stoves were well suited to Russian cooking – or rather, Russian cooking developed in a way that was well suited to these stoves. Katerina Avdeeva explained how one might prepare *shchi* or another soup in just such an oven:

> Russian cooking is just as well and as tastily prepared in a simple oven as on the stovetop; just make sure of the following: put a clay pot with *shchi* or with soup in the oven once the wood is already well burning and the smoke has cleared; make sure that

pots with bouillon do not boil dry; skim off the foam cleanly;
if the foam is removed cleanly, then there is no need to strain;
it is better to salt [the soup/bouillon] when the foam has
been skimmed off. For a *funt* of beef add two bottles of water;
choose a pot that will be filled to the very top, for a pot that
is not full will burn and the food will get an unpleasant
taste; when the oven is stoked and the heat is building, then
do not put the pot near the heat, but put it in a place where
it will simmer but not boil over.[63]

Kasha was also cooked in a clay pot, first brought to a simmer, then covered and placed further from the fire to keep warm. Bread and *pirogi* were
baked in the oven. So too were blini. Meats could be roasted; *kisels* could
be thickened. The oven could be brought to the task of preserving foods,
as well – drying mushrooms, for example. It was, in the end, perhaps the
single biggest influence on the food practices of Russia.

The trick to cooking in the oven was regulating its heat. In 1838, one
author gave advice on how to know that the oven was the proper temperature for baking bread. 'If a little bit of flour thrown in the oven does
not burn, but browns, then that is a true sign that the oven has warmed.'

This illustration jumbles together many different kinds of sleds that might be seen in
Russia against a largely imaginary landscape, but gets at the idea that the sled was one of the
particularities of the country – and one that did in fact make its vast distances and frigid
weather slightly less forbidding for the traveller.

Another problem was knowing when the bread was done; because it was baked of darker rye flour, colour was not a sufficient indicator. This author, though, had a solution:

> at the same time that you put the bread in the oven, break off a little piece of dough and put it in water in a glass; when the dough floats to the top of the water then that is a sign that it is time to take the bread out of the oven.[64]

Of course, just as Russia had cold winters, it had hot summers. Although they were short, they could be intense. For peasants, this was the season of heavy labour and *tolokno*, the ground oatmeal that was eaten uncooked. For nobles, it was the season of *botvinia*, the iced, cold soup that so shocked many foreign visitors. It could also mean the season of moving cooking outdoors, or at least into separate quarters. Summer kitchens were a part of noble estates. As the summer houses known as dachas began to spread out from St Petersburg and Moscow, first among nobles in the eighteenth century, then among the growing middle class in the nineteenth century, so too did different ways of cooking. Even now, an Internet search for 'summer kitchen' in Russian brings up countless variations on grills and brick ovens and set-ups meant to make summer cooking its own separate world.

Before the products of the land got to the stove, they were processed or preserved in all sorts of ways. Perhaps above all, there was the question of processing grain into the groats or flour to be cooked into porridges or bread. First, individual kernels of grain had to be separated from their chaff. East Slavic peasants – that is, encompassing Russians, Ukrainians and Belarusians – used a kind of large mortar and pestle for the job, sieving out the chaff as they went. Archaeological sites from the medieval era contain examples of pestles that look much the same as those still used in the nineteenth century.[65] So ubiquitous was the practice that in Russian folk tales, the fearsome witch Baba Yaga flies around in such a mortar, carrying a pestle as a weapon.

This process gave peasants grains to use for porridge, but not for flour. For that, they developed hand- and water-operated mills. The early hand-operated mills used two stones to grind grain between them, producing flour of consistent size. They were small enough to sit in the corner of a peasant cottage. Larger water- and then windmills came later; watermills with vertical wheels – known as 'German wheels' due to their foreign

One of the classic characters in Russian folk tales was Baba Yaga the witch, who lived
in a house built on chicken legs, and who, as in this illustration by Ivan Bilibin,
flew around in a mortar wielding a pestle. You can see the narrow shape of the Russian
mortar – something preserved in archaeological digs and still in use much later.

origins – came into regular use in the sixteenth century.[66] Mills for grinding
larger quantities of flour for the people of a village or a region were often
built on a landlord's land and rented out to a miller.

In towns, rye and wheat flour were commercial products. By the end
of the nineteenth century, flours of different fineness were in regular use.
Moscow regulations allowed for six kinds of rye flour, from the lowest
'common' to the highest 'baking', and three kinds of wheat flour. The
best, most expensive wheat flour was known as *krupchatka* or *krupichataia*

muka; it was the flour often called for in recipes for *pirogi*.[67] It was also produced with a different grind than other flours. This was a kind of flour 'characterized by notable graininess', which meant it was less fine than some other flours, 'prepared only in Russia, primarily from hard sorts of wheat'. It absorbed less water than other wheat flours, but could be stored for longer. 'Foreign bakers cannot work with *krupchatka*, which explains the unsuccessful export of it abroad,' according to one description.[68]

The mortar was used as the first stage of another important process: oil-pressing. Russians consumed large quantities of seed oils. Early in its history, flaxseed and hempseed oil were the most common; in the twentieth century, sunflower seed oil took over. In those earlier years, the seeds

Sunflower Seed Oil

In part because of the need for non-animal fats during the extensive periods of fasting in the Orthodox calendar, Russian cooking has long relied on various kinds of seed or nut oil. Through the eighteenth century, this oil was most often hempseed or flaxseed oil, or, for the most elite, possibly walnut oil or even olive oil. The former could be produced even in the northern lands of Russia, the latter imported. In the nineteenth century, however, sunflower seed oil came to predominate. It was already an important part of the produce of the southern Volga region by the middle of the century, produced particularly by the German colonists around Saratov, and became the dominant non-animal oil during the Soviet era. Sunflower seed oil was already well on its way to ubiquity when it made a startling appearance in the opening pages of Mikhail Bulgakov's *The Master and Margarita*, in which the devil comes to early Soviet Moscow. As the novel begins, a man named Berlioz meets the devil in disguise, who tells him that his death by decapitation is foretold in part because 'Annushka has already bought the sunflower oil, and not only bought it, but spilled it, too.' Berlioz storms off in disbelief, only to slip on spilled sunflower oil in front of an oncoming tram. It is a dramatic appearance of what came to be a homely, everyday good.

were cracked in the mortar before being put through an oil press. Later, these oils were produced in larger institutions and sold at markets.

Seed oils were so important because of the fasting calendar of the Orthodox Church, which regularly forbad not only meat but dairy. Also as a result of that fasting calendar, Russians had all sorts of ways of preserving milk. Of course some was drunk fresh, but most milk was not. The simplest preparation was *prostokvasha*: controlled soured milk, which kept for longer than fresh. When it was soured enough to separate into curds, that simple cheese was known as *tvorog*, and served as a filling for pies and pastries or as a treat on its own. *Varenets* was a kind of baked milk, essentially: whole milk was put in the oven, and when it foamed up, that foam or skin was stirred back into the milk; this process was repeated until the milk took on a reddish colour, at which point it was pulled out of the oven and placed on ice to cool.[69] *Varenets* could be eaten alone or along with another food, including other dairy products like *tvorog*. And, of course, there was *smetana*, or sour cream, skimmed from the top of milk as it soured. It could be further processed, used as a 'whitener' in soups, cooked with *kasha*, added to doughs to enrich them or used as a dressing for salads.

Russians made butter, too, but their butter was not the sweet butter of puff pastries (although that eventually became common, as well). Instead, they came up with other ways of making butter that lasted longer. There were two major sorts of butter in use other than plain sweet butter. The first, *chukhonskoe* butter (after an old term for the Finnic peoples of the Baltic region), was made of sour cream rather than sweet. It was used primarily for baking. The second, known as 'Russian' butter, was a kind of clarified butter. To produce Russian butter, *chukhonskoe* butter was melted, and impurities and liquids were poured off, leaving just the fat behind. Some home instruction manuals recommended melting the butter with a larger proportion of water. The water collected the solids and impurities and was then poured off after cooling. This process was repeated several times until the water ran clear.

These processes also produced by-products that were then used in various ways. Traditional buttermilk – the liquid left over after making butter – was called *iuraga*. The liquid by-product of making Russian butter was also saved. Avdeeva recommended using these liquids to make buckwheat *kasha*, and listed that variant of *kasha* as its own speciality (*iurazhnaia kasha*) of the Russian table.[70] One account from the early nineteenth century described all the things that might be made out of a measure of fresh, whole milk. Ideally, the author noted, a farmer who produced too much milk for domestic consumption could sell milk in a nearby town. In Moscow, for example, a *shtof* of milk sold for 30–40 kopeks. A *funt* of *chukhonskoe* (sour) butter sold for 40–50 kopeks, but was a much worse return on the milk that went into it. To produce that *funt* of butter, a farmer needed to use at least 7 or 8 *shtofs* of whole milk. The skimmed milk could then be used to make *tvorog*, probably worth another 40 kopeks, and the remaining whey (*syvorotka*) could fetch another 10 kopeks.[71]

One thing that Russians did not have until relatively recently was cheese – at least, not cheese in the sense of aged or ripened cheese. The British visitor George Forbes, writing in the 1730s, noted that Russian 'Cows give abundance of Milk of which they make a Strange Kind of Butter but not Cheese at all.'[72] They did make *tvorog*, a slightly sour, soft, white, fresh cheese. This is mentioned in early chronicles; the word *syr*, now used for all sorts of cheese, appears there, too, but probably meant a variety of *tvorog*. Starting at least in the reign of Peter the Great, however, some Russians developed a taste for ripened, imported cheese (Peter was said to love a good slice of Limburger as a dessert). Swiss and Dutch cheeses, Stilton and Parmesan, all were imported in sometimes surprising quantities through the nineteenth century. After small-scale attempts to produce Swiss or other cheese on Russian soil beginning in the late eighteenth century, only in the 1860s did larger scale cheese production start to take off.[73]

Meat and fish, too, were preserved in different ways, at times by smoking or drying but most of all with salt. Russia got most of its salt from salt lakes, but also some from mines (though not generally from the sea, being cut off from such sources for much of its history). The famous Stroganov family built up its fortune as salt boilers in the far northeast reaches of Muscovite territory in the sixteenth century. Their seat was called Solvychegodsk – *sol* means salt. Later, production moved to giant salt lakes in the southern Volga region. For a while in the nineteenth century these salt sources could not keep up with demand, but by the end of the century, as transportation issues were resolved, Russia became largely self-supporting when it came to salt (and the third largest producer of salt in the world, after the U.S. and Great Britain).

Salting and drying was a common method of preserving fish for future use, although not a perfect one. At one point in the 1840s, newspapers were filled with accounts of people who had died from 'fish poison' found on 'damp dried fish' that had not then been properly cooked through. Still, drying was a simple and largely effective method. Beef was more common than pork in the northern latitudes of the Russian Empire, even in the bones left behind in archaeological sites, and so salt beef (*solonina*) was possibly a more 'traditional' food than ham or salt pork. Nineteenth-century accounts noted that it above all 'served as a principal food of peasants and household serfs in winter'.[74] There were pigs, though, particularly when Russia began to extend further south, and from them ham (*vetchina*) and salt pork and cured pig fat (*salo*) and sausages (*kolbasy*).

Perhaps the most significant 'technology' that affected Russian consumption of meat was a feature of the environment: the cold. The *Domostroi*, a sixteenth-century guide to housekeeping, recommended storing leftovers and things like aspic on ice to keep them edible for longer. Meat and fish could be frozen and stay frozen. This shocked and amazed foreign travellers in the eighteenth and nineteenth centuries, who saw this most of all in the frozen meat markets of Moscow and St Petersburg. The places were filled with strange sights: fish were 'attractively beautiful; possessing the vividness of their living colours, with the transparent clearness of wax imitations'. The slaughtered livestock were viewed as either miraculous or as 'a far less pleasing spectacle. Most of the largest sort being skinned, and classed according to their species; groups of many hundreds are seen piled up on

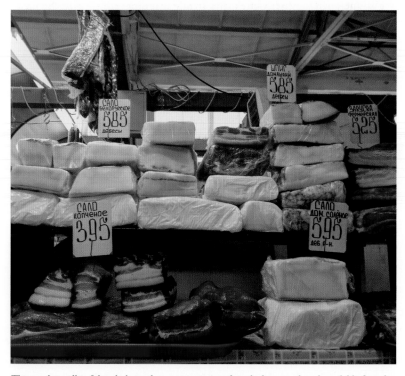

This market stall in Izhevsk shows the many varieties of smoked or cured pork available for sale.

their hind legs against one another, as if each were making an effort to climb over the back of its neighbor.'[75] Thomas Raikes described the benefits of this kind of market: 'here the march of corruption is stopped; the sheep which was killed a month ago will be fresh a month hence; and the fish, which has been brought from the Volga might travel another thousand wersts [*versts*] without losing its delicate flavour.'[76] He also, however, described a bad side-effect: he described frozen meat as 'very tasteless'.[77]

Raikes may not have been wrong – or at least, he was probably right that frozen meat was not part rotten, which had long given some kinds of game and other meats a certain tang on the edge between fermented and putrid. Vladimir Odoevskii, writing in the 1840s as Doctor Puf, believed that this was part of the reason why the existence of frozen meat created a real difference in food practices between Russia and other parts of Europe: 'the essential difference between inhabitants of the south and of the north', he wrote, 'consists in the fact that the first do not eat frozen meat, while the second eats it.'[78] This was important, because much of the cooking advice available in Russia at the time had simply been copied and translated from foreign sources, and said not one word about how best to deal with frozen meat. Odoevskii went on to give general advice – thaw the meat in cold water and let it sit a day or two before cooking – and a specific recipe: stuffed turkey.

Odoevskii noted that freezing was only effective for preserving meat, not vegetables. He was at that point right, for freezing plant products requires different methods and storage. But Russians used other methods to preserve the produce of the garden and orchard and forest. Mushrooms, particularly the large milk caps and boletus, were often dried either whole or sliced. Molokhovets gave advice on how best to dry herbs and greens, as well, to preserve some of their flavour for the winter. Salt and fermentation (*kvashenie*) preserved other vegetables. Beetroot, cucumbers and turnips were all preserved with salt or a lightly salted brine, often also with some degree of fermentation. Eventually tomatoes were preserved in the same way, allowing their taste of summer to take on a slight tang for the winter.

Above all, though, there was *kvashennaia kapusta*: fermented cabbage, sometimes also called *kislaia kapusta*, or sour cabbage. Preparing cabbage for the winter was an important part of the autumn work of peasant men and women. To make it, cabbage was chopped or shredded finely, mixed with salt and lightly pounded to release liquid. This was usually women's work, but according to one reporter:

in nearly all the western provinces, the chopping of cabbage by
serf-owners and some peasants is done in a totally different way
to that common in the northern provinces of Russia . . . this
method consists in the fact that the cabbage is chopped not
in a trough or a tub with cutters but in a big box, usually with
scythes, and therefore not by women but by men.[79]

Before the twentieth century, cabbage was stored in tightly covered barrels
and kept in cellars. One author claimed that 'if the lid is often doused with
brine the cabbage will be preserved for the duration of the winter, even
though it will acquire a not totally pleasant odour,'[80] but others noted
that no matter the precautions, it was hard to keep from spoiling over the
winter: 'every spring we see that people who run corner shops throw out
huge masses of this putrefied pickle.'[81] As glass jars became more common,
they began to replace barrels. And in the twentieth century, people left
behind the country but not the desire to make and keep cabbage for the
winter. Because many buildings in towns had double windows with a good-
sized space between them, that space became a storage spot for large jars
of cabbage or other preserves, kept cool by the outside temperatures but
not frozen by the heat from indoors.

Fruits were preserved, too. Although Russia only developed a significant sugar beet industry in the nineteenth century, it imported sugar or
used honey for preserving. *Varenye* were Russian fruit preserves: fruit
cooked with sugar until syrup forms. *Varenye* is not usually cooked until
the syrup gels – it is a softer, more syrupy form of fruit preserves. Other
fruits – apples, most notably, but also certain forest berries – were
'soaked', which meant packed whole in a container and covered with a
sugar/salt brine. Dried fruits also became part of the culinary world, both
domestically produced and imported from places further to the south.

ALL OF THESE ELEMENTS, environmental and technological, affected the
ways in which Russians ate. At times they constrained what could appear
on tables; at times they brought more and more goods to the market.
There were many continuities through the centuries: rye and buckwheat
as centrally important crops; honey and mushrooms as both potent symbols of Russianness and delicious parts of many meals. But of course there
were changes that came in as well, as the Russian state grew and as the
Russian people changed in their economic position. The ways in which

these changes played out and our understanding of what has remained the same helps to trace out the longer history of food and drink in Russia from the earliest times, when the written record is scarce, to the present day, when a desire to return to 'tradition' at times tries to turn its back on the changes brought in by the centuries.

THREE

Eating and Drinking in
the Earliest Days of Russia

In Ivan Bilibin's illustrations, old Russia takes on a distinct Art Nouveau vibe. Swirling shapes and distinct, crisp lines make up his images of an imagined past world, half historical, half magical. In one of them, an illustration for the folk tale 'Salt', a royal figure, thick and flowing of beard, sits at a table, knife in one hand, goose leg in the other. Before him lie a piece of bread, a cup, the roast goose and a flask of some beverage. Behind him stand two men holding tureens of more food – perhaps *shchi* and *kasha*? This particular version of a past tsar is eating a meal that looks much like one that could have been eaten at any time over the centuries leading up to the time the image was created (1931).

In many ways, Bilibin's illustrations often get at a problem with knowing what people ate and more generally how people lived in earlier times. The written sources are few and inclined towards discussion of less everyday subjects. We have lists of products, we have statements of bad harvests, we have tangential descriptions of the fact of meals, if not specifics of what they contained. The archaeological record helps a bit, as it uncovers the shape of people's everyday lives, the objects they used to cook and eat, even fossilized remnants of the food they ate. In a lot of ways, however, our understanding of what people ate in the earliest years of the development of Russia is based heavily on what we know people ate in much later times, and on our belief that many of the same foods carried through from those early centuries into close to the modern era. There is good reason to believe this. Archaeologists note that the mortars and pestles used to grind grain that are found in digs from the tenth century CE look remarkably like those now in ethnographic museums from the late nineteenth century. It is hard not to conclude that those who used them not only ground grain in the same way but then went on to prepare it in much the same way.

All the same, for the earliest years of Russian habitation of the northeastern European lands, our knowledge remains scanty in many ways. There is something incredibly evocative, though, about the image of small groups moving ever further north and east into the forests, which themselves become more challenging environments with longer winters and poorer soils. Somehow, though, for these early settlers, movement to the north, despite all its hardships, must have seemed an option of greater security in comparison with their lives further south. Did people move at

Ivan Bilibin often imagined an ancient Russian world for his illustrations of folk tales.
In this illustration a king gnaws at a leg of perhaps goose, with bread easily at hand.
Servants hold tureens filled with soup or perhaps a stew.

the first sign of frost, new harvest in hand, hoping to settle by the onset of deepest winter? That might not give enough time – was there instead some moment when the days got just short enough that signalled the moment to move? As a result, in order to start to think about what the earliest inhabitants of the Russian lands ate, we have to think about the larger story of their social and economic organization in order to hope to piece together the meagre evidence from texts and from archaeological digs.

Everyday Life in Early Rus

According to many, if not most, general histories of Russia, the origins of the Russian state lie in a distinctly different state known as Kyivan (or Kievan) Rus, centred on the city of Kyiv (Kiev). The city was located on the Dnieper river, near the line where the forest gave way to the steppe, and it emerged and came to prominence at the end of the first millennium CE.[1] Spreading north from Kyiv to the city of Novgorod, located on the river Volkhov, and encompassing lands that at times spread even further to the south and north, this Rus state brought together the various Slavic, Finnic and Iranian peoples that had been living in this wide region, not always peacefully. It also found some stability between the stronger forces to the north (the Vikings/Varangians) and to the south (the Byzantine Empire and, on the steppe, a series of different nomadic groups, most recently the Khazars). The throne of Kyiv was held by the Grand Prince, who at least in principle sat above the princes of other fortress towns scattered throughout the earliest Kyivan lands. In practice, though, these princes often made war among themselves. As a result, as Valerie Kivelson and Ronald Suny have put it, Rus was not so much a state as 'a mafia-like network of merchants and warlords' and 'a non-territorial, quite mobile system of tribute-collection and constant warfare'.[2]

With all this war, it is no surprise that a military elite developed, supported by a broader population in towns and villages. The *Tale of Bygone Years*, as the earliest chronicle of these Rus lands is known, is mostly concerned with the wars between Kyiv and Constantinople or between various Rus princes, not with how the bulk of the population lived their lives. But still, it makes clear the fact that everyday life in medieval Rus was difficult: the land was 'rich and fertile', but in furs and forest products, not in grain. The climate was severe and the world was therefore uncertain. There were princes, and each prince had a retinue of elite military men. Towns had townspeople who engaged in crafts and trade both locally and further away, and who usually also engaged in agriculture. And there was a larger population more fully engaged in agriculture and in wresting something from the harsh natural environment. Princes owed something to their towns – protection, above all – and the towns and peasants gave back taxes and support (the degree of coercion involved in these basic structures is what is most uncertain). There were slaves, some born into slavery, some taken in war or otherwise coerced. But most historians agree that there was also a larger free peasantry, able to move and to migrate into the forests of the north.

However their social world was ordered, people gathered together in towns and in villages, building homes and sowing the ground, figuring out ways to live as comfortably as they could despite harsh environmental conditions and threats from the world around them. Archaeological evidence from Novgorod and its region gives the fullest details about the ways in which everyday life was ordered in this world. It may not be generalizable to the entire Rus lands – in fact, it is almost certainly not generalizable – but it nonetheless offers some vision of the ways in which these early Slavic peoples interacted with their environment and with each other. Above all, they relied on the earliest version of the Russian stove to keep them warm and to prepare their food. It was different in shape but not in size or function compared to the stoves still visible today. The stove was a necessity but in towns, at least, it was also an ornament: stoves were whitewashed and decorated with elaborate designs.[3] People in Novgorod cooked with iron or layered metal pots and pans; they ate and stored things in ceramic bowls and pots. Glassware was rare but present; metal cups were more common, although that may be in part a reflection of their greater durability. Spoons were above all made of wood, though some made of bone or metal have survived.[4] Most households even in towns had at least a cellar, if not an entire separate storehouse or two. Town households also generally had space for a garden and to keep livestock. The Russian historian M. G. Rabinovich has concluded that this organization meant that most town dwellers continued to grow much of their own food and to store it themselves, and furthermore that most town dwellers were eating primarily their own products and not imported goods.[5]

In Novgorod itself, however, clearly at least some foods were brought into the town from further away. Walnut trees did not grow in the area, for example, but walnut shells turn up in digs dating back to the tenth century – they must have come in via trade.[6] Seeds from cucumbers, from dill, from apples, cherries and plums all turn up in digs dating back to the

These are 19th-century log houses in Arkhangelsk province in Russia's north, but the earliest settlements may not have looked much different. Carved out of the forest, a few households came together to form villages. The only major difference may have been the method of heating – in this photograph, individual houses have chimneys, but Russia was home to an older tradition of the so-called 'black' cottage without a chimney. Smoke stayed inside the house, mostly likely causing health problems, but also keeping all the warmth produced by a fire within.

tenth or eleventh centuries CE, and never disappear.[7] Most of these were foods not originally native to the area around Novgorod, but instead from further south. They were either traded in or, eventually, cultivated locally, which would surely have meant putting in real effort to bring them to maturity before the winter's frosts.

Russian settlements also spread out to the north and east of Novgorod itself. The city eventually held lands that reached all the way to the northern Urals, although 'holding' lands meant above all collecting furs from the people who lived on those lands, not any kind of regular administration. Settlements of East Slavs began moving into these lands intensively in the centuries around 1000 CE (mostly after that date). These were not temporary settlements of those looking to hunt furs, although furs were a valuable commodity of the forest, and one that served to pay taxes. Instead, archaeological evidence suggests that people moved to new places, usually near a lake or a river, and began to settle, felling forests and planting crops.[8]

Excavations carried out since the 1990s have uncovered a world of surprising prosperity even beyond the city walls – or at least, of prosperity beyond what the written record ever suggested. Settlements in the far northern reaches of Russian territory (between Lake Beloe and the town of Vologda) had the same kinds of two-room houses with large stoves that Novgorod did. Those houses were not scattered through the countryside, but instead placed in orderly fashion along streets. The digs show dense settlement in these villages, as well as new houses built on the same sites as older ones. That is, communities stayed together over the years, rather than spreading out more widely.[9] Metal jewellery, decorated pottery and glass beads have all been found in significant numbers at the sites. People kept some pigs, some goats, some sheep, but more cattle, for both milk and meat; they fished and perhaps also traded for bigger fish from further away. They caught and then processed large numbers of fish at once, probably to preserve them for later consumption.[10] And so, these early Russians, both in towns like Novgorod and in more distant settlements along its northern edge, farmed, kept animals, plied crafts and engaged in trade.

It is hard to know exactly how the lists of fish and fowl and animals and plants discovered in archaeological digs actually appeared on the tables of these early Russians. Based on continuities in stove design and in cookware, we can assume that there were soups and stews and porridges and occasional roasts similar in preparation to those cooked centuries later, when records were clearer. In places like Novgorod itself, particularly once the city was well established in trade, archaeological evidence suggests that

Another illustration by Ivan Bilibin, for *The Tale of Tsar Saltan* (1905), shows an imagined feast from Russia's past.

cattle were being kept for beef, not just for milk or for hauling. Everywhere, though, dairy production was important.[11] So in all likelihood, the early inhabitants of Rus ate something very like *shchi* and *kasha*, sometimes with fresh or more likely salted beef, sometimes with *smetana*, sometimes *tvorog*. They ate bread, as well, for grains used to bake bread feature heavily in things like the Novgorod birch-bark scrolls. An early Kyivan account of the lives of monks, the *Paterik*, mentions both bread baking and possible disruptions to that process: evil spirits upsetting the flour and *kvas* used as leavening, or finding a frog in the kneading trough. Beer and mead and *kvas* were the common drinks, as birch-bark documents from Novgorod mention brewing rooms, hops, malt and barley, and archaeological digs have found casks, barrels and jugs.[12]

Although written sources like the *Tale of Bygone Years* rarely mention food or eating, they do regularly mention something else: famine. The first famine described in any of the various chronicles occurred in 1024 in the Suzdal region. As one nineteenth-century historian put it, famine must have been known before then because in that year the people of Suzdal already had a partial solution – to go and purchase grain from the Bolgars to their south – and because famine was already understood as a punishment by God for a people's sins.[13] In Novgorod in 1128, a terrible famine raised the price of rye to unimaginable levels, forcing people to use moss, birch bark, leaves, even pine needles to bake some sort of bread. Sickness came on top of hunger, leaving bodies piled in the streets. According to the chronicler, parents begged foreign merchants visiting the city to take away their children to safety. A few decades later, the chronicler was even blunter: 'oh, there was sorrow: at the market – corpses, on the streets – corpses, in the fields – corpses.'[14]

Famine was usually tied to crop failures, which could themselves be caused by weather that was too wet or too dry, both in the heat of summer and in the cold of winter. Too little snow in winter could be just as devastating to crops as too little rain in summer because of the practice of planting a winter crop, usually rye, which relied on snow cover to protect germinated seeds from the bitter cold. A crop failure in 1303 was caused by 'no snow through the whole winter', which meant that the winter crops failed.[15] These crop failures caused by climate could be made even worse by wars and invasions, whether due to sieges or to the extra extractions of men and supplies demanded by war. According to a later chronicler, fighting between princes of Moscow in the middle of the 1400s combined with bad harvests led to 'ten years of general famine'.[16]

Because the chronicles were compiled by monks in monasteries scattered throughout the Russian lands, their descriptions are local. They describe fifteen 'serious' famines that affected more than a single region or were times of 'terrible death', but even more local incidents of famine – only local, but significant enough to move beyond a crop failure and a resulting time of tightened belts – between the beginning of the eleventh century and the end of the sixteenth.[17] There may have been even more. These were, in other words, centuries in which a basic life of basic sustenance could be disrupted by famine at any time. The famines caused people to move in search of food: peasants came to towns, townspeople fled to the country. Entire settlements were emptied, sometimes to recover, sometimes to fade back into the forests.

Despite their terrors, and despite their possible long-term impact on individual communities and lives, famines were not the norm. For the most part, people sustained themselves. A few other glimpses of how people did that come from the first statements of law in medieval Russia. The first version of the *Russkaia pravda*, often translated as 'Russian justice', probably dates to the early reign of Prince Iaroslav (the beginning of the 1000s CE), as he moved from his initial base in Novgorod to seize the throne in Kyiv. To do that, he had to have an extensive military force, many of them mercenaries, supporting his claim. The *Russkaia pravda* may have been above all an effort to keep order among his military followers. Its rules certainly read like they are intended to keep order within a group of people inclined to violence. 'If a man kills a man, then a brother may avenge a brother,' it opens, and hardly gets less violent from there.[18] Murders are avenged, injuries are satisfied with fines (startlingly, the fee for cutting off someone's moustache or beard is four times the fee for cutting off someone's finger) and the rights to certain kinds of property – horses and slaves, most of all – are affirmed.

Crimes against other kinds of property are also included in the *Russkaia pravda*, providing another window into the ways in which people in the area lived their lives. The *Russkaia pravda* set fines for killing oxen, cows, calves, lambs and rams; for stealing chickens, doves, ducks, geese, swans, sheep, goats and swine. It notes that 'ploughing across a border' was a serious offence garnering a fine of 12 *grivnas* (killing the prince's horse came with a fine of only 3 *grivnas*) – so agricultural land was understood as belonging to certain individuals. So too were beehive trees; the destruction of one, at least one belonging to the prince, came with another hefty fine.

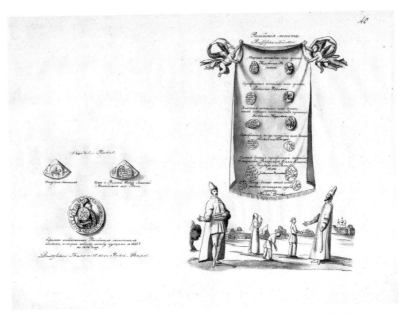

One of the challenges when looking at a long period of history is understanding how money changed over that time. In Rus, the standard monetary unit was the *grivna*, with smaller units known as the *nogata* and *rezana*. Later, small coins known as *dengi* (now the word for money) in units of kopeks or half-kopeks appeared, as in this illustration from the Mayerberg Album. Peter the Great established a new standard in the early eighteenth century: one rouble was equal to 100 kopeks. Over the next century and a half, however, the state released multiple versions of the rouble: a gold rouble, a silver rouble, and also paper bank notes, known as *assignaty*. Before 1840, one silver rouble was worth 3½ *assignaty*.

At some point over the next century, the initial short document was expanded with more regulations covering additional sorts of crimes. Many of them were similar, identifying fines for violent crimes, but others indicated an expanded vision of property, and as a result give an expanded vision of the economic world of Rus. There are references to stealing grain from 'the threshing floor'. There are more detailed references to swine and suckling pigs. There are more descriptions of the kinds of boundaries that marked off land: boundary markers and boundary oaks. There are references to beehive trees and the markers that were placed on them to claim them. There are references to traps and snares.[19]

The two versions of the *Russkaia pravda* also set out a 'schedule of fees' to be given to the bloodwite collector, the man tasked with collecting fees payable to the prince. The expanded edition describes the food portion of those fees thus (*nogatas* and *kunas* are coins):

the bloodwite collector is to take seven buckets of malt for
a week, and a ram or half a carcass of beef or two *nogatas*;
and on Wednesday a *kuna* or cheese, and on Friday the same;
and two chickens per day, and seven measures of bread, and
seven measures of millet, and seven measures of peas and seven
of salt; all this [is to be provided] for the bloodwite collector
and his deputy.[20]

These were the supplies out of which a person of good status could be
expected to feed himself. That meant buckets of malt – which in this case
most likely meant not the roasted grain that served as the basis for brewing
beer or other alcoholic beverages, but the beverages themselves. It meant
bread (which could mean grain, the basis for porridge, rather than baked
bread), millet, peas. It meant meat, cheese, fish, chickens. This was hearty
eating of a kind recognizable not just in Novgorod or Kyiv but through
much of Europe.

The first, shorter edition of the *Russkaia pravda* includes one other
clause in its instructions for supplying the collector: 'if it happens to be
Lent, give the collector fish; [he is entitled to] take seven *rezanas* for
fish.'[21] That is because not long before it was written, the Grand Prince of
Kyiv had declared that Rus was henceforth part of the Christian world.
That had huge implications for the future development of Rus within the
larger European world, of course, but it also had huge implications for
the world of Russian food. Orthodoxy, the variant of Christianity that
came to Russia, had well-developed and elaborate dietary laws that came
to influence the kinds of foods that Russians ate and the ways that food
helped to shape the calendar by which nearly every Russian lived.

FASTING AND FEASTING: ORTHODOX CHRISTIANITY

The tale of how Rus became a part of the Orthodox world is one of the
best-known stories from the *Tale of Bygone Years*. Rus had been in regular
contact with the Byzantine world as it developed and grew, and that
also meant contact with Christianity. For the most part the people of
Rus worshipped a multitude of gods of Slavic, Iranian and Finno-Ugric
origins, but a few people had certainly converted to Christianity by the
middle of the 900s. At the end of that century, Grand Prince Vladimir
(r. 980–1015) became the figure most responsible for turning Rus towards
Christianity. He consolidated his authority in Kyiv around 980, fighting

off his many brothers to do so. Almost immediately, he turned to religion, although not yet to Christianity, in order to bolster his claim to the throne. Initially he chose a subset of the many gods worshipped in his lands and made of them a standard pantheon for future worship; he recognized the many peoples of his lands, giving them all someone to pray to within this pantheon.

A bit less than a decade later, Vladimir turned to religion again. As the story in the *Tale of Bygone Years* goes, he declared an interest in some of the other religions of the world and sent out several of his men to investigate them and report back. Not every version of the text includes all these versions, but in its maximal account, Vladimir and his men decided against the Western/Roman Christian world because 'we beheld no glory there' (they visited the recently converted German lands, not Rome itself, which may have had something to do with that); against Islam (which they visited via the Bolgars), either because they did not like the way worship was practised in mosques or because they did not want to give up pork and alcohol; and against Judaism (which they learned about via the Khazars, recently their great enemy on the steppe whose elite had converted to Judaism), because they believed that God had turned against the Jews and scattered them from their homeland.

Vladimir's envoys also went to Constantinople to visit the Eastern Christian church. They reported back:

> we knew not whether we were in heaven or on earth. For on earth there is no such splendor or such beauty, and we are at a loss how to describe it. We only know that God dwells there among men, and their service is fairer than the ceremonies of other nations. For we cannot forget that beauty.[22]

Obviously, this seemed the right choice, although it took several more twists and turns in the tale for Vladimir to make his final decision. Once he did, many of his retinue immediately followed suit, and he went on to order that the rest of his people convert to Orthodoxy, as well.

There is quite a bit of debate over what this conversion story means for the larger history of religion in Russia. It is clear that the elite of Rus converted, that they endowed or built churches and monasteries in cities and in the countryside throughout the Rus lands, and that Christianity in Rus cleaved to the Byzantine/Eastern/Orthodox, not the Christianity of Rome. Initially, that distinction was minor, and Rus was simply the easternmost part of a larger European Christian world. Marriage ties linked the ruling house of Rus, the Riurikids, to the royal houses not just of near neighbours like Poland, Sweden and Hungary but even to France and England.[23] Eventually, though, Rus was caught up in the schism between the Eastern and Western churches. The date of the Great Schism between East and West was 1054, when the heads of the two churches mutually excommunicated each other, and by extension all their followers. But that was neither the start nor the end of the story when it came to how people lived within the church.

Well before this schism, the Eastern church already had many distinct practices that went beyond the matters of doctrine that led to the break between the church hierarchies. For one thing, the Eastern and Western churches used different kinds of bread for their communion. The Western church used unleavened bread, while the Eastern church not only did not but viewed that practice with deep suspicion. This suspicion may have been based as much on cultural interpretations of bread as on religious ones. Within the Byzantine world, unleavened bread was eaten primarily by Jews and by Armenians, the latter of whom practised a version of Christianity deemed heretical by the Byzantine church. When it turned out that the Western church was using it too, that seemed proof that their Christianity was not the true one.[24]

In addition, the Eastern church had stricter dietary regulations than the Roman church. Some had to do with meats. Pork was fine, but at one point veal was not. Animals killed by snares or nets were also not to be consumed (or, more generally, animals that were strangled and not bled).[25] Fast days (*postnye*) were distinct from meat-eating or non-fast days (*skoromnye*) and were weekly features of the calendar: every Wednesday and Friday was a fast day. On fast days, the Orthodox faithful were expected to abstain from all animal foods, avoiding not only meat but all dairy products (although, as the list of the bloodwite collector's provisions suggests, not everyone held to this rule). Most fast days also required abstention from fish, although it was allowed when a holiday fell on a fast day. On some days, even vegetable or seed oils were forbidden. As a result, Orthodox dietary rules were both stricter when it came to fasts, but also more complicated because there were distinctions between different kinds of fast days.

There were also a lot of fast days. On top of the weekly fast days, there were four extended fast periods over the course of a year: 'Great' Lent (the forty-day fast before Easter); the Apostles fast (of apostles Peter and

Праздникъ Пасхи въ С.-Петербургѣ.

The Orthodox calendar in many ways revolved around Easter. It was preceded by the Great Lent – 'Great' in a calendar that included three other extended fast periods – which was itself preceded by the festival of *Maslenitsa*, or Butter Week. Easter came to be celebrated with particular foods, and also particular ways of eating them together. In the earliest years of Orthodoxy in Rus, celebrating Easter would not have looked quite like those in the illustration above, but the elements of later celebrations would have been in place.

Paskha

Easter is the most important holiday of the Orthodox year, and the whole panoply of celebrations and fasts that surround it make it the most marked by special dishes. In many ways the run-up to Easter begins with *Maslenitsa*, the week of celebration that precedes Great Lent. During *Maslenitsa* snow forts and ice slides appear outdoors, and indoors everyone eats blini, fried and slathered with butter, which is soon to be put aside. During the Great Lent, no animal foods are eaten – no butter, no milk, no cheese. If a religious holiday falls in the middle of Great Lent, the fasting rules are slightly eased to allow fish, but otherwise, it is forty days of abstemious eating. It is no wonder, then, that the treats most associated with Easter itself are celebrations of the foods that have just been avoided. *Kulich* is a yeasted cake enriched with eggs, butter and milk. *Paskha* – the Russian word for both Easter itself and a celebratory dish – combines the slightly sour fresh cheese *tvorog* with sour cream and butter. The resulting mass is usually slightly sweetened and possibly studded with dried fruit. The whole is put into a mould and pressed for a day. One cookbook from 1834 suggested a possible refinement: carving a sheep out of butter, covering its horns with gold leaf and placing it on top of the *paskha*.[26]

Paul, held between the second Monday after Pentecost and the feast of Saints Peter and Paul; because Pentecost itself depended on the date of Easter, this fast could last anywhere from just over a week to six weeks); the Dormition fast (two weeks in August before the Feast of the Dormition); and the Nativity fast (from 15 November to Christmas). Each of these had a slightly different set of dietary rules. *Maslenitsa* – the festival before Great Lent – and Holy Week also had their own dietary rules.[27] One visitor to Muscovy in the early 1500s claimed that Great Lent was kept even more strictly than the rules demanded – that many contented themselves with bread and water, or even maintained a full fast, abstaining from all food for anywhere from three to five days a week.[28]

Of course, this system had an enormous effect on the ways in which people ate. It ordered their weeks, it ordered their years, it marked out the end of winter and the end of summer. It also either demanded ways of preserving foods not allowed during fasts for sometimes extensive periods or perfectly fit an existing spectrum of preserving techniques. Some have, in fact, argued that the Orthodox fasting calendar was particularly well suited to Russia. As one British traveller put it:

> nothing can be contrived with more ingenious policy to suit the habits of the Russians. When Lent fasting begins, the stock of frozen provisions is either exhausted, or unfit to use, and the interval which takes place allows sufficient time for procuring, killing and storing, the fresh provisions of the spring.[29]

Others believed that the many meat-free days of the Orthodox calendar made a positive out of what others might consider a lack of animal foods. One nineteenth-century doctor, Ivan Zatsepin, even argued that a largely vegetarian diet – that is, a diet following the fast rules – was the reason why Russians were by and large healthy. For him, it was an essential part of the Russian world.[30]

It is of course hard to know exactly how well these tenets spread through the population beyond the elite. In fact the presumed slow adoption of Orthodoxy – or at least the slow penetration of Orthodoxy beyond a mere label – gave rise to the concept of *dvoeverie*, or double-belief: the idea that Russian peasants might be Orthodox in principle but still held on to certain pre-Christian beliefs and traditions in practice. During the Kyivan era it is entirely possible that large swathes of the population were barely Orthodox. But that would soon change, in part due to the greatest disaster to fall on the Eastern Slavic world: the arrival of the Mongols and the onset of what came to be known as the 'Mongol Yoke'.

DEVASTATION AND RECOVERY:
THE MONGOL ERA AND THE RISE OF MOSCOW

The larger effect of the Mongol era in the history of Rus and Russia is a subject of huge debate. Some later thinkers and historians claimed that the era had created dramatic changes in the everyday life of Russians. Vissarion Belinskii, one of the great intellectual figures of the early nineteenth century, viewed the Mongol/Tatar (sometimes written Tartars) influence as the source of all that he disliked about Russia's past:

The seclusion of women, the habit of burying money in the ground and of wearing rags from the fear of revealing one's wealth, usury, Asiaticism in the way of life, a laziness of the mind, ignorance, contempt for oneself – in a word, all that Peter the Great was uprooting, everything that was in Russia directly opposed to Europeanism, everything that was not native to us but had been grafted on to us by the Tatars.[31]

Others believe this to be an overstatement, and instead argue that the everyday interactions of the Tatars and the Russians were simply not strong enough to 'graft on' anything so personal.

Nonetheless, the arrival of the Qipchaq Khanate – the westernmost part of the larger Mongol Empire allotted to one of the sons of Chinghis [Genghis] Khan – was a turning point, and a dramatic one at that. The *Tale of Bygone Years* first makes mention of a new, terrifying military force called the Tatars in 1224, when they appeared, engaged Rus troops in fierce and deadly battle, and then left. 'We know neither from whence they came nor whither they have gone,' the chronicler wrote. 'Only God knows that, because he brought them upon us for our sins.'[32] This was just a taste of what this new force could do. They showed up again more than a decade later, in the late 1230s, ravaged the northeastern parts of Rus and disappeared again. And then in 1240, they returned to sack Kyiv itself.

'They attacked Russia, where they made great havoc, destroying cities and fortresses and slaughtering men,' wrote the papal envoy Giovanni de Plano Carpini a few years later. 'Going on from there, fighting as they went, the Tartars destroyed the whole of Russia.'[33] That was perhaps a slight overstatement of the effect the Qipchaq Khanate had on Rus, but not much of one. The Mongol army was a hugely efficient and effective military force, and the ruling khans made use of it first to expand their control and then keep it in place by making sure that their conquered territories stayed conquered. This involved both force – there were major Mongol invasions of Rus lands eleven times between 1237 and 1327 and many more smaller-scale raids – and less violent ways of making sure that those territories kept up a steady stream of taxes and tribute.

There were a number of significant outcomes. The Novgorodian lands to the north and northeast remained largely outside the sphere of direct Mongol control. At the same time that the Mongols were appearing on the steppe in the south and southeast, Novgorod was fighting with would-be conquerors from the west and the north: the Swedes and the Livonian

Order. The Prince in Novgorod, Alexander (1221–1263), fought off both forces, most famously trouncing the Swedes in a battle on the ice of the river Neva in 1240. He was henceforth known as Alexander Nevsky. He also travelled to treat with the Mongols before they attacked Novgorod itself (although they had come quite close). He obligated Novgorod to pay tribute to the Mongols, and as a result the city continued to serve as a conduit for Russian goods out to the West and for Western silver to come back into Russia.

The rest of Rus was not so lucky. Not only did the violence of the initial invasion cause harm but the tribute demands of the Mongols depressed economic development for a century or more. There was virtually no building of stone (that was true in Novgorod, as well) for half a century; stone building began again in the north at the end of the thirteenth century, but failed to recover at all in the southern reaches of the Rus lands until the middle of the fifteenth.[34] On top of this, there was the Black Death, which came to Rus in 1352, several years after it had first appeared in Western Europe – a sign, it has been said, of the ways that Rus was cut off from potential sources of wealth like the Silk Road because of its position vis-à-vis the Qipchaq Khanate. It too killed thousands upon thousands.

The Mongol era also affected the ways in which people ate in the Russian lands in part because it clearly disrupted some sorts of trade that had earlier allowed for the spread of certain foods. Digs in Novgorod, for example, show walnut shells from the pre-Mongol era, but almost none in layers from the thirteenth to the fifteenth century. Wine almost disappears from mention in texts other than as part of religious services, as well. What wine still came in was imported through Novgorod via the Hansa trade.[35] As people moved away from the border with the steppe in order to find more safety in the forests, they also had to contend with the relatively poorer soil and relatively harsher climate as they figured out a way to feed themselves.

Despite these hardships, some institutions eventually managed to prosper and even to begin to expand their domains. Hundreds of monasteries were built during these centuries, some because of donations by a rich patron, some growing around a single holy figure. They spread through the Russian lands: 150 new monasteries in the 1300s, 250 in the 1400s, more than 300 in the 1500s.[36] Among other effects, this brought Orthodoxy and the church closer to more people. Some regions prospered, as well. Novgorod was one, and the other region that turned out to be its greatest rival was Moscow. In some ways, this was a surprise. Its princely house

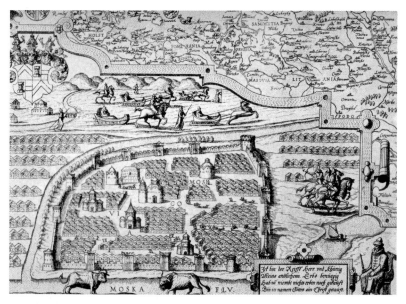

This detail from a 16th-century map shows the walled city of Moscow, lying on the Moskva river (mislabelled Moska on the map), and with extensive settled lands just outside the walls. The river was hugely important to Moscow's rise, as it was one way of connecting the city with a wider region. The map shows another option, too – sleds, here carrying people, but in reality at times also carrying supplies for the city.

claimed Riurikid roots, through Daniil, a younger son of Alexander Nevsky. Moscow was a relatively young town in the northeastern frontier region of Vladimir-Suzdal at the time of the Mongol invasion. As a result, it did not have the longstanding trade networks of Novgorod, nor was it relatively protected from direct contact with the Khanate.

It did have some advantages, though. Its environment was relatively mild, its soil relatively rich, and so it could support itself better than some of its neighbours.[37] Most of all, though, it had ambitious princes who combined their ambition with clever politics. They negotiated with the Mongols for the right to collect taxes from other regions (which got them a bit of profit, as well). They convinced the Metropolitan of Kyiv to move the seat of the Russian church to Moscow. They fought with their neighbours, but they also negotiated with them to gain influence and lands. By the beginning of the 1400s they had expanded their dominion such that they seemed a true rival to Novgorod. Then there was a bad period, when civil war pitted brothers and cousins against one another, devastating their lands once again. But once it was finished, and once Muscovy had recovered, its princes moved onward and outward, annexing Novgorod, the White Sea region, Pskov and Smolensk – all by the beginning of the 1500s. And it was Moscow's princes who declared that the people of Rus would no longer pay tribute to the Tatars (whose empire had fragmented to the point that this was a largely symbolic statement, but still a potent symbol). Muscovy was the new regional power. It is in almost every way the true origin state of the Russia we know today.

EVERYDAY LIFE IN MUSCOVY

Compared to the era of Rus, there are a few more written sources for the Mongol and early Muscovite eras that move beyond chronicle writing – few letters or personal statements, but accounts of saints' lives and other ecclesiastical sources, charters and other records of monasteries. These are not necessarily concerned with the minutiae of how people lived, but nor do they entirely ignore it. Some saints' lives mention all the stages of baking bread: of grinding grain into flour, kneading and leavening it, baking it.[38] There are mentions of both ordinary rye bread and of fancier wheaten *kalach* in written sources; these baked loaves were counted by number, not by weight, which led the Soviet historian Artemy Artsikhovskii to conclude that they were usually baked to a relatively standard size.[39] That means that bread had a cultural form – it was a loaf of known size, and probably known shape, as well.

Written sources made a few mentions of cabbages or of apple trees, although not enough to draw conclusions about how widespread their cultivation was. Archaeological excavations show the same array of animal bones that were found in the earlier periods: among livestock mostly cattle, then pigs, then sheep; fish of all sorts and chickens and ducks. According to Artsikhovskii, mead and beer were the only drinks mentioned in documents from the era with any frequency, and mead was much the more common. It was the alcoholic beverage warned against in church writings on fasts (where wine might have been the norm to the south). It was something used to fulfil obligations, it was what people mentioned as the source of unpleasant popular drunkenness. Beer appeared occasionally, but rarely without mead, as well.

These basic foods were consumed by people who were in many ways probably not that different to the people of the Kyivan era. For one thing, their social organization was largely the same. There were princes, still, with retinues of boyars and military supporters. Now they were more firmly based in specific territories (hence the princes of Moscow), although not in Novgorod, where the people of the city picked which prince they wished

These illustrations show two villages in northwestern Russia in the 17th century. Both depict clusters of houses surrounded by cultivated fields or pastures; this kind of geographical layout governed the agricultural world, and as a result the culinary world, of most of Russia's inhabitants.

to accept. There were still peasants who tilled the land and who therefore supplied the economic base of the entire society, by growing the grain and by paying taxes or rents to support the military elite. As Moscow expanded, it rewarded loyalty on the part of local elites with grants of land, often taken from those whose loyalty was suspect. Not only did Moscow grant the land but the peasants who lived on that land, who made it productive. Although initially those peasants could leave if they found their new landlords too rapacious, starting in the fifteenth century, that right started to disappear. Not for everyone, and not entirely – only peasants who had debts, and even they would still be allowed to move during the two weeks around St George's Day in November. By 1497, however, the St George's Day restriction was extended to all peasants, a first major step in the process of binding Russian peasants to the land.

This meant that there were clearly distinct social strata in Muscovy, with different ways of life – and different ways of eating. At the top was the Grand Prince of Moscow, at this point occasionally called 'tsar' and soon to take that name more formally. The boyar elite was a military elite, which came to prominence through service. Individual boyar clans were often at odds over matters of precedence and over matters of influence. Elite women lived in seclusion known as the *terem*, in part to guard the honour of their clans. Towns were home to other people: traders, craftspeople and, particularly in Moscow, chancellery servitors of various kinds. Many were elite slaves; other kinds of slaves and indentured servants played important roles in household economies. The countryside was home to the peasantry, living and farming on lands that were not considered theirs.

At the beginning of the sixteenth century, the Austrian diplomat Sigismund von Herberstein visited Muscovy on two long trips and later wrote out a lengthy description of what he saw. The area around Moscow was a difficult one, he thought, with sandy soil and a severe climate – he personally saw the result one winter, when severe frosts killed off an entire year's fruit harvest.[40] He described huge variation in agriculture just in this one region: on the one hand, he noted, although there was generally sufficient grain and vegetables, there were no cherries, no walnuts (only hazelnuts), and not much in the way of tree fruit grown locally at all. And yet, he claimed that Muscovites put great effort, even 'particular care', into growing melons, using manure to fertilize the soil and growing them in a sort of cold frame. (Historians wonder whether he could really have seen melons grown in Moscow.)[41] He found the livestock smaller than that he was used to and also claimed there was no honey to be harvested there.[42]

Herberstein's entourage was brought into Moscow in great state, given a place to stay, and then also given someone to see to all their needs (and perhaps also to keep an eye on their actions). According to him, his Muscovite hosts had a clear idea of how much of different supplies were necessary per person in any given group; so, they supplied the basics – like bread, drinks, meat, oats and straw for horses, salt, pepper, oil, onions 'and other trifling things' – usually 'sufficiently and even in excess'. The Muscovites regularly supplied five different drinks: three kinds of mead and two of beer.[43]

He described differences to what he was used to in other food practices, as well. In particular, he reported trying to buy live fish at markets as a treat for himself and his entourage. His hosts, however, were horrified at the idea. Live fish for purchase at a market were simply not a part of their understanding of how food got bought and sold; they expected fish to be on sale frozen, dried or salted.[44] At elaborate meals with the tsar, the table was carefully arranged as to precedence, of course, but also set with particular accessories that Herberstein read as particularly Russian. Placed along the table were sets of three dishes: one with salt, one with pepper, one with vinegar, such that every four guests had access to one set. At the meal Herberstein was ceremonially offered bread and salt, and he described the shape of the bread as being like an oxen's yoke, which he interpreted as a symbol of the slavery of the Russian people. The main dish – roast swan – was eaten with vinegar 'like a sauce', or with soured milk (perhaps really sour cream), or with salted cucumbers or pickled plums. He saw these sour accompaniments as a particular Russian practice, one that might be shared with Russians of other social status. The drinks served at the tsar's table were indications of social stratification, however– there was actual 'Greek wine' as well as the usual assortment of meads.[45] Herberstein saw other signs of a growing rift between the wealthy and the common folk. According to him, wealthy Muscovites – the boyars, in particular – saw holidays as times to 'feast and drink and go about in fancier clothing', but the common folk, instead, generally just worked as normal, 'saying that to be festive and to refrain from work – that's the master's affair'.[46]

It is still difficult to know exactly what people, even elite ones, regularly ate during this period, but there are more descriptions of what was going on. One source for this kind of information is the *Domostroi*, compiled most probably in the 1550s.[47] This text, which could almost be translated as 'Housekeeping', was a set of instructions for running a good, economical, Orthodox household. Perhaps Orthodox should come first, for Orthodoxy and good Orthodox behaviour is centrally important to its directives. Its chapters are filled with quotations from the Bible, reassuring its readers of the source of its advice. Even topics like 'how to be hospitable to guests in your house' begin with the need to pray before a meal, not with the meal itself. The text also imagines the ideal Orthodox household as a patriarchal one. The male head of the household was to instruct his wife, his children and his servants both in good home economics and in good religious behaviour, using fear if necessary. Furthermore, the *Domostroi* tells him, he has something to fear, too: if he does not behave properly God will punish him.

The *Domostroi* was addressed to the master of the house; he was to instruct his wife, who was then to instruct the servants, in proper behaviour. In this illustration from the Mayerberg Album, dating to around a century after the *Domostroi* was compiled, we see three women who might be found in Muscovite households like the one depicted in the household guide: a boyar, or noble, woman; a townswoman, meaning most likely a merchant's wife; and a 'simple town maiden', in this case apparently a servant.

The *Domostroi* also has a more practical side to its instructions (although avoiding everlasting punishment might be considered a practical goal): how to run a kitchen and feed the household through the long, often cold, year. The household of the time was an expansive one, with a main living structure, gardens and outbuildings for cooking and storage. There were servants (possibly slaves) as well: a cook, a housekeeper (or keeper of the keys), a baker, as well as more cooks and kitchen servants. The *Domostroi* advises the master and mistress of the house to talk each day about the state of the household, to watch over the expenses of their servants and to set them tasks for cooking and for purchasing supplies. It was the master's responsibility to make sure that the Orthodox dietary rules were kept and to order foods, either with meat or Lenten, appropriate to the specific day. They were to keep good accounts, too, to make sure that money was not lost. Uneaten food was to be put aside on ice, not thrown away. Anything that had not been touched could be served again to the master and mistress and their guests; other food could be given away.

The *Domostroi* echoes some of Herberstein's descriptions. Like him, it also describes dishes for salt, pepper and vinegar, and the idea that Russians had a particular taste for the salty and the sour. 'Vinegar, and brine from pickles, from lemons, or from plums' could be served if strained – and the pickles, too, of course. (A century later the Dutch traveller Nicolaes Witsen [Nikolaas Vitsen] would say of his meal with the tsar that although the baked goods were tasty, 'the meat was so strongly studded with garlic, onion, lemon and marinated cucumbers that our tongues could not bear it.'⁴⁸) A meal would probably include 'dried fish or anything dried, and various aspics, either meat or Lenten, and caviar and cabbage'. Drinks should be 'clear, strained through a sieve' and most likely home-brewed beer or *kvas*.

This household manual is also much more detailed in its descriptions of what a normal meal, or what the normal foods eaten in a day, was likely to be: 'on meat-eating days – bread of sifted flour, *shchi* every day and thin *kasha* with ham, or sometimes, instead of it, thick *kasha* with fatback, and meat, if there is some, serve for dinner; and for supper *shchi* and milk or *kasha*'. Lenten days were similar: '*shchi* and thin *kasha*, sometimes with jam, at times peas, at times dried fish, at times baked turnip, and for supper cabbage *shchi*, *tolokno* and sometimes *rassolnik* or *botvinia*'. Or there could be even more variety:

> use hemp-seed oil, groats and flour from one's stores: make any
> kind of *pirogi* or blini, and make roulettes and various *kashas*,
> and noodles with peas, or thick peas, and soups, and dumplings,
> and preserves and sweet *kashas* and foods – *pirogi* or *blinchiki*
> with mushrooms, with poppy seeds, with *kasha*, with turnip,
> with cabbage or nuts in sugar, or rich *pirogi*, whatever God sent.

Even during the strictest of the fasting periods, Great Lent, the table was hardly tasteless: 'swedes/rutabagas, horseradish, cabbage, strong brine and various vegetables' gave variety. When fish was allowed, the options were even greater: 'fish and caviar and dried or boiled fish, and *ukha* from dried or smoked fish and dried German herring'.

Holidays and Sundays had fancier foods: 'some kind of *pirogi* or thick *kashas*, or vegetables, or *kasha* with fish oil, blini and *kisel*, and whatever God sends'. All these were the foods served to the men of the household and their (male) guests; women (who lived separately), children and servants got the leftovers.⁴⁹ Major holidays were to have even bigger feasts: on Easter, all sorts of wildfowl (including swans), mutton, chicken, *kasha*, salt beef, tongue, ham, 'double *shchi*'. Or, for a fish meal, smoked fish (including imported ones), dried salmon and osetra, *viziga* and multiple different varieties of *ukha*. Long lists of similar foods appear under other holidays as well – abundance suggested as much by the huge variety of meats or fishes as by any particular way of preparing them.

Luxury was above all suggested by quantity, for the most part, because when it came to preparation these were at base simple foods, as further instructions suggested. 'Cabbage or beetroot or pickled vegetables: chop them up finely and wash them well, and cook them and steam them well.' 'On meat-eating days take meat or ham or salt pork, put it [in a pot], add sour cream or sprinkle in groats, and steam it too.' Salted or dried meat was to be washed, scraped, cleaned and boiled well. 'And prepare every dish for the servants of the family, and knead and sour breads for them, and roll them out well, and bake them, and [bake] *pirozhki* for them too. All food for them should be prepared well and cleanly, like for yourself.'[50]

Although the work was done by servants, the mistress of the household was supposed to know how everything was done. She ought to assign tasks to her servants – 'who is making the food for the day, who is baking the breads' – and she ought to

> know how to sift the flour, how to make and knead the dough,
> how to shape and bake the bread, both sour and rich, and
> *kalach* and *pirogi* too, and she should know how much flour
> each takes, and how much the finished bread should weigh,
> and how much one should get from [different measures].
> And how to bake and cook meats and fish, and all sorts of
> *pirogi* and blini, various *kashas* and *kisels*, all sorts of dishes
> – all this the mistress of the household should know herself
> so that she can instruct her servants how to do it.[51]

The *Domostroi* even gives glimpses into the thrifty origins of some of these foods. It suggests that when baking bread, any extra dough should be used to make *pirogi*, 'on meat-eating days with meat fillings, whatever there is, on Lenten days with *kasha* or with peas or with sweet things or with turnips or with mushrooms and with cabbage or with whatever God gives'.[52] Or it suggests the many things that a 'housewifely wife and a good cook' could think up to do with a whole sheep once its meat had been eaten and its hide had become a coat (essentially, stuff, roast or otherwise cook every type of offal).

In addition, the *Domostroi* gives all sorts of advice on filling storerooms with foods for the long winters (and for other times of year, as well).

It gave good economic advice: buy everything at the time it was produced, harvested, or first brought to the city to get the cheapest prices. Preserve whatever was not consumed right away. The mistress of the household was expected to have all the knowledge 'to make beers and meads, and distilled things, and malted things, and *kvas*, and vinegars, and fermented foods and every store for the kitchen and for baking'. (Women were only supposed to drink the *kvas* or other non-alcoholic beverages, though.) In the autumn, 'salt the cabbage and put up the beetroot, store the turnips and carrots.' Everyone should keep a milk cow or two; in summer they were easy to put out to pasture, and in winter they could eat all sorts of things, particularly the mash left over from brewing beer, *kvas* or *kislye shchi*. With a milk cow and a few chickens, a household had all it needed 'so that any day can have festive treats and pleasures not bought at the market. All sorts of *pirogi*, blini, roulettes, *kisels* and kinds of milks – whatever you want, everything made at home.'[53] Nor were these sorts of foods the only things to be stored. The world of Moscow had opened up beyond the borders of Muscovy – as the mention of 'dried German herring' already suggests. But there were other signs of this, as well. Herbs which might be home grown were to be stored along with imported spices like cloves and nutmeg, for example.

Books like the *Domostroi* present ideals, not necessarily realities, but records from some religious institutions suggest that its description was not too far off from the world in which it was created. Of course, a monastery was not the same as a household – it was much bigger, for one thing, and organized in totally different ways. But there are things about life in monasteries that echo the concerns of the compiler of the *Domostroi*. After all, the *Domostroi* described a perfect form of domestic economy as experienced in a perfectly Orthodox household, one that had access to markets but which also produced much of its own food itself. Monasteries were larger, but organized in not such a different way, and with similar concerns for the moral bases of their institutions.

One vivid set of records come from the Resurrection Convent in Goritsy, far to the north of Moscow. In 1563, Tsar Ivan IV (the Terrible) forced his aunt Evfrosinia Staritskaia to take religious vows and then confined her to the convent in Goritsy. Although she took a new name, becoming the nun Evdokiia, she continued to live in the convent as a member of the elite, supported by a household of fourteen servitors. She had her own tailor and guards, and also her own chefs and 'stewards in charge of beverages and the pantry'.[54] In other words, although she was within

Monks ate together in refectories (*trapeza*) like this one in the Valdai Iverskii monastery, founded in 1653.

the walls of the convent, she was in other ways living in a household of a status like that described in the *Domostroi*. According to the decree that had forced Evdokiia into her new position, she and her suite were also to receive certain provisions: each member of her suite received measures of rye, oats, salt and meat; the group was to share additional measures of oatmeal and *tolokno*. Historian Ann M. Kleimola has calculated what this actually meant: they received enough rye to bake three-and-a-half loaves of bread per person each day.

In addition, Evdokiia was supported in her household by six nuns. The *Domostroi* told wives and daughters to abstain from alcoholic beverages, but apparently there was no such suggestion for the nuns. Nor was their table modest. They too received rye flour, oat flour, oatmeal and *tolokno*, but they also received significantly different provisions: barley malt for beer, buckwheat, honey and barrels of fish (beluga, sturgeon and pike).[55] Not only did Evdokiia's personal household receive grants from Ivan but the convent as a whole received supplies for special holiday meals – supplies meant to provide four feasts a year for seventy nuns. They received fish, both salted and fresh, as well as wheat and other flour; millet and poppy seeds, nut and hemp oils; honey for brewing mead as well as already brewed mead and wine; pears, apples, cherries, dried figs and raisins as well as syrups for sweets; and finally spices: pepper, saffron, ginger, cloves, cinnamon.[56] Again, the domestic and the imported are already intertwined.

The significant amount of fish was key to one particular version of Russian cooking that had developed by this time: the food of the Russian religious establishment. Of course this was linked to the general Orthodox dietary regulations, but those regulations were given new form in monasteries and convents. In the early seventeenth century, Patriarch Filaret (who was himself from an extremely well-connected and well-off family: the Romanovs) ate meals that brought this Orthodox fish-based cuisine to new levels. A single meal might include a dozen different kinds of fish – fresh, salted or smoked – served on their own (perhaps with cucumber or with garlic) or cooked into an *ukha*; plates of caviar; and more fish and *viziga* cooked into *pirogi*. There are very occasional mentions of other foods – *shchi*, of course! – but for the most part, this version of monastery cuisine was almost monotonous in its plenty.[57] In addition, this was a very specific kind of plenty tied to Orthodoxy and to the environment of Muscovy. It was perhaps the apotheosis of early Russian cooking as much as were the foods described in the *Domostroi*.

THE BOYARINA EVFROSINIA was forced to become the nun Evdokiia because of the actions of her nephew: Ivan IV, the Terrible. The *Domostroi* dates to his reign, as well. The era of Ivan IV was a watershed for Russia in many ways. Born in 1530, he succeeded his father in 1533 as a small child and was formally crowned tsar in 1547. Although he was still a teenager, this formal coronation marked the moment when he threw off boyar guardianship and ruled as an adult. Ivan would come to be known as Ivan Groznyi, Ivan the Terrible, for his military victories, but also because of the many, many stories of his troubled and troubling character. His most infamous act is probably the *Oprichnina*, a period in the middle of his reign during which he handed over responsibility to a small group of *Oprichniki* who proceeded to terrorize the wider population, boyar and peasant alike. Then there were the many wives (sequentially – had he lived in the era of Henry VIII and not of his daughter Elizabeth, this part of his reign might not have seemed so shocking to foreign observers), and the killing of his son, and many, many stories of petty cruelty.

Because of this, Ivan the Terrible's reign has often been read as a preview of later autocratic, even totalitarian, excesses. That is debatable, at best. But Ivan's reign was incredibly important for the later development of Russia (and for that matter of the Soviet Union) because it began Muscovy's transformation into the Russian Empire. His father's and grandfather's military efforts had already been in some ways imperial, as Moscow annexed most of its neighbours in the 'gathering of the Russian lands', as it was sometimes called. Most of the inhabitants of these lands were ethnically and/or religiously contiguous with the people of Muscovy, so it was not an imperial expansion involving certain kinds of difference, but the inhabitants of Novgorod certainly felt the weight of external, foreign control. Furthermore, particularly in the far north and northeast, non-Russians had lived under Novgorodian control, and now lived under Muscovite control.

With Ivan the Terrible, however, an era of extensive colonial expansion began. War led to expansion in new directions and resulted in the absorption not only of new lands but new peoples and new religions. This led, of course, to significant changes in the self-conception of the Russian state and in the lives of the many non-Russians who came to live under the control of Moscow, and then St Petersburg, and then Moscow again. It also meant that Russian society and Russian culture were altered in significant new ways, as Russians moved out of the forests of the Russian north, eventually to expand into the southern steppe and through the vast terrain of Siberia. They brought with them certain practices, but then also adapted to their new environments in ways that transformed those practices and often travelled back to the old 'heartland' of Rus.

FOUR

Russia Becomes an Empire

When English merchant adventurers in search of a northeast passage to Asia stumbled instead upon a northern sea route to Muscovy in 1553, they were probably initially disappointed. After all, what was there in this far off, far northern land? No one knew that much about it; reports from people like the traveller Sigismund von Herberstein had circulated, but they were few and far between. There was a young new tsar there, too, a man named Ivan IV who had just conquered the Khanate of Kazan, one of the remnants of the Qipchaq Khanate to Moscow's east. That was certainly something to pay attention to, particularly as he would go on to conquer the Khanate of Astrakhan just a few years later.

Quickly, though, these men realized they had stumbled across a place of great wealth in commodities that were particularly valuable to an island country that needed a healthy navy and merchant armada to stay powerful. Muscovy turned out to have immense stores of hemp, pitch, tar and timber, all materials necessary for seafaring. And so, when they returned to London, these adventurers gathered more backers and founded the Muscovy Company, the first of the great joint-stock companies that began the march of the British Empire around the globe.

These military/naval commodities were central to British trade with Muscovy and central to negotiations to keep that trade going over the following few centuries.[1] When Giles Fletcher was sent to Moscow in 1588, firming up Anglo-Russian trade was his top priority – but in his account of his stay, less practical commodities also come to the fore. After introducing the geography and environment of Muscovy, Fletcher moved on right away to 'The native commodities of the Countrie'. Of course, this was of central interest to someone engaged in trade negotiations. But he began his account with something that suggests that he was as struck

139

by what he ate and drank while in the country as with its potential as a trading partner:

> For kindes of fruites they have Appels, Peares, plummes, cheries, redde and blacke, (but the blacke wild) a deen [*dyn*, or melon] like a muske millian, but more sweete & pleasant, cucumbers & goords (which they call *Arbouse* [actually, watermelon]) rasps, strawberies, and hurtilberies, with many other bearies in great quantitie in every wood and hedge. Their kindes of graine are wheat, rie, barley, oates, pease, buckway, psnytha, that in taste is somewhat like to rice. Of all these graynes the countrie yeeldeth very sufficient with an overplus quantitie, so that wheate is solde sometime for two alteens or ten pence starling the *Chetfird*, which maketh almost three English bushels. Their rye is sowed before the winter, all their other graine in the spring time, & for the most parte in May.[2]

He went on to describe the more standard trade commodities of the country – or at least the more exportable. Furs, of course. But also wax, honey ('besides an exceeding great quantitie spent in their ordinary drinks (which is *mead* of al sorts) & their other uses, some good quantitie is carried out of the countrie'), tallow, hides, 'trane oyle' (a term later used primarily for whale oil, but in this case oil from the blubber of seals), flax and hemp, salt, tar, mica, saltpeter, brimstone, iron, beasts of the forest and fish.[3]

Fish brought him back to consumables:

> For fresh water fish besides the common sorts (as Carpe Pikes Pearch, Tench, Roach, &c.) they have divers kinds very good & delicate: as the *Bellouga,* or *Bellougina* of 4 or 5 elnes long, the *Ositrina* or *Sturgeon*, the *Severiga,* & *Sterledy* somewhat in fashion and taste like to the *Sturgeon*, but not so thicke nor long. These 4 kinds of fish breed in the *volgha,* & are catched in great plenty, & served thence into the whole Realme for a great food. Of the Roes of these foure kinds they make a very great store of *Icary* or *Caveary* as was said before.
>
> They have besides these that breed in the *volgha* a fish called the *Riba bela,* or white salmon which they account more delicate then they do the redde salmon wherof also they have

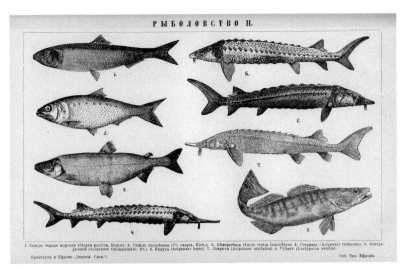

РЫБОЛОВСТВО II.

1. Сельдь черная морская (Clupea pontica, Eichw). 2. Сельдь каспійская (Cl. caspia, Eich.). 3. Бѣлорыбица (Lucio trutta leucichtys). 4. Стерлядь (Acipenser ruthenus). 5. Осетр русскій (Acipenser Güldenstädtii, Br.). 6. Бѣлуга (Acipenser huso). 7. Севрюга (Acipenser stellatus). 8. Судакъ (Lucioperca sandla).

Брокгаузъ и Ефронъ „Энциц. Слов.".   Соб. Тип. Ефрона.

Giles Fletcher lists the well-known fish of the Volga that came to play a role both for their flesh and for their caviar: these were the sterlet (*Acipenser ruthenus*) (4), osetr (*Acipencer Güldenstädtii*) (5), beluga (*Acipenser huso*) (6) and sevruga (*Acipenser stellatus*) (7). This later illustration also shows herrings common to the Black (1) and Caspian (2) seas, the *belorybitsa* (*Stenodus leucichthys*), literally white fish, then common to the Caspian Sea basin (3), and the *sudak*, or zander (*Sander lucioeperca*) (8).

exceeding great plentie in the rivers northward, as in *Dvyna*
the river of *Cola*, &c. In the Ozera or lake neere a towne called
Pereslave, not far from the *Mosko*, they have a smal fish which
they call the fresh herring, of the fashion, and somewhat of the
taste of a Sea-hearing.[4]

Fletcher's description of commodities not only gives another insight into
the kinds of foods that were eaten in Russia but recognizes the ways that
Moscow's imperial expansion was already beginning to transform them. It
was not only furs or the seal oil that came from the far-reaching expanses
of the Muscovite state. Honey, he noted, was particularly a product of the
area near Kazan; the major fishing sites that produced fish not just for local
consumption but for 'the whole Realme' were Kazan and Astrakhan. These
were areas that had only been annexed into Muscovy a few decades earlier.
Already they had a significant effect on the foodways of the Muscovite
lands more broadly. In addition, Fletcher's mere presence also hinted at
another element of the changes that began in the reign of Ivan IV: ever
more interaction with Western European peoples. Those interactions, too,
would affect foodways in Russia proper, introducing new products, new
dishes and eventually a new vision of Russian culture.

MUSCOVITE EXPANSION

Ivan IV was formally crowned in 1547. Within a decade he had conquered the Kazan and Astrakhan Khanates, thereby extending Muscovy's control over the entire length of the Volga. In many versions of Russian history, this marks the moment when Russia moved from a regional power to an imperial one. Now it had to incorporate new peoples: Tatars, Mari, Mordvy, Chuvash. Of course, the expansion carried out by Ivan's father and grandfather had also had its imperial aspects; for one, it involved incorporating clearly separate polities, and for another, the Novgorodian territories were home not just to Russians but also to Komi and Sami, Finnic peoples of the Arctic and sub-Arctic. Nonetheless, Ivan's reign and conquests did see a dramatic new turn to the East and as a result a dramatic new phase of empire building.

Beginning at the end of the 1550s, Ivan also turned to the northwest in his effort to make Muscovy into a Baltic Sea power. His lengthy Livonian War (1558–83) was briefly a success: he gained new lands and a new foothold on the Baltic. But most of those gains were short-lived, and the war's exorbitant costs outweighed its scant benefits. Ivan funded his military efforts by farming out tax collection and other administrative duties in his wider realm. His high-ranking military servitors – those who perhaps lived according to the rules of the *Domostroi* – funded themselves by collecting rents from peasants living on their lands; those lands could be inherited lands passed down within a family, or lands granted for service. They were also responsible for supplying a certain number of soldiers to fight in Ivan's wars. That meant providing both the soldiers and the provisions that would support them as they fought.

Those rank-and-file soldiers shocked and amazed observers with their valour when compared with the apparent poverty of their provisioning. Fletcher noted that soldiers ate

> a kinde of dryed bread, (which they call *Sucharie*) with some store of meale, which they temper with water, and so make it into a ball, or small lumpe of dowe, called *Tollockno*. And this they eate raw in steade of bread. Their meate is bacon, or some other flesh or fish dryed, after the Dutch manner.[5]

Of course, dried fish or meat was not 'after the Dutch manner' but a long-standing practice. Overall, though, this description highlighted the ways in which Russians had developed technologies to make their basic foods portable. *Tolokno*, ground oats prepared in such a way that they did not have to be cooked to be consumed, would continue to play an important role in the peasant agricultural world, brought out to the fields for a quick meal. *Sukhari* were dried rusks, common in Russia as similar dried bread or hardtack would be in other military or naval contexts. Dried fish or meat likewise turned an everyday food into something that peasant soldiers could bring from home as provisions as they marched to the site of battle.

Those soldiers also played a role, although a secondary one, in the other major area of expansion of the Muscovite realm: Siberia. This new phase began later, in the 1580s, and through an entirely different mechanism. Rather than being a conscious effort at expansion on the part of the ruler of Muscovy, the annexation of Siberia began with Russian merchants and traders who wanted to protect and expand their interests. The prime movers in the initial push beyond the Urals were members of the Stroganov family of merchants, who had received the right to develop lands far to the northeast of Moscow. They were above all engaged in the salt trade around their stronghold of Solvychegodsk. This had long been a sure source of profit because of its centrality to food preserving.[6] During the reign of Ivan IV the family also moved to expand their influence further to the east.

As a result, in 1558 the Stroganovs were granted a permit by Ivan IV allowing them to colonize 'empty lands' on the northeastern boundaries of Muscovy. They were furthermore given various tax breaks on their profits, but with one duty, as well: to protect Russian settlements in the region. That meant protecting them from the Khanate of Sibir, one of the last remaining branches of the former Mongol Empire. The Khan of Sibir, Kuchum, was based just east of the Urals among the various Indigenous peoples of the region. The khanate collected tribute from many of these peoples, and worried about the growing number of Russians to their west. At the time that Ivan was conquering Kazan and Astrakhan, the khans of Sibir agreed to pay him tribute in furs to avoid formal annexation. Kuchum, though, stopped paying tribute – perhaps out of a belief in the growing weakness of Ivan's reign, perhaps out of concern that the new settlements were infringing on his territory.

These tensions came to a head in the 1570s. In 1572 Kuchum's forces attacked Russian settlements in the region and killed a Muscovite ambassador who had travelled to Sibir to collect tribute once again. This led to a new movement of Muscovite settlers into the region; in particular, in 1574 the Stroganovs were given permission to establish settlements on the eastern side of the Urals, thereby moving into the territory of the Siberian khanate. Their presence was intended both to stake a claim to land and to serve as a buffer between the more established Muscovite lands to the west and the khanate to the east.

Finally, in 1581, a man named Ermak Timofeevich set off with around eight hundred Cossacks to cross the Urals and take on Kuchum. The force was probably sent by the Stroganovs to protect their investments in the area. And Ermak was successful: his forces routed the Siberian khanate, due both to their technological superiority and to divisions within the Siberian forces, and began to raid up and down the Ob and Irtysh rivers in a display of Muscovite authority. Although Ermak and his troops were killed in 1585, their deaths were not enough to stop the expansion of Muscovy into the region and beyond. Instead, more and more Russians poured into the region.

Russian forces reached the Pacific coast by 1639. Along the way they founded Tyumen in 1586, Tobolsk in 1587, Surgut and Tara in 1594, Tomsk in 1604, Yakutsk in 1632. In the middle of the seventeenth century they founded a series of other fortress towns: Okhotsk on the Pacific in 1648, Irkutsk on Lake Baikal in 1652. A treaty established a border with China and Mongolia in 1689. This rapid movement (the distance between Moscow and Okhotsk is some 5,600 kilometres/3,500 mi.) proceeded unevenly, and was accomplished by a range of people. Traders and trappers and

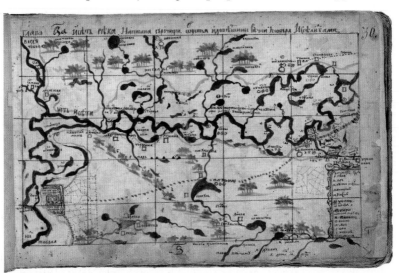

As Russians spread through Siberia, they founded settlements, and began to develop not only the fur trade but agricultural activities. This map from Semën Remezov's *Khorograficheskaia kniga* (Cartographical Sketch-book), sketches out some of those fields outside the city of Tobolsk, here in the lower left-hand corner of the map.

merchants went in search of furs. Cossacks were frequently hired as part of groups travelling through these lands. Soldiers and also administrators and church servitors followed, settling in the fortress towns and helping to establish regular trade (and regular tax/tribute paying). Indigenous Siberians also themselves moved through the wider space in part as a result of the Russian advance. Some were pushed out or killed; some joined with Russian forces to serve as interpreters and guides, or were forced to provide cart duty to help transport goods. Some also saw benefit in allying with the Russians against other Indigenous groups; the Khanty came to describe themselves as allies of the Cossacks against 'traitors and rebels, the Kalmyk people and the Tatars, and the Ostiak, and the Samoed, and the Tungus and the Buliash people, and all kinds of rebels'.[7]

PROVISIONING THE EXPANDED MUSCOVITE STATE

One of the major questions that came up with this movement of Russians into the region was provisioning.[8] Siberia had long supported its Indigenous population, but the arrival of relatively large numbers of new people (by the end of the seventeenth century there were somewhere around 25,000 households of Russians living in Siberia) placed strains on its resources and also created new demands because of the different tastes of the new-comers.[9] Above all, the newcomers were used to consuming grain. As a result, getting agriculturists to Siberia to support the fur traders and mer-chants in the area was an early priority. Starting at the end of the sixteenth century, peasants were resettled into Siberia either 'by decree' (that is, forced) or 'by choice' (although that also at times involved some degree of compulsion). Initially, their actual agricultural successes there were limited.[10] Eventually that changed, though, as Russians moved not quite throughout Siberia, but into scattered pockets of settlement throughout Siberia. Furthermore, as peasants came to settle in Siberia, they brought with them their familiar agricultural practices – 'if they were able to,' the historian Janet Hartley writes, 'they brought seed with them to grow the main staple crops of European Russia, as well as their own livestock and agricultural implements.'[11]

The Russians who had moved to Siberia by choice or by force brought with them their own culinary traditions. These were certainly related to traditions elsewhere – Russians in Siberia also ate rye bread and *kasha, shchi* and *pirogi*.[12] The nineteenth-century writer and cookbook author Katerina Avdeeva even argued that Siberia was by then the home of the true Russia,

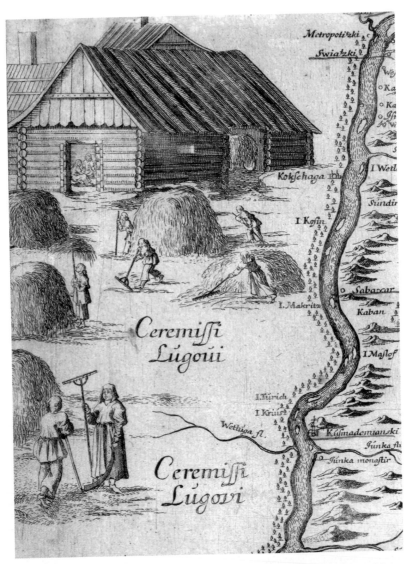

As Russians moved into newly conquered territories, they brought with them many of the same kinds of farming techniques they had used in the Russian heartland. This detail from Adam Olearius's 17th-century map of the Volga shows peasants at work mowing hay; although the area is labelled as lands of the Cheremis, now known as the Mari, this stretch of the Volga reaches into the older Russian territories.

where 'old Russian' habits and foods had been best preserved. But there were differences, too, based in part on climate, in part on other particularities of way of life. The *kasha* might more probably be of millet or barley, not buckwheat. Wild leek replaced onions.[13] Commentators at the end of the nineteenth century stated that Siberians had a particular taste for all that was rich and fatty: their *kasha* and their *pirogi*, even their *shchi*, were said to 'swim in fat and butter'.[14] Siberians also reportedly ate more meat than Russian peasants in the old core: 'nearly half the householders eat meat every day, except for fast days.'[15] On the other hand, fruit trees did not survive well, leading some to claim that there was no fruit there at all. There were berries, though, 'no less than twenty different kinds', and by some reports 'Siberian housewives are famed for their preserves.'[16]

In other ways, the Siberian context created a world of Russian peasant food that was a variant on the foods eaten in European Russia. Siberia's legendary cold also helped to create new variations on traditional Russian foods. Salt beef (*solonina*) was a traditional way of preserving meat in European Russia, but late nineteenth-century authors described a Siberian variation on it. The Siberian speciality was cold-cured 'hung' beef (*provesnaia goviadina*). It was prepared in a way similar to salt beef, but relied on the drying properties of the Siberian cold and wind. To prepare it, once the hard frost set in, a lightly salted piece of beef was hung outside on a rack to dry in the cold and wind.[17] And, of course, Siberia was the legendary origin of *pelmeni*, the small, meat-filled dumplings that later became ubiquitous throughout Russia. As the story goes, these were Siberian not so much because of their preparation, but because of how they were stored. These small dumplings were a winter food, prepared first in large quantities and then stored, frozen, in wooden boxes outside the home.

Above all, Siberia came to be known as the home of *pelmeni*, the small, meat-filled dumplings that have become a freezer staple for many.

147

The prolific German playwright August von Kotzebue found himself briefly exiled to Siberia in 1800, and eventually wrote a colourful account of his travels to Kurgan, now on the border with Kazakhstan. His host (or jailer) in Kazan fed him plentifully:

> early in the morning was served coffee, with bread and butter; an hour after *pirogue* (a kind of meat pie) with brandy; two hours later, more brandy, with soused fish, sausages, and such things. Afterwards came in dinner, consisting of four very large dishes; then at three o'clock coffee and biscuits; at five tea, with several kinds of pastry, and at night, after all this feasting, came a plentiful supper.[18]

Once he had moved on to Siberia proper he was no less impressed with the abundance he saw before him. In Tobolsk he found a rich variety of 'people of all nations, particularly Russians and Tartars, Kirgists and Calmucks' buying the provisions. He went on to describe what was to him 'a very novel spectacle' – the fish market:

> Great quantities of different kinds of fish, which I had hitherto known merely by description, were exposed, both dead and alive, in tubs and barges, for sale. Esterlets (*acipenser rutkenus*) sold for a mere trifle. The *huso*, or royal fish (*acipenser huso*) the *silure* (*silurus glanis*) &c. with *caviar* of every colour, were equally reasonable. Had it not been for the disagreeable smells in this market, I should often have loitered there.[19]

Only in Kurgan itself did he find some problems (and a contradiction to the laws of economics): on the one hand, prices were extremely cheap and quality was often excellent (he claimed never to have eaten better butter 'in any part of the world'), but on the other, supplies were often lacking. As he described it:

> there is neither baker nor butcher in the whole town: once a week, on Sunday afternoon, a kind of market is kept, in which the inhabitants must provide themselves with bread and meat for the whole week. It often happens too, that this market is without a supply of meat.[20]

Many travellers described fish sold in the frozen markets, but Kotzebue describes fish sold 'dead and alive, in tubs and barges'. This illustration suggests that fishmongers might even have pulled tubs of live fish around towns to attract more customers.

These were later developments, though, and in the initial years of Russian expansion into Siberia life was much more difficult. Siberia was also used early on as a place to send people whom the state considered to be undesirable. One of them, the Archpriest Avvakum, implicated in the great seventeenth-century schism in the Russian Orthodox church, happened also to be the author of the first autobiography in Russian history. His tale of his initial exile into Siberia in the 1650s was filled with drama – and with hunger. While living beyond Lake Baikal, he described the terrible conditions of his encampment, largely, he claimed, due to its unscrupulous and cruel overseer:

> It was the fourth summer of my journey from Tobolsk. They were floating logs for the building of houses and towns. There began to be nothing to eat, the folk began to die of hunger and from ceaseless working in the water; shallow was the river, heavy were the rafts, merciless were the taskmasters, stout were the sticks, gnarled were the cudgels, cutting were the knouts, cruel were the sufferings – fire and rack; the folk were so spent with hunger that let him, Afanasy, but start tormenting one of them, and lo! he was dead on his hands. Ah, me, What a time! It would

149

almost seem that he was out of his mind. There remained to
Dame Avvakum one Moscow gown that had not been rotted
with damp. It would have fetched twenty-five rubles and more
in Moscow; but in these parts they gave us four sacks of rye for
it, and we dragged on for another year, living on the Nercha
River, and keeping ourselves alive with the roots and herbs that
grew on the banks. One after another the folk died of hunger,
and he saw to it that none of them ran away, and they were
circumscribed within a small space, and they would wander
over the steppes and fields, digging up grasses and roots, and
we with them. And in winter we would live on fir cones, and
sometimes God would send mare's flesh, and sometimes we
found the bones of stinking carcasses of wild beasts left by the
wolves, and what had not been eaten up by the wolves that did
we eat; and some would eat frozen wolves and foxes – in truth,
any filth they could lay their hands on . . . Ah, me! What a time![21]

Avvakum was influenced by earlier accounts of saints' lives, and therefore may have been writing with a degree of exaggeration. His was also
certainly a story of a particular kind of forced settlement in Siberia. That
said, the idea that hunger was a part of the Russian movement into Siberia
– in part due to the difficulties of the terrain, in part due to differences
between Siberian and Russian foodways, and in part due to the distances
that affected the movement of supplies – rings true. One reason is that
hunger was also far from unknown in the old core of Muscovy itself, for
famine was one of the major stories of these years of expansion and growth.

FAMINE AND THE SEVENTEENTH CENTURY

One of the signs of the stresses that Ivan IV, the Terrible, placed on his
domains was the regular reappearance of famine. In 1553 there was 'terrible
mortality from famine'; in both 1557 and 1570 'a great famine in all Rus and
death'.[22] These lined up with his great military campaigns and the excesses
of the *Oprichnina*, which were events that created hardship not only for
Ivan's soldiers and boyars but for the wider population forced to fund his
wars and support his followers. When Giles Fletcher visited a few years
after Ivan's death, he described both great potential wealth but also the
signs of stress that recent years had placed upon the population. Many
towns of the realm, he noted, 'have nothing that is greatly memorable, save

many ruines within their walles'. Why? The ruins 'sheweth the decrease of the *Russe* people, under this government'.[23]

All of that paled in comparison to the famine that hit Russia at the very beginning of the seventeenth century. The ruler at the time was Boris Godunov, the first non-Riurikid tsar, who had served as a virtual regent during the reign of his brother-in-law Fedor Ivanovich (the only son of Ivan IV to survive his reign). Fedor died without children in 1598, leaving a question regarding the succession. Boris Godunov parlayed his position within the court and his family's connection with the Riurikids into his election as the new tsar. His authority was never quite secure, however, in part due to his own persona, in part due to the world of boyar politics. It was challenged even more by bad harvests three years in a row – in 1599, in 1600 and in 1601. The country more or less absorbed the first two, but the scale of the crop failures in 1601 were too much. Rain fell without a halt for ten weeks, so nothing could be harvested. Then a hard frost hit shockingly early, on 15 August, destroying the rest of the harvest.[24] With few or no stores left after two prior years of bad harvests, the result was famine on a dramatic new scale that lasted until the spring of 1603.

One of the problems that faced Godunov's reign was the very method he used to try to stave off famine. First he opened the tsar's own granaries to the public – but greedy lords bought up that cheap grain to sell for a profit. Then he reportedly offered to hand out alms to his people to allow them to purchase grain to feed themselves. The problem was that news travelled too fast: when rumours of this 'tsarist mercy' spread through the land, thousands upon thousands of people came to Moscow itself in search of aid. But of course, that put a huge strain on the limited grain supplies in the city itself. As a result, the reports of the famine within just Moscow are horrifying. In the end, thousands died in Moscow, thousands more on the roads leading to the city.[25] Some estimates suggest that 100,000 people died in Moscow alone, and that the wider death toll may have reached a third of the entire Muscovite population.

In the end, Godunov tried other methods to help improve the next year's harvests and end the famine conditions. He started public works projects in Moscow to spread some wealth. But, more importantly, he found more grain, reaching out to more distant areas that had not suffered from crop failure, buying up grain stores and having it brought to the suffering regions. The grain was not necessarily given away, but it was brought in to bring prices down. Slowly the famine conditions abated, and the population began to regroup and recover.

Even long after famine conditions ended, the memory of the disaster remained strong. For the rest of the seventeenth century, Russia's leaders began to play a more active role in attempts, largely successful, to avoid famine's return. These were much the same as those taken by Godunov: trying to keep prices down by bringing in more grain when scarcity began to drive prices up. And, in addition, there were efforts to make sure that others who possessed wealth did something to help the poor during such times. Lords were supposed to ensure that their slaves were fed even during times of high food prices and famine; they were furthermore told they were not to try to avoid that responsibility by freeing their slaves during such periods. And in the middle of the seventeenth century decrees asked (they tried to demand, but demands did not always work) that 'Metropolitans and powers and all sorts of people' bring their own grain supplies to market to sell to local authorities for a reasonable price.[26] Although there continued to be localized conditions of dearth, there were no more famines on the scale of that of the beginning of the century – and in fact, there would be nothing like it again until the waning years of the tsarist empire.

SERFDOM AND SOCIAL CHANGE

Boris Godunov's reign also saw the onset of the 'Time of Troubles', a period during which Muscovy was torn apart by social upheaval and a foreign invasion.[27] It can be seen as beginning with the death of Fedor Ivanovich, the last Riurikid prince, in 1598; that sparked a dynastic crisis that Boris Godunov's accession to the throne did not quite solve. Or it could be seen as starting with the devastating famine a few years later, which led to social upheaval. At the latest, it began in 1604, when a young man backed by Poland-Lithuania turned up claiming to be Ivan IV's son Dmitry, thought to have been killed in 1591 (and probably actually killed in 1591). This False Dmitry, as he came to be known, did eventually seize Moscow, but could not hold on to the throne in a time of such upheaval. He was killed (and his body burned and the ashes shot from a cannon towards Poland), but a Second False Dmitry soon appeared, again with support from Poland. Sweden invaded, as well, taking advantage of the upheaval in its neighbour's lands.

In the end, Moscow was retaken by Russian forces only in 1612. The following year a new royal house was acclaimed by an Assembly of the Land: the Romanovs. In 1617, a peace treaty was signed with Sweden; in 1618, with Poland. Muscovy lost some lands along its western border, but survived. The events of this period gave shape to the seventeenth century that was to come. Military action sought to regain lands lost in the first decades of the century – and then to expand beyond them, annexing lands settled by the East Slavs, who came to be known as Belarusians and Ukrainians from Poland-Lithuania. The tsars of the new Romanov dynasty sought to consolidate their own authority in part through making laws and giving deals to their supporters.

Both of these elements combined in the *Ulozhenie*, or Law Code, of 1649. A new tsar, Aleksei, had come to the throne just a few years before, in 1645. Aleksei was young, still a teenager, when his father died, and he very quickly found himself faced with a need to assert his authority as the reigning autocrat. Initially, he went about it in exactly the wrong way. There were no formalized representational systems in place in Russia, no parliament. The Assemblies of the Land were called irregularly and to discuss specific issues, not to serve as a general means for the population to make its needs known. Instead, there were petitions. Petitions were the ways in which individuals or groups of individuals addressed the tsar or other authorities in an effort to get aid or to get policies changed or otherwise to make their needs heard. Petitions were an essential part of the functioning of the autocratic system, and it was well understood that petitions had to be accepted. They might not be acted upon or granted, but they had to be heard.

In the summer of 1648, a group of petitioners approached Aleksei's entourage as they returned to Moscow from a pilgrimage. There was at the time significant resentment over taxes, in particular a very unpopular salt tax that he had allowed soon after coming to the throne in an effort to fill his coffers. After all, salt was a necessity of life, one that allowed the produce of summer to stay edible through the long, long winter – taxing it made sense fiscally, but was also a hardship for the wider population. Although the salt tax was eliminated after many complaints, other direct taxes were levied to replace its income. The petitioners were complaining primarily about the taxes, although also about a particular unpopular local official. Unwisely, Aleksei refused to accept the petition – and even worse, he ordered that some of the petitioners be arrested. When news got out about this sequence of events, riots broke out in Moscow. Not only did the common people of Moscow protest but the *streltsy*, musketeers and therefore servants of the state, as well. In the course of the riots the man deemed responsible for the salt tax was killed and his body, cut to pieces, dumped on a dung heap. Fires raced through the city, too.

The illustrations above depict scenes from the 1626 wedding of tsar Mikhail Fedorovich, the first Romanov tsar, to Evdokiia Lukianovna. In the first (top left), boyars carry *karavai* in a procession; in the second (top right), nobles bring ceremonial pots of kasha. In the third (above left), one item on the banquet table is labelled – it is the wedding cheese, cut as part of the ceremony (the early *Russkaia pravda* noted that a man who called off the wedding after the cheese was cut faced a fine for dishonouring the bride), and in the fourth (above right), everyone enjoys a grand feast.

In order to quell the unrest, Aleksei ordered a commission to produce a new law code for the land. The commission jumped to work: it pulled records from all the chancelleries in Moscow to figure out what laws currently governed their operation and it looked at other law codes to add certain provisions. It also addressed the demands (petitions) of various social groups, adding certain provisions they had asked for. The whole was accomplished with remarkable speed: in January 1649 a new Assembly of the Land was called to approve the new code, and copies were made and sent around the state. The *Ulozhenie*, as this law code was called, is a dramatically larger document than earlier law codes. With 25 chapters and hundreds of separate laws, it covers everything from robbery and murder to counterfeiting to treason, and as a result serves as a remarkable window into the everyday life of seventeenth-century Muscovy.

Among the most notable changes that the *Ulozhenie* makes apparent is one that came to play a major role in Muscovite and then Russian eating and drinking patterns: the appearance of vodka. Distilled spirits, or what we would now call vodka, began to appear regularly in records only in the sixteenth century. It was possibly known and consumed a few centuries before that, but was also almost certainly not a major part of the world of Russian food and drink. One of the causes of uncertainty in dating its appearance is the fact that the word most often used for the clear alcohol distilled from grain was *vino* (which also means wine), not vodka. But it is clear that vodka/*vino* in the form that we think of it today was enjoying regular consumption by the end of the sixteenth century.

One of the reasons we know this is because it already played what came to be its perpetual double role as both a pleasure for the people and a source of income for the state. Giles Fletcher described the situation thus:

> In every great towne of his Realme [the tsar] hath a *Caback*
> or drinking house, where is sold *aquavitae* (which they cal
> *Russe wine*) *mead, beere, &c.* Out of these hee receiveth
> rent that amounteth to a great summe of money. Some
> yeeld 800, some 900, some a 1000 some 2000 or 3000
> rubbels a yere.[28]

Nearly a century or so later, their income was said to be yet higher – 10,000 or even 20,000 roubles each year.[29] These drinking houses therefore played an important role in bringing income to the state, and of course also in bringing drinking to the masses. Fletcher was scathing on the subject: these were 'base, and dishonourable meanes to encrease his treasurie', where 'the poore labouring man, and artificer, manie times spendeth all from his wife and children.'[30]

It was in this way – as a source of state income – that vodka came into the *Ulozhenie*. The entire last chapter of that law code gives laws for 'illicit taverns' and for illegal home distilling. The sale of distilled spirits (and to an extent of mead and beer, as well) was to be strictly regulated not in order to safeguard public health but in order to safeguard the income of the tsar. Distillers and sellers of illicit spirits were fined 5 roubles for a first offence, 10 for a second and 20 for a third. Anyone caught drinking illicit spirits was also punished: ¼ rouble for a first offence, ½ for a second and a whole rouble for a third. Repeated offences also came with physical punishments: for a second offence sellers were to be beaten with a knout, consumers with the (less severe) bastinado; for a third offence, sellers were to be imprisoned and consumers beaten with the knout. A few years later, in 1652, distilling for sale was banned except when controlled by the state, in essence creating the first of several vodka monopolies. Drinking continued, but in domestic spaces or in state-controlled taverns known as *kabaks*.[31]

According to travellers, these limits had no effect on the demand for strong spirits. Instead, by the early seventeenth century regular consumption of distilled spirits seems to have become quite common. As Adam Olearius travelled around Muscovy in the 1630s while serving as the secretary to an embassy sent by the Duke of Holstein, he regularly reported being served aquavit or 'strong-water', seeing people drinking it (at one point 'the Musketeers, who had been somewhat busy with the Aquavitæ, entertain'd us with some feats of their activity') or supplying it to others.[32] 'There's no place in the World where drunkenness is more common than in *Muscovy*,' he claimed. 'All, of all conditions, Ecclesiasticks and Laicks, Men and Women, Old and Young, will drink strong-water at any time, before, at, and after their meals.'[33] Others who came to Muscovy during the century were similarly struck both by the amount of distilled spirits drunk by both men and women, by people of all statuses, and by the strength of those spirits. (It is hard not to wonder whether some of the English visitors would have been as struck by both a few decades later, when the gin craze sparked similar concerns about the drinking habits of people much closer to home.)

Although the *Ulozhenie* gives glimpses into all sorts of facets of Russian life in the seventeenth century, from property to family relations, perhaps its most important contribution involves the establishment of serfdom in Muscovy. It was the end point of the process of binding what had been a free peasantry to the land. In the fifteenth century, peasant movement had been limited to a period of two weeks around St George's Day in the autumn. There it had stayed until late in the reign of Ivan IV. In the waning years of his reign, Ivan instituted so-called 'Forbidden Years' during which peasants were forbidden to move at all. In principle these were temporary institutions intended to allow landowners (although of course not necessarily peasants) to recover from the depredations of the *Oprichnina* and his own monetary demands. In practice, they were made permanent.

There was one small glimmer of opportunity for movement that still remained. When these Forbidden Years were extended to all peasants in 1592, the duty of return had a statute of limitations. That is, if a peasant were to leave his home and stay away, undetected, for five years, he could remain where he was. It was this small opportunity that was eliminated with the *Ulozhenie* (the time for return had been extended several times in the interim). From this point forward, all peasants could be returned to their village of origin (and, for that matter, all townspeople could be returned to their town of origin) until the day they died. The result was a world in which landowners counted their wealth not by the area of land they owned but instead by the number of people who lived on it. This practice was already ensconced by the time Paul of Aleppo visited in the 1650s:

> the grandees of the empire do not reckon their possessions
> after the manner of our country, by the number of their
> farms and gardens and vineyards . . . they reckon the houses
> on their estates with their families, and say, such a Kniazi has
> three thousand Mojik or peasants, or eight or ten or twenty
> thousand; calculating the value of their lands only by the
> capacity of the houses upon them, and their actual inhabitants.[34]

In addition, the institutionalization of serfdom eventually helped lead to the creation of distinct cultures associated with Russia's elite and its peasant masses. Through the sixteenth and even through much of the seventeenth century, this distinction was not so strictly drawn. Instead, there was a general culture based in Orthodoxy and its practices with certain differences based on social status. Most famous is the *terem*, the seclusion of elite women, who lived in separate quarters and remained hidden from men not in their family. This was impractical for the masses,

Here, travellers stop at the Ponedele monastery on Lake Ilmen, near the town of Novgorod, to take refreshment outside the monastery proper. In many of the early travel accounts of Muscovy, monasteries became places to stop for a meal; Olearius and others described being served spiced bread or gingerbread, cherries, cucumbers or turnips, and strong drink.

of course. As a result, it served as a method both of protecting family honour and perhaps also as a method of emphasizing social rank.

The ways people ate reflected both broad commonalities across the social spectrum and distinctions based in status. Samuel Collins, who worked as Tsar Aleksei's physician in the 1660s, described the abundance of mushrooms everywhere in Russia as 'the poor mans food, the rich mans dainties'.[35] In other words, they were a food common to people of all ranks, but entered their diets in different ways. It is hard to know precisely what the masses of peasants and lower ranking people in towns ate, because visitors to Russia, who provide some of the best descriptions of food, tended not to talk about it. Collins noted that 'to his Houshold Servants [the tsar] gives allowances of Meal, Honey, Fish, Nut-Oyl, Oates, Beer and Mead.'[36] This was a sufficient if not luxurious diet, with some pleasures. The scant evidence suggests that the basic meals of bread or *kasha*, *shchi* or preserved cabbage and *kvas* to drink were still the most common foods to be found in the land. Adam Olearius wrote:

> they are not acquainted with our delicate meats and sawces. Their ordinary food is coarse Meal, Turneps, Coleworts, and Cowcumbers, both fresh and pickled. Their great delicacy is Salt-fish, which being not well salted, infects the places neer it, so that you may smell their Fish-market at a great distance.

And, he noted, there were some specialities:

> Among other things they make a sort of Pies, which they call *Piroguen*, about the bigness and fashion of a two-penny Loaf. They fill the crust with Fish or minc'd meat, with Chibols [spring onions] and a little Pepper, and fry them in a Pan with Butter, and in Lent with Oil.

These were, he thought, 'no ill dish'.[37]

If the expansion of Muscovy brought some new foods, or made familiar ones more available, on some level it did not change the essence of Russian foodways. At the beginning of the sixteenth century Herberstein had been struck by the use of salt, pepper and vinegar as particular condiments; in the middle of the century the *Domostroi* called for their regular use, as well. Fletcher, too, described the Russian diet as based in strong flavours. The emperor, he noted, feasted regularly on upward of seventy dishes at a single meal, 'dressed somwhat grosely, with much garlicke, & salt, much after the Doutch manner'.[38] More generally he believed the Russian people ate a 'diet that standeth most of rootes, onions, garlike, cabbage, and such like things that breed grosse humors, which they use to eate alone, and with their other meates'.[39] Half a century later, Olearius largely agreed: he described foods 'dress'd with Onions and Garlick' to the point that his group found them unappealing.[40]

In part, Olearius and his embassy tried to hold themselves separate from the world of Russian cooking by preparing their own food, but they still received provisions that reflect the kinds of foods consumed in Muscovy itself. When the embassy first arrived in Moscow itself, the tsar sent provisions, including 'eight Sheep, thirty Capons and Pullets, great store of white and brown bread, and 22 sorts of drinks, Wine, Beer, Hydromel and Aquavitæ'.[41] On Olearius' second visit, the embassy received another huge supply of food:

> every day, sixty two Loaves, a quarter of Beef, four Sheep,
> a dozen of Pullets, two Geese, one Hare, and one Heath-cock,
> alternately, fifty Eggs, ten pence towards Candles, and five
> pence for small things us'd in the Kitchin, one Pot of Sack,
> eight of Hydromel; three, of Beer; and three small pots of
> Strong-water. Besides all this, for a common stock, a Tun of
> Beer, a lesser Tun of Hydromel, and a Barrel of Strong-water.
> With this we had, by way of extraordinary in the week, a *poude*,
> that is, forty pound, of Butter, and as much Salt, three Pails
> of Vinigre, two Muttons, and a Goose.[42]

The embassy's own cooks prepared it all, but the provisions are suggestive of what was considered right and proper foods for people of good standing.

Olearius was also present at various dinners and official 'collations' along his route to Moscow proper. At one such collation he was served 'spic'd bread, some gobelets of a very strong kind of Aquavitæ, and with two sorts of very bad Hydromel'; at another 'Ginger-Bread, Cherries newly preserv'd, and Aquavitæ'.[43] And he had other occasions to observe or partake in meals. As his troupe passed by a monastery on the way from the border to Moscow itself, he was given 'a Present of Turneps, pickled Cowcombers, some green Pease', and more cucumbers and turnips later.[44] A few decades later, when Macarius, the Patriarch of Antioch, travelled to Russia, his entourage was greeted with similar 'collations' along the way.

Voevodas (local governors) treated the travellers with copious strong drink and trays of cucumbers and radishes, or generous supplies of melons and 'such apples, that we blessed the Creator at the sight of their beauty and size, and for their smell, and colour, and taste'.[45]

At a royal feast in Moscow during fast time, Olearius was served 'forty six dishes, most fish, boil'd, broil'd, and fry'd in Oyl, some Sallets and Pastry; but no flesh, by reason of the Fast which the *Muscovites* very rigorously observe before Christmas'.[46] This, he noted, was one of the peculiarities of the Russian table:

> for that their year hath more fasting dayes than flesh days,
> they are so accustomed to Fish and Pulse, that they care not
> for Flesh. Add to this, that their continual fasts have taught
> them so many wayes to dress their Fish, Herbs, and Pulse,
> that a man may well forbear those dishes of meat which
> are much esteemed elsewhere.[47]

Paul of Aleppo gave even more detailed descriptions of the kinds of fish dishes his party was served at a dinner with Tsar Aleksei:

> Dishes were brought in of fish, dressed with such art, that
> they appeared to contain stuffed lambs. From the abundant
> variety of the finny tribe in this country, they are enabled to
> cook them in a multiplicity of ways, as we had long heard.
> Throwing away all the rough and bony parts, they pound
> the remainder in mortars, till it becomes a paste: this they
> mix with a great quantity of onions and saffron, and put
> into moulds of the shape of lambs and geese: then they fry
> these artificial animals with oil, in very deep pans as deep as
> a draw-well, so that the frying penetrates them to the inmost;
> and serving them up, carve them as if they were cutting into
> solid muscles of white flesh: their taste is excellent, and an
> ignorant person might suppose them to be real lambs. In this
> manner they make various kinds of pastry, with the flour and
> with cheese fried in butter, long and round, as cakes, lozenges,
> &c. Then they have puddings like those usually made of bread,
> composed of small fish, as small as worms, and baked or fried
> in the same way.[48]

Paul of Aleppo was impressed with meals like this, but found other elements of Russian cuisine quite difficult. He never came to like Russia's sour black bread, although he did eventually find *kvas* to be a cooling, pleasant drink. Lenten foods, particularly on days when fish was not allowed, however, he found quite difficult in comparison to the Lenten foods of his southern world. Pickled cabbages and cucumbers, a few beans – this was not to his taste, and 'on this account we were in great distress, such as cannot be described ... There was not a man, I swear most solemnly, among us, who, after this experience, continued to complain of Lent as kept with us.'[49]

As Olearius noted, however, the many dishes of 'herbs and pulses' were not a sign of scarcity. According to a number of seventeenth-century writers, Muscovy – particularly the Muscovy that had resulted from the territorial advances of Ivan IV – was generally well able to provision itself. Both Paul of Aleppo and Guy Miège described abundant livestock (Paul believed it was in part because Russians avoided eating veal, and therefore had more cattle grow to adulthood).[50] Olearius described the fruits of the land near Moscow as a picture of abundance:

> there are excellent fruits, as Apples, Cherries, Plums, and Goosberries. I have seen Apples in beauty & colour much like those which are called *Appians*, and so transparent, that holding them between your sight and the Sun you may easily tell the Kernels ... They have also all manner of Pulse, Pot-herbs, Asparagus, Onions, Garlick, Roots, Cowcombers, Citruls, or Gourds, and Melons, and of these last abundance, excellent good, and so big, that at my being in Muscovy in the year 1643, a friend presented me with a Melon, that weigh'd forty pound. The Muscovites are very expert in the ordering of their Melons.[51]

Some of this abundance, though, reflected another major change that had been coming into Muscovy over the past century, and which would also eventually add greatly to the growing distinction between elite and commoner. Asparagus, he noted, was new: 'the *Holand*, and *German* merchants have but lately planted [it] there, which take very well, and are as big as a man's thumb.' In addition, he noted, 'nor have the *Muscovites* been long acquainted with Lettice and other Salad-herbs, and laugh'd at the Strangers who fed on them; but now they begin to like them.'[52]

Olearius was here writing of the ways in which more contact with the Western European world was beginning to alter internal Russian practice.

This had been a slow process, and not without controversy. The Russian church was concerned with what it saw as the dangerous influence of foreign culture. Early in the reign of Ivan IV, a church council compiled the *Stoglav*, or the book of a hundred chapters, to set out and formalize current practice in the Russian Orthodox church. It emphasized the dangers inherent in 'foreign customs' to true Orthodox believers. In particular, 'Latin and heretical' habits were condemned as leading men away from their true path to God. Most famously, it affirmed that adult men were not supposed to shave their beards – shaving was foreign and radical and wrong, as it made it impossible to identify an Orthodox believer.[53] In other cases, it was Western products that seemed to bring danger. The Western import tobacco, for example, was seen as distinctly dangerous, and was banned with harsh measures. Between the church and seventeenth-century tsars who also wished to restrict tobacco usage for economic reasons, it remained a subject of harsh penalties (a person caught smoking tobacco 'many times' was to be punished by having his nostrils slit). This was all the more noteworthy because of the great efforts that British merchants made in an effort to expand their trade, and in particular to find a commodity to export to Russia (the Anglo-Russian balance of trade was much in Russia's favour until the end of the eighteenth century).[54] Although the repeated bans on tobacco certainly imply that tobacco was finding smokers or sniffers in Russia, the strength of the combined church and state stand against it did limit its role.

By the end of the seventeenth century, though, efforts to ward off foreign habits faced serious challenges. For one thing, there were simply more foreigners in Muscovy, both merchants and mercenaries. Perhaps more importantly, although the Orthodox church certainly had not waned in its influence, it was also riven by a great schism in the middle of the seventeenth century. The specific issues of the schism were many, but in essence the problem was one of interpreting foreign customs. In the seventeenth century, new influences started to make waves in church circles. These were 'foreign' influences, in that they were not the practices accepted in the Russian church, but nor were they from the 'Latin and heretical' world. Instead, they were from the wider world of Orthodoxy. In particular, some of them emerged from an exercise in comparing Russian church texts (the Eastern Christian world had long been more open to translating religious texts into vernacular languages) to Greek originals. Over the centuries, whether through initial translating error or later copying error, the two had diverged. What should be done about this?

The answer, according to the new Patriarch Nikon in the 1650s, was to correct the Russian texts. He commissioned new translations, and adapted some of the rituals of church services and practice (most famously by changing the hand position for making the sign of the cross) to reflect what he and a group of scholars believed to be more truly Orthodox. But these changes led to an outburst of dissent, led in part by Archpriest Avvakum. For him, the new practices were an outrage: 'it was as if winter was of a mind to come; our hearts froze, our limbs shook,' he wrote of first hearing about Nikon's new policies.[55] Although the church as a whole adopted the reforms (even after removing Nikon from his position a few years later), a breakaway group who came to be known as the Old Believers refused to do so. This was seen as something actively dangerous not only to the church but to the authority of the autocrat, as well. The tsars were divine-right rulers, whose charismatic authority was bound tightly with the rituals of the church. The schism called that relationship into question.

As a result, for the rest of the seventeenth century Old Believers were brutally suppressed. Avvakum was exiled to Siberia, then recalled to Moscow and eventually burned at the stake; other Old Believers were either burned at the stake or, shockingly, self-immolated in protest against the demands of church and state. Despite this, Old Belief continued to spread, particularly in areas far from Moscow, or among social groups who felt themselves to be increasingly dispossessed by the Muscovite state. Although in the eighteenth century the state came to tolerate Old Believers, it did so only very grudgingly, and with strict controls. Nonetheless, as a result Old Believers came to occupy a place slightly outside the norms of Russian culture and society. They viewed themselves as the carriers of the true Old Russian religion and culture – including of Russian culinary traditions. This association with tradition became central to Old Believer self-identification, not only because of the changes within the church but because of changes within Russia more generally. In particular, the eighteenth century was ushered in with a new man as tsar, one who envisioned a different Russia from the Muscovy he had inherited, and who took steps to make his vision a reality – Peter I, who came to be known as Peter the Great.

PETER THE GREAT seems like a character out of a fairy tale, not out of reality. Hugely tall, with a twitch and a personality described kindly as exuberant or less kindly as crude, he threw himself into everything. He spent much of his childhood among the foreign specialists and mercenaries who lived in one neighbourhood of Moscow. After an adolescence that took place against the backdrop of family conflict driven in part by a desire to keep him off the throne, eventually, in 1696, he became the sole ruler of Muscovy. As tsar, Peter did many, many things. Much of his energy went into military pursuits, and many of his reforms supported those military goals. Peter's eventual military successes set the stage for a century of remarkable further expansion and military action, all of which made Russia an empire in every possible way. Although some ambassadors had referred to the rulers of Muscovy as emperors, Peter was the first to take on the title officially, and to call his state the Russian Empire. Over the course of the century, too, Russia became ever more a multi-ethnic empire, with different schemes of control over its widely varying population.

Perhaps even more famous than all of these changes, however, were the radical alterations Peter made to Russian culture. At least, to elite culture. Peter's early enchantment with foreign artisans working in Moscow never faded. A year after his first military successes in Azov, he set off on a tour of Western Europe, his Grand Embassy, where he travelled 'incognito' (or as incognito as a 2-metre-/nearly 7-ft-tall Russian man could), visiting courts but also shipyards. Almost as soon as he returned, he began to make changes intended to pull Russia into what he saw as the modern world, the modern world of Western Europe. Peter's most famous interventions involve the outer appearance of the person. He demanded that men shave their beards (at least most of them), and he instituted new styles of dress modelled on Western European fashion. He was also interested in the inner person, too. His chief ideologue, Feofan Prokopovich, wrote of 'the duty of tsars . . . to maintain their subjects in felicity and to formulate for them every kind of good instruction for piety, and also for honest living'.[56] He wanted his nobles to give their children a better education, founding schools to encourage them and establishing rules to punish those who did not (illiterate sons of nobles could not inherit property, for example). He wanted Russians to socialize in new ways, to engage in the exchange of ideas. He gave instructions for holding assemblies, which meant instructions for how to throw a proper party open to men and women of quality to come visiting – supplying one's visitors with places to sit and food and drink were necessities, he specified.[57]

As a result, Peter I's reign has come to be seen as a time of major change for Russia. Those changes were both geopolitical and internal. Russia was now an empire, but its ruling people, the Russians, were themselves divided by a cultural division between noble and peasant created in large part by his reforms. That cultural division, which of course also reflected a real social division of privilege and lack thereof, became one of the motivating features of the next two centuries of Russian history. In the eighteenth and nineteenth centuries, maintaining privilege or attaining privilege were perpetual goals of different social groups. Mediating their conflicting aims was a perpetual struggle for the Russian state. And thinking of ways either to ameliorate the cultural division, to understand it or to blow it up and start anew became a perpetual focus of Russian intellectuals from the artistic to the revolutionary.

Food and drink intersect with health in many ways; one is the rise of interest in mineral
water as not simply a healthy drink but as something with healing properties. As interest in
discovering the natural resources of the Empire's lands grew in the 18th century, explorers
were advised to look for mineral water sources that might be exploited for health and profit.
Things really took off in the 19th century with Russia's expansion into the Caucasus. Spa towns
sprang up to take advantage of the natural springs in the area. One such place, Borzhom, in
the modern-day Republic of Georgia, became a place both to go to take the waters (top) and
a place that bottled water for consumption elsewhere (above). Borzhomi mineral water is still
the water that is the normal accompaniment to a meal at a Georgian restaurant.

FIVE

Champagne and *Kvas*: Russia Divided

In 1719, Peter the Great released a personal decree giving guidelines for those who wished to travel to Olonets, a province in northern European Russia, in order to take the healing mineral waters that had recently been discovered there.[1] This was one of many, many laws and decrees that were released during Peter's reign. He either wrote these himself or gave specific instructions regarding more than half of some 3,000 or so separate decrees or laws released during the last five years of his life. According to the Russian historian Evgenii Anisimov, the reason was that 'Peter attributed great significance to written legislation. He sincerely believed that the "right" law, promptly issued and consistently implemented in practice, could do everything, starting with providing the people with bread and ending with the correction of manners.'[2]

In principle, the autocrat was supposed to pay attention only to the 'most important' things, but Peter, at least, clearly had a broad understanding of what might be considered 'most important'.[3] A decree on healing waters, like this one, hardly seems a 'most important' issue for the ruler of a country that was at this time in the final years of the lengthy Great Northern War (1700–1721) (although at this point Russian success was largely ensured, and all that remained was to finalize a peace treaty with Sweden). But for Peter, who was interested in the scientific, the technical and the odd (which at that time were often one and the same), making sure that his newly civilized subjects used a newly discovered medical wonder in the most effective way probably seemed like a perfectly normal object of an emperor's attention.

The instructions turn out to involve most of all what people were supposed to eat and drink while taking the waters in order that their healing properties would be fully effective. First, meals were to be eaten at

167

least three hours after taking the waters, and the last meal of the day was to be finished at least two hours before sleeping. Those meals, too, were to include or exclude (or at least to limit) specific foods and drink:

> Before dinner those who are used to it may take a shot of vodka [a *charka*, around 122 ml (4 fl. oz)], particularly of anise vodka, and after dinner one may drink around three glasses of Burgundy or Rhine wine or light French wine; also, to quench one's thirst, half-beer, or drinking a little light beer is not forbidden. And anyone who due to poverty has no Rhine, Burgundy, or French wine, that one is allowed to drink another shot of vodka, but no more, and *kvas*, *kislye shchi* and such fermented things are totally forbidden.

The rules for eating were also strict: 'do not eat anything gelatinous after dinner; one should first eat a soup and then a roast, that is have mutton, veal, beef, chicken, wildfowl, turkey, rabbit, venison . . . also fresh eggs cooked softly, but anything baked or boiled hard is forbidden.' And, finally,

> the following foods are totally forbidden: every kind of salted, sour, or smoked meat, also any salted and also fresh fish; milk, fatty dishes, cucumbers, cabbage, turnips, garlic, onion, radishes, mushrooms, which are a great danger to those who take these waters; and in the summer strawberries, blackberries and other berries, or peas, beans, carrots and other vegetables are totally forbidden to eat, both fresh and salted.[4]

What must those who went to take the waters have made of these instructions? They certainly indicate a style of eating that was very far from the normal world of Russian cooking that most of them had probably always known. No *kvas* or *kislye shchi* – no salted or otherwise preserved meat or fish – no cabbage or mushrooms! The bread and porridge that was the mainstay of many tables was not forbidden, but neither was it included. Plus, because Russian bread was normally sour, it was likely to be excluded by the ban on fermented foods. The instructions seem if anything to be suggesting that Russian foods were to be avoided for the best health.

On the one hand, this fits with many visions of Peter's reforms, which sought to pull Russia, or at least its elite, out of its set ways in order to make it a more properly European state. But on the other, because its prescriptions would have been unimaginable for most of Peter's subjects, the decree also highlights the ways that those reforms created two different worlds. For all that the decree also states that it was aimed at more than the most wealthy, most elite, of the Russian state by giving alternatives for those with less money, that 'poverty' was hardly the poverty of Russia's serfs.

This distinction between elite and popular culture was visible in many ways, most famously in matters of dress. Peter demanded that his noblemen shave and that all nobles henceforth dress in Western clothing. These reforms took hold with speed, and so by the end of the century there was a distinctly different visual culture: Russia's nobles dressed much like elites throughout Europe, while its peasants continued to dress much as they always had.[5] Foodways, though, were a place where these distinctions were more blurred. Of course, the wealthy ate (and drank, as Peter's decree suggests vividly!) differently to peasants in all sorts of ways, but there were also many areas in which they shared commonalities. Their tables held some of the same foods and drinks, from *shchi* and *kasha* to *pirogi* and *kvas*, and they interacted in many spaces, from country estates to towns. There was a Russia divided into worlds of the privileged and the unprivileged, but those worlds were not entirely separate. There were both common foods and zones of interaction. Still, the idea of the period of serfdom, in particular, as an era of a starkly divided Russia is a powerful one that grew out of earlier practices and also shaped much of what was to come.

The period from the reign of Peter the Great, or perhaps more properly from the reign of Catherine the Great (r. 1762–96), until 1861 was the height of the regime of serfdom in Russia, with all its attendant social, political and cultural results. The bulk of the population had been bound to the land in 1649; those on land belonging to private individuals were increasingly bound to their lords, not the land, by the end of the century. Peter then made reforms that had implications for how serfdom was experienced. He established a regular standing army staffed most of all by peasants conscripted for life. He established a new poll tax, known familiarly as the 'soul tax' as it was levied on every male 'soul' (not nobles, though, and eventually not priests or merchants, as well). He established a semi-regular count of the population in order to make sure that these new duties were fulfilled. Serf-owners became responsible for drawing up these counts and for making sure that their peasants' duties were paid. In addition, though, Peter also decreed that nobles, who were the bulk of the serf-owners, themselves owed a duty to his state: service. In 1722, he organized the civil administration and military command into a hierarchy known as the Table of Ranks, and at the same time declared that all nobles must serve in some official position, as a military officer or as a state servitor.

Something very different happened in 1762: Peter III, a grandson of Peter the Great who had been on the throne only a few months, 'emancipated' the nobility by eliminating their duty to serve. 'We judge it to be no longer necessary to compel the nobles into service, as has been the practice hitherto,' he wrote.[6] Although this Peter was removed from the throne by a coup on the part of his wife Catherine only a few weeks after this manifesto, she confirmed its provisions. As a result, it is the reign of this Catherine, who came to be known as another 'the Great', that in many ways set up the world of Russian serfdom that later became familiar through the great works of nineteenth-century Russian literature. Thanks to this manifesto, a nobleman was no longer required to spend all his time in St Petersburg or Moscow serving in the bureaucracy or the military. Now he could also choose to retire to his hereditary estate and live the life of a landed proprietor, a country gentleman. While not every nobleman had the financial wherewithal to retire, many did. The richest built great palaces with extensive formal gardens.[7] More built more modest manors, but nonetheless moved to the country in search of some vision of a rural utopia.[8] As they did they interacted more with their serfs but also felt themselves to be more distinct from them.

Like Peter the Great, and like a true Enlightened ruler, Catherine the Great believed in laws and their potential to remake both her administration and her subjects. She reorganized the provincial structures of the empire in an effort to spread her administrative resources (which were somewhat limited) more effectively and efficiently throughout her realm. This reorganization demanded new towns; she founded more than two hundred of them and then promulgated a charter to the towns that laid out new rules for their administration and also the rights and duties of townspeople. The same day as the charter to the towns, she also released a charter to the nobility, affirming their rights, as well. Alongside these were hundreds upon hundreds of decrees and manifestos and charters.

The one topic she did not address directly was the peasantry in general and serfdom in particular. Of course, some laws touched on peasants, but there was no real attempt to rethink their status within the empire. At least, no successful attempt. Catherine did draft a charter to the state peasants – that is, to peasants who did not belong to any particular person but who were still bound to the land – that was largely parallel to her charters to the towns and the nobility, but never released it. Instead, serfdom actually

Although the changes brought by the eighteenth century are generally seen as marking a new era in Russian history, peasant life continued along many of the same patterns as it had before. Here, in a hand-tinted photograph from 1862, peasants sit around a table, with some sort of simple meal laid out before them, and a drink being poured out by the man standing on the left.

spread during her reign, as she continued the practice of her predecessors by giving her noble supporters gifts of land and the peasants who lived on it (she had more land to give, too, because she also declared that all monastery lands now belonged to the state, which meant she could then allot them to people at will).

Her successors did not do much about it, either. Catherine's son Paul (r. 1796–1801) acted extraordinarily arbitrarily towards his nobles to the extent that he got himself assassinated for his pains. At the same time, though, he also had a streak of public consciousness for people beyond the nobility. He limited the amount of labour that serf-owners could demand from their serfs in order to ensure that they were able to grow enough of their own grain; he established grain stores in towns and some villages to guard against potential famine; he introduced measures that were intended to keep food in towns affordable even for their poorest residents. His son and successor Alexander I (r. 1801–25) had been raised by his grandmother to be the most Enlightened of Enlightened autocrats. Anyone who hoped he would intervene in the peasant question was disappointed, however. He made some changes meant to remove the worst excesses of serfdom (banning the sale of serfs without land and banning advertising the sale of serfs in newspapers) and made it easier for serf-owners to free their own serfs en masse, but the system still remained. After all, his reign also saw the great victory over Napoleon, when serfs, too, joined in the fight to expel the invaders. The Russian Empire seemed secure, serfdom be damned.

The reign of Nicholas I (r. 1825–55) in many ways brought these questions to a head. These years saw the first great explosion of Russian literature, with the poetry and prose of Pushkin and Lermontov, the fantastical world of Gogol, the realism of Goncharov and Turgenev, even the earliest works by Dostoevsky and Tolstoy all first appearing in print. In part through these works, it also saw the growth of an intellectual tradition of dissent. Much of that dissent was concerned about the split between the Russian elites and the Russian masses; 'Westernizers' wanted that split to be resolved by moving the masses toward 'rational', 'Western' culture, while the 'Slavophiles' wanted the split to be resolved by moving the elites back towards 'tradition'. In both views, serfdom was one of the major problems that kept the rift between the two sides in place. Because political writing was not allowed, there were no voices that called out publicly for an end to serfdom, but the social critique embedded in much of the literature and particularly in literary criticism naturally drew such a conclusion.

The official world also found itself increasingly concerned with the peasant question. A series of localized but significant crop failures raised fears about whether Russia's peasants were in an economically perilous position – and whether Russia might be facing famine again. An upturn in peasant disturbances was likewise disturbing to all. Although Nicholas was among Russia's most conservative autocrats, he fully realized that there were problems in this world. Over the course of his reign he established ten secret committees to look into various elements of the peasant question. And in 1842, in a statement to the State Council, he noted that 'there is no doubt that serfdom, in the form in which we have it now, is clearly and obviously bad for everyone.' At the same time, he also doubted whether there was anything to be done about it: 'to attack it at this point would be even more destructive.'[9] Only the shattering of the Russian state's confidence caused by its defeat in the Crimean War (1853–6) eventually pushed it finally to take on this vexed question.

The World of the Russian Peasant

Peasants made up the vast majority of the Russian population through the entire tsarist period (and, in fact, well into the Soviet era, as well – it was only in 1961 that the rural population of the Soviet Union fell below 50 per cent of the total population).[10] From 1600 until almost the middle of the twentieth century, peasants made up 80–90 per cent of the entire Russian population.[11] The first tax census of the Russian empire, carried out in 1719, counted 5,722,332 male peasants, or just over 90 per cent of the total male population; by the first modern census, carried out in 1897, their numbers had grown to 25,866,082 male peasants, or 86 per cent of the total.[12] They were the dominant group in society by any quantitative measure.

Most of Russia's peasants lived in villages and farmed lands held communally. Peasants lived in cottages (*izba* sing., *izby* pl.) gathered together along a street or two and went out to the fields to farm. Each household had an allotment of land scattered in small strips across the fields belonging to the community. The proceeds from the farming of these lands went to feed the family and to pay taxes and other duties. In many, although not all, villages, a practice of regular repartitioning of those lands tried to make sure that each household had enough to survive – a household that had

Both men and women contributed agricultural labour to the household, which is why land allotments were calculated by the *tiaglo*, a work unit that comprised both a man and a woman. Here, a pair of peasants from Iaroslavl province are heading to the fields armed with a scythe and a rake – and perhaps a meal in the covered basket hanging from the woman's arm.

lost members might have some of its lands taken away, while those that had gained hands might receive more. Both men and women counted in this allotment; allotments were usually made per *tiaglo*, a work unit consisting of a man and a woman, because everyone's labour was necessary for the proper functioning of the peasant world.

All peasants owed taxes; additional duties varied depending on the circumstances of individual villages. Consistently, around half of all peasants were privately owned serfs. Their numbers (in terms of their proportion of the entire population) peaked at the beginning of the nineteenth century. Serfs owed their owners either *obrok* or *barshchina*: *obrok* was a form of quitrent, a payment in kind or later mostly in cash; *barshchina* was labour duties on the lord's own land. The former was viewed as less onerous than the latter, because it allowed serfs to guide their own economic life, as long as they came up with the money to pay their rent. Peasants on *obrok* often also engaged in significant work off the land, travelling on passports to towns to work as craftsmen for part or all of the year, working in transportation (most famously hauling barges along the rivers that were central to the Russian economy) or even engaging in small-scale trade. A few became wealthy through their work off the land. Some were able to purchase their freedom, but not all landlords wanted to let a wealthy serf go.

Barshchina was a different matter. The practice became more common after the 1762 'emancipation' of the nobility, when serf-owners gained the freedom to move to the countryside and take a stronger hand in the governance of their estates. In villages with *barshchina* agreements, peasants were still allotted some land, which they worked to feed themselves and pay taxes to the state. They also worked the rest of the estate's land, and the income from that land went to the aristocratic owner's pocket. By many accounts, most famously that of Aleksandr Radishchev, nobles abused this kind of labour duty, demanding so many days labour on their lands that serfs were forced to farm their land for sustenance at night and on Sundays.[13] Emperor Paul intervened in this, stating firmly that this was not acceptable. Instead, Sundays should be a day of rest, and the remainder of the week should be divided between labour on the lord's land and on peasants' land. In other words, peasants should be required to work a maximum of three days a week on the lord's land.

Although things shifted a bit at the end of the eighteenth century, after Catherine's annexation of the steppe lands north of the Black Sea, and as peasants moved (or more often, were moved) into the area, the agricultural world of the Russian peasant was primarily one of short, intense summers and long, cold winters. Peasants called the summer season the 'suffering time' because of the hardships of the work; in the 1830s, one provincial governor declared in a report that 'the whole life of the Russian peasant is constant, heavy labour.'[14] Some travellers, in particular, called the Russian peasant 'lazy', but that description was sharply contested by many Russian observers. At the end of the eighteenth century, the Russian writer Ivan Boltin published a lengthy response to the French author Nicolas-Gabriel Leclerc's description of the Russian Empire and its inhabitants. To Boltin, Leclerc's description of the country seemed absolutely wrongheaded – he found fault everywhere in Leclerc's text. One specific target of his ire was Leclerc's dismissal of the agricultural prowess of the Russian peasant. Boltin claimed this was utterly wrong and argued against Leclerc in two ways. First, he noted, Russia was no less inclined towards agriculture than any other nation: 'this is proved by the fact that Russia has never purchased and does not purchase grain from neighbouring powers but instead yearly sells not a small amount of it to others.' Second, Russia's peasants were not 'lazy', as Leclerc claimed, but instead 'so busy with work that they have no day of rest', at least during the short summer months.[15]

Over the course of 1861, the journal *Selskii listok*, which was itself aimed at a peasant readership, featured a different illustration of the agricultural world of the Russian peasant as the frontispiece of each issue. The first image alone moves away from the agricultural world. Instead, it featured an image of the inside of a peasant cottage, with a family clustered around a table. A young woman spins as a man sits under a smoking lamp reading, presumably aloud, to the group. The rest of the images show other elements of the peasant world as it changed throughout the year. For the remainder of the winter, peasants take advantage of the freeze to use sleds to move goods, both sacks of grain and frozen carcasses, to market. They cut blocks of ice, repair tools and repair thatched roofs. Then comes the planting season, as the peasant ploughs (notably using a modern metal plough, not an older peasant scratch plough), sows seeds and harrows the earth. Women draw water in buckets to water young plants in a vegetable garden. Sheep are sheared, and then the haying season begins, as men wield scythes and women collect and sheaf the hay. Later in the year, peasant women are pictured harvesting apples and milking cows, while men chop and stack firewood (huge stacks for the long winter to come), thresh grain and bring it to a mill and work on repairing walls and fences. The journal may have presented Russian peasants at their most industrious, but even should

In 1861, the yearly labour of the Russian peasant was depicted in a series of etchings in the journal *Selskii listok*. These images showed the labour involved in field agriculture, including (from top to bottom) ploughing the fields, sowing grain, threshing and separating the grain from the chaff by tossing it into the air for the chaff to blow away.

actual peasants have done only a fraction of all of these tasks, their lives were filled with heavy labour.

In many ways, this world of heavy labour, particularly in the summer, was reflected in the Russian peasant diet. In the 1830s, the university professor (and part-time censor) Ivan Snegirev tried to describe the world of the Russian peasant in a multi-volume work on 'Russians according to their folk sayings'. According to Snegirev, folk sayings gave a 'more lively and stronger' vision of the Russian peasant than 'all descriptions by outside observers'.[16] One of the reasons is that sayings gave insight into everyday life – into how peasants viewed the climate, their homes, their clothing and of course their food, in ways that were not always obvious to those passers-by.

'The food of Russians is simple, coarse and filling, fitting to their cold climate and tough stomach,' Snegirev wrote. 'It is more vegetable and starchy than animal, as among the English, who live under dank clouds.'[17] He went on to describe the specific foods common to Russians, linking each to a particular saying. First came rye bread, usually eaten with salt alone; the combination (*khleb i sol*) formed the basis of the concept of hospitality (*khlebosolstvo*). Although 'heavily salted thick slabs of rye bread' was normal working peasant food, it could also form the basis of *tiuria*: here bread was doused with *kvas* or water and hempseed oil and eaten with onions. The wheat bread known as a *kalach*, Snegirev noted, was 'a treat, not a filling food', as peasant sayings made clear: 'you won't get full on *kalach*' or '*kalach* soon palls, but bread never does.'

In addition, there was 'austere *shchi*', the vegetable (and usually vegetarian) basis of the meal. *Shchi* was so important that 'people get married for *shchi*'. There was also variation due to the fasts and fast days, Snegirev noted, which were not only characterized by 'abstinence' but served as a 'guard against sickness'. The prevalence of fish in the diet owed something to the fasting rules but also something to 'age-old habits of the Slav-Rus', who had often settled near rivers and lakes. Mushrooms were also part of the Lenten world, giving rise to the saying that during the Lent before Easter, there were 'seven foods, all of them mushrooms'. *Kisel* and beer and *kvas* rounded out the menu. All in all, 'the Russian table is depicted by the following saying: the bitter, the baked, the salted, the vinegary, the cold, the sour.'[18]

Finally, Snegirev summed up his discussion of peasant food with a vision of the ways in which it was innately suited to the Russian lands and the Russian people – and also of a potential problem lurking within the norms of Russian peasant life:

The moderate and filling food offered to the Russian person
by mother earth does not irritate the body with excess juices,
[but] gives it the strength to bear the hardships of labour in
the field at the harvest, of battles, of heat, of cold and of hunger.
On campaign or during fasts he can survive without food for
several days . . . If drunkenness and other vices associated with
it did not sometimes exhaust his strength even more than
labours that no other European could endure, then every
Russian by his nature would be a hero and the earth would
be for him mother and nurse.[19]

In these sections, Snegirev gets at a whole series of issues regarding the food
of the Russian peasant. It was 'moderate and filling' but not luxurious.
It was usually sufficient, but when it was not, the Russian peasant could
cope and even prosper. It was drawn from the Russian environment and
was suited to the health of the Russian person. The lurking problem was
drink and drunkenness, not dearth.

Vodka was in fact coming to be seen as a real danger for the Russian
people, but one that was particularly difficult to solve because it was
inextricably linked both to culture and to the interests of the state and
its revenue. Drunkenness was not seen as a problem because it inclined
people towards violence. Indeed, a number of foreign writers particularly
noted that drunkenness in Russia tended towards at most sleepiness, not
meanness. A French traveller at the beginning of the nineteenth century
claimed that

a drunken Russian is gay, he is a talker, a gesticulator, a singer,
a dancer. His drunkenness has nothing of sadness and silences;
in this state he does not have dark humour and evil genius.
The drunken Russian is the friend of the whole world . . .
it is not rare to see him dead drunk, but rarely does one see
him mean.[20]

Half a century later, another visitor similarly stated that 'the Russians
drink enormously' and yet 'when drunk and reeling, they are invariably
affectionate'.[21]

Instead, the problem was above all that vodka cost money – it was
associated with peasant poverty and not with peasant violence. In the
nineteenth century, this came into greater prominence because of changes

in the overall patterns of vodka consumption that began to affect peasants. At the end of the eighteenth century, Catherine the Great had instituted a system of tax farming for vodka distilling. There were a limited number of licences to distil vodka which the imperial state sold off for its own profit (a huge portion of its profit: a quarter of the state's income).[22] Those tax farmers, then, opened as many taverns as they could in order to increase their profits (or so critics said). That meant that older patterns of community-based drinking at festivals and celebrations were beginning to be transformed by the spread of taverns out of towns and into larger villages. These made access to vodka an everyday occurrence, not just something that went along with holidays.[23]

Drinking in the village was associated with poverty. Some serf-owners boasted that they were committed to controlling their serfs' alcohol consumption by controlling the amount of alcohol available in the village. One, for example, noted that he allowed no permanent taverns on his estate, but only temporary sale of alcohol on holidays – and only after holy services were complete.[24] But others seemed not to care or not to pay enough attention to avoid the problem. In a didactic story written for an imagined peasant audience, Vladimir Burnashev described a 'typical' village brought nearly to ruin by 'two big taverns built with the approval of the overseer, without the consent of the lord' – in other words, where the lord did not care enough about the everyday world of his village and instead handed off its administration to a hired overseer more concerned with profit. According to the story, those taverns had drawn peasants from the church and 'enriched the tavern-keepers as much as they impoverished the peasants'.[25]

There were hopes that other beverages – particularly tea – might replace vodka as the preferred drink of the common man. In 1860, a newspaper correspondent in Kazan, for example, praised a new tea shop with lower prices in part because it gave more reason for the 'lower estates' to switch to drinking tea rather than the more expensive vodka. (His editor doubted that this would ever happen, however. He noted that 'many people here drink tea, true, but that does not mean that it serves as a substitute for vodka. Look at the evening spread of a townsman: before anything a guest is given a shot of vodka, after it another, and sometimes a third ... It is called: *before tea*.')[26]

In any event, the idea that peasants might switch their allegiance from vodka to tea was not without its own set of worries. Tea was not intoxicating, to be sure, but it still cost money. In 1846 an author claimed that 'today, in every village lying near cities and on great roads it is possible to see

This *lubok* – a kind of print aimed at a peasant audience – from the late 18th century warned of some of the dangers of excessive drinking, including violence, vomiting and voluptuousness.

samovars glowing in the windows of houses.' Furthermore, those samovars did not require only water and coals, but tea and sugar. 'How much does it cost a peasant to keep this tea equipment, even if he and his family only use it twice a week?' the author asked. Seventy roubles a year, he claimed, on top of the cost of the samovar itself.[27] Egor Alipanov, himself born a serf, wrote a didactic vaudeville work that poked fun at this problem, as well. The heroine, Dunia, wished to marry a fellow serf named Grigorii, who was the most successful farmer in the village in part because he borrowed books on agriculture from his owner, Ekonomov. Dunia's mother, however, wanted her to marry a different serf, Ivan Chaev, because he had a samovar in his window – to her a sign of his wealth (*chai* is the word for tea in Russia, so his name also signified his association with the beverage). In the end, Grigorii tricks Chaev by substituting grass for his tea; when Chaev's undeveloped palate cannot tell the difference, Ekonomov takes

These three details
highlight some of the
dangers of drinking,
from illicit sex at the
top to a headache
or depression at the
bottom. The image in
the centre may seem
to be innocent — an
elegantly dressed pair
gathering grapes —
but the sinuous vine
wrapped around
a tree clearly recalls
the serpent tempting
Eve in the Garden
of Eden, just as too
much drink tempts
all to bad behaviour.

The Samovar

Although tea had old roots in Russia, in the nineteenth century it became a sign of modernity both in and of itself and in the specific way in which it was consumed. This was above all to do with the samovar. As the traveller Henry Sutherland Edwards described it, 'the samovar, which, literally, means "self-boiler", is made of brass lined with tin, with a tube in the centre. In fact it resembles the English urn, except that in the centre-tube red-hot cinders are placed instead of the iron heater.' This traveller believed that its heat source gave it 'no advantage then, whatever, over the English urn, except that it can be heated with facility in the open air, with nothing but some charcoal, a few sticks of thin dry wood, and a lucifer; hence its value at picnics, where it is considered indispensable'.[28] Others, though, were impressed. Louise Hunt, the wife of the U.S. ambassador to St Petersburg in the early 1880s, wrote that she planned 'to get a brass samovar; they are the best things for tea I have ever seen'.[29] The samovar heated and then kept water hot; a small porcelain teapot placed on top to keep warm held a strong brew, which a drinker could then dilute with the water in the samovar. Most accounts state that samovars appeared in Russia in the early to mid-eighteenth century. Audra Yoder argues that its origins are probably the very English tea urns that Edwards referenced, and that it caught on so well because it heated water more quickly and efficiently than the Russian stove, which excelled at slow cooking rather than high temperatures.[30] The town of Tula, first associated with armaments factories, became the centre of samovar production by the early nineteenth century. By the end of the nineteenth century the samovar was a sign of affluence, often a prop in staged photographs. Now, although many Russian households still own a samovar, it often sits on a high shelf, brought out only on special occasions – the electric kettle has become the norm there as in so many other places.

Not simply tea but particularly the samovar became symbolic of Russian peasant life in the early nineteenth century. In one image, three peasant women from Novotorzhskii district are pictured with a fully kitted-out samovar. This region lay on the main road from St Petersburg to Moscow, which may explain both the relatively fancy dress and the samovar at this fairly early date. In the second, two peasant men sit at a table, talking and drinking tea. In this image, too, you can see a particularity of Russian tea drinking: cooling the hot tea in the saucer, and drinking directly from it.

НОВОТОРЖСКІЯ ЖЕНЩИНЫ И ДѢВУШКА.
1830. г.

МОСКОВСКОЙ ГУБЕРНІИ СТАНЦІЯ ЧЕРНАЯ ГРЯЗЬ 1848 г

this as occasion to give a lesson on what not to spend money on, and Grigorii wins Dunia's hand.[31]

Another change that was beginning to affect peasant foodways came from the top: new encouragement to cultivate and consume the potato. The potato seemed a potential miracle food that might assuage any fears of famine; the example of its spread already in parts of Europe appeared to promise great returns even in the poor soils of the Russian north. The Imperial Russian Free Economic Society, founded in 1765, was particularly interested in pushing potato cultivation. In its early years, the society set a series of questions on economic issues to be answered by its noble members as they described the lands on which they owned estates. Among the questions were 'are potatoes planted in the given region, or are such underground fruits completely unknown?' Members wrote in; a few had begun planting potatoes themselves (or, rather, they had ordered their serfs to plant potatoes in the fields), with varying degrees of success. One, Fridrich Vulf, claimed that potatoes had great potential when grown in good soil, but also noted that on his own poor soil, they grew to be no larger than a large pea.[32] For the most part, though, even someone who asked around among the local peasants discovered that 'no one had yet heard of this kind of root vegetable'.[33]

There was a bigger push for potato cultivation beginning in the 1830s, when a series of bad harvests raised the fear of famine. The newly formed Ministry of State Domains, which governed non-privately-owned peasants, started competitions for potato cultivation, granting prizes to peasants who were successful that included shirts decorated with modern farming implements. It also encouraged the publishing of new journals and a new agricultural newspaper that pushed potato cultivation. These were aimed mostly at an audience of landlords, who might then encourage their own serfs to plant potatoes.

Potatoes also featured in didactic stories aimed at a peasant audience. In one such story, Burnashev described a meal served to a priest at the end of the great Petrov fast (that is, when meat, dairy and eggs were not allowed, but fish was). In Burnashev's story, the priest was invited to

a big oaken table, covered in a snow-white cloth. On this table there were placed a tureen with excellent *ukha*, a cold fish dish and a trout fried in poppy-seed oil; as an accompaniment there was prepared a delicious dish called *salad* out of potatoes, beetroot and cucumbers in beer vinegar. The residents of the village learned how to prepare salad from Polikarp, who had eaten this dish more than once while a guest of some students from the District Agricultural School, who lived at the school in model cottages. Father Nikandr ate all of this with particular pleasure, and praised the father, mother and children for their industry, their zeal for good, and for their introduction of good order in their household.[34]

Burnashev here describes a method by which information about new foods might be transferred from one peasant to another, but is also himself engaged in exactly that effort. He was describing this 'new' dish, salad, which intentionally included a new and still not entirely popular ingredient, the potato. By claiming that the priest ate this meal happily, including the potato, he was also doing a bit of proselytizing for the tuber, given that peasants were said to be loath to eat potatoes out of fear that they were not allowed to do so on religious grounds.

Potatoes took a long time to catch on in Russia. Introduced in the 18th century, and then touted by agricultural reformers in the early 19th century, they still remained more of a curiosity than a staple. By the early 20th century, they were finding their place, as this photograph by Sergei Mikhailovich Prokudin-Gorskii suggests – here monks line up to plant potatoes in newly cleared lands near a monastery in the forested north.

There certainly were changes coming into peasant diets by the middle of the nineteenth century. Potatoes were still far from common, but they had begun to appear on peasant tables. Tea, too, was making its way into everyday life. But for the most part, by just about every account, peasants were eating much the same way they had been for centuries, with a cycle of Lenten and meat foods every week, and longer intervals of fasting and feasting every year, all based on the rhythms of the church calendar and on the harvest.

THE AGE OF THE RUSSIAN NOBILITY

The world of the Russian noble, on the other hand, underwent a profound change from the reign of Peter the Great to the middle of the nineteenth century. Much of that change happened in the eighteenth century. Peter's commands to shave and to dress differently, to interact in different ways, via school or assemblies, even to move to the new capital of St Petersburg, all affected noble life. The process has often been called 'Westernization', as Peter wanted to make the boyar elite he inherited into something more akin to a proper Western European nobility (although one with a voice limited to their active participation in state service).

Particularly when it came to culture, Peter more or less succeeded. The Russian nobility simply looked different at the end of his reign, and certainly by the end of the eighteenth century, in comparison to what they had been before him. They dressed like their peers across Europe; they built the same kinds of Palladian-inspired manors that were appearing not just in Europe but in the Americas, too. As nobles came to learn French and German as well as Russian (or even instead of Russian), they read the same books.[35] And, they came to eat many of the same foods, as well.

The changes that came into the world of the Russian nobility were rapid and profound, involving both everyday practices and the world of consumption. When it came to behaviour, Peter seemed to want to make his nobles no longer 'rude and barbarous' in the eyes of foreigners. He even commissioned a guide to behaviour for his young nobles. Among other things, it gave advice on how to behave at table: a young noble ought not 'to blow into soup so that it sprays everywhere' nor to 'lick your fingers . . . gnaw bones, clean your teeth with a knife . . . cut bread while holding it against your chest . . . make a fence of bones, bread crusts, etc. around your plate'.[36] When it came to food itself, the changes that entered Russia involved both new foods, many imported either from the edges of the empire or from abroad, and new cuisines which came along with new methods of preparation. Both of them together meant a world of Russian elite food that was a cosmopolitan mix of the traditional and the new.

In 1772, the journal of the Free Economic Society published sample budgets for noble households of different income levels.[37] The budgets listed all the provisions that a household might need, and then recommended how much of each provision a household should buy based on yearly incomes ranging from 3,000 to 32,000 roubles. The provision lists are extensive, and reflect this kind of new mixed table that had already become common among Russia's elite. They include:

Butter
Wheat flour
  (*krupichatka*)
Wheat flour (sieved)
Rye flour
Rice
Pearl barley
Farina
Sago
Buckwheat groats (fine
  and simple)
Oatmeal (fine and
  simple)
Barley groats (fine
  and simple)
Millet
Carob pods
Peas
Grey peas
Beans
Lentils
Turkish beans
English cheese
Parmesan
Dutch cheese
Swiss cheese
Dutch butter

Holstein butter
Neapolitan pasta of
  various sorts
Salt
Dried cherries
  (Swiss)
Raspberries
French prunes
Simple prunes
Raisins (two sorts)
Currants
Pears and apples
  (sweet and dried)
Almonds in the shell
Sweet almond
Bitter almond
Pistachios
Chestnuts
Mushrooms
  (including
  champignons
  and mousserons)
Truffles
Black pepper
White pepper
Yellow ginger
White ginger

Cinnamon
Nutmeg
Mace
Cloves
Cardamom
Hartshorn
Sunflower
Sage
Chopped oysters
Indian birds nest
Asimanga and Asibomba
  [?]
English mustard
Sugar (simple, refined,
  Canary)
Black tea
Green tea
Coffee
Dutch herring
Anchovies
Capers and olives
Wine vinegar
Olive oil
Crabs
Oysters
Caviar (grain)
Shallot
Cumin
Anise
Coriander
Ham ('common'
  and Bayonne or
  Westphalian)
English bacon
Speck

Smoked goose
Smoked sausage
Smoked salt beef
Smoked salmon
Smoked herring
Dutch cod
Common cod
Plaice
Ruff
Osetrina
Beluga
Caviar
Narva lamprey
White cabbage
Cucumbers in salt
Cucumbers, small, in
  vinegar
Preserved (soaked)
  apples, plums, berries
Salted beans, mushrooms,
  green parsley
Dried peas

For drinks and zakuski:
White French wine
Red French wine
Expensive wine
French vodka
Gdansk vodka
English beer
Half beer
Liqueurs
Sweet snacks
Vegetables and fruits

Not every budget could afford every food on this list, of course. But even the poorest household on the list was assumed to have access to English and Dutch cheeses (although not Parmesan or Swiss), to French prunes, to imported herring, to tea and coffee, to anchovies and capers and olives, and to a hogshead each of white and red French wines every year. In other words, according to this image of what noble households ate, everyone had been touched by new tastes coming in from abroad.

That same year, another author, Iosif Regensburger, also ventured to offer his thoughts on the ideal budget for a 'married but childless man with an income of 20,000 roubles a year' – quite a high budget, but not unheard of.[38] According to him, on an average day, the main meal would involve the master and mistress of the house along with eight guests. For those ten people, the chef should prepare twelve dishes, including soup and salad (seven dishes were enough for a late supper).[39] Those dishes were increasingly drawn not just from the Russian tradition but from foreign cuisines, as well. As the cookbook author Sergei Drukovtsov put it in his *Cooking Notes*, first published in 1779, the human body could be satisfied with very simple foods, but often preferred something with a bit more panache. 'This truth', he went on, 'is proved by the way of life of our peasants . . . who have very few extras beyond their rye bread and water.' His readers, however, had become accustomed to a different world of food. 'Our habits and practices have changed with an increase of luxury, and with that our tastes so that we are no longer satisfied with simple foods.'[40] Although his was a very simple cookbook (a typical recipe was: 'take a ham, roast it on a spit, under it serve a sauce of sour onions with mustard'), it also included a dictionary of 'cooking terms' taken from foreign languages. These were mostly cuts of meat, but also techniques (*oblanshirovat*, to blanch), ingredients (*sharlot*, shallot) and preparations (*farsh*, 'chopped meat with eggs and greens', or, forcemeat).[41]

Other cookbooks went much further in terms of including foreign cuisines, culminating in Vasilii Levshin's multi-volume *Cooking, Serving, Confectionery-making and Distilling Dictionary, Containing in Alphabetical Order Detailed and True Instructions for the Preparation of Every Sort of Food from French, German, Dutch, Spanish and English Cookery, Pastries, Desserts, Preserves, Salads, Waters, Essences, Spiced Vodkas, Liqueurs, Double Vodkas and the Like; Also for the Order of Tables with Plans, Menus, Servants and the Like and with as an Addition, in Separate Paragraphs, a Complete Bourgeois and New Cookery; and In the Same Ways Austrian, Berlin, Bohemian, Saxon and Russian Cookery.*[42] His was a huge compilation: six volumes, each over 400 pages long, with lengthy sections on each of the national cuisines identified in the title. Nothing later came close to its length, complexity or completeness, but the wide array of foods he considered would become more and more of a standard in cookbooks. They always included something Russian, if only *shchi*. But foreign words and dishes grew to be accepted, no longer needing translation.

As a result, the tables of the Russian elite came to astound visitors with their luxury and their complexity. One way of displaying the wealth of an individual noble involved not just the fineness of the preparations served on his table but also the profusion of goods he served, brought in from all over the empire and, indeed, the world. As one British visitor put it in a letter from 1800:

> at the same table we see, veal from Archangel, mutton from
> Siberia, sterlet from the Volga, apples from Astrachan, grapes
> from Persia, porter and strong beer from London, wines
> from France, Spain, Italy, &c., strawberries from Lapland;
> in short, the whole world is ransacked to supply their
> sumptuous banquets.[43]

Ideal budgets and recipes listed in cookbooks do not necessarily reflect any real world of eating, of course, but records of household stores and purchases show a noble dining culture that had indeed evolved to incorporate both foreign foods and foreign dishes. This was visible in everything from the vegetables and fruits that nobles actually planted, to the imported foods they bought, to the dishes they served on their tables. Perhaps not all the different foods described in the sample budgets were purchased by any individual noble household, but many of them were. And the meals they served similarly came to draw on the many different foods that had come into general usage.

There are many examples of these practices. In the 1850s, the exceedingly wealthy and posh Durnovo family ate meals consisting of multiple courses of soups, roasts and sauced dishes, many of them of French origin, but some still classic Russian dishes.[44] Or there are records from the household of Dmitry Golokhvastov (1796–1849), a well-educated state servitor splitting his time between a house in Moscow and his estate just outside the city. His household was well off, but not excessively so; he was not among the wealthiest of nobles, but nor was he anywhere close to impoverished. Golokhvastov consistently spent hundreds of roubles on wine, usually from the Belgian wine merchant Philippe Depret, whose store in Moscow was one of the better-known ones in the city. In 1826 he bought Sauterne (12 bottles for 36 roubles), champagne (12 bottles for

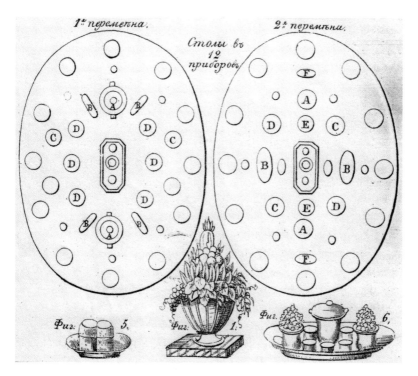

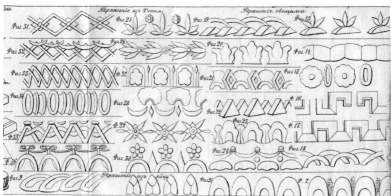

Katerina Avdeeva claimed that her cookbook was aimed at modest households – it was not for the extremely wealthy, but instead for the middling strata of Russian society. This middle-class table was increasingly opulent, as suggested in these two illustrations from her cookbook.

In the first, table settings for the first two courses of a meal for twelve are shown above a series of potential table decorations that are anything but modest. In the second, she includes suggestions for decorating: those on the left are decorations made of dough, presumably to be placed on a fancy *pirog*, and those on the right are decorations made of vegetables, cut out and placed perhaps upon an aspic or a whole cooked fish.

129 roubles, 60 kopeks), Malaga (2 bottles for 10 roubles, 80 kopeks), St Julien (a Bordeaux; 12 bottles for 30 roubles) and, most expensively, Clos Vougeot (a Burgundy; 2 bottles for 25 roubles). He continued to buy wine from Depret through the 1840s, when he also bought Rhenish wine and English porter.[45] He was also a buyer of Parmesan and olives for *zakuski*, so part of the wider world in that way.

Other examples come from the Vorontsov family, one of the most prominent noble families in the eighteenth and early nineteenth centuries. Two brothers, Aleksandr (1741–1805) and Semën (1744–1832), served in the military, then as diplomats (both represented the Russian Empire in London, Semën for more than twenty years). At the beginning of the nineteenth century Aleksandr served as State Chancellor in St Petersburg while Semën served as ambassador in London. Their sister Ekaterina (1743–1810), whose married name was Dashkova, became the most decorated Russian woman of her time (other than her good friend Catherine the Great, of course).[46] Semën's son Mikhail went on to serve in the military against Napoleon.

In 1802, Count Aleksandr Vorontsov gave his factor, Ignaty Bogdanov, instructions 'on conducting the household economy and on constructing menus when the Princess is present'. The princess was probably his sister, Princess Dashkova-Vorontsova. First and foremost in his instructions came the demands of the stomach:

1st. The table must consist of two bowls of soup, *pirogi* and cold dishes and for the change of course, boiled beef, one day roasted and the other boiled mutton. Salt beef, ham, two hot sauces, roast, whatever kind of vegetable and pies. And sometimes blancmange.

2nd. A dessert of four dishes, watermelon, apples, dishes of raisins with prunes, a dish of jam. And when there are no watermelons replace it with another dish of jam and sometimes with sweets and 'soaked' grapes when they are imported [and therefore available].

3rd. Make sure that fish is served, too, that each week stock fish should be served in a *pirog*, or macaroni, which should be in a *pirog*. Vary the soups, so that they are not all the same, and also vary the *pirogi*. And vary the sauces too.[47]

In other words, this worldly Vorontsov commanded a menu that reflected plenty, and variety, and some fancy ingredients, but also relatively modest foods like soup and baked *pirogi*. Even the most elite liked their homely comforts. At around the same time the cellars of the Vorontsov household in Moscow also showed this combination of the epicurean and the everyday. Around 1806, the wine cellar of the Vorontsov household in Moscow contained 27 barrels and 6,523 bottles of wine; 199 bottles of various sizes of vodka; and 100 bottles of mead flavoured with birch and with raspberries, as well as 175 bottles of olive oil, more than 400 kilograms (880 lb) of sugar and nearly 100 kilograms (220 lb) of coffee.[48] The mead and the vodka spoke to one set of tastes; the wine, olive oil and coffee to something very different.

The generation of Vorontsovs prominent in the 1830s and 1840s had tastes that were even more inclined towards the elite. Mikhail Semënovich, the head of the family at this point, had spent his early years in England while his father served as a diplomat there – his sister even married an English peer. Starting in the 1820s, this Vorontsov came to serve as a military governor in the southern steppe (and also eventually of the Caucasus region); his household thus spent time both in Moscow and St Petersburg and in these other areas. Later, in the 1840s, a register of pantry stores from his household shows a taste for coffee, cheese and probably salad dressed with tarragon vinegar:

Olive oil, best: 200 bottles
Parmesan: 1 round
Stilton: 1 tin
Swiss cheese: 1 round
English Chester: 20 *funty* [8 kg/18 lb]
Tarragon vinegar: 6 bottles
Mustard powder: 20 *funty* [8 kg/18 lb]
Coffee, Moka: 5 *pudy* [81 kg/180 lb][49]

The count signed employment contracts with butlers and chefs and gardeners over the course of several decades. In all likelihood he did not have to do this; as a serf-owner, he could have trained his own serfs to serve in these capacities. But clearly these men had particular skills that made their employment worth his while. In 1825, while he was stationed in the south near Crimea, he hired a gardener to watch over the vineyard he established there, paying the man 1,000 paper roubles a year and supplying him with a horse and a cow. In 1832, he signed a contract with a freed serf named Mikhail Stepanovich Skubilin to work as a cook in his household in Odessa. Count Vorontsov agreed to pay for Skubilin's move to Odessa, to give him a salary of 720 (paper) roubles a year and to supply him with an extra payment of 80 roubles to fit himself out with proper chef's whites. In 1849, he gave a contract to another chef, Gerasim Timofeev Bekenskii. The new chef agreed to travel with Count Vorontsov 'wherever it is convenient for His Excellency' and to 'prepare according to the orders of His Excellence foods both for His Excellency's table and also for all guests and servants, while maintaining strict economy in expenses and ensuring that provisions of the best quality are used'. In return, he received a salary of 50 silver roubles a month, 'from which I must supply all my own needs'.[50]

Although these chefs were clearly Russian, the meals they prepared were a much more varied mix, reflecting the varied tastes of the Russian nobility of the time. On Friday 19 May 1837, the count and his guests dined on a multi-course meal that included Russian favourites (albeit in French forms, like the *ukha* represented as *ouca* and the *pirogi* represented as *petits pâtes*) and foreign imports – the sturgeon garnished with lettuce, the beef with Brussels sprouts, the apple charlotte and soufflés for dessert:

Le Potage ouca maigre
Le Potage au macaroni
Les Petits Pâtes
Les Turbots sauce Crevelles
Le Boeuf garni de choux de bruxel
La Morue maigre
Les Croquettes de volaille
Le Sauté d'esturgeon garni de lettuces
Les Vaneaux (Rot)
Les Petits Soudacs (Rot)
Les Choufleurs sauce au beurre
Les Charlottes de Pommes et Soufflés

The record of the menu was accompanied by a list of expenses for the meal:

Beef	18 roubles
Veal	7 roubles, 20 kopeks
Mutton	3 roubles, 80 kopeks
Fish	32 roubles, 80 kopeks

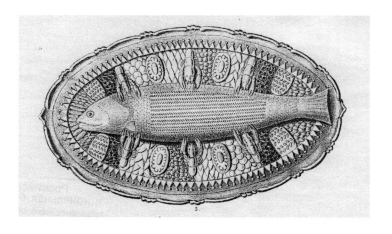

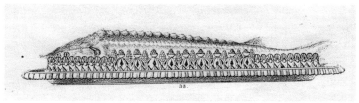

If Avdeeva's cookbook provided its readers with the building blocks of decorations, Ignaty Radetskii's cookbook, *St Petersburg Cooking*, showed them something much, much more elaborate, as in these three illustrations of decorated fish and fowl. Radetskii was also the author of a series of cookbooks titled *The Gastronome's Almanac* – his was an elite audience of fine taste, who wished their food to be both tasty and beautiful. (According to their labels, the dishes are: trout à la Chambord, sterlet Russian style with garnish, horn of plenty with paté, swan of whipped cream, and hot paté of pheasant.)

Poultry	18 roubles
Game	12 roubles, 60 kopeks
Fruit	14 roubles, 40 kopeks
Groceries	23 roubles
Cream	2 roubles, 40 kopeks
Apples	3 roubles, 60 kopeks
Butter	6 roubles
Bakery	1 rouble, 20 kopeks
Lemon	2 roubles
Herbs	1 rouble, 20 kopeks[51]

On 5 May 1837, the household kitchen prepared three different dinners at a total cost of 76 roubles, 88 kopeks. The first was for the main household and included:

Le Potage viennois
La Soupe russe
Le Turbot sauce hollandaise
La Pièce de Boeuf flamande
Les Filets de Veau pigné sa pointes d'asperges
Le Suprême de volaille aux champignons
La Petite Poulet rôtie
Les Asperges
Les Beignets crème
Les Charlottes russes a la vanille

Next came a separate meal for the children:

Le Potage au vermicelli
Les Beefsteaks maître d'hôtel
Les Choufleurs
Les Côtelletes d'agneau
Les Compotes
Le Pudding

Finally, a meal for the office staff:

Le Poisson
La Salade

La Soupe au selleri
Le Bouille
Le Foie de gras
Le Rôti de veau
Les Gâteaux de riz[52]

Of course, these are all the meals of the very wealthy. There was a wider world of nobles whose lives were more constrained by finances. Some were still living lives of comfort in the provinces, mostly avoiding the more luxurious and more expensive world of Moscow and St Petersburg society. According to some, this led to lives in which the supposedly sharp division between noble and peasant cultures was blurred. A traveller at the end of the eighteenth century claimed that 'the picture of Russian manners varies little with reference to the prince or the peasant,' by which he meant that if a Russian nobleman were to settle in the countryside on his estate, he would take on 'a mode of life little superior' to that of the peasants. Practically, that meant that he would spend his days 'with his neck bare, his beard lengthened, his body wrapped in a sheep's hide, eating raw turnips and drinking quass [*kvas*], sleeping one half of the day, and growling at his wife and family the other'.[53]

In addition, there was a wider world of impoverished nobles that was constantly growing because of the very cost of living up to their status.[54] The most famous vision of that world is the painting *The Aristocrat's Breakfast*, in which a well-dressed man in a well-appointed room rushes to hide away the evidence of his breakfast of simple black bread. Food was an easy place to cut corners for those who were trying to keep up appearances despite limited finances. The nineteenth-century poet Afanasy Fet remembered that his father kept a strictly limited table (he 'satisfied himself with unchanging oat porridge with oil') – except when guests were to dine (when 'dinner was served with a new soup and five new dishes').[55]

The two different worlds could coexist within a single family. In one memoir, the noblewoman O. Verkhovskaia described the sharp difference between the home of her wealthy grandmother and that of her parents, a difference that manifested most visibly in the kinds of foods that she ate in each:

On the same terrace where tea was drunk in the morning, [a table] was set for breakfast. What wasn't there on that table! There was a huge skillet of scrambled eggs with sour cream, another such with fried potatoes and then a dish with *sochenki*. *Sochenki* were a family dish, passed down from generation to generation. They were thick pancakes, cut in half, with *tvorog* in the middle and fried in butter ... As for me, my mouth even watered from such a multitude of dishes. We were used to breakfasts at which were served yesterday's warmed-over meat or cutlets for father, and we were served only buckwheat gruel or bread and butter.[56]

There was nothing particularly exotic in this meal, but there were ample quantities of rich things. Wealth could mean fricassees and truffles, champagne and pineapple, or it could mean a rich, filling breakfast with comfortable, old-fashioned things.

IN THE MIDDLE OF the 1780s, at the height of the reign of Catherine the Great (r. 1762–96), just after she had promulgated some of her most important reforms, the conservative noble Prince Mikhail Shcherbatov wrote a lengthy disquisition 'On the Corruption of Morals in Russia'. Shcherbatov came from an old noble family. Born in 1733, he had an early career in state service – mandatory for nobles as of the reign of Peter the Great. But as soon as that duty was abolished, he retired and lived as a gentleman of leisure with a penchant for history and philosophy. He served as a representative of the nobility to Catherine's Legislative Commission at the end of the 1760s, where he staunchly defended noble privilege and lamented that Petrine reforms had allowed commoners to enter the nobility. Although he was himself a man of education and the Enlightenment, he found much to dislike in the courtly world around him. Publicly, he eventually produced a multi-volume *History of Russia* that looked to the time before Peter the Great for lessons for the contemporary Russian state. Privately – or at least, not for publication in a time of censorship – he wrote pieces that took a harsher view of the world in which he lived.[57]

'On the Corruption of Morals in Russia' is his strongest statement against the current noble and courtly world. Although he criticized many elements of noble society, in his mind 'corruption' had been caused above all by luxury – by 'voluptuousness' in dress, in entertainments and, of course, in food and drink. He explicitly contrasted this contemporary love of excess with the world before Peter the Great had come to the throne:

[In the past] although there were many dishes, they were all
composed of simple things. Beef, mutton, pork, goose, turkey,
ducks, chickens, grouse and suckling pig were enough to make
up an extravagant table with the addition of a mass of baked
goods, not always made of white wheaten flour; veal was not
much in use, and milk-veal and capons were unknown. The
height of luxury was when the bones of roast and ham were
decorated with gold leaf, *pirogi* were gilded and so on. Then
they did not know capers, olives, other preparations to awaken
the appetite, but satisfied themselves with salted cucumbers,
cream, and they considered it a great treat to serve an aspic
with salted lemons. Their dessert was just as simple, for raisins,
currants, figs, prunes and honey *postila* made up all the dried
things; in summer and autumn fresh things were: apples, pears,
peas, beans and cucumbers; and I think that they did not even
know melon and watermelon ... they also brought in preserved
grapes in molasses [*vinograd v patoke*] but they did not have
the knowledge to bring in fresh grapes, for even in my memory
during the reign of Empress Elizaveta Petrovna, by the efforts of
Ivan Antonovich Cherkasov, cabinet-minister, they started to
bring in fresh ones.[58]

In Shcherbatov's telling, the problem dated back to the reign of Peter the
Great but was due not so much to Peter's own habits as to larger changes
in society. In his view, Peter was himself a modest man, who liked simple
things, but did introduce some foreign luxuries: Hungarian wine, Dutch
aniseed vodka and, although Shcherbatov did not focus on it, apparently
Limburger cheese.[59] He admitted, somewhat grudgingly, that figures like
Grigory Orlov – the nobleman who had helped Catherine seize the throne
in 1762 and who played an important role in the early years of her reign
– or even Catherine herself were also moderate in their tastes. In fact, he
said, Catherine was perhaps 'even too moderate'.[60]

There were two problems, Shcherbatov felt, that had turned the introduction of some new goods into a problem that corrupted morals. One
was individuals close to power who set a bad example for the court and
the larger society. He cited figures dating back to the reign of Elizabeth
whose individual epicurean tastes promoted luxury. He singled out one
of the Shuvalov brothers, important state figures during her reign, as an
example of luxurious living, above all because he created the first pineapple

In the 18th century, nobles began constructing elaborate greenhouses (orangeries) on their estates in order to produce their own tropical (and other) fruits. This is one of the greenhouses on the former imperial estate Tsaritsyno, in what used to be the Moscow suburbs. The original greenhouses date back to the middle of the 18th century; this reconstruction was completed in the early 21st century.

plantation in Russia (presumably under glass).[61] This was an outrageous transgression not only of the edicts of simplicity and logic but of natural law. The bulk of his ire, however, was aimed at one of his own contemporaries: Grigory Potemkin, the erstwhile lover of Catherine who was still an important figure in her reign. According to Shcherbatov, Potemkin was guilty of introducing

> love of power, ostentation, pandering to all his desires, gluttony and hence luxury at table, flattery, avarice, rapaciousness and, it may be said, all the other vices known in the world, with which he himself is full and with which he fills his supporters, and so on throughout the Empire.[62]

Shcherbatov did not extend his criticism of the world of noble luxury to a criticism of the larger social world based as it was in serfdom. He was, in fact, an ardent supporter and defender of serfdom. In another piece of writing unpublished during his lifetime, however, he explicitly linked luxury to a problem of poverty among Russia's peasant masses. Russia was facing a potential famine, he wrote, caused not by a poor harvest but by soaring grain prices. There was a whole series of reasons for this danger: an increase in the population; the decreasing fertility of agricultural lands and a failure to ameliorate this with new agricultural techniques; the growth of the distilling industry; exporting grain without a thought to internal conditions. First of all, though, was something else: 'the emergence of voluptuousness in all state ranks and even in the peasantry'.[63] When it came to the nobility, this voluptuousness was evident 'to anyone looking at our tables, rooms and buildings'. His evidence for the voluptuousness of the peasantry was more circumstantial. What used to supply two families only supplied one, now, he claimed. Even worse, peasants were leaving aside agricultural labour to move to towns and engage in trade or crafts there.

Shcherbatov's hope that these trends would be curtailed was not to be met. Instead, the later nineteenth century saw the end of serfdom and the rise of the town. Russia's population would still be overwhelmingly agricultural at the end of the nineteenth century, just as it had been at the time Shcherbatov was writing, but that population would be altered by changes in the social and economic order, particularly the end of serfdom and the rise of industry. The coming century would make Russia not entirely modern when viewed overall, but definitively part of the larger world of modernity, with all its pleasures and pitfalls.

SIX

Russia Becomes Modern

In 1883, Alexander III was crowned emperor of Russia in a grand ceremony in Moscow. This was not unusual – although the centre of the government had moved to St Petersburg during the reign of Peter I, coronation ceremonies were always held in the old capital, symbolizing the longer history of the Russian lands and the house of the Romanovs. Although the coronation ceremony itself took place over several hours on one single day, Alexander and his family stayed in Moscow for two weeks, meeting and greeting and being feted at banquet after banquet.

Alexander's stay in Moscow was shorter than those of his predecessors, but that shorter period was due to heightened security concerns (his father, after all, had been assassinated), not to any particular disinclination to stay in the old capital. In fact, Alexander was himself a staunch Russophile who believed himself to be linked if anything more strongly to the Muscovite tsarist past than to St Petersburg's Western, outward-looking gaze. That Russophile turn would come to play an important role during his reign, as Russification policies sought to bring the larger empire more and more firmly under a unitary Russian control. There were cultural elements of Russification, as well: Alexander's reign saw the rise of a new 'Russian-style' architecture, beards came back into fashion and the Fabergé egg became a symbol both of imperial opulence and of older Russian Easter traditions.[1]

Some of these elements were already visible during the coronation celebrations, perhaps nowhere as clearly as on the elaborate menus produced as souvenirs for the many, many feasts and banquets held around the old city. Two produced for official banquets held within the grounds of the Kremlin itself explicitly drew on the imagery of the old fortress. Both were designed by the painter Viktor Vasnetsov, who was at this moment moving away from the realism of mid-century Russian art to a more fantastical style grounded not in current reality but in an imagined past. The menu images are part of that new way of interpreting Russia's history. On one menu, bearded men in elaborate caftans from the era before Peter I walk down the stairs, with the symbols of Orthodoxy and the Romanov dynasty around them. On another, two men face the viewer, one dressed in the same kind of robes, the other wearing armour and astride a warhorse. Shields with the symbols of the emperor and empress make up part of the framing of the image. Both had the same image and text on the reverse: a group of men and women in traditional peasant garb, the man in the centre holding a tray with a huge loaf of bread – together with salt, one of the symbols of hospitality in Russia. The text was a poem by Apollon Maikov hailing the tsar.

The images of the menus, then, spoke to tradition and Russianness. The list of foods, however, spoke to the ways that tastes were more complicated than that. The menu for a dinner held on 27 May 1883 included:

Soup-purée of mushrooms	Roast turkey and snipe
Bouillon with root vegetables	Salad
Pirozhki	Asparagus with
Sterlet with cucumbers	Hollandaise sauce
Boiled beef	Hot *pirog* with pineapple
Quail with mashed peas	Ice cream
Cold dish of crab	Dessert

The meal was a fusion of Russian favourites and foreign imports that had become favourites: ice cream, pineapple, asparagus, salad. There were many other meals held in honour of the occasion around the empire, as well, and many of them featured similar mixes of dishes. A meal in Samara held on 17 May included *botvinia* with osetra and salt fish, soup *printanière*, roast beef with truffle sauce, steamed sterlet, asparagus and peas, roast fowl, pineapple gelatine, fruit, and tea and coffee. Others were simpler. A dinner held by the city of Moscow for the troops stationed in the city featured cold salt beef, filled *pirogi*, noodles with beef, roast mutton and a sweet pastry, all washed down with vodka, beer, mead and red wine.

All of this spoke to an agreeable mix of foods, reflecting an image of a comfortable state of affairs in the empire. Of course, that was only part of the story. On the one hand, the reign of Alexander III's father had seen sweeping reforms that tried to modernize Russian administration and

This menu for one of the elaborate dinners that marked Emperor Alexander III's coronation features self-consciously 'traditional' Russian imagery – but a meal that was a fusion of Russian and imported favourites.

society. The congenial world of the banquets could be read as an example of their successes. But on the other hand, the security of that world was challenged on two fronts: by a mass of peasants who were affected by the reforming urge but still left out of its ultimate hopes, and by a small but growing cohort of Russians who believed that more radical change – even revolution – was necessary. Some of them had even managed the ultimate act of terror in an autocratic society: killing the tsar himself in 1881.

If these banquets came to symbolize Alexander III's accession to the throne, a very different sort of event came to symbolize his son Nicholas II's coronation less than fifteen years later. Nicholas also travelled to Moscow for the events, and again there were banquets and balls around the old capital and the empire in celebration. This time, though, the event that was most remembered was not one of the elegant balls with elaborate menus, but instead the feast for the people held in conjunction with the more elite festivities. This was again not something new. Previous coronations had also been joined by popular feasts held outdoors in a field near the city. A French visitor described the popular feast held when Alexander II (r. 1855–81) was crowned:

The festival was set for two o'clock, and, at the signal of the
Emperor, the people were to set themselves at the provisions
which garnished the tables; but unfortunately, at a false signal
given at six o'clock in the morning, the impatient ones rushed
at the promised delights displayed before their eyes, and at two
o'clock nothing remained any more . . . nothing remained of
a repast prepared for two hundred thousand people, nothing
of the fifteen hundred steer, of the four thousand sheep with
gilded horns garnished with red calico . . . nothing of four
thousand hams, of one hundred thousand chickens, of one
hundred thousand ducks, of four thousand shoulders of pork,
of one hundred thousand cakes with cream, of two hundred
thousand kalatches (so they call a certain bread in the form
of a knot which the people eat in Russia).[2]

When Nicholas was crowned, a similar false start led to a disaster. Nicholas
had wanted the popular festival to be grander than any before, a symbol of
what he believed to be his mystical unity with the Russian people. A site
on Khodynka field was chosen for the event. News of the feast spread, and
hundreds of thousands of would-be revellers trekked to Moscow to take
part. Perhaps because the day was unusually hot and people were thus
exhausted and on edge, perhaps because the crowds were simply too big

The public festival at Khodynka for Nicholas II's coronation was supposed to proceed
like this: elite guests on view for the masses of common folk feasting on the fields below.
A failure of crowd control led to a tragedy instead.

to control, in a moment everything went wrong. A false start caused the crowd to push forward, but the barricades were still up. Hundreds were crushed against them, and then once they fell, were trampled under the feet of those behind them. In the space of mere minutes, more than 1,000 people were injured. The death toll in the end was somewhere around 1,500.[3]

The Khodynka tragedy became a symbol of the reign of Nicholas II not only because of the awful event itself but because of the way that Nicholas reacted to it. The feast went on even as the injured and the dead were being pulled from the scene. Nicholas came, and made no mention of what had happened just hours before. Later, he went on to dance at a ball held by the French ambassador – something intended to demonstrate resilience, but which was interpreted instead as tsarist indifference to suffering. As a result, the tragedy became a symbol of the increasing distance between the tsar and the people, even as he continued to believe they were somehow innately bound, and a sign of simmering discontent that would soon erupt.

The story of Russia from the middle of the nineteenth century to the beginning of the twentieth is one of contradictions. Russia was changing dramatically during these decades in ways that made it more and more modern. It industrialized (at least to a point), its population grew dramatically and began to spread out from the old core more and more intensively, and it engaged in a more consciously colonial imperial expansion in Central Asia. On another level, Russian subjects produced some of the most lasting works of world literature – this was the era of Dostoevsky and Tolstoy and Chekhov – and music – it was also the era of Tchaikovsky, Rimsky-Korsakov and the rest of the 'mighty handful'. But although many of these trends hoped in some way to reduce the distance between the privileged and the unprivileged, that distance not only remained but became the centre of political dissent that would bring the empire to its end.

After an eighteenth century notable for military victory after military victory, culminating with the triumph over Napoleon, the Russian Empire found itself in a very different position in the middle of the nineteenth century. Already embroiled in a lengthy colonial struggle in the Caucasus, in 1853 it entered into war with the Ottoman Empire. That proved to be a disaster. British and French forces joined the Ottomans, leaving Russia alone and forcing it to face the ways in which it had failed to innovate and modernize its military (and perhaps its economy as a whole). Emperor Nicholas I died as the war still lingered on, and his successor and son

Alexander II soon brought it to an end. The treaty that ended the war was a humiliation, and Alexander as a result inherited an empire that seemed in need of radical change.

At this point, that radical change took the form of a series of reforms that were so wide in their scope and deep in their effects that they have come to be known as the Great Reforms. The most fundamental of them was the 1861 Emancipation manifesto freeing Russia's serfs. From this point on, they were subject to no owner. All of Russia's peasants were now juridically equal. They received land as part of the Emancipation settlement, as well, but other than those living in a very small number of wealthy communities who were able to purchase the land outright or those who chose to forego a land allotment, they had to pay the state back for it. These 'redemption payments' were again assessed communally, and other provisions of the manifesto also affirmed a certain degree of control by peasant communities over their members.[4]

There were other reforms, as well. Educational reforms altered the governance of universities and also set up a network of primary schools intended to give every peasant at least a basic education (they were slow

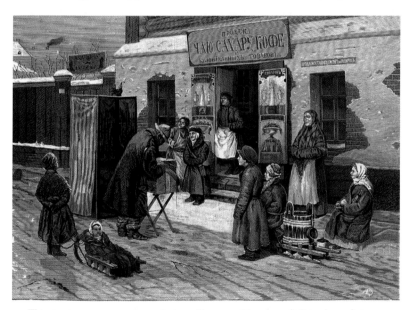

This street scene, purporting to be in a village near Moscow or St Petersburg, features a shop front offering 'Tea, Sugar, Coffee and Colonial Goods'. 'Colonial' was the term used as a shorthand for imported foods or ingredients from the larger colonial world like tea, coffee and spices, but which could also stretch to include things such as Swiss cheese. The illustration suggests that the sharp divide between wealth and poverty – or at least between worlds of eating – was beginning to fade at the end of the 19th century.

to grow, but were improving literacy rates by the end of the century). Secondary schools with an agricultural focus were also intended to improve peasant, and thereby the state's, economic health. These were run by provinces now governed by new provincial administrations called *zemstvos* that had an electoral element. There were reforms to the judicial system, to the censorship system, to municipal government. A reform of the army eliminated the old method of drafting peasant soldiers for life and instead instituted short-term universal (that is, now including all men, not just the lower ranks of society) military service.

Many of these reforms aimed at making the broader population more engaged in its own governance, but only at a local level. There were no attempts to create similar empire-wide institutions – governance from St Petersburg was still governance by ministries that answered only to the emperor. This meant that political dissent had no legitimate outlet, and so those who wanted more rapid or more intensive change came to meet and eventually act outside the boundaries of the law. In the 1870s, these revolutionaries came to be known as populists, as they believed they were acting in the best interests of the common people, though most of them were of more elite backgrounds. In 1881, a group of the most radical populists succeeded in their ultimate goal: killing the tsar.

The new tsar, Alexander III, also brought changes to the governance of the empire, but his changes aimed to increase centralized or elite control over the larger imperial world. Some of the *zemstvo's* autonomy was reduced, peasants found themselves subject to new Land Captains drawn from the ranks of the nobility, and policing was ratcheted up to a new degree. Alexander also pushed an image of himself as a truly Russian tsar, via innocuous actions such as wearing a beard and much less innocuous actions like promoting anti-Semitism and Russification policies through the wider empire. At the same time, Alexander's regime also began to push for a rapid industrialization of the empire, something that seemed necessary for the state's economic health, of course, but that also carried with it a potential for radical change.

Alexander died young, of natural causes perhaps exacerbated by injuries sustained in a train accident several years before. His son, the young Nicholas II, continued and expanded on Alexander's patriotic pretensions. Unfortunately for him, they did not serve to hold the country together, despite the efforts of groups like the thuggish Black Hundreds. Instead, Nicholas faced two crises, both sparked in part by military failures, the first in the Russo-Japanese War, the second in the First World War. The

Russo-Japanese War led to the first all-empire elective body, the Duma, and to the promise of more civil rights – but not to the dismantling of the policing structures of the regime. The First World War led to the entire collapse of the tsarist regime.

The Rural World After Emancipation

Emancipation brought radical change to rural life in Russia. From the point of view of the tsarist state, agriculture was still the basis of popular and state well-being. In particular, the state hoped that the Russian Empire could move from being self-sufficient in grain production to becoming a grain exporter. And so, efforts to improve agricultural productivity became a major focus of state intervention in the lives of its peasant population. This was not something entirely new, of course; in the earlier nineteenth century, when the Ministry of State Domains was founded to oversee state lands, including lands occupied by state peasants, part of its goal was to improve peasant agriculture. It sponsored agricultural journals and contests, promoted potatoes and other new crops and otherwise tried to get peasants and serf-owners to take agriculture more seriously. It also drew on agricultural societies like the Free Economic Society, founded during the reign of Catherine the Great, and a series of other regional agricultural societies that appeared over the course of the first half of the nineteenth century. In these, mostly noble landowners shared ideas for improving their estate economies through agricultural innovation.

After the abolition of serfdom, agricultural improvement remained a concern of noble landowners, the tsarist state and now, increasingly, peasants. Although the basis of the noble estate economy changed with the end of serfdom, some nobles continued to think about agriculture as a way of increasing their profits. The number of different agricultural societies, some only regional, some larger, continued to grow in ever increasing numbers. There had been one at the start of the nineteenth century, around thirty by the 1860s and up to three hundred (including regional outposts of main societies) by the end of the century.[5] They benefitted from increasing state resources aimed at improving agriculture. The Ministry of State Domains pushed its agricultural reform agenda to the fore and was in the 1890s renamed the Ministry of Agriculture. In addition, agricultural schools primarily aimed at peasants appeared in many localities; these were the major kind of secondary school available to peasants, training them for positions as agronomists.

These efforts, combined with other changes in markets and in the economy as a whole, created both large-scale and small-scale agricultural changes. The small-scale changes often varied by region. In New Russia – now split between southern Ukraine and Russia – peasants began to engage in more conscious production for nearby urban markets like Odessa. Fruit, vegetables, honey – all were demanded by urban consumers and increasingly supplied by local peasants.[6] On the southern steppe, too, agriculturists began more and more to cultivate wheat for both domestic consumption and export. One American traveller claimed that 'the best bread I ever ate was in the cities of Mexico and of Moscow . . . The reason of this excellence is, no doubt, the fine wheat, which is raised in both countries.'[7] Other regions came to specialize in particular commercial crops like tobacco or sugar beet.

In the late nineteenth century, too, the Russian state encouraged peasants to move to Siberia to take advantage of lands there that had not yet been cultivated. Millions set out in the 'great Siberian migration'.[8] One of the successes of this new Siberian agricultural effort was a rise in butter production around the city of Omsk. In the last decades of the tsarist era,

> this butter trade has grown to such an extent that to handle
> the traffic the railway . . . had to provide 1,080 refrigerator
> cars, each of which was reckoned to carry fifteen tons each.
> A weekly service of seven trains was arranged for, and each
> train had a full complement of some thirty-five cars. These
> carried their freights to Petrograd, Riga and other Baltic
> ports, whence steamships carried the butter to England.
> It was not an infrequent event for a thousand tons of
> Siberian butter to be delivered in London in a single week.[9]

The successes of Siberian butter aside, the major large-scale change in agriculture was above all Russia's emergence as a global supplier of grain. The change was significant and rapid. In the early 1860s, Russia exported nearly 80,000 *pudy* of grain each year; a decade later, the number was just under 195,000 *pudy*; a decade after that, just over 300,000 *pudy*; and in the early 1890s just over 440,000 *pudy*. This was a huge amount, bringing in by the end of the period just under 300 million roubles in foreign currency – or just under half of the empire's total income from foreign trade. And yet it was also a relatively small proportion of the grain produced in the country as a whole – an enormous 4 billion *pudy* of grain each year,

Russia's imperial expansion allowed it to produce not only tobacco and sugar beets on the southern steppe but even more delicate crops, such as tea. Russia imported tea overland from China starting in the 17th century, but as its empire expanded it acquired territories southern enough to produce tea. One was in what is now the Republic of Georgia, at Chavki, beginning in the late tsarist period. This photograph shows tea being measured out and packed. The tea produced here never amounted to a large share of the tea consumed in the country, but let the Soviet Union lay claim to growing 'the northernmost tea in the world'.

consumed either at the point of production or through the vast network of the empire's internal trade system.[10]

The cultural world of the Russian peasant was of course also transformed by the end of serfdom. Above all, its end took away the most egregious way in which serfs had been disadvantaged and unprivileged by the social and political order: they were no longer subject to the whims of individual owners. The other provisions of the Emancipation settlement were a more mixed bag in the minds of many peasants. The process of dividing lands between landlords and peasants was slanted in favour of the landlords, so peasants often received (or at least believed they received) inferior lands. Peasants had to pay for land that they had viewed as essentially theirs because they were the ones who farmed it. And because those payments were made communally, peasants were not entirely free to move about as they wished. If they took a land allotment at the time of

Although Emancipation brought real change to the countryside, many everyday
aspects of peasant life continued largely undisturbed. Most were still heavily engaged
in agriculture, which meant summers of hard labour and meals taken out in the open air,
as in this photograph from 1909.

Emancipation, they were bound to their commune by their redemption
payments.

In many ways, Russian peasants lived much the same lives after serfdom
as they had as serfs. Even at the very end of the nineteenth century, travellers
who stopped at peasant villages reported much the same kind of greeting
as had their predecessors several centuries before. The American Francis
B. Reeves reported being served 'excellent' tea along with 'a small bottle of
vodka, a large loaf of black bread, a dozen hard-boiled eggs, and four salted
cucumbers' when he visited a village in the early 1890s.[11] Peasants still largely
farmed, and still largely remained within the commune, where households
structured everyday life. If they wished to travel away from the village, they
needed a passport or other travel document to do so. Larger trends in the
economy, particularly the rise of industry late in the century, gave them
greater incentive to do so. So, too, did challenges internal to the village. In
particular, population growth in the second half of the century began to

put real strains on the capacity of peasant lands to support them. Peasant land allotments fell significantly over the course of the century despite the fact that peasants purchased more and more lands.

Although there had always been differences between Russia's northern forested zone and its southern steppe lands, those were if anything magnified by the end of the tsarist period. The former were the heartland of the old Russia, with long traditions of work off the land made necessary by its poor fertility and by the long winters. The latter had been settled as Muscovite and then imperial authority moved south, accompanied by the spread of serfdom, often with labour duties that demanded physical presence. This came to have a significant influence on peasant diet. At the beginning of the twentieth century the average daily energy intake of a peasant was 4,500 kcal, 15.3 per cent of which came from animal foods. But in some (not all) northern provinces the norms were closer to 5,000 kcal a day, 20 per cent from animal foods, while in some southern provinces it was as low as 3,111 kcal a day, with only 4.2 per cent from animal foods.[12]

One thing that did not change either over time or through much of the empire's geographical expanse was the hospitality of the Russian peasant (at least according to foreign travellers). August von Kotzebue, who was exiled to Siberia in the late 1790s, found Russia's peasants to be among the most hospitable people he had ever encountered, freely offering bread and *kvas* and accepting small amounts for 'poultry, cream, and eggs'.[13] Through the nineteenth century, other travellers often agreed. Robert Pinkerton stated that 'brown bread, eggs, milk, salted cucumbers, radishes, &c. &c., are readily produced by the mujik and his wife, in their humble izba; and it is seldom that they will consent to accept any compensation.'[14] Even much later and in much starker circumstances, peasants were reported to be generous to passers-by, whatever their reason for passing. A late-nineteenth-century traveller claimed that

> even in Siberia the peasantry do their best to lighten the journey of the weary pilgrim on the great post road that leads to the Pacific. Enter a village after sunset and you will see on every doorstep a bowl of milk and wedge of black bread. They are placed there for the brodyag, or escaped convict, who dare not by day emerge from the dark, pathless wood, but who is, at night at any rate, free from molestation and sure of a meal.[15]

The Smirnov vodka brand dates back to the middle of the 19th century, and by the end of the
century it had become a thriving concern – its display at the 1896 Industrial Exposition in
Nizhnii Novgorod features seals that showed the prizes and awards its vodkas had won.
Of course, it was about to face a huge reverse: the state vodka monopoly.

Another source of continuity was vodka – and worries about its consumption. Although concern over drink had a long history in Russia, it reached a new peak at the end of the nineteenth century. Over the course of the 1890s, concerned citizens founded temperance societies in many parts of the Russian Empire. According to an account from 1895, 'every day provincial newspapers bring news from various parts of European Russia of the rise of temperance societies and of the resolutions of rural societies to close taverns.'[16] But it also hinted at the continued central tension when it came to strong drink: there were both 'state sales of spirits' and 'provincial and district committees to oversee public temperance'. How could both of these be goals of the state?

These tensions had played out in various ways over the course of the nineteenth century. One of the Great Reforms abolished the system of tax farming established by Catherine the Great, which had been blamed for increasing alcohol consumption. Instead, the state levied taxes on both distilling and selling vodka. Although it was hoped that this system would slow a perceived rise in the number of taverns and in the presence of drunkenness, it did not. Early in Sergei Witte's tenure as the Minister of Finance (1892–1903), his ministry introduced a new state vodka monopoly to control the production of hard spirits. In principle, the monopoly was supposed to restrict vodka consumption (in particular, vodka could only be purchased at stores, not in taverns or restaurants where food was served). To make an even better claim that the monopoly helped to control popular drunkenness, an imperial temperance society also became an official state office. But in practice, alcohol consumption continued to rise, and the state's claims seemed hollow when compared to its enormous profits.[17] From 1803 to 1914, alcohol accounted for an average of 31 per cent of the imperial state's revenues; that proportion had been falling after a peak just before the Great Reforms, but began to rise again with the establishment of the monopoly.[18]

Some saw a tendency to drunkenness as a particular problem for the peasants, others for certain regions. One traveller claimed that everyone in Siberia was inclined to drunkenness to 'frightful proportions'.[19] Another noted that both rural and urban Russians 'may differ in their hats, [but] they do not differ in their taste for vodka'.[20] T. V. Privalova, however, argues that the degree of drunkenness among the peasantry was probably overstated. In 1913, the average consumption of alcoholic beverages ranged from 18 to 43 litres (approx. 4–11 UK/U.S. gall.) per person per year in

By the end of the tsarist era, vodka consumption had come to seem like an enormous problem to at least some Russian (and foreign) observers – and for many of those observers, the fact that the vodka monopoly tied drinking directly to the interests of the tsarist state made it seem particularly damaging. This poster from around 1917 shows elites including the tsar himself standing in front of a state vodka shop, ready to take a humble peasant's money.

towns to 4.5–8 litres (approx. 1–2 UK/U.S. gall.) per person per year in the village; and Privalova notes that these were lower numbers than around the same time in France and Britain.[21] Even so, the idea that Russia was facing a crisis of drunkenness was incredibly strong and discussed in ministries and in the pages of Russia's press. It may in the end have more to do with the fact that Russia was changing dramatically in these years – and nothing changed more than the rise of the town in the vision of what it meant to be Russian.

The Rise of the Town

The Russian Empire was still a predominantly peasant, agricultural world even at the turn of the twentieth century. According to the first all-Russian census, held in 1897, agricultural labour was by far the most common occupation: 75 per cent of the population listed it as its primary occupation (in both the empire as a whole and in European Russia in particular). But that large number hid some radical differences that were already coming into the Russian world. In many of the European Russian provinces both north and south, locals were even more likely to engage primarily in agricultural labour: in relatively southerly Voronezh province, 85 per cent of the population were agriculturists; in northern Viatka province, 89 per cent were. Vladimir province, on the other hand, had historically been home to a growing textile industry, and by 1897 only 58 per cent of its residents farmed as their primary occupation. Numbers were even lower near the two capitals: in Moscow province only 28 per cent of the population farmed; in St Petersburg province, only 25 per cent did so.[22] Most of the reason for those radical differences in occupation had to do with one simple fact: Moscow and St Petersburg provinces were home to by far the largest cities in the empire – the only two with populations of more than 1,000,000 – and so had significantly larger urban populations than did any of the other provinces. In smaller towns, agriculture was still an important part of the local economy. But here and near other large towns around the empire, town populations were moving away into very, very different worlds.

In an imperial Russian town, food was everywhere. At the beginning of the nineteenth century, one German visitor had described the scene:

> the farmer who brings his goods to sell in town, is not bound
> in Russia to expose them to the purchasers in the open market

Street vendors roamed around Russia's towns, bringing their wares out from central markets to residential neighbourhoods. This illustration shows a whole series of such vendors, selling food and drink of all kinds (and toys and balloons and even chairs).

only; on the contrary, he has the liberty to hawk them about the town, and his customers willingly pay a few copeques more for the advantage of supplying their wants at their own doors.[23]

All sorts of foods and drinks were freely sold on the street by vendors. Foreign visitors were startled by this array of, as one put it, 'iks', after the

The Corner Shop

By law, shops in imperial Russia were categorized in three ways: who could run them, where they could be located and what they could sell in them. Only people classified as merchants could run certain high-status shops in merchant arcades. People of lower social status, however, were allowed to sell wares in *melochnye* shops – after the word *meloch*, small change. These corner shops were allowed anywhere in Russian cities, not only in central trading areas, in part to be sure that the larger population had convenient access to supplies. The shops might be trivial according to their name, but they were filled with not only necessities but some luxuries. An 1826 list of the various wares they were allowed to sell included: tea, coffee, sugar and various spices; olives, capers, olive oil, mustard, pepper and vinegar; '*prianiki* and assorted peasant treats'; herring and various salted and dried fish; baked bread of various sort and rolls; fruits, berries, vegetables and greens of domestic production and preserves; preserved cabbage, cucumbers and other local vegetables; salt, molasses, honey, chicory coffee and eggs; oil of various sorts; groats of various sorts and flour; milk, *tvorog* and sour cream (as well as assorted non-food items like soap, candles and ribbons).[24] After a period of much more restricted sales, in many ways, post-Soviet Russia has returned to a similar world of small food shops that offer a bit of everything, scattered throughout major (and not so major) cities.

suffix denoting a vendor: *chaichik* (tea-seller), *khlebchik* (bread-seller), *kolbasnik* (sausage-seller).[25]

In addition, there were shops and markets scattered around the cities. St Petersburg, for example, had not only huge trading areas filled with shops but smaller shops dispersed around the city on the ground floor of buildings, the wares 'in just one of which would be sufficient to provide for a good-sized provincial town'.[26] In the early 1830s St Petersburg had more than 200 taverns, inns, restaurants, not counting food shops. Even the working people: day labourers, masons, guards, bridge watchers, barge haulers – everyone can drink tea and coffee in restaurants decorated with such taste, and furnished with such furniture, that one cannot but be amazed by the contrast between coarse caftans and the fine material of couches, armchairs and the like.[27]

There were restaurants, too, where an elite but increasingly socially mixed crowd came to dine. There were different types of restaurants and cafés, all regulated in different ways. A restaurant (*restoran*) could serve certain foods and drinks, a *traktir* (often translated tavern, but serving food as much as drink) a different array and another type of tavern called a *kharchevnia* yet another. The last was explicitly regulated as an establishment intended to feed the 'working people' or 'people of the lower class' in growing cities. The restaurant, on the other hand, was regulated so that 'people both bound to service [that is, imperial bureaucrats] and otherwise finding themselves in towns have meals appropriate to their condition'. The *traktir* was somewhere in the middle. The *kharchevnia* and the restaurant were places where distinctly different people ate. In fact, in 1834, a decree stated that peasants were not allowed 'to enter coffeehouses, restaurants, and *traktiry* in simple peasant dress'.[28]

By the end of the tsarist era, the number of such eating establishments had grown enormously and the simple association of restaurant with elite dining had been blurred. According to an 1880s travel guide to Moscow (for Russians), a *traktir* of the 'first degree' served 'portions from 80 kopeks. A single man will be satisfied with a half-portion for dinner. In restaurants it is cheaper, but the portions are smaller.' The guide went on to recommend the Hermitage for its 'French cuisine, satisfying the most exquisite taste' and the 'Big Moscow *traktir*' for its French and Russian cooking as well as its handsome look, which had, the author noted, recently brought it to the attention 'even of foreigners'. This guide recommended *traktiry* above all, describing the city's restaurants as 'mostly bars for beer, frequented by Germans, artists and theatrical musicians'.[29]

A St Petersburg guide from 1896 noted that a dinner at a restaurant there would cost 1 rouble or more; at a good *traktir* 50 kopeks; and at a *kukhmisterskii stol*, a cooking-master's table, 30–50 kopeks. In addition, St Petersburg had canteens (*stolovye*), 'in which dine primarily trading people. In these canteens dinners are undoubtedly always of the very

One of the most famous restaurants in Russia was the Trinity *traktir* in Moscow. Usually a *traktir* was a lower-status eating establishment than a restaurant, but the Trinity catered to an elite crowd, and was known as much for its waitstaff as for its clientele.

freshest provisions; they are not only remarkable for their service, but are completely fine.' In these, a dinner might cost only 20–30 kopeks. (The guide also advised avoiding so-called 'Greek kitchens' – the cheapest version of a canteen – other than in the direst situation.)[30] A 1913 guide to 'all business-industrial Russia' listed nearly 150 restaurants in St Petersburg, ranging from the Aquarium to the Iar, and 67 in Moscow including the Alpine Rose and the El Dorado.[31]

In the nineteenth century, Moscow's most famous restaurant was the Trinity *traktir* (sometimes also called the New Trinity *traktir*) on Ilinka street, one of the streets radiating out from Red Square:

> In twelve nicely decorated rooms around fifty tables are set,
> and bureaucrats, merchants, artists, travellers come to feast.
> A mixture of voices is heard, someone demanding food,
> someone Champagne, Madeira, Margaux, beer, and forty-
> three waiters hustle, hurry, scurry. They are dressed the same,
> in long tunics almost to the ankle of white buckram, very
> proper, with moustaches and muttonchops . . . As soon as
> one person leaves, another enters, and the tobacco-filled

atmosphere rarely clears. In the winter up to half a *pud* [about 8 kg/18 lb] of tea and up to three *pudy* [49 kg/108 lb] of sugar are drunk, and the income is up to 2,000 roubles.[32]

Diners consumed a huge amount of other foods, too: each day they went through the meat of three milk-fed calves and 270 kilograms (600 lb) of other meats, 50–60 sterlets, 100 bottles of champagne and more than 2,000 servings of different breads. Descriptions of meals there emphasize both luxury and the homely and domestic. One meal consisted of 'first and as always, caviar', then *shchi* served with *pirogi*, then several courses of meats and fish – a suckling pig, beef, sterlet – and at the end grapes and tea. Champagne was served throughout the dinner along with *lompopo*, a beverage one French visitor described as a mixture of beer, lemon, sugar and toasted black bread – 'a mixture agreeable to drink, but disagreeable to see'.[33]

The French traveller Boucher de Perthes ate several meals at the Trinity when he visited in the 1850s. His last meal there was a grand affair, served, he was told, 'entirely à la russe'. His neighbour, a merchant, had invited Boucher de Perthes and another guest to dine. Their meal was extravagant:

The meal was what our guide promised. It began with a cold soup which had *kvas* for bouillon, in which cucumbers had been cut up; there was added some sugar, pepper, salt, mustard, olive oil and slices of sturgeon. This is the favourite soup of Russians. Here, contrary to the proverb, it seemed to me that it was the fish that made it possible to eat the sauce ... Another national dish followed, no less renowned: a sort of pastry, of which the crust is soft and fairly light, but tough and hard to break. Under this crust is a filling of meat mixed with sturgeon. One dips the whole thing in a fatty or lean bouillon, served on a separate dish ... As another course, we had slices of a raw fish, very red and very salty, which we were presented before the soup, but which the Russian and the young woman were the only to enjoy ... A quarter of suckling pig followed the red fish, and at the end as a finale came the classic sterlet decorated with olives and pickles. This fish is good, but it seemed to me no better than the sturgeon, which it resembled in form although it was much smaller ... The dinner finished with a plate of mushrooms and of some sweets. We drank raspberry *kvas*, very fresh and very good; then, a glass of a liqueur in which, the waiter told me, there were forty kinds of herbs; it was no better … This meal cost us one and a half rouble and ten kopeks per person, or around seven francs, which seems to me little for the number of plates; the expense would have doubled if we had drunk wine.[34]

By the end of the nineteenth century restaurants in Russia's great cities had become sites of luxury and display that also came to change Russian cuisine. In the middle of the century, the restaurant at L'Hermitage in Moscow was home to a chef named Lucien Olivier. He created a composed cold dish of potatoes and pickles, grouse and crayfish, all with an olive-oil-based mayonnaise. The separate ingredients came to be mixed together to form 'salad Olivier'. It was revived in the 1930s and became a staple of the Soviet canteen – and even more, it moved outside Russia to become 'Russian Salad' in many other cuisines.[35]

The masses of people, of course, never set foot in such temples of gastronomy, nor tasted their wares. But towns did have many other sorts of restaurants or cafés that catered to a wider clientele. The *kharchevnia* or *traktir* took the place of the tavern or pub or cafés that might feed a broader population; by the end of the tsarist era so too did the first canteens. Other than unusual examples like the Trinity, rarely were they visited by anyone elite – in the middle of the century, one Russian writer joked that he needed a chaperone/guide even just to enter a *traktir*.[36] A few decades later an early budget travel writer (the author of *A Tramp Trip: How to See Europe on 50 Cents a Day*) nonetheless recommended the *kharchevnia* for an affordable meal: 'very good dinners are served for twenty or thirty kopeks – ten or fifteen cents. Hard-boiled eggs, pickles, salted or smoked fish, and pastry filled with mushrooms, rice, and meat, form the ordinary bill of fare in these places.'[37] (Although he did not mention it, they probably also had soup.)

Particularly at the start of the twentieth century, and through much of the Russian Empire, not just its old Russian parts, some of these many new restaurants and cafés and *kharchevni* and *traktiry* advertised in cheap kopek newspapers to try to lure diners not just from the affluent few but from the masses, as well.[38] In Odessa, the 'people's restaurant' The Bear promised 'light, air and hygiene! Fresh, tasty and cheap! Tea, dinners, suppers and drinks.' In its third-class dining room, it offered tea for 8 kopeks for a single diner, 12 kopeks for two diners and 20 kopeks for four.[39]

This ad for the restaurant at the Hotel Versailles in Tiflis (now Tbilisi, Georgia) features two gentlemen having a conversation about the delights that await within, from 'coffee, cream and tea' in the morning to 'foreign drinks and Russian cordials too'.

Утромъ кофе, сливки, чай
За журналомъ не скучай;
Завтракъ, водка и вино
Удовольствіе одно!
Обѣды сытные всегда
Не дороги никогда.
И порціо нно кушать можно,
Какъ дешевле невозможно
Цоцхали идетъ очень ходко
Для любителя находка,
Загр аничные напитки,
Есть и русскія наливки
Гдѣ же? гдѣ жъ, все это?
Догадаться очень трудно
Коль не знаешь ресторана
Подъ гостинницей ,,Версаль''
Это правда а не враль!

960 10—3.

In Kiev, the restaurant Iar promised that 'all its dishes are prepared with fresh butter'.[40] An Odessa restaurant ('the newly refurbished BIG café at the Onipko bakery') also promised fresh butter, as did Logovskii's establishment in Saratov and the Café Paris in Tiflis. (Perhaps the rise of the Siberian butter industry made butter such a focus.) The Café Paris offered meals 'of European and Asian dishes under the care of an experienced chef' – here 'Asian' almost certainly meant Georgian, as the one food specifically highlighted with capital letters is the (delicious) Georgian cheese bread *khachapuri*.[41]

These various cafés and restaurants were the site not only of meals but of a new way of living in the world. Even in the pages of kopek newspapers aimed at anything but an elite audience, restaurants and cafés advertised both meals and entertainment in ways that aptly demonstrate the hybrid nature of late tsarist culture. In 1913, the restaurant North Pole in Saratov

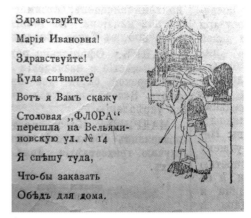

These two ads for the Tiflis canteen Flora show two distinct potential customers.
In one, three men have a conversation about the great value of eating at the canteen.
In the other two women discuss ordering food from the canteen to eat at home –
for them, public eating was not yet quite a done thing.

promised daily performances by 'a male choir in boyar costumes' as well
as Ukrainian dancers.[42] Others promised Romanian or Italian orchestras
or, at The Bear in Odessa, 'cinematographic pictures of an educational
character'.[43] At the Nizhnii Novgorod restaurant Apollo, a diner could
even make use of the restaurant's automobile to go for a ride after his meal
(price subject to agreement).[44]

Such establishments also promised the beginnings, but only the barest
hint of beginnings, of a different world for women. Restaurants were an
almost entirely male environment through most of the nineteenth century.
When Boucher de Perthes visited the Trinity in the 1850s, he noted that
his party created a commotion among the other diners because it included
a woman, a fact that he noted 'shocked me; this lady was pretty without a
doubt, she was well dressed, yet there was nothing in either her beauty or
in her toilette, that could motivate the sensation that she produced'.[45] The
sensation was, of course, her mere presence in a generally all-male environment. Most of the advertisements from the end of the tsarist era also suggest
that dining out was a male realm: they are almost entirely addressed to
possible male diners, who are often portrayed as chatting over the value of
a meal.[46] One exception is an ad for the Tiflis cafeteria Flora, in which two
very well-dressed women have a brief conversation that suggests that such
institutions were beginning to reach out to women consumers, albeit in a
restricted way: 'Hello Maria Ivanovna! Hello! Where are you rushing off
to? Well, I'll tell you – the cafeteria Flora has moved to Veliaminovskaia
street No. 14. I'm rushing there to order a dinner for home.'[47]

The world of multi-course dinners with live orchestral accompaniment promised to the readers of late imperial Russia's kopek press was probably not much more than a dream for most of them. Those readers were not the wealthy, but the urban masses, whose numbers were growing during the late tsarist period. Over the course of the second half of the nineteenth century more and more workers came to towns or industrial regions to work in factories. Industrialization was a conscious goal of the imperial state in the aftermath of the Crimean War, which was a debacle in part because Russia's military was technologically behind its foes. As a result, more and more factories appeared throughout the Russian Empire, although clustered in particular regions and around cities, and more and more workers came to them to work, at least part of the time. Peasants had to purchase passports to travel to work in towns, but only a few were able to turn that permission to permanent residence. Few had individual homes or even apartments with individual kitchens; instead, renting a room or even just a corner of a room was common. By the early twentieth century the problem had become acute. According to one Russian journalist, residential buildings in London held an average of 7.9 people. Moscow's buildings held 28 and St Petersburg's 52 people. This was not simply a reflection of the size of the buildings. A single room in a St Petersburg or Moscow building housed just over 8 people, compared to 4.5 in London (and even slightly fewer in Vienna, Berlin or Paris).[48]

As a result, all sorts of different practices developed to feed the itinerant working population. The fact that there were many sources of cooked foods, either from wandering sellers or from informal stands, helped to supply many eaters and had done so from much earlier periods. Earlier in the century, August von Haxthausen, who was interested in the communal forms of labour and peasant organization he saw in Russia, had been struck by the way that much of Odessa's labouring population ate:

> I was particularly interested with the old bazaar, where are the cook-shops and booths for bread. In the market here are to be seen, at all times of the day, but particularly at noon, crowds of people sitting upon benches in the open air, eating. The beggars and vagrants, as well as the greater part of the labouring classes, have no houses of their own; instead of cooking at home, they get their dinners from the cook-shops in this bazaar. Here may be seen the habits of the various peoples; the Russians for instance are distinguished by a

certain kind of ceremonial which they go through. Before
sitting down to dine the Russian takes off his cap, turns his
face toward the nearest church, and makes the sign of the
cross. His dinner is always brought to him by waiters with
white aprons, and he never eats without seating himself at
table; in short he always shows himself a man of breeding
... This way of living appears expensive and luxurious, the
common man thus receiving substantial nourishment,
generally animal food and fish, but it is in fact the cheapest
and most suitable. The wife, not having to purchase and cook
the provisions, can herself earn money by work; and the food
is provided wholesale by the people in these shops much more
cheaply than the people could obtain it for themselves.[49]

Several decades later, another traveller described something similar in the
major trading city of Nizhnii Novgorod:

near the 'Siberian Line' that skirts the Volga are several soup-
kitchens well worthy of a visit. For the sum of five copecks
(about 1½ d.) labourers are supplied in them with an ample
dinner consisting of soup and black bread *ad libitum*, and of
about one pound of *kasha*, or buck-wheat porridge – the staple
food of the Russian masses. The average consumption of bread
alone is one and a half pound per man, but it is not at all rare to
find a labourer capable of disposing of three pounds. No spirits
or ale are allowed, but tea is available throughout the day, at a
charge of three copecks, or less than a penny.[50]

As larger factories appeared, employing larger numbers of workers in
close quarters, other systems developed. In many cases, Russian workers
fed themselves using a collective *artel* system. This had a long history in
Russia associated with the all-male environment of the military. There,
soldiers grouped together to purchase and prepare their food as a unit.
The same practice came to Russia's factory centres. The English traveller
Henry Sutherland Edwards was particularly struck by this system: 'the
workmen elect one caterer or steward, who buys for all, presides at the
general banquet, and is re-eligible every month.' This was, he thought,
very significant. He noted:

The associations of operatives at the Russian fabrics [factories] are formed only with a view to buying provisions on the cheapest terms, and cannot offend any theorist, or indeed any one at all, except, perhaps, the neighbouring butchers and bakers, who would evidently gain more money if each workman bought his food separately.[51]

Even more significant was his conclusion:

it seemed to show, however, what I had often been told by Russians of all opinions, that the Russian peasants are a sensible, dutiful, well-behaved, manageable class, having confidence in one another, and respecting, as individual members of a community in which each member has a voice, the general decision of that community.[52]

Little did he dream that this 'dutiful, well-behaved, manageable class' would soon take part in revolution.

The Return of Famine and the Collapse of the Tsarist Regime

All of this change, all of this growth, all of these new possibilities, were breathtaking. And yet, despite it all, at the beginning of the 1890s the Russian Empire faced a famine the likes of which it had not seen since the Time of Troubles. 'Here in Russia famine is still even now a terrible guest, thanks to the poverty of our agricultural population, poor cultivation of land, the absence of a sufficient quantity of good and cheap roads and means of transportation,' wrote a historian in 1913.[53] Russia might have appeared to be becoming modern, but famine suggested otherwise.

Through much of the nineteenth century various arms of the tsarist state had actively tried to combat the threat of famine. In some ways, the Russian Empire had been lucky. The terrible famine at the beginning of the seventeenth century was the last such event for nearly three centuries. Although regions of the empire had faced bad harvests with some regularity, those events generally led to short-term, localized distress rather than mass famine. In principle, during the time of serfdom lords were supposed to make sure that their serfs did not starve, although there is some evidence that that did not always happen. And there were other efforts to make sure that both peasants and townspeople stayed fed. Starting in the early eighteenth century, the *taksa* – set prices on certain goods – tried to make sure that people in towns had access to food. Prices were set on bread, and on meat and fish, and were adjusted in part based on the actual fluctuation in the cost of raw materials and in part on the petitions of bakers. In the countryside, this method would not work. Instead, starting at the end of the eighteenth century, peasants were required to deliver grain every year to a communal granary to be held in reserve should a bad harvest wipe out a new year's seed. Initially, this was limited to court peasants, those that belonged to the Romanov dynasty personally, when Emperor Paul ordered them to start keeping such stores. In the early nineteenth century, when a series of bad to very bad harvests made everyone worried that famine was again around the corner, all peasants were forced to keep them.[54]

Up until the very end of the nineteenth century, this seemed to work, at least mostly. There were regular bad harvests, just as there always had been. There was still suffering as a result. Reports regularly circulated describing the many surrogates for bread that peasants ate in times of particular dearth: moss, bark, acorns, grass, hay. For the most part, though, the state could believe that it had managed to put into place a system to stop these difficulties from getting dramatically worse in the way that they had in the past – or even than they had more recently in different parts of the world.

Then, the system failed. In the good grain-growing regions of the Russian Empire, 1890 was a bad year – dry, with an early deep frost. The winter of 1890–91 was bad, too, with snow but also wind that dried up the ground already sown with winter crops. A late frost in 1891 was followed by early extreme heat. The result was predictable: a terrible harvest.[55] According both to observers at the time and to later historians, however, the terrible harvest was made into a terrible famine in part by bad decisions on the part of the tsarist state.

A. S. Ermolov, a high-ranking official in the Ministry of Finance who would soon become the Minister of Agriculture and State Domains, recalled travelling through southern Russia in the spring of 1891 and seeing all the signs of the bad harvest to come. He travelled through the area on a train, and was disturbed both by the devastated country he saw outside the window and by the newspaper articles he read on the way, filled with plans to raise grain prices and improve Russia's balance of trade by increasing grain exports. He also recalled sending a memo to the Minister of Finance, Ivan Vyshnegradskii, warning him of the bad times to come and

Famine conditions ranged from Arkhangelsk in the north to Astrakhan in the south, from Poltava in the west to Ufa and Turgaisk in the east. This illustration highlights some of the ways that the famine was interpreted – peasants facing a cold, uncaring bureaucratic state exemplified by uniformed soldiers – and hints at the ways that the famine was part of the undoing of the tsarist system in what turned out to be its waning years.

hoping that 'the most decisive measures' might soon be taken to ward off famine. Vyshnegradskii, who was set on improving Russia's balance of trade in order to get the rouble on the gold standard, angrily threw the memo into the rubbish.[56]

Ermolov proved to be correct. Famine conditions hit 29 provinces and regions of Russia: Arkhangelsk, Astrakhan, Kaluga, Kazan, Kharkov,

Kherson, Kostroma, Kursk, Nizhnii Novgorod, Olonets, Orel, Orenburg, Penza, Perm, Poltava, Riazan, Samara, Saratov, Simbirsk, Tambov, Tobolsk, Tula, Ufa, Voronezh and Viatka provinces as well as the districts of the Urals, the Don Cossacks, Akmolinsk and Turgaisk (that is, what is now southern Ukraine and Kazakhstan). All thoughts of getting Russia on the gold standard by exporting grain were forgotten, at least for the moment. Instead, central tsarist state offices and local administrations spent around 175,000,000 roubles on aid to those suffering from famine.[57] More money and aid in kind came from private donors: the Red Cross, local groups, individuals.

Despite this aid, the death toll was high – perhaps 500,000 in excess mortality during these two years, much of it caused by the wave of cholera that travelled along with the famine conditions. The tsarist state took the crisis seriously enough not only to put into action immediate relief efforts but to begin collecting information from the provinces in the hope of overhauling the laws on provisioning. Opinions on the best way forward varied widely, however. In the end, new regulations were produced in 1900. According to Ermolov, one of their main components was taking responsibility for provisioning in times of need away from villages themselves and also away from *zemstvo* administrations, which were responsible to the people of the provinces, and placing it instead on regional offices of the tsarist state.[58] In other words, it made the tsarist administration, and by extension the tsar himself, responsible for provisioning. In this moment that seemed an expression of the tsar's own care for his peasants. Soon, however, it would prove to be his undoing.

Everything came crashing to an end during the First World War, for the Russian Empire's experience of the Great War was not one of nation building but instead one of imperial destruction. Only a decade before, the Russian Empire had gone to war with Japan in the hope of reasserting itself as a major player on the world stage. Instead, it found itself soundly defeated on its far periphery and embroiled in unrest throughout its European lands. Called the Revolution of 1905, this unrest hit every part of society. Workers went on strike, eventually paralysing the normal functioning of towns including the capital, St Petersburg. Soldiers and sailors mutinied, most famously on the battleship *Potemkin*, a mutiny sparked by maggot-infested meat. Peasants rioted, almost always in the name of the land they worked and believed they ought to own. This revolution led to the creation of Russia's first assembly, the State Duma, though in the end it failed to put an end to dissatisfaction with the working of the autocracy.

The First World War made the traumas of the Russo-Japanese War pale in comparison. Although Russian forces eventually had some success in the south and southwest against the Ottoman Empire and Austria-Hungary, their initial experience of the war involved a rapid retreat until the front stabilized in extensive networks of trenches. All of this led to one of the major problems that faced the Russian state on the home front: a problem of supply. The scale of the war led to a refugee crisis as people fled its violence. By the end of 1915 official sources counted 3.3 million refugees; by the beginning of 1917, the number had risen to 6 million.[59] The infrastructure and resources of Russia's towns were already stressed by the influx of new workers that had accompanied the rise of industry, and the millions of refugees now also needed to be fed and sheltered.

Discontent was growing on the home front, and food was at the heart of that discontent. This came as a surprise to the tsarist state. As Lars Lih notes, the government did not expect provisioning to be a problem because the empire had seemed so firmly established as a grain exporter by the onset of the war. (Of course, this ignores the famine that had hit just over two decades before and the continued concern over the potentiality of future famine.) Instead, as he puts it, 'food supply soon came to be seen as a problem, then as a crisis, and finally as a catastrophe.'[60] Grain production fell, not dramatically but enough to be felt. The relatively modest decline, though, was magnified by a need to extract more food from the country-side to feed soldiers and by the lack of a transportation infrastructure in the areas where those supplies needed to go as the war continued.[61] Farm workers were called up into the military – something like two-fifths of the labour force in the countryside left during the initial mobilization – and horses were, too. Exports largely stopped, but the falling productivity still created pressures on the ability of the empire to feed itself. The army had to purchase more and more to feed its soldiers and horses, and people in towns were left feeling the brunt of the shortages. The tsarist state did not introduce rationing, instead trying to fix the problem through compulsory grain levies or fixed prices, but these practices did little to get more grain out of the countryside and to those in towns who needed it.[62] Provisioning became a crisis not just in the largest towns but in provinces, as well. Both those that were traditionally grain exporting and those that were traditionally grain importing were hit by the crisis.[63]

As a result, it is perhaps no surprise that, on International Woman's Day in 1917 (8 March internationally, but 23 February according to the calendar then in use in the Russian Empire), women workers in Petrograd,

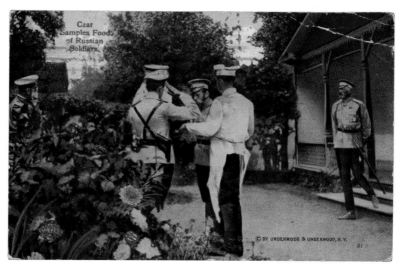

The mutiny on the battleship *Potemkin* during the revolution of 1905 was famously sparked by soldiers refusing maggot-infested meat that had been declared fit to eat. Provisioning the massive military force required by the First World War's extensive network of trenches along Russia's long western border was of course a huge challenge. Here, a postcard implies that Emperor Nicholas II was personally interested in the quality of the food his men ate – a caption on the back notes 'not satisfied with the reports that everything was of the best, the Czar himself, as the photo shows, is sampling the food of his soldiers to be convinced that his men were well provided for'. The image may not have been read as intended, as Nicholas's environment, in a courtyard filled with flowers, must have posed a sharp contrast to the experience of the trenches.

as St Petersburg had been renamed in a fit of anti-German sentiment, walked out of work in protest over problems with bread distribution in the city. Food supplies had been straitened over the course of the winter, and rumblings of discontent on the city streets had been becoming louder and louder. In response, Petrograd authorities gave out an increased measure of flour to the city's residents in early February. That strained available supplies to the point that the city government had to restrict flour supplies to bakeries, causing yet more shortages. Bread queues grew and grew, making it harder and harder for people both to stand in them and to do their other daily tasks, including work. Finally, women workers at one factory asked for the factory either to supply them with bread or to reduce their working hours so they had enough time to stand in queues. When the factory did not agree, they walked out.[64]

THIS ONE MOMENT, a protest by women about bread, was the spark that led to the collapse of the tsarist state. More workers in the capital joined the women, culminating in a general strike around the city on 25 February. Although the government called in soldiers to put down the strike, one regiment revolted against their orders, and soon others joined; by 27 February, striking workers and soldiers spread through much of the city, paralysing its functions and demanding not only bread but radical change in the government they blamed for their plight. Over the next several days, the tsarist ministers were arrested or fled, the State Duma created a Duma Committee that stepped into the vacuum of authority at the top of the administration, and a general strike council – the Petrograd Soviet – became a parallel or shadow government. On 2 March, Nicholas II abdicated on behalf of himself and his son, Aleksei. The following day his brother Mikhail stated that he refused to take the throne, as well.[65]

The Romanovs and the empire of the tsars were no more.

SEVEN

Hunger and Plenty: The Soviet Experience

When ethnographers set out to describe the inhabitants of the Soviet Union in the 1950s and 1960s, they were looking for evidence of the 'socialist cultural transformation' that the revolution of 1917 had created.[1] 'The nutrition of worker and peasant families has sharply changed for the better in comparison with the past and continues to improve,' they claimed. Above all, the ethnographers went on to state, Russian peasants and workers now ate much more meat and dairy than they had before the revolution, when 'the greater part of the working population suffered a serious deficiency in them', because of their impoverished state and lack of cattle.[2]

Other than this reported change, however, much of their description of the Russian peasant and worker diet seems very familiar. Soured or cooked dairy products intended for medium-term storage were common: *prostokvasha* and *varenets* and *riazhenka*. 'Russian' sour butter instead of sweet cream butter was still 'characteristic'. Meat was eaten roasted or in soups, baked into *pirogi* or cooked into aspic. Now cured sausages were 'a beloved snack, particularly on holidays' – they were a sign of modernity, too, for they were purchased in shops, not produced at home.

Sour rye bread was losing ground to white wheat bread. Boiled dumplings and fried or baked *pirogi*, *kalachi* and *vatrushki* might be filled with meat, cabbage, carrots, mushrooms or berries. Pancakes (*oladi*) and blini were treats. *Kasha* was cooked out of millet, out of barley, out of oats and, of course, still above all out of buckwheat; farina and rice were becoming more and more common as children's foods. *Kisel* – juice thickened with starch – was 'loved'. *Tolokno*, the oat flour that had long served as the basis of a quick meal in the fields, still 'enjoyed a great popularity' in some regions.

Vegetables were still central to the peasant diet, but now their variety was different. Cabbage was still important, eaten fresh in summer, salted or fermented in winter and as soup all the time; cucumbers, too, were salted or eaten fresh. Now, however, potatoes had become the most common vegetable, 'eaten fried, boiled, as a side dish to meat and as a separate dish'.[3] Some vegetables once common only in the far south were increasingly known further north too, particularly tomatoes and squash. Borscht, a soup 'characteristic for Ukrainians', was also increasingly common among Russians, though mostly in towns. Onions, garlic and carrots were 'eaten raw or as a condiment for food'. Radishes and horseradish added zing, as well. Turnips, which had been among the most common vegetables in the north, were losing ground to the potato. Mushrooms were still collected everywhere, and food was often prepared with some sort of vegetable oil, including old familiars like hempseed and flaxseed oil, but increasing amounts of sunflower-seed oil, as well. Apples, pears and plums made their way to tables, as did berries, and increasingly watermelons and other melons.

The authors also described some of the other ways that the Soviet experience had changed village food habits. Collective farmers now received wages and had access to shops. They now purchased relatively exotic things like macaroni, sugar and confectionery, as well as homely foods like bread. Ice cream, too, was being produced in some villages, the authors claimed.[4] Tea was the most common drink (*kvas* and beer were not far behind, and vodka and wine were purchased for holidays). But tea was now drunk differently: the samovar, in particular, was disappearing, replaced generally in towns and increasingly in villages by kettles heated on a stove.

For all that *kolkhozy* (collective farms) were increasingly getting access to things, the authors admitted that cities still had more goods. They benefitted from more imported fruit: the ethnographers listed persimmons, peaches, apricots and citrus fruits. Canteens, canned foods and 'half-prepared' foods helped ease the process of feeding families. The urban Soviet population continued to eat 'characteristic Russian foods, like *shchi*, *okroshka*, *pelmeni*, blini, crêpes, pancakes and also traditional baked goods (*pirogi*, *kalachi*, Tula and Viazma spice cakes)'. And also, the ethnographers noted, 'city dwellers eat many things from the cuisines of other peoples: Ukrainian borscht, Central Asian *plov*, Caucasian *shashlik* and many other dishes from both eastern and West-European cuisines.'[5]

The changes that the ethnographers identified were in many ways modest. Mostly the same range of dishes, supplemented by some new

The picture above, from 1915, shows a woman in a traditional peasant cottage that includes two signs of modernity – the samovar (certainly placed in what could not have been its normal spot in order to include it in the image) and cooking on a range instead of in a traditional Russian stove. The second, opposite, from 1952, shows a different vision of the modern world of food – a range with prominent gas lines, and plenty demonstrated by meat and an abundance of canned foods. This was at the heart of the vision of Soviet abundance.

pan-Soviet cuisine; some changes in ingredients that implied changes in agricultural practices, in food production and in how goods moved around the vast country. There were a few more fruits and vegetables more widely used, more meat and dairy consumption, more white bread instead of rye and more processed foods. These changes had developed in part because of

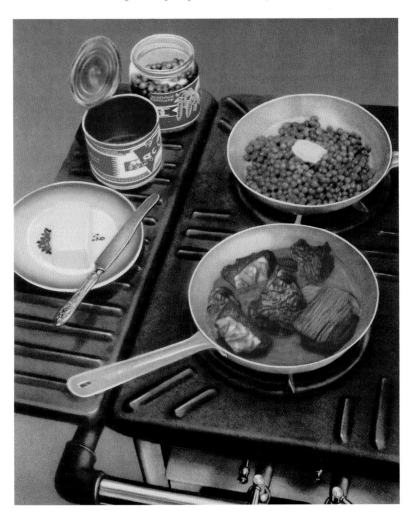

increased contact with cities, the ethnographers implied, and also because of central efforts to promote 'social nutrition' (*obshchestvennoe pitanie*). Those efforts had brought cafeterias and shops and as a result new foods not just to towns but to villages, as well. Otherwise, the ethnographers were silent as to the mechanisms of change that had altered, though hardly erased, Russian cuisine.

Of course, this meant that they were silent about a great many things. They were silent about Stalin's crony Anastas Mikoyan, whose particular, peculiar vision of abundance via mechanization created many of the new networks of food supply and demand. They were silent about the collectivization drive that had forced peasants into the *kolkhozy* in the early 1930s and about the amalgamation drive that had removed most of the last traces of the pre-revolutionary village in the years since the Second World War. And, most of all, they were silent about the effect of the repeated famines in the early 1920s, in the early 1930s and in 1946–7.

On the other hand, this volume of ethnography was published in 1968, when those hard times and horrors might have seemed to be of the past. The Khrushchev Thaw was ending, but had seemed a time of increased opportunity and relative freedom. More practically, during the Khrushchev era cities got more housing, and *kolkhozy* were for the first time supported by the state rather than drained by it. Although the late Brezhnev period (1964–82) started to be known for shortages and so-called 'deficit goods', its first decade or so seemed a time of relative general abundance when the hardships of the past could be imagined to have given way to a prosperous present, at least if you lived in Moscow or St Petersburg.

All of this together makes up the story of Russian food in the Soviet era. It was an era of shortages and harsh transformations caused by state decrees that were at best poorly conceived and at worst actively violent. It was an era of utopian plans that believed in the transformative power of cafeterias and public kitchens, of sausages and champagne, to create new, happy, prosperous Soviet citizens – but at the same time, they were often only plans on paper, unmet in reality. And it was an era of lived experiences that at times veered between the two and in the end perhaps reinforced the importance of eating not only as a necessity of physical life but as a necessity of social life.

The Soviet era was ushered in by a revolution in 1917. Or rather, by two revolutions. The February Revolution, sparked by a women's bread protest, ended the Romanov dynasty. The October Revolution, led instead by active revolutionaries, established the beginnings of the new Soviet State. Of course, the story is much more complicated than that. The word 'Soviet' means council, and the new state was in principle based on the workers' strike councils that had sprung up not only in Petrograd but in cities around the empire. The October Revolution, however, was spearheaded by the most radical faction of the Petrograd Soviet, and as a result although in principle the Soviets as a whole were the new authority, increasingly it became clear that members of one political party held the true power: the Bolsheviks. The Bolsheviks were members of the Russian Social Democratic Workers' Party who followed the particular interpretation of Marxism espoused by Vladimir Ilich Lenin. Lenin became the leader not just of his faction, but of the entire political system. Within a few years, other forms of political expression (as well as many individuals who had expressed them) were eliminated, and the Soviet state became a one-party state. The RSDWP(b) became the Russian Communist Party and eventually the Communist Party of the Soviet Union.

In the October Revolution, the Soviet seized control of Petrograd, the capital. Soviets in other cities followed suit. Soon the capital was moved further away from the border, back to Moscow, the old heart of the country. From there, Soviet/Bolshevik forces began to contest a lengthy and extraordinarily costly, terror-filled Civil War that sought to incorporate most of the lands of the former Russian Empire. Eventually a few of its former imperial holdings gained independence, but the remainder of the former empire was reconstituted in 1922 as the new Union of Soviet Socialist Republics: a union of initially four and at its maximum fifteen separate republics organized on national bases. By far the largest both in size and in population was the Russian Soviet Federated Socialist Republic.

After its violent and radical beginnings during the Civil War, the new Soviet state briefly slackened its breakneck rate of change in order to recover. Those early years had seen rapid nationalization of industry, the

Although the new Soviet state saw itself as above all the champion of industrial workers, the realities of the wider Russian Empire meant that it had to grapple with many different kinds of labourers. This poster from the Civil War era shows one of the ways that it tried to speak to peasants (in this case, the man's moustache suggests that he is Ukrainian): 'Peasant! The Red Army is protecting your crops from predators.'

establishment of grain requisitioning in the countryside and the repression of the political and class enemies of the new Bolshevik authorities. The 1920s, known as the era of the New Economic Policy, or NEP, saw a relaxing of some of these policies. Certain kinds of private production (particularly those involving consumer goods, including food) were relegalized, requisitioning turned into a tax and the need for 'bourgeois specialists' was grudgingly accepted as a reality. But the 1920s also saw a change in leadership. Lenin suffered a series of strokes that sidelined and eventually killed him. The next few years saw a struggle for power within the highest echelons of the Party. By the end of the decade, one man had eliminated his rivals: Joseph Stalin. He would become the leader of the Party and thereby of the Soviet Union for the next quarter of a century.

Stalin brought the relatively relaxed era of NEP to an end. Now everything was a battle: the battle for industry, the battle for collectivized agriculture, the battle for class purity, the battle for socialist culture. In the mindset of the time, the Soviet Union was surrounded by class enemies that wished to destroy it and therefore it needed to struggle to survive. That struggle seemed to demand or to pardon harsh measures – for all of this happened with shocking harshness. The effort to collectivize agriculture went along with a drive to 'dekulakize' the countryside. *Kulaks* were so-called rich peasants whose lands were confiscated by the new collective farms and whose families were deported into settlements, often in Siberia or the far north. The rapid urge to industrialize was merciless in a different way, with painful workloads and entire new towns springing up with severe living conditions. Class enemies were dismissed from their positions in what has been called a kind of cultural revolution, as well.[6]

The 1930s saw a Soviet Union settling into a new normal. Industrialization and collectivized agriculture were the bases of the economy, and any problems with these goals were either covered up (as happened shamefully when famine struck Ukraine and other grain-growing regions) or blamed on class enemies and saboteurs. A vision of Soviet culture also coalesced during these years, a culture that was surprisingly traditional in many ways. The radical art forms of the 1920s were pushed out in favour of a new focus on so-called 'socialist realism', which portrayed not exactly reality, but an idealized version of reality. This had implications for everything from music (no more dissonance) and literature (straightforward stories of hero-workers, please) to clothing (the Soviet House of Fashion) and food (champagne for everyone, for life has become more joyous!).

All of this continued as the heightened repression of the Great Purge inflicted another trauma on the Soviet people. From its very beginning, the Soviet state had used terror in pursuit of its goals. Already in December 1917, the Cheka (an abbreviation for the All-Russian Extraordinary Commission for Struggle against Counter-Revolution, Sabotage and Speculation) began to use imprisonment and execution against political opponents and class enemies. The pace of executions fell off after the Civil War, but not the use of prisons and forced labour camps. Scattered labour camps were united under the new State Administration of Camps (GULag) in 1930, in the midst of the great pushes to industrialize and collectivize. They were filled with political prisoners (who could have been charged with crimes against socialist labour for being late to work) and also with violent criminals, a fact that many of the political prisoners recalled with horror. In 1937 and 1938, signals from above sent the system into a frenzy of arrests and hasty prosecutions of the supposedly politically unreliable. Hundreds of thousands were executed, even more were funnelled into the Gulag system.

Although this round of terror was curtailed by the end of the 1930s, another threat remained: Nazi Germany, which had been staunchly anti-Bolshevik from its very beginnings. Despite this, in 1939 the Soviet Union and Germany signed a non-aggression pact, one that also secretly divided the lands between the two states. Almost immediately, Germany invaded Poland, prompting the end of policies of appeasement and the onset of the Second World War. The Soviet Union annexed lands that had belonged to the former Russian Empire – the eastern parts of Poland as well as the Baltic states; it fought a harder war in Finland, too. But of course the pact did not last (despite Stalin's apparent and inexplicable trust in it). On 22 June 1941, German forces staged a massive invasion of the Soviet Union. Although this would eventually lead to the demise of the Nazi regime, that was not apparent in the early days or even early years of the eastern front. Instead, the Red Army was pushed ever further back in a sickening retreat. Leningrad, as the old capital St Petersburg had been renamed in honour of the late leader, was placed under siege in September. German forces came at Moscow from several sides, reaching only 41 kilometres (25½ mi.) from the Kremlin itself. They were fought off and pushed ever further into the southern steppe, leading to the massive confrontation at Stalingrad on the lower Volga. A months-long siege during the winter of 1942–3 led to an eventual Soviet victory – one of the first signs that the tide of the war was turning.

By the end of 1944, Soviet forces had pushed the German army out of the pre-war borders of the Soviet Union and begun to move into the

Balkans, as well. In 1945, Soviet troops were the first allied troops to enter Berlin, wreaking vengeance as they went, for the eventual victory came at an enormous cost. Although estimates vary widely, there were probably around 26–7 million deaths as a result of the war, both civilian and military. (The Soviet Union also absorbed the vast majority of Germany's military activity during the war: at the end of it, 80 per cent of German military casualties came from the eastern front.) Huge expanses of Soviet space had been under occupation for months or even years; both death tolls (including the extension of the Holocaust onto Soviet territory) and the physical destruction of cities and agricultural regions were high.

The Soviet Union rebuilt, with the victory over Germany a source of unity that forgave much (and particularly before Stalin's death, there was still much to forgive). Resources taken from the Soviet Union's new satellite states in Eastern Europe helped to support it. So too did a punishing pace set from above that strained the countryside yet again – but so also did the promise of a materially better life once rebuilding was complete, something that began to appear more and more in films and stories and even cookbooks, though not yet in everyday life for anybody outside of an elite few.[7] For almost a decade after the war, Stalin still held sway in the Kremlin, growing more erratic but still in charge. These last years of Stalinism saw new waves of people entering Gulags – most famously and egregiously, former POWs or other captives of the Germans, who found themselves deemed politically unreliable upon their return to Soviet soil – or otherwise repressed, as were the great poet Anna Akhmatova and other artists.

After Stalin's death in 1953, things changed. Following a period of uncertainty, Nikita Khrushchev emerged as the new leader of the Party and therefore of the Soviet Union. He ushered in a period of political de-Stalinization that included a degree of openness in the cultural world and a rapid reduction in the size of the policing and Gulag apparatus (and a release and rehabilitation of many prisoners). In addition, he also ushered in a new period of attention to the material well-being of everyday Soviet people. His promises often went further than his ability to fulfil them, but Khrushchev started putting more money and effort into agriculture, opening up the 'virgin lands' and bringing in new crops (he famously became interested in maize (corn) after a stop in Iowa on his tour of the U.S.). New apartment construction in cities also tried to deal with the perpetual space crisis that had begun in the late tsarist period and continued through the entire Soviet era, as more and more people flocked to cities to find work.

Through Khrushchev's era and then the era of his successor, Leonid Brezhnev, relations with the outside world thawed and froze and thawed again, and efforts to control internal order likewise went from relatively open to relatively shut (though never again to the levels of repression as under Stalin). In principle, attention to the material needs of the population never went away – the idea that the Soviet Union was a place of general prosperity was strong. But in practice, that prosperity had always been unequally distributed across the entire Soviet Union, and toward the end of the Brezhnev period in the late 1970s, supply problems began to affect even those areas that had been relatively well supplied. So-called 'deficit goods' brought the same kinds of long queues and extra labour that had sparked the women's protest over bread that had led to the collapse of the tsarist regime in 1917.

Nothing like that happened in the era of shortages, but the Soviet Union nonetheless collapsed in 1991. Mikhail Gorbachev, the last leader of the Soviet Union, in some ways echoed Khrushchev in his efforts to reform and rebuild after a period of stagnation. His policies of *glasnost* (openness) and *perestroika* (rebuilding) were not intended to end one-party rule or to eliminate the role of the state in economic planning. But on the one hand they relaxed cultural and political controls enough to allow the rise of dissent, and on the other failed to resolve the economic problems plaguing the system. The trigger for the collapse this time was an effort on the part of Soviet hardliners to wrest control away from Gorbachev in August 1991. Their effort led to a popular protest in Moscow that brought Boris Yeltsin, the head of the Russian SFSR, to the fore. In the aftermath, the various constituent republics of the Soviet Union largely voted for independence, and each set out on its own path to a separate, non-Soviet future.

HUNGER

Hunger was part of the Soviet experience from the very beginning. The First World War had strained the country's resources. The Civil War that followed was possibly even more damaging, disrupting supply lines further and pushing people either to retrench in the countryside or to run to the cities. Neither made the overall food situation better. Instead, rural officials tried to extract more and more grain from the peasantry, who responded by hiding grain or reducing production. By 1921, Russia's grain production had fallen to only 31 per cent of its pre-war levels.[8] As a result, town officials found themselves in an ever more challenging position, as they attempted to institute food rations but simultaneously found themselves unable to maintain them.[9] By the beginning of 1921, although the new Soviet state had largely defeated the so-called White armies that had opposed it and its Red Army, it found itself now facing other sorts of opposition from within: peasant revolts against requisitioning and worker unrest due to their own sorry economic position. In response, the harsh economic measures from the era of the Civil War were relaxed, leading to the relative openness of the New Economic Policy. One of its elements was the elimination of grain requisitioning in favour of a fixed tax on grain and other food supplies, which among other things now left peasants with grain to sell – something they could also now do with the elimination of the grain monopoly and a return to (limited) markets.

Although the NEP would eventually lead to growth and recovery, it did not immediately alleviate what quickly turned out to be a crisis. Instead, in 1921–2 the Soviet Union faced the first of a series of major famines and other food crises that would eventually kill millions. This first Soviet famine struck widely, eventually killing some 5 million people. It was fairly clearly tied to the grain monopoly established during the years of the Civil War, by which grain was extracted by Soviet/Bolshevik agents from a resisting peasantry. Already in the spring of 1921 officials were reporting famine conditions along the Volga, as peasants planted all the seed they had in hopes of a better harvest that year. A widespread drought, however, eliminated that hope, and instead by the end of the year famine had become widespread along the Volga and also spreading west to Ukraine and east to the Urals.

In this case, Soviet authorities responded to reports of famine with rapid efforts – not all of them successful – to stop it. News of the famine was widely shared and was tied to a campaign against the Orthodox church. Why did the church hold on to its treasures in the face of widespread famine, the argument went. Ought it not give them up to fund famine relief work? Efforts to confiscate church property in the name of famine relief sparked more opposition, and the church's own famine relief organization was disbanded. Other efforts at famine relief received official sanction, however: a Central Commission for Famine Relief run through the government and another All-Russian Famine Relief Committee with famous figures like Maksim Gorky as its public face. That committee also reached out for foreign aid, which in the end played an important role in ameliorating the famine conditions.

Two good years of harvests in 1922 and 1923 helped bring the famine to an end. Changes in Soviet economic policy did so, as well. Officials

The Civil War brought with it the first of several Soviet-era famines. In this poster, the viewer – whose meal is far from luxurious! – is exhorted to 'Remember the starving!'

kept tweaking the system, altering levels of the grain tax, adjusting the price paid for grain by state officials and allowing markets to absorb more grain.[10] But some elements of the era, in particular a continued fear that wealthy peasants known as *kulaks* had too much power in the countryside, meant that many members of the Soviet elite were deeply uncertain about the reliability of the peasantry. This fear came out in force at the end of the decade. A war scare in 1927 led peasants to hold on to grain rather than sell it, something that had potential to destabilize the entire country's food supply. The newly ascendant Stalin urged strong measures against peasant 'hoarding': coercion, prosecution, searches, roadblocks to ensure that grain was not being illicitly sold rather than brought to state purchasing centres.

Finally, in late 1929, Stalin announced a new policy of collectivization and dekulakization. The first aimed to turn peasant villages into collective farms, the second to bring class war to the countryside in the name of eliminating *kulaks*. Over the winter, thousands of urban youths went out into the countryside to persuade – but really to force – peasants to collectivize. The result was chaos and resistance both passive and active. Women were particularly likely to protest. Peasants slaughtered livestock rather than hand it over to the collective. Others protested through flight. But the threat of dekulakization served as an effective coercive measure to make collectivization happen. Being labelled a *kulak* meant not simply being forced into the collective farm but being forced into involuntary resettlement in far-off places. It was too great a threat. Although Stalin signalled a slight relaxation in policy in early 1930 when he described collectivizers as 'dizzy with success' and therefore inclined to excess, the pressure of dekulakization remained an effective force to compel compliance. Although there was an initial drop in collectivization measures, by the end of 1931 more than 60 per cent of the Soviet peasantry had been collectivized. By 1937, 93 per cent were.[11]

Collectivization had far-reaching goals of creating a new properly Soviet society with properly Soviet class and economic relations. What collectivization might mean in the grain-producing regions seemed clear in principle: peasants using tractors to produce ever more grain to support the larger Soviet project of rapid industrialization. The Soviet world, however, was incredibly varied in its existing social and economic structures, which meant that collectivization played out in at times strange ways. In the Siberian north, Indigenous groups with traditions of reindeer herding were forced to collectivize their reindeer herds. On the Kazakh steppe, where most Kazakhs had lived as pastoral nomads, collectivization combined with an effort to sedentarize the population, transforming them into something more 'modern' and also opening up the steppe for larger-scale agriculture.

Collectivization was not only disruptive but deadly. Famine went along with collectivization, in the end killing somewhere between 5 and 9 million people. It hit first, lasted longest and destroyed the largest percentage of the population on the Kazakh steppe, where the Indigenous pastoral nomads were forced to sedentarize and to collectivize their herds. The Kazakh famine had already started in the winter of 1930, but only in

1933 did the Soviet state begin to introduce measures to help, though the famine continued until the next year. Through the course of the famine, 1.1 million people fled, some abroad into China, and more than 1.5 million, most of them Kazakh, died. That meant that around one-quarter of the entire population of Kazakhstan – and one-third of the population of ethnic Kazakhs – died, and nearly that many ethnic Kazakhs moved out of Kazakhstan, disrupting life there entirely.[12]

The other major site of famine was Ukraine, where some 3.9 million people (out of a pre-famine population of 31 million) died in a famine that began to appear in 1932 and peaked in 1933. There is little debate over the scale and horror of the famine, or about the shameful decision to hide it rather than to act to prevent it. Likewise there is no real contention about the fact that it was clearly exacerbated by practical decisions on the part of the Soviet regime – that it was a man-made famine caused by the extreme levels of grain requisitioning during this first phase of collectivization and failure to correct course in time to stop it. There are, however, questions over the reasons that lay behind this decision. Some, calling it the Holodomor, see it as a deliberate, genocidal act aimed against the Ukrainian people. Others argue that it had no specifically ethnic component and was instead based on a complete failure to understand agricultural reality, a failure that reached beyond Ukraine, and beyond the heavily Ukrainian Kuban region of the Russian republic, to again bring death to the major grain-producing regions along the Volga.[13]

There is no doubt that the collectivization famines were based on a prioritization of a particular vision of Soviet society and an especially strong need for grain to fund the massive industrialization drive going on simultaneously. That the Soviet state's actions compounded the problem rather than immediately reacting to ameliorate it is also unquestionable. Although eventually relief efforts tried to bring the famine to an end, they were late and also secret. While the famine at the beginning of the 1920s was publicized, this one was hidden. That first famine could be explained away as a remnant of the tsarist past, or as caused by *kulaks*. Now, though, *kulaks* had supposedly been eliminated and the Soviet state could not shirk its responsibility if it made it public. As a result, no aid came, no one spoke openly, and yet the memory of the famines even now remains as a still-painful scar among the communities most affected by them.

There was one more major Soviet famine, this one almost forgotten in comparison with the others in large part because it came at the tail end of a greater trauma: the Second World War. In 1946–7, another 1–2 million people died due to famine conditions that again struck the Soviet Union's great grain-growing regions. The countryside had of course been strained by the war; horses were drafted, livestock killed, the number of workers was down due to the persistent demands of the Red Army, tractors were in short supply. The end of the war brought some relaxation but not enough. Although some demobilized soldiers moved back to the collective farms, many decided to strike out for new lives in urban centres instead. A drought brought with it another bad harvest. And once again the Soviet state wanted to take as much as possible from the countryside. The result was yet another famine, this one happening to people whose lives had already been turned upside down several times over by the war.

Like the collectivization famines, the post-war famine was hidden away from outside view because it did not fit the story of a Soviet Union recovering faster than its capitalist counterparts from a devastating war. For example, the Soviet Union eliminated wartime rationing in 1947, nearly a decade before Great Britain, not because its supply issues had been solved but because doing so allowed it to say that it had solved them faster. Recognizing a famine that was still not fully solved would call into question this image of the Soviet Union's great triumph.

Another reason might be that hunger plays so many other roles in the story of the Soviet Union's experience of the Second World War. The German war effort required extracting massive quantities of grain and foodstuffs (and oil and other resources) from the Soviet Union with no concern at all for preserving the lives of Soviet citizens. As a result, the German occupation, which spread through Ukraine, western Russia and the entire southern steppe to the Volga, was a violent, harsh affair. Of the 13.6 million civilians who are estimated to have died in the occupied zone, 7.4 million were simply killed (2 million of them Jews) and another 4.1 million starved.[14] The experience of occupation was the experience of the struggle for survival against hunger.

Even in areas not under occupation, hunger was ever present, as well. The scale of the occupation meant that the Soviet Union was suddenly without its normal supply of foodstuffs. In principle, agricultural production became part of the struggle against the 'ravenous hordes of German fascism'. There were efforts to produce more in other areas: party officials in the Arctic and sub-Arctic Komi Republic, for example, responded in part by vowing to 'increase the production of potatoes in collective farms, state farms, on suburban lands, in the private plots of *kolhozniki* [collective farm workers] and the individual gardens of workers and bureaucrats'.[15]

But of course there was a reason why the Soviet Union's south, now largely occupied territory, was its breadbasket. Efforts like these could at best help their own regions to become more self-sufficient, but could not solve the problems of the country as a whole, particularly when there was a massive army to feed.

The Soviet state moved rapidly to institute rationing to try to solve some of the problems of supply. The ration system was based on a hierarchy of importance: workers in industries necessary for the war effort got more calories, workers in other fields fewer calories, non-working dependents even less. No one other than a few officials received rations that fulfilled their actual energy needs; miners and some special workers came close, but even a worker on a 'special list' entitling him or her to a higher ration received only 40–50 per cent of their caloric needs. These rations were supplemented by other foods, particularly the potato, but many people's experience of the war was of chronic undernourishment if not out-and-out starvation.[16]

During the war no single place was as hard hit by hunger as Leningrad, held under siege from September 1941 to January 1944. Somewhere

This photograph from the Soviet Information Bureau shows a vision of plenty at the Moscow Grocery no. 1 in 1946 – captioned as 'one of the largest food stores in the world'. The reality within the country was much starker, as a third major famine ravaged the countryside as it began its recovery from the war.

between 700,000 and 1 million people died in Leningrad during the siege, almost all from outright starvation or illness exacerbated by hunger. Life behind the blockade was one of extreme scarcity, particularly during the first long winter of 1941–2, when the sudden onset of the siege left the city entirely cut off from its usual sources of food. An even stricter system of rationing was instituted there than in the country as a whole; bread rations fell to as low as 125 grams (4½ oz) per person per day, and the rationing system became almost as much a symbol of their suffering for Leningraders as the Germans were.[17] Although the situation improved in 1942 as gardens were planted in the spring and summer and a new supply system was established over the ice of Lake Ladoga in the winter, the situation was still fraught. Food was an all-consuming (though little-consumed) passion during the blockade. One diarist described how conversations within the blockaded city had changed: 'wherever two or three people happen to meet, at work, on watch duty, or in line, the conversation is only about food. What are they giving out based on ration cards, which norms, what one can get, etc. – this is everyone's cardinal, vital, question.'[18]

Life during the blockade was so different so quickly that already in November and December of 1941 doctors were describing what they saw around them as an entirely new kind of illness: what they called 'nutritional dystrophy', a complex of multiple illnesses associated with starvation. The

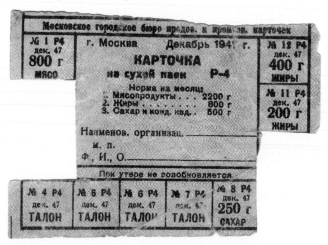

The devastation of the Second World War brought strict rationing to deal with a crisis of provisioning that continued after the war ended. This December 1947 ration card from Moscow could be used to purchase 2,200 g (4 lb 13 oz) of meat products, 800 g (1 lb 12 oz) of fat, and 500 g (1 lb 2 oz) of sugar or candy. This card still has tabs remaining – for 800 g (1 lb 12 oz) of meat and for 600 g (1 lb 5 oz) of fat.

same term found another home in another very Soviet site: the Gulag. So prevalent was hunger and illness related to it that one former inmate believed the term had its origin in the camps of the 1930s – it seemed so much a part of Gulag life that it had to have its origins there.[19] During the blockade Leningraders described their particular obsession with food, the way that they no longer ate like well-fed people, but instead 'we revel [in eating]; it resembles a liturgy'.[20] In one of his works about Gulag life, Aleksandr Solzhenitsyn described something similar in the actions of his protagonist Ivan Denisovich Shukhov:

> The only good thing about soup was that it was hot, but Shukhov's portion had grown quite cold. However, he ate it with his usual slow concentration. No need to hurry, not even for a house on fire. Apart from sleep, the only time a prisoner lives for himself is ten minutes in the morning at breakfast, five minutes over dinner, and five at supper.[21]

Although it was in the end extraordinarily inefficient, the giant Gulag system was an essential part of the larger Soviet economic system. The labour of inmates felled trees, dug canals, mined gold, even built skyscrapers in Moscow. Food played a central role in compelling that labour. As the historian Golfo Alexopoulos notes, 'hunger represented the Gulag's fundamental labour incentive and food was insufficient by design.'[22] Even if Gulag camps had received their full allotment of supplies, they would have been insufficient to feed everyone well. Not only was there not enough but the monotony of the Gulag diet – unchanging bread and potatoes – meant that illnesses associated with vitamin deficiency were rampant. Rations differentiated prisoners by work ability and productivity and served as an additional means of punishment. On top of this, rarely did camps receive their full ration of supplies. Many camps were located in the Arctic or on permafrost; supplementing their allotment was difficult if not impossible. If the Gulag serves as the ultimate metaphor for Stalinist society, then hunger was at its core.

VISIONS OF PLENTY

Hunger was one of the stories of the Soviet experience. Plenty, or at least the promise of plenty, was another. The Soviet Union needed new Soviet men and women, who worked and dressed and played and ate differently from their tsarist predecessors or their capitalist contemporaries abroad. Very quickly, the new Soviet state began to promote policies intended to create these new Soviet people. That meant changes not only in the scale of agriculture (that is, collectivization) but in its contents (that is, new crops). That meant changes in the food production and distribution system, particularly in the form of a new concept of *obshchestvennoe pitanie*, *obshchepit* for short. And that meant the creation of a new pan-Soviet culinary world that epitomized the idea that the Soviet Union was not an empire but the home of the 'friendship of nations'. In it, Russian food predominated but was joined by the cuisines of the other republics to create a new transnational fusion.

Above all, the Soviet state wanted its population to eat differently to how it had under the tsars – 'better', in ways that were defined both by nutrition and, somewhat surprisingly, by the pleasure that food could bring. From its earliest years, it was concerned that the Soviet masses were marked as backward and impoverished, in part by their diet and in particular by a reliance on grain for calories. Already in the middle of the 1920s, authors were trying to find some signs of improvement in peasant/worker diet. The statistician Elena Kabo was among the first to investigate the diet of the Russian worker 'before and after the war'.[23] She included early infographics to indicate the ways that diet had been improving: more white bread compared to rye, more meat compared to potatoes. Increasing meat consumption was a particular and lasting concern. The idea that Russia's peasants were primarily vegetarian had a long history; it was a claim used to bolster vegetarianism abroad and also debated by Russians who saw it as a slight on their own national development.[24] The Soviets wanted above all to catch up with American meat consumption – a desire that they had little chance actually to do, given that even their targets, themselves rarely met, would not come close.[25]

Even so, there were real changes in consumption by the middle of the twentieth century. A calculation of the normal daily ration of foods consumed by peasant families in one village in Voronezh province suggests some real alterations in everyday practices of food consumption:[26]

Product	g [oz] in 1900	g [oz] in 1956
Rye bread	709.5 [25]	198.9 [7]
Wheat flour	11.1 [⅔]	300.8 [10½]
Groats and legumes	125.1 [4½]	44 [1½]
Noodles	—	40 [1½]

Potatoes	233.85 [8¼]	576 [20¼]
Cabbage	94.06 [3¼]	98.8 [3½]
Cucumbers	2.74 [¹⁄₁₀]	80 [2¾]
Tomatoes	—	102 [3½]
Vegetable oil	2.49 [⁹⁄₁₀₀]	12 [½]
Sugar	0.78 [³⁄₁₀₀]	31 [1]
Confectionery	—	50.0 [1¾]
Meat	36.62 [1¼]	62 [2¼]
Lard	0.34 [¹⁄₁₀₀]	16.4 [½]
Fish	6.37 [¼]	10.5 [⅓]
Herring	0.28 [¹⁄₁₀₀]	23.6 [¾]
Whole milk	220.37 [7¾]	561.4 [19¾]
Butter	0.7 [²⁄₁₀₀]	13 [½]
Eggs	3.1 [¹⁄₁₀]	10.2 [⅓]

There had been some big changes, particularly a drop in dependence on rye bread and an increase in potatoes. Meat consumption had nearly doubled, as well; and the consumption of cucumbers, which had long been considered a Russian favourite, and tomatoes, which were largely new, skyrocketed. The larger amounts of milk, butter and eggs may also have reflected the waning influence of Orthodoxy in the officially atheist Soviet Union. In other words, these changes, which were perhaps magnified in towns, represented new emphases in the worlds of agriculture and food industries, in the forms of provisioning, and in the wider culture.

Much of the effort to change agriculture focused on large-scale modes of agriculture and particularly on the cultivation of grain. The first round of collectivization at the turn of the 1930s aimed at securing a reliable source of grain both to feed the Soviet Union and to export in order to fund industrialization. It also had other goals, too, including introducing larger-scale, mechanized agriculture. Tractors were the ultimate emblem of that transformation: they were to be supplied to all collective farms (at least through access to a tractor station) and used to amalgamate the separate plots into single large fields, worked with what was in principle the greatest degree of efficiency.

Officials also paid significant attention to the cultivation of vegetables and potatoes, but mostly by pushing it off into peasant hands. After the initial radical collectivization at the beginning of the 1930s, in which all lands and livestock were brought into a single collective whole, Soviet

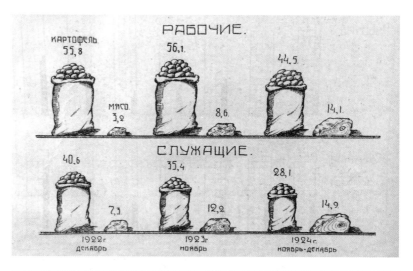

These infographics compared how the diets of 'workers' and 'white-collar workers' had changed in the years right after the Civil War; in one (top), meat consumption rose (while potato consumption remained very high!), in the other (above) the proportion of rye to wheat bread fell.

authorities quickly relegalized private plots of land on which peasants could grow their own vegetables and potatoes and allowed trade in *kolkhoz* markets. Soon these private plots came to account for half of the income of most peasants, and by the end of the 1930s it was private plots that came to supply the majority of the Soviet Union's vegetables.[27] This only continued in the post-war world: at the end of the 1950s, a Soviet report claimed that private plots were outperforming collective farms as a whole in the production of milk, meat, vegetables and eggs – they produced 50–80 per cent of collective farms' entire output in these categories. That percentage dropped somewhat over the next decade, but private plots continued to be an important source of necessary foods.[28]

Particularly in the Khrushchev and Brezhnev eras, collective farms became a source of social security rather than a purely extractive resource for the Soviet state. At the same time, though, Khrushchev in particular also attempted to increase agricultural production. For one thing, he promoted the cultivation of the 'virgin lands', primarily in southern Siberia and Kazakhstan. This was a massive undertaking intended to fix the Soviet Union's grain supply problem as quickly as possible – 41.8 million hectares (103.3 million acres) of new lands were cultivated between

The potato harvest remained an important part of the agricultural world until and beyond the end of the Soviet era – although people were eating more protein and fewer carbohydrates, potatoes and bread were still staples.

1954 and 1960. Initially Khrushchev could claim success, as yearly grain production increased by an average of 40 per cent in the initial years of the campaign compared to the five years before. Other reforms seemed to have succeeded, as well: more milk production, more meat production. And yet, the Soviet Union soon found itself needing to purchase grain; as Khrushchev put it, this was because it had chosen not to follow what he called the 'Stalin-Molotov method of securing grain' – that is, ruthless extraction at the expense of those who farmed it. If the Soviet state now wished to ensure that everyone ate, it might find itself producing more and yet still purchasing grain from abroad.[29]

Although agriculture and heavy industry always got more attention from the Soviet state, food networks and food industries became ever more vital to the actual well-being of the Soviet population as more and more people moved to cities. During NEP, the Soviet state allowed food industry and other light industries to remain largely in the hands of private traders while it concentrated on heavy industry. That changed in the early 1930s, when, along with the larger Stalin revolution in heavy industry and collectivization, light industry and food production were brought into the state's fold under a series of different people's commissariats (of trade, of provisioning, of food industry). The leading figure in food production, through the 1930s at least, was Anastas Mikoyan (1895–1978), a Bolshevik from before the revolution, who was somehow able to survive the many traumas of the Soviet leadership from Lenin to Brezhnev.[30] In many ways, he was the figure who was supposed to turn Stalin's 1935 claim 'life has become better, comrades, life has become happier' into a reality on the table.

In response to that claim, Mikoyan stated in 1936 that 'the provisioning question – one of the greatest difficulties of the Russian revolution ... has been solved.'[31] This was of course a gross overstatement, coming as it did only a few years after famine had killed millions, but was part of his and Stalin's imagined world of Soviet abundance. Despite the difficult realities of Soviet life, this imagined abundance was so present in posters and advertisements and shop windows and film that it entered people's memory as reality: in the post-Stalin years, people wrote letters demanding a return to Stalinist abundance, an abundance that was a powerful fiction.[32] It was a part of the world of Soviet culturedness that emerged in the middle of the 1930s, which involved everything from respect for Pushkin and Tchaikovsky to keeping plants on the windowsill to having clean linens on the table.[33] And, of course, it meant abundant food to consume, as well.

Now the worker could drink champagne ('Soviet champagne', of course), not just the bourgeois. At least, so went the rhetoric and the memory.

The new Soviet world of abundance included many features, but when it came to food above all it wanted two things: more technology and more meat. Technology was modern and made food into a part of the larger world of Soviet industry. Meat was important because national differences in meat consumption had long been read as signs of prosperity or backwardness, with the basic formulation that more meat signified more prosperity. The Soviet Union simply could not be in the vanguard if its population was not properly supplied with meat (eventually Khrushchev explicitly promised to match and surpass the U.S. in consumption of meat and dairy). These two strands met above all in the desire to produce more sausage. Sausage could be produced industrially and also found a ready pool of consumers, who hungered (unfortunately sometimes literally) for the good.[34] When a food industry collective put on a theatrical performance devoted to the theme of abundance, sausages played a particularly important role: a chorus of sausages sang 'we are soviet sausages, widely available to the masses. There are one-hundred-and-twenty-five sorts of us. We only wait for your mouths. You can smear us with mustard, you can boil us in water, you can fry us in a pan.'[35]

Improvements in refrigeration technology after the Second World War had a particularly big effect on food production and consumption. Ice cream became one of the most visible signs of post-war prosperity – and perhaps also the greatest success of the post-war economy of food.[36] Ice cream was not new. Ice-filled carts carried the treat around Leningrad in the 1920s, Mikoyan dreamed of ever greater production of ice cream in the 1930s, and large modern plants in Moscow had already begun to produce tons of ice cream even then.[37] After the war, and particularly once Khrushchev tried to emphasize abundance now rather than abundance always off in the future, the Soviet regime was willing to put real resources into making ice cream a regular part of life. The technology of production was there already, but the war helped by, of all things, improving cooling technology via dry ice. The result was not just ice cream production, but a different way of getting ice cream to the people, by sales from carts on the street.

Another major change in food supply was the rise of conserves and convenience foods. Canned peas, canned fish, canned meat: all of these were intended to be symbols of the new modern Soviet Union and a convenience for Soviet consumers. This turn is particularly visible in what

This woman dressed in a smart white smock is signalling two major changes in Soviet foodways: the rise of canned goods, and a particular focus on finding new sources of protein. Here, canned fish (anchovies and rollmops) are prepared 'for Moscow', according to the photograph's label. The photograph from the Soviet Information Bureau is from 1946, and was likely intended to show idealized recovery from the war as much as it showed actual recovery.

came to be the standard Soviet cookbook: the *Book of Tasty and Healthy Food*, first published in 1939 with a print run of 100,000.[38] It would appear in fourteen more revised and expanded editions between 1945 and 1990, with a total printing of 3.5 million copies. Its first few editions were illustrated, but in black and white; by the 1950s, though, its luxurious colour images of a new Soviet life were something very different indeed. They promised many of the same things as the larger world of food industry: canned goods, 'half-fabricated' frozen foods, all sorts of conveniences that would free the Soviet woman (never quite stated as such, but always implied) from kitchen labour. As the historian Irina Glushchenko puts it, the cookbook 'portrayed the old world as a complete hell. In it there was nothing good, it was only possible to remember it in order to compare the horrors of the past with the achievements of the present.'[39]

In addition to alterations in agriculture and food industry, the Soviet state also invested in the concept of what it called *obshchestvennoe pitanie* or *obshchepit*. This was a concept of social nutrition or what the historian

The *Kommunalka* Kitchen

People began to flood the towns of the new Soviet state in ways that placed its housing infrastructure under enormous strain. One of the results was the rise of the *kommunalka*, the communal apartment. Large pre-revolutionary apartments that had once housed a single noble family were nationalized and divided up among many families, each living in a single room (or, sometimes, in half or a corner of a single room) – and everyone sharing a single kitchen. At its best, the *kommunalka* kitchen could be a place where people gathered and even celebrated together. At its worst, it was a site of perpetual battles over ownership of pots and plates and brushes, of usage of the stove or sink. In Mikhail Zoshchenko's 1924 short story 'Nervous People', a fight between two women spills over to include nearly the entire apartment's occupants, despite (or perhaps exacerbated by) the fact that the kitchen itself barely held them all. In principle, *obshchepit* was supposed to relieve the pressures on the *kommunalka* kitchen by establishing canteens and even larger communal kitchens. In practice, the promises that *obshchepit* might 'free women from kitchen drudgery', as a poster put it, never really worked. Instead, women continued to carry the burden of feeding their families as they simultaneously took on the burdens of industrial or other labour.

Diane Koenker translates as public catering – a blanket concept that included everything from pavement kiosks to buffets in theatres to canteens in factories and schools to restaurants in hotels.[40] In principle, at least, all of these were intended to alter everyday food practices in a way that helped in 'the battle of the Soviet people for socialism, for a prosperous, cultured life, for the improvement of the conditions of labour and of everyday life and for the speedy solution of provisioning problems'. In particular, it was intended to move responsibility for feeding people from the individual household to public services. This had 'completely obvious advantages', according to one account – it was more efficient, for one thing, and also was part of a campaign to free women from the kitchen (and perhaps also was intended to reduce private spaces in a world increasingly under surveillance).[41] Utopian plans for new apartment complexes in the 1920s included spaces for canteens that would eliminate the need for private kitchens. 'Factory-kitchens' were intended to feed the workers of the new workers' state.

As in so many fields, there was a push for greater development of public catering in order to improve nutrition and culture at the beginning of the 1930s. Of course, in retrospect there is a terrible irony to this push, which occurred just as hunger and famine were recurring in the wider Soviet space. And, furthermore, it came about in part because the privately run restaurants and cafés that had been allowed during NEP had been eliminated at the end of the 1920s (according to Natalia Lebina, the more than 28,000 privately run eating establishments in place in 1927 were entirely eliminated by the beginning of the 1930s).[42] Even so, in 1931 a Central Committee decree on public catering described some successes (3 million children fed hot breakfasts at school! 13,400 individual public catering outlets!) but also a great need for improvements in everything from the poor sanitary conditions in many canteens, to unqualified cooks, to weak labour discipline, to theft of supplies. It presented a series of tasks to ameliorate each of these problems and declared in the end that

> the Central Committee considers that every worker, every member of the Party and the Komsomol [Communist Youth League], and, in first place all those working in public catering institutions, are obligated to take part in the work of the successful battle with all deficiencies of public catering and to turn it into a most important link in the work for the improvement of the life of the working class.[43]

As in food production, one of the main tenets of the concept of public catering was mechanization.[44] When Mikoyan introduced a new journal devoted to the concept, he noted that 'it should expand the battle for mastery of new technology of cooking, for the mastery of systems of new production, of powerful enterprises, for the introduction of scientific conquests in the everyday practice of catering workplaces.'[45] The new factory canteens that were proudly lauded in brochures and other publications were prime examples: they are pictured as places not furnished with huge stoves but instead with huge thermos canisters, where only foods that could be boiled or stewed or steamed were prepared. Even later, printed

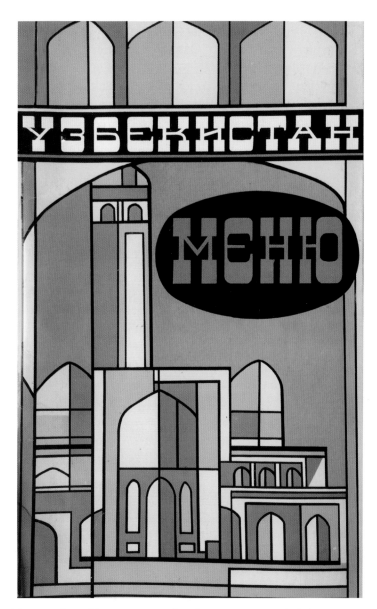

This menu from a Moscow restaurant shows how restaurants were linked to creating a grand Soviet space that crossed national boundaries. Here, the menu for the restaurant 'Uzbekistan' clearly links it to a part of the wider Soviet world that was different from its Moscow environment.

guides to running restaurants or other types of public catering prioritized technology above nearly all else.⁴⁶ Or, they focused more on the standards of the facilities than on the food they served; in one 1936 account of 'The Best Canteen in the City' (of Kemerovo, in Siberia), the three women who had banded together to improve the quality of their local factory's canteen talked of all their efforts in 'capital repair', not in improving the quality of food.⁴⁷

By the post-Stalin period, the big cities were home to restaurants often housed in hotels that also created a vision of a connected Soviet space. In Moscow, the restaurants Ukraina, Uzbekistan, Aragvi, Ararat, Baku and Minsk were linked on some level with the other Soviet republics; the Praga, Sofia, Budapest, Havana and Pekin (where even after relations between the USSR and the PRC grew strained one could still order a 'Chinese Friendship Assortment') all linked the Soviet Union to the wider communist world.⁴⁸ These did not necessarily serve widely varying foods – in many ways, their menus were mostly standardized, with gestures towards the places their names evoked. But particularly in the Brezhnev era, there was increasing interest in making them representative of varied cultures in both their decorations (bringing in wooden carvings from Bulgaria for the Sofia restaurant, having consultants from Czechoslovakia come in to advise on both the decor and foods served at the restaurant Praga).⁴⁹ Even Russian cooking, as opposed to a general Soviet cuisine, gained a new prominence in the rebirth of the pre-revolutionary restaurant named Slavonic Bazaar, now decorated in old-fashioned Russian style and featuring *ukha*, borscht, blini and new 'Russian' creations.⁵⁰

In both restaurants and other catering institutions as well as cookbooks, this vision of a particularly Soviet plenty that drew on the strengths of its constituent republics (while privileging the Russian) became a central part of the post-war culinary landscape. Earlier cookbooks had included recipes for Georgian foods, and Stalin's own taste for the foods of his homeland (he was by birth a Georgian man named Dzhugashvili) ensured a supply of Georgian ingredients and increasingly restaurants in Moscow and eventually elsewhere.⁵¹ In the post-Stalin era, the standard cookbooks for catering establishments forthrightly stated that they included the best of all the republics: 'Russian pies, Ukrainian borshches, Uzbek pilafs, Georgian kebabs, Armenian tola, Azeri piti'.⁵²

There was also a side of the idealized world of plenty that cast a more troubling light on the Soviet world: alcohol. As in earlier periods, alcohol was both a source of income and a source of concern. The Soviet era began in a period of temperance instituted by Nicholas II as a war measure. *Samogon*, or home-distilled vodka, which had hitherto been essentially unknown, came to fill the gap. By the early 1920s, it even contributed to a rise in alcohol consumption in the villages from its pre-war levels.[53] Even before the famine in the early 1920s, officials were linking the rise in *samogon* to hunger; in 1919, according to one account, it had already 'reached the degree of a national tragedy'.[54] In the end, the Soviet state bowed to necessity and re-established official vodka consumption – and a new state vodka monopoly – which came into effect in 1925.[55] However, as historian David Christian points out, the arrival of *samogon* during the period of prohibition meant that the state's control over vodka production was never as absolute as it had been, which meant that alcohol consumption, hard to control at the best of times, became even more a possible subject of concern.

And a concern it definitely turned out to be. In the post-war period, and particularly during the Khrushchev and Brezhnev eras, alcohol consumption increased dramatically: according to Soviet sources, alcohol sales increased 7.4 times between 1940 and 1985.[56] This increase, visible well before the 1980s, began to worry Soviet authorities. It was difficult to work out how to talk about it, however, because officially alcohol abuse had no place in a properly proletarian society – it was an illness of capitalism that ought to die out with the establishment of socialism. It did not, however. A Khrushchev-era decree aimed to 'strengthen the struggle against drunkenness' by limiting vodka sales. Instead, it led to vodka drinking moving into homes and onto streets. In 1972, another decree took on drunkenness by limiting vodka production and increasing wine and beer production to compensate. But it did not even succeed in limiting vodka production, which instead actually increased.[57] There is no better (or more terrifying) expression of late-Soviet drunkenness than Venedikt Erofeev's 1973 novel *Moscow-Petushki* (also sometimes translated as *Moscow to the End of the Line*), which follows a central figure as he travels on a suburban train, drinking and discoursing as he goes.[58]

In reaction, one of the first acts Mikhail Gorbachev took upon becoming the General Secretary of the Soviet Union in 1985 was a law 'on measures to overcome drunkenness and alcoholism'. As had the tsarist state in its waning years, the Soviet state tried to promote temperance societies as a bottom-up method of combatting drunkenness. It also did something that the tsarist state only carried out as a response to war, and which Brezhnev's Soviet Union had made gestures toward but never

In this anti-alcohol poster from 1954, an ideal Soviet man simply says 'No!' to the shot of vodka he is being offered.

properly undertook: it cut alcohol production dramatically. The result, it is said, was not a reduction of drunkenness but instead a huge rise in the production of *samogon* and an accompanying disappearance of anything that could be used to distil alcohol.[59] Culinary writer Anya von Bremzen remembers a trip back to Moscow in late 1987, when the campaign had led

264

This anti-alcohol poster from 1990 uses folk motifs to make a point that echoed those of more than a century before: drinking could lead to violence, but a family that drank tea together was a happy family.

to empty shelves: not only no Soviet champagne, but no yeast, no sugar, no fruit juice, no hard sweets, no tomato paste. 'Resourceful Soviet drinkers could distill hooch from anything,' she writes.[60]

EVERYDAY REALITIES

In the last decade of the Soviet Union, these visions of plenty were mostly a mirage. By this point the mirage hid not outright famine or hunger, at least for the most part. It did, however, hide a blander, more monotonous world of food and one that required significantly more effort than the image of abundant canteens and ready-made meals suggested. Of course, there were some who enjoyed Soviet abundance, just as there had always been a privileged elite who enjoyed plenty. Early in the Soviet era, the conception of abundance and plenty went along with an acceptance that rationing was necessary. During the Stalin revolution, as the state was pushing for collectivization and industrialization at the expense of living standards (and at the cost of famine), a ration system tried both to distribute food and to create a new social hierarchy based on access to food and other goods. This system of rations ended after a few years (even the rations instituted during the war a few years later were cut short almost as soon as the war ended), but the 'hierarchy of distribution', as the historian Elena Osokina has called it, remained in the network of different shops stocked with different goods open to different consumers.[61] The result was a Soviet society divided by access to goods, including food – it was a society of haves and have nots.

At base, the Soviet Union found itself perpetually stymied in its efforts to ensure an abundant food supply, in part because it found itself perpetually facing problems in its agricultural system. Despite the fact that the Soviet Union continued to put more and more resources into agriculture, the return on that investment grew only slowly. Even in the Khrushchev era, when so much effort was put into new crops and new lands and increased production, the Soviet state had to import grain. Late in his tenure, breadlines began to form once again, and the Politburo even discussed reintroducing rationing. These failures were an essential part of Khrushchev's downfall.[62] In the 1970s and early 1980s, the Soviet Union turned from a food exporter to a consistent food importer, and yet those imports failed to solve its persistent supply problems. Mikhail Gorbachev, who held the position of Secretary of Agriculture before taking on the role of General Secretary, loosened some of the restrictions on private plots and private livestock in an effort to increase domestic agricultural production. As General Secretary, he worked to implement further reforms in agriculture, even at one point declaring 'we need decollectivization' to the Politburo, but found his efforts hindered by a central bureaucracy that did not want to give up its authority.[63] Abundance remained elusive.

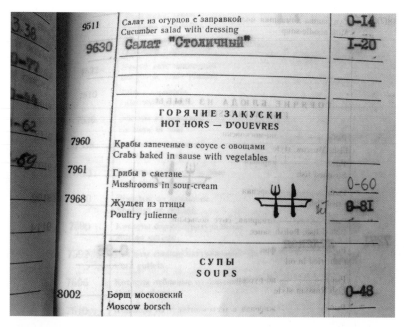

In principle, restaurants had elaborate menus. In practice, they often lacked certain goods. This menu from the restaurant 'Moscow' lists three dishes available as hot *zakuski* – but in small pencilled letters, one of them, poultry julienne, is marked 'нет' – none.

Produkty

A Soviet-era grocery – marked with a sign proclaiming it sold *produkty* – was usually set up in a way that emphasized the power of the seller, not the consumer. Each store was divided into separate sections – dairy, meat, canned goods, fresh foods and so on – with the goods all kept behind counters that displayed what was for sale, each guarded by a sales assistant. A purchaser had to walk around to see what was available and make a note of the prices. If the item was sold by weight, she asked to have a portion measured out, and was told the price. All money was handled at a separate cashier window. There, the purchaser listed which sections and how much she wanted to pay – 2 roubles at section 1, 50 kopeks at section 3 – and got receipts in return. She then returned to each section, handed over the receipt and got her goods. In times of shortages, at least according to rumour, individual sales assistants came to have a lot of power over access to goods, keeping particularly desired goods like sausages for certain customers. It was a form of *blat*, the everyday world of exchanges and favours that kept the everyday Soviet economy running. Satirical journals often poked fun at the rudeness of sales assistants, and the day-to-day reality of shopping for food could be wearing, making a misery of an already difficult task.

The shortages that resulted meant the return of long queues for certain goods. There was still cabbage, there were still potatoes, there was – on a base level – enough to eat, but there were not the luxuries promised by films and magazines. Or at least, there were not luxuries in the quantities promised. Shortages of so-called 'deficit goods', foodstuffs among them, meant that people came to use connections (called *blat*) to get access to scarce goods. If they lacked connections, they were always on the look-out for goods – women carried string shopping bags called *avoski* or, 'just in case', men used their briefcases as they stopped in at any shop where there was a queue.[64]

The bulk of the labour involved in finding and preparing food fell on women. Revolutionary slogans had promised to 'free women from kitchen drudgery', but the reality was that they still cooked, and still shopped, and now simply did so on top of work outside the home. In the early decades of the Soviet Union, that could also mean coping with shared kitchens in communal apartments. After the Second World War, and particularly in the Khrushchev and Brezhnev eras, single-family apartments became more common, but the stresses of the kitchen in some ways even increased due to the rise of a vision of domesticity and motherhood in the wider culture. Its goal was to emphasize motherhood in order to recover from the demographic catastrophes of the late 1930s and 1940s. It ended up having the effect of placing extreme pressure on women – what has been called their 'double burden'. As Anastasia Lakhtikova and Angela Brintlinger put it, 'the burden to care for and feed the family is on a fully employed (and therefore seemingly emancipated) woman' who was furthermore limited by the fact that 'access to food is not as straightforward as in capitalist society because it does not depend on income level.'[65]

Overall, there was a perpetual belief that things should be better, somehow. Already in 1933, and even in the official journal of public catering, a headline could read 'The Workers of Rostov Say: WHY IS HOME COOKING TASTIER THAN IN A CANTEEN?'[66] Later, in the Brezhnev era, when standards of living actually did rise to levels not seen before, there was also perpetual dissatisfaction with the state of things.[67] Sausage had come to play a central role both in actual diets and in the imagined world of abundance during the Brezhnev era. In 1960, official Soviet statistics reported that the USSR produced 20.3 kilograms (44¾ lb) of meat, including sausages, per person. By 1980, production had more than doubled, to 34.4 kilograms (75¾ lb) of meat and 11.6 kilograms (25½ lb) of sausage per person.[68] But that production was spread unequally throughout the state. It was widely believed that Moscow got more than its fair share of sausage, creating 'sausage envy' among those who lived elsewhere.[69] By the end of 1990, this sense of a lost abundance became the norm. There was, as von Bremzen remembers, 'Nichevo – nothingness. The glaring existential emptiness of the shelves.'[70] What was there to hold onto, given this nothingness?

THE SOVIET UNION in many ways owed its existence to a food crisis. The March (February) bread protest that grew to topple the tsars set in motion the revolutionary year of 1917; success in the Civil War that eventually followed was based not only in the Red Army's ability to mobilize people but in Bolshevik ability to extract grain. In the three great waves of famine, in continued challenges with agriculture and with food supply, and even in the use of food to create a vision (and eventually a partial reality) of Soviet abundance, food underlay the horrors and the successes of the Soviet era. At times, food even made its way back into a source of protest. When prices on meat and dairy were increased in 1962 (and when wages had fallen), workers in Novocherkassk protested – even rioted. Although the protest was put down with all haste, it shook the Soviet leadership, probably hastening Khrushchev's removal.[71]

The Soviet experiment came to an end in 1991 in a complicated cascade of collapse. In one way, its end was clear: citizens in the constituent republics of the Soviet Union, some of whom had long been clamouring for independence, voted to secede from the larger Union. As of the beginning of 1992, fifteen independent states, one of which was the Russian Federation, succeeded the old Soviet state.

Exactly how it got to that point is still essentially puzzling, however. For all the nothingness on the shelves, for all the unpopularity of Gorbachev due to his anti-alcohol campaign in the 1980s and his turn to violence in an effort to preserve the Soviet Union at the beginning of the 1990s, it was notable that, when an old-school, hardline group of Party faithful tried to remove Gorbachev and take over the Soviet state in August of 1991, everyday people came out to stand in front of tanks to stop them. The chaotic events of the failed putsch in Moscow reverberated through the Soviet Union. The putsch began the end of everything. When Gorbachev returned to power, it was clear that it was to be a short-lived return. A new figure had emerged as Russia's next leader: Boris Yeltsin, who had left the CPSU (Communist Party of the Soviet Union) but who had nonetheless been elected the President of the RSFSR in its first presidential elections. A chastened Gorbachev and a boisterous Yeltsin became the lead actors in the events of the dissolution of the USSR, one brought down and one raised up by the events of August. The Soviet leader would sign away the end of his state, and the Russian one oversee the transition to a new Russia.

Russia Again

I first travelled to Russia in the autumn of 1992, at the end of the very first year of the new Russian Federation's life. I was an undergraduate student and journeying on a language programme to Krasnodar, in what is now again called New Russia, close to the Black Sea. Revisiting the journal I kept I am struck by the things I've forgotten (endless harassment by men, my own pretentiousness), but somewhat relieved to see that one of my central memories was indeed part of my consciousness at the time: an almost all-consuming preoccupation with food. It is not that I ever went hungry – armed with dollars, I always had enough to eat – but finding and preparing food was so much more complicated and took so much more time than anything I had experienced that it held and still holds an outsized part of my memory of that trip.

In one of my final entries, I thought back to how things had changed over the course of the autumn (we arrived in September and I was at this point writing in the middle of December):

> Upon our arrival we were overwhelmed by the produce in the markets. Tomatoes, grapes, cucumbers, eggplant, raspberries . . . The variety of fruits and vegetables seemed endless . . . And not only was there plenty of produce, but many other foods were available. The state store across the street often had butter, cheese, milk, *tvorog*, sour cream, plus a healthy variety of bread. Eggs were not hard to find. Meat was fairly plentiful (although amazingly expensive). As fall deepened, however, food at the markets began to diminish and prices continued their steady rise. Now, at the beginning of December, the markets have persimmons, wildly expensive *mandariny* [mandarin oranges],

apples, and a few tomatoes that now cost 100 rubles / kilogram instead of 30, maybe potatoes, maybe onions, maybe garlic. The store usually has fat, not butter, and today while I waited in line they ran out of bread.

Elsewhere in the journal I rhapsodize over ice cream, which I ate almost every day on my trips into the centre of town to shop at the main market, and over foods from the wider Soviet world that I had never known. *Lavash*, a wood-fired flatbread, and *adjik*, a spicy paste, both from the Caucasus and available at the market, became staples of my meals. The *lavash* emerged from a hole in the fence at one end of the market, handed over so piping hot that it almost burned my hands. Women sold small jars of the *adjik* along with jars of mayonnaise – both mixed together turned out to make an excellent dressing for shredded cabbage. I also fell hard for 'carrots Korean-style': thin strips of carrots in a fiery-hot dressing sold in little plastic bags by another woman in the market. Although I did not know anything of this at the time, I eventually learned that their 'Korean'-ness came from the ethnic Korean population that had been forcibly resettled by Stalin from the Soviet border with Korea to Kazakhstan. These together became one of my staple meals, perhaps with a small container of *plavlennyi syr* – gooey processed cheese, the only kind we could reliably find.

I ate fried *pirozhki* from a stand near the main market, filled with cabbage or mushrooms or potatoes (or liver, a word I had not known and learned to avoid). I learned both that the word for a clove of garlic in Russian is a 'tooth' of garlic and that sliced raw garlic on bread was considered an effective way of fighting a cold. I had my first experience with *pelmeni*, eaten in a little restaurant in the centre of the city that served only them, dished up in bowls with a generous helping of sour cream, to be sprinkled with greyish salt from a communal bowl on the table – delicious and warming (I became curiously un-American about germs). On our group trips I also experienced a version of *obshchepit* in Intourist hotels, where mysterious, tough meat was the norm and I learned to envy the vegetarians in the group. (They regularly received only noodles and cheese, but that seemed a better deal than some of the odd cuts we got.) I must have had soup, as well, given how prominent it has become in my understanding of Russian food, but it is oddly absent in my journal or my memory.

I was given advice on how to tell the difference between proper vodka and *samogon* sold in official-looking bottles. The fear was that *samogon* was

Along with a (Soviet) rouble, a map of the Moscow metro (now very out of date), and a
ticket from the St Petersburg Philharmonic (still printed on its Soviet form), I glued three
pop labels on the journal I kept in 1992: for Pepsi, Fanta and Fiesta.

likely to be methyl alcohol, and therefore deadly, instead of ethyl alcohol,
simply intoxicating. (The advice had something to do with swirling the
bottle and looking for bubbles, but basically I was scared and avoided the
whole issue.) Mostly I drank Pepsi or Fanta, both of which were somehow
in steady supply. Pepsi had entered the Soviet market in 1974, when it
opened a bottling operation inside the Soviet Union. Initially, it traded
its syrups for Stolichnaya vodka in return, selling the vodka on; as the
Soviet economy grew more strained, it took on other goods in exchange,
including most startlingly $300 million in tankers and freighters in 1990.[1]
Fanta, part of the larger Coca-Cola brand, came in a few years later, as did
the Pepsi version – Fiesta.

I was also introduced to generous displays of hospitality and gen-
erosity even in the face of increasing problems with supplies. I was fed
endlessly, it seemed – making and eating *blinchiki* at one person's house,
soup at another's. I stayed in a dorm, but I was assigned a host family for
Russian language practice; they wanted to send a grapevine cutting from
their dacha home with me, though I regretfully had to decline because I
would not be allowed to bring it into the u.s. After a few of the members
of our group went to a primary school to sing songs with the children
there (we mangled some 'American' songs, the teachers sang a beautiful
version of 'Yesterday' in Russian translation), the teachers served us an

absolute feast of foods brought by the parents of the pupils. Jars and jars of *varenye* (preserves), blini and *blinchiki* and other fried treats, biscuits and buns and *pirogi*. Cup after cup of hot, sweet tea, or of instant coffee with sweetened condensed milk.

In the middle of the trip we went up to St Petersburg and Moscow for two weeks. It was November, and cold, and I found St Petersburg thrillingly beautiful and Moscow incomprehensibly big. There were more strange hotel meals and things we had not seen in months, from the exotic (people standing outside metro stops with tables set up, selling bananas and pineapples) to the more mundane (Twix bars). I remember almost nothing about a dinner at a Moscow restaurant except for a single dish: sliced tomatoes covered with a garlicky grated cheese mixture, which I now recognize as a common starter, but which at the time sang out to me after several months of only processed cheese. And although I am somewhat ashamed to admit it, I cried a little bit when I saw the first McDonald's in Moscow. It had opened only two years before, in January 1990, bringing with it 'milkshakes and human kindness', as a *New York Times* reporter put it.[2] Its menu boards promised 'a free smile!' and that meant as much as the hamburgers and fries.

I recognized even at the time that although I never myself went hungry during that autumn and early winter, that had everything to do with the fact that I had time – my language classes were over by midday, so I could spend the afternoon going to multiple markets and standing in queues – and dollars. Even the 30 roubles a kilogram (2¼ lb) for tomatoes I paid at the beginning of the trip was well out of the reach of many people searching out food in the markets, let alone the 100 roubles at the end. For me, the price was pennies (at the start of the trip I got 250 roubles to the dollar, by the end 500), but for the people around me, it was something very different. A survey of wages in the new Russian Federation found mean monthly wages of 296 roubles at the start of 1991; it had risen to 18,672 by February 1993 but had actually decreased in purchasing power because of the staggering rate of inflation.[3]

What I did not fully understand was that all of this had to do with the 'shock therapy' introduced in an effort to reform and rebuild the new Russia's economy after decades of Soviet stagnation. It had a huge effect on everyday life, though, in part because of the many things it involved. It was not just privatization of formerly state economic concerns, a process that itself went along with significant traumas as shares were sold by those who needed money immediately and purchased by those who had money to spare, in part leading to a world of extreme inequality: oligarchs and everyone else. It was also a much broader set of changes to the market and to the social safety net that had eventually covered the Soviet population. These new measures included in particular the elimination or dramatic reduction of food and agriculture subsidies. Those had accounted for 20 per cent of the Soviet Union's expenses in 1990 – their elimination saved money, but also led to a huge fall in agricultural production and stresses on the food system.[4]

The shock to the agricultural system was only part of the problem during the 1990s – the economic situation more generally ricocheted widely during this decade. First and foremost, real incomes continued to fall, only recovering and stabilizing at the very end of the decade. Although wages recovered slightly in 1992, they then fell again by the end of 1995. By the beginning of 1996, 73 per cent of the population earned wages below 'a reasonable average subsistence income'.[5] Their fall was caused in large part by soaring inflation and a plummeting value of the rouble through the early years of the decade. A comparison of wages and prices in Moscow from August 1993 showed just what this meant in terms of the choices people now had to make when it came to feeding themselves. The monthly income of a university professor was the equivalent of $31, a medical doctor $50, a bus driver $80, a government worker $150 and a business manager $600 (the monthly minimum wage was at the time equivalent to $7). At the same time, 2.3 kilograms (5 lb) of potatoes cost $0.91, 0.5 kilograms (1 lb) of salami $2.21, a bottle of Coca-Cola $0.45, 10 eggs $0.30 and a Big Mac $1.40. Bread, at least, was still cheap: $0.07 per loaf.[6] It was a return to a diet of bread and potatoes for many. As dire as this seemed, there were some signs of more stability in the middle of the decade. At the end of 1997 a currency reform slashed the final three digits off banknotes (a 10,000-rouble note became a 10-rouble note) because at least the inflation rate had more or less stabilized.

I was in Russia again when that currency reform happened, a Russia that was similar to the one I had first experienced, but which had already begun to change dramatically. The currency reform brought with it a lot of confusion, not so much for the banknotes but for the smaller coins – old 100-rouble coins were now the same as the new 10-kopek coins – and I spent a fair bit of time holding handfuls of coins up to kiosk windows where a seller picked through them to find what I owed. That was one of the big changes: the explosion of different places to buy things. On my first trip, there were official shops with price controls that made them cheaper than anywhere else, but which came to hold almost nothing by the end of 1992. There were official markets based on Soviet-era *kolkhoz* markets, where prices were higher but food was relatively plentiful, and there were a few semi-official market spaces, as well. By my next trip, in 1996, stores had goods in them again, but markets were cheaper. There were now all sorts of kiosks, too, which sprang up on main streets, outside metro stations, in pedestrian underpasses, selling bootleg videotapes, hosiery, juice, pastries, fruit – just about anything one might need. One estimate suggested that in 1994, St Petersburg had 8–10,000 kiosks in operation, compared to 2,815 officially registered shops.[7] They were notorious for their connection with organized crime, but they still got things to people.[8] In a lot of ways, it was a return to a kind of urban world of food that visitors in the eighteenth and nineteenth century had experienced – food was everywhere and available at any time, though in ways that could be confounding in unexpected juxtapositions of goods.

Food was everywhere, but in each of the places I lived over the course of a long stay in 1997–8 I found particular pathways through the maze. When I lived on my own in an apartment in St Petersburg at the end of a metro line, I found my way through the mass of kiosks at the station to a particular one with a friendly shopkeeper and *lavash* that was not quite as good as what I had eaten on my first trip, but still delicious. I went to a tiny grocery shop on a street a block or two away from the Hermitage where there was good imported Italian pasta sauce, and also to the closest thing to a supermarket, in the basement of the pre-revolutionary 'Passazh' shopping arcade, now reborn. There I bought Finnish hot cereal and locally produced ricotta cheese. As I walked between the library and the archives, a trip that took me along the main street of St Petersburg, Nevsky Prospect, I stopped into the giant bakery that offered everything from frozen puff pastry to fresh-baked bread, grabbed an apple *pirozhok* and continued on my way. I started going to an aerobics class, and my teacher invited me on an excursion to Kronstadt one Saturday; on the way we stopped for a picnic of open-faced sandwiches with sausage or *salo* (smoked pig fat), cream puffs and very sweet red wine. Eventually I found my way to the 'Idiot' café, still today located in the same low, cosy rooms along one of the canals, just down from the Iusupov Palace where Rasputin met his end. There I drank pots of tea and ate plates of *syrnyki*: small patties of sweetened *tvorog* and raisins, pan fried and served with sour cream. Nothing was as comforting as winter came and the days grew shorter and shorter.

In Moscow I stayed in a dorm, cooking for myself in a communal kitchen. The Finnish cereal I had eaten every morning in St Petersburg turned out not to be on sale this much further from the Finnish border, so I switched my morning routine to oatmeal – and discovered that it still held on to its Soviet-era brand name 'Hercules'. On the train between Moscow and St Petersburg, the man sitting next to me disapproved of my simple meal of bread, water and an apple and tried to get me to eat a giant boiled sausage he pulled out of a Thermos (I declined as politely as I could). I almost broke a tooth on a frozen chocolate bar bought from a street vendor on the way to the archives on a bitterly cold winter day. I found that one of the shops near my dorm sold a decent Australian cheddar. I discovered the glories of Georgian food, going regularly with friends to a place called Mama Zoya, where we feasted on *khachapuri*, hot and oozing with cheese, and the sharp garlicky flavours of its many vegetable treats. I ordered bowl after bowl of *pelmeni* at a little restaurant in the Moscow Conservatory and ate countless cheese- and apple- and cabbage-filled *pirozhki* bought piping hot from a man who stood with big wooden trays of them outside the entrance to the library. My German friends, in particular, loved the fact that many of the new small grocery shops were open around the clock. After walking past it many times, a couple of other American friends and I decided to try a small neighbourhood restaurant, Kristina's Place, where we were faced with an incomprehensible menu: it listed names of dishes that had meaning to those who had grown up in the Soviet system but which were at that point unknown to us. Fortunately, whatever we tried turned out to be good – 'pork peasant-style' was topped with slices of pickles and tomato, covered with melted cheese, for example – and we returned often.

I spent a month in Kazan, a twelve-hour train ride east of Moscow, where I stayed with a family. The city was of course much smaller than either Moscow or St Petersburg, but it had a similar mix of older shops, newer shops and kiosks. My host Natasha cooked me breakfast and dinner every day and I immediately realized that I had lucked into the home of an excellent cook. Mornings I feasted on *kasha* or eggs or, my favourite, *syrniki*. Every evening we had soup; one weekend day I sat in the kitchen with Natasha as she made and narrated the process of making borscht, and hers is still the borscht I make myself. Soup was the beginning of the multi-course Russian meal that I was coming to recognize as the standard: soup, salad (usually tomatoes and cucumbers in a simple vinaigrette with fresh herbs), meat and starchy 'garnish', bread. Every morning I stopped at the same bakery to buy a roll or two to eat for lunch. I was clearly an object of some curiosity, but it was not until I was interviewed on the local news simply for being an American at the archives that the cashier asked me 'and how are you finding it here?' Another researcher at the archives, an older professor, seemed dubious of my topic when I told him what I was working on – food in eighteenth- and nineteenth-century Russia – but he started dropping a couple of sweets on my desk when he left for the day. My host Oleg proudly told me of Kazan's brewery, Krasnyi Vostok ('The Red East'), and I started buying bottles of beer to bring home to dinner most days.

One of the reasons I brought beer home with me was that I knew that it was too expensive for Oleg and Natasha to buy regularly, even with the rent I was paying. In fact, all through this period I knew that my way was still eased by dollars. Nothing was as cheap as it had been half a decade before, and there were certainly expensive places I could not dream of visiting, but for me there was nothing particularly difficult, just somewhat idiosyncratic, about the ways that the food system worked. That was not the way of it for most of the Russians around me, though. Overall calorie consumption did not drop significantly, but the percentage of household income going to food increased over the course of the 1990s, and calories from grains increased in comparison to calories from meat and dairy, reversing the trends of the later Soviet period. Households spent 38 per cent of their expenditures on food in 1991 and 50 per cent in 2000.[9] Some groups were harder hit, as well: famously, pensioners found themselves

Gardening was and is both a necessity and a passion for many Russians across its great expanses. In this photograph from 2003, a lush garden in the Siberian province of Cheliabinsk promises an abundant supply of fruits and vegetables for the long winter.

living on pensions that were first of all dramatically out of step with the current cost of living and second often in arrears for months.[10]

This all went along with larger changes in the world of agriculture. Some things did not change, of course. For one thing, private plots remained an important part of the ways in which people kept themselves fed during some of these years. If in 1991 private plots accounted for 31 per cent of all agricultural production, by 2000 they accounted for 57 per cent of the total. Access to land could remove at least some of the sting of a tiny pension. In 1998, a pensioner with an official residence in the town of Tula spent much of her time at her mother's house in a village an hour away. There, they counted on potatoes, carrots and beetroot, and 'an ocean of pickles in huge glass jars' for much of their food. Her pension (when it was paid) helped with sugar and meat and other necessities.[11] Even as the economy has stabilized in the 2000s, the private plot is still significant. By the middle of the 2010s, around 50 per cent of the population of giant Moscow has access to some sort of plot of land for gardening; slightly more do in St Petersburg, and in smaller cities the numbers are more like 62–6 per cent.[12] Now, however, along with practices like picking berries and hunting mushrooms, these garden plots are as tied to a sense of authenticity, of tradition, of being part of the natural world, as they are to necessity.[13]

As the private plot retained its importance, both practically and symbolically, the larger agricultural world began to change more significantly. After the crisis caused by the removal of subsidies at the beginning of the 1990s, agricultural concerns had to figure out how to survive in the new semi-capitalist Russian world. A major influence turned out to be the rise of the fast-food restaurant. That first McDonald's was quickly joined by more and more restaurants in Moscow, in St Petersburg and then throughout the country. By the middle of the 2000s, the chain accounted for 43 per cent of the market share of fast-food restaurants in the country – a 194-billion-dollar market.[14] Initially, that first McDonald's was supplied mostly through imports and, as it grew, by production in its own complex outside Moscow (the McComplex). Steadily, though, Russian businesses started to produce most of what McDonald's needed. A *kolkhoz* just outside Moscow started supplying lettuce almost as soon as the first McDonald's opened. As McDonald's grew, so did it, and now the Belaya Dacha company supplies not just shredded lettuce to fast-food restaurants but also dozens of varieties of lettuce to supermarkets. In 2010, as the first Moscow McDonald's turned twenty, 80 per cent of the restaurant chain's needs were supplied by domestic producers.[15]

The Russian economy as a whole began to recover in the 2000s, helped significantly by rising commodities prices. Wages increased and diets improved, although the poor, and particularly the urban poor, still faced and face challenges of subsistence.[16] In particular, the transformation of the agricultural sector has largely made it possible for Russia to feel food-secure in a way it had rarely done in the past.[17] Already by 2013, it had gone from importing more grain than any other country at the end of the Soviet era to the third-ranked grain exporter in the world. It did so via methods that in many ways reflected the Soviet past. In the early 2000s, around 80 per cent of agricultural land was controlled by large-scale agriculture enterprises that mostly evolved out of the Soviet-era *kolkhoz*. Small-scale farms cultivated only 10 per cent of agricultural lands. But those small-scale farms were responsible for 50 per cent of agricultural production, compared to only 40 per cent by the large-scale farms.[18] Small-scale production has fallen since, but the role of smaller farms is still important. Overall, however, the transformation of post-Soviet agriculture has made Russia into the agricultural powerhouse earlier leaders always believed it to be. In 2017, it was the fourth-largest producer and largest exporter of wheat in the world (it was also the largest exporter of buckwheat, flaxseed and sugar beet pulp); it was the largest producer of barley and third-largest of potatoes and milk.[19]

This feeling of greater stability has been palpable not only on the streets of Moscow and St Petersburg but much more widely within the Russian Federation. After my long trip in the late '90s, I returned for a stay in Moscow and St Petersburg during the summer of 2002 and then not again until 2007. That trip in 2002 is something of a blur in my memory – it felt mostly of a piece with my previous stay. The major difference was more restaurants and particularly a mini-explosion of sushi restaurants and fancy cafés. Otherwise I revisited some of the same shops and restaurants I had before, though I was saddened that my favourite bakery on the main street of St Petersburg had turned into a clothing shop and that one of my favourite cafés in Moscow had become a much more expensive coffee shop. That was another change: with the stabilization of the rouble, prices were no longer as cheap as they had been for me, though there were also now apparently more consumers who could enjoy these places.

Starting in 2007, I have travelled to Russia about every other year for stays in summer and winter, for a few weeks or a few months. I spend most of my time in Moscow and St Petersburg, but have also visited other cities: Riazan, Iaroslavl, Saratov, Novgorod. Although there is more of everything in the two big cities, there are things that bring all of these places together when it comes to food. Of course, there are McDonald's everywhere now. There are also all sorts of other restaurants and cafés aiming to be places not just for the super wealthy. There are Russian fast-food chains like Teremok, which serves blinchiki and buckwheat *kasha* filled or topped with cabbage or mushrooms or ham and cheese. They started as kiosks at the end of the 1990s, along with Kroshka Kartoshka, which offered baked potatoes filled with similar things. In the last five or so years, the *stolovaia* – the canteen – has made a huge comeback, with new versions offering soup and *kotlety* but also aubergine with pesto popping up even on the fancy shopping streets of Moscow and St Petersburg. So too has Georgian food, which seems to have replaced the sushi restaurants in its ubiquity (there were always a few Georgian restaurants, but their numbers have risen dramatically in the last few years). On my last few trips, I've eaten Neapolitan pizza (excellent) and Thai food (delicious) and tacos (not as successful, alas) and drunk both craft beers and fair-trade espressos.

Shopping is different, too. In the 1990s, there were a few large supermarkets, dozens of small grocery shops that stuffed a surprising amount of

Unofficial distribution systems outside the world of stores have continued throughout the post-Soviet era. One day in the autumn of 2009 I noticed watermelon stands like this one spring up around St Petersburg. The cage stayed in place overnight, filled with watermelons that were at first replaced with fresh shipments from the south, and later with dwindling numbers (and a thicker layer of broken-up boxes to guard them from the encroaching cold).

In the autumn
of 2018, Moscow
celebrated the
harvest with vivid
displays of vegetables
and other foods
in and around the
historic city centre.
Here, in the centre
of the giant shopping
arcade GUM, a
display of (fake)
milk cans labelled
cream, sour cream,
milk and *tvorog* show
off post-Soviet dairy
abundance.

food for sale into small central city spaces, and even more kiosks. Those smaller groceries have not really disappeared, particularly in the old centres where space is at a premium. There are also now larger supermarket chains that seek to serve different clienteles. Perekrestok is an all-round super-market often located in the basement of the many shopping malls that have also sprung up around Russian cities. Azbuka Vkusa – 'The ABCs of Taste' – features beautifully wrapped produce and much higher prices. The most startling change to come to Moscow is the decline of the kiosk. Literally overnight, on 9 February 2016, bulldozers throughout the city razed dozens of kiosk structures, part of a larger beautification campaign by the city's new mayor.

On every trip to Moscow I have taken since 2007, I have stayed at the same place, renting a room in a slightly out-of-the way neighbourhood from a retired woman named Emma. Doing this has let me get a feel for how a residential neighbourhood in Moscow has changed over this past decade and more: I saw the old grocer's shop in the neighbourhood, which even on my first trip was still reminiscent of a Soviet-era grocery (but with more food), shut, reopen and be joined by multiple new grocery stores in the area. I saw the kiosks close, except for the ice cream one by the bus stop. Of course, it has also let me get to know Emma, and we have had many conversations and even arguments about books and music and history (which Emma calls her third profession, after a number of historians like me have stayed with her). And, of course, we talk about food.

Although I mostly cook for myself, Emma feeds me from time to time, more and more, in fact, as I get older. (She is usually reluctant to eat anything I make, alas.) She now always greets me with soup and *vinegret* (or more recently with a Georgian vegetable dish called *pkhali*) and a lemon *pirog*, her speciality, for my first meal. She tells me I have to finish this dish or that dish that she made too much of. Now she will actually go out to a restaurant occasionally, though when I first stayed with her she thought that was a ridiculous extravagance. We talk about the fact that GUM – the big shopping complex along one side of Red Square – still has the best Soviet-style ice cream in the city and she sends me pictures on WhatsApp of herself and friends that I know enjoying it.

In many ways, all this change means that food has become a simpler part of life. There are no more queues, for one thing. But as my conversations with Emma suggest, food still holds a central place in the mental world of many Russians. Cookbook sections in bookshops are huge; magazines and newspapers feature recipes and culinary advice. The Russian-language Internet is filled with recipe sites and message boards answering questions about the difference between forms of ham or of sour cabbage. There is a particular interest in the history of Russian food, as well. The Soviet-era cookbooks and food histories written by the late Viliam Pokhlebkin are printed and reprinted. Other authors and culinary figures, notably Maksim Syrnikov, strive to uncover the Russian dishes lost during the Soviet era and even during the Europeanizing centuries before.[20] Although the exact way this plays out is new, the interest in food beyond the purely utilitarian certainly is not. Anastasia Lakhtikova has written about the recipe notebooks kept by women in the late Soviet era. They copied recipes on anything that came to hand, including old library cards or punch cards, in an effort to make that time of shortages into one of pleasure, as well.[21]

Starting in 2014, there was another reason to talk a lot about food, at least for a while. That year, Western countries applied economic sanctions on the Russian Federation for its annexation of Crimea. In response, the Russian regime levied what it called 'countersanctions' against those countries – members of the EU, the U.S., Norway, Australia and Canada. The countersanctions above all banned the import of most foods from these places, from fruits and vegetables to sausages and cheese. Although initially intended only as a short-term measure, they have been extended again and again.[22] Although these countersanctions include many, many foodstuffs, somehow cheese has taken on outsized importance in discussions of their effects. Soon after, an Internet poll claimed that if asked to choose between Crimea and cheese, 64 per cent of Russians would choose cheese.[23] The following year, when smuggled cheeses and other banned foods were uncovered, officials decided to make a show out of destroying them, bulldozing them into a pit or even setting fire to them – quite a dramatic statement that Russia no longer needed to worry about having enough food, on top of a statement against the imports.[24] Since then, the domestic cheese industry has seen a huge influx of interest and support in its efforts to create a Russian-made alternative to Camembert or Brie or even Parmesan.[25]

IN 1859, BAYARD TAYLOR, a traveller to Russia, wrote a remarkable description of Moscow:

> No other city in the world presents so cosmopolitan an aspect.
> The gilded domes of Lucknow – the pagodas of China –
> Byzantine churches – Grecian temples – palaces in the style
> of Versailles – heavy inexpressive German buildings – wooden
> country cottages – glaring American signs – boulevards,
> gardens, silent lanes, roaring streets, open markets, Turkish
> bazaars, French cafés, German beer-cellars, and Chinese
> tea-houses – all are found here, not grouped exclusively into
> separate cantons, but mixed and jumbled together, until Europe
> and Asia, the Past and Present, the Old World and the New, are
> so blended and confounded, that it is impossible to say which
> predominates. Another city so bizarre and so picturesque as
> Moscow does not exist. To call it Russian would be too narrow
> a distinction: it suggests the world.[26]

With slightly different language, one could write nearly the same description of Moscow today. The city's architecture has grown even more complicated, with the layers of Soviet and post-Soviet buildings adding the gothic and the utilitarian and the gaudy to the mix. Streets have become more roaring, but there are still surprisingly silent lanes just off them. There are still French cafés and German beer-cellars and Chinese restaurants, at least.

Travellers in the nineteenth century often noticed a similar sense of Russian food, at least on the tables of the elite, as being similarly 'mixed and jumbled together', with Western European foods and drinks and Russian ones served up together. Again, there are many ways that that is still true, in large part because the history of food in Russia has long involved layer upon layer of influences, from within what turned out to be an enormous empire and from outside its borders. It is almost impossible to imagine 'Russian cuisine' without potatoes or borscht, but both only began to play such a role during the nineteenth century, one coming from far outside the country's borders, one from its western empire. Vodka is much older, but not as old as beer and mead. Some foods have been forgotten, others have triumphed. All of those layers, all of these influences over a millennium or more of history, have made the food of Russia what it is today.

Recipes

A note on units: the recipes below are all direct translations from original sources, which means that their units of measurement are not necessarily reliable. When they give specific measurements at all, nineteenth-century recipes often use units of 'a cup', 'a bottle' or 'a spoonful'. A 'cup' was around 273 ml (a little over a U.S. cup); a bottle was just under a litre (just under a U.S. quart). The Soviet Union joined the metric system in 1925; after that point, measurements are mostly given in grams.

ZAKUSKI AND SALADS

Mushroom Caviar (1835)
Having taken cooked white mushrooms, chop them finely, mix with walnut oil, add pepper and salt in proportion and put on a plate; along the edge place chopped green onion and serve.[1]

Okroshka (1848)
Take leftover roast, whatever you have (except for pork and ham, which are not suitable because they are very fatty), cut it into small pieces, chop green onion, dill, cucumbers, hard-boiled eggs and, if you have it, some crab meat, then mix it all together, pour in good *kvas*, season with salt and let it sit. It is also possible to add a couple of spoonfuls of sour cream.[2]

Okroshka, *Meat* (1891)
[Molokhovets lists this as a 'cold soup' along with *botvinia*]
Take little bits of roast or boiled beef – salt beef, ham, veal, everything that is meat – cut into small pieces of equal size so that there is a total of

2 cups. Add 1 or 2 fresh, cleaned cucumbers, 1 or 2 hard-boiled eggs, finely chopped green onion, dill; put it in a soup tureen, pour in ½ cup of sour cream or a cup of whey, add 1 bottle of *kvas* and a bottle of *kislye shchi*, salt it, add a piece of ice.[3]

Studen *from Ox or Veal Feet and Head* (1891)

Clean the feet and head, put in a clay pot, pour in water, put in the oven for about eight hours, or boil in a pot on the stovetop, with a bay leaf, English and simple pepper, salt and onion. When the meat has cooked, take it out, clear it from the bones, chop finely, put it in the mould, strain the bouillon, pour it into the mould, let it chill. To serve, turn out onto a plate. Eat with mustard, vinegar or horseradish with vinegar.[4]

Studen (1945)

Cut scalded cow's lips and feet into pieces, chop up the bones and let soak. Then strain and clean everything, put it in a pot, pour in water and boil for 3–4 hours, then add a carrot, a celery root and an onion, a bay leaf and pepper and cook for another 30–40 minutes, after which, having taken it out of the bouillon, carefully separate the meat from the bones and chop the meat. Strain the bouillon, mix it back together with the chopped meat, salt to taste, cool to the consistency of a thick *kisel*, pour it into forms and cool thoroughly.[5]

Vinegret (1848)

It can be made from game, from any sort of meat: veal, mutton, beef, or whatever; sometimes there is a little bit of different kinds of roast left over and rather than serve it all together as the roast course, it is better to make *vinegret*. Separating the meat from the bones, put it on a plate in parts or having chopped it into small pieces. Take boiled potato, beetroot, fresh or pickled cucumbers, and cut them into thick slices; you can also grate the potato and beetroot; then put it all in rows on the plate on top of the meat or, if [cut into] little pieces, in a circle. In the *vinegret* you can put soaked apples, cherries, pears, capers, olives, cooked mushrooms, salted milk cap. Having put whatever of the above on the plate, sprinkle [chopped hard-boiled] eggs on top, or add a galantine. Then take vinegar, mustard, olive oil, salt, mix it all together and pour onto the plate.[6]

Vinegret (1945)

3–4 potatoes, 500 g beetroot, 100 g carrots, 2–3 cucumbers, 100 g green onion, 100 g cabbage, 1 tablespoon oil, 2 tablespoons vinegar, mustard, sugar and salt to taste.

Trim cooked potatoes, beetroot, carrots and fresh or salted cucumbers, cut into pieces and put in a bowl, adding shredded sour cabbage. Mix the mustard, sugar and salt with the oil and vinegar. Pour this dressing into the bowl with the vegetables and let it sit for 15–20 minutes, so that the vegetables soak up the dressing.

Before serving the *vinegret* put it on a salad server or on a plate, piling up the salad in the shape of a little mountain, and decorate with the vegetables that went into the *vinegret*. As you wish you can add to the *vinegret*: apples, green or yellow onion, tomatoes, salted or marinated mushrooms, eggs. You can dress it with a spoonful of sour cream; colour it with various marinades, from cherries, plums, grapes, berries and so on. *Vinegret* may be prepared with an addition of cooked fish, herring and also meat or meat or fish conserves.[7]

First Course: Soups

Ukrainian Borscht (1835)

Having soaked in river water good dry white mushrooms, so they are well reconstituted and there is no more sand, boil them until they are done; when they have cooked, separate the stems from the caps; chop up the stems finely and put them in the caps, cramming them in well; having added white bread soaked in almond milk, stuff it all together. Take two spoonfuls of walnut oil, add flour in proportion so that it combines, also salt, pepper, nutmeg, green dill, mix it again and make fish quenelles. Having sautéed beetroot, cabbage, onion, roots, carrots, the stuffed mushroom caps, sauté them in walnut oil and, having added a small amount of flour, add mushroom bouillon and let boil; when it is halfway done, having boiled a head of sour cabbage in water a little, cut each leaf in half and, removing the stem, wrap up some of the quenelles and put in the borscht. The rest of the quenelles put in the borscht with a teaspoon. Sour with good *kislye shchi*. Serve with almond milk and a sprinkle of green dill.[8]

Borscht (1891)

Make a bouillon from 1 or 2 *funty* of fatty beef, or pork, or from 1 *funt* of smoked pork fat, without root vegetables but with an onion, 1 or 2 dried mushrooms, a bay leaf and 3–4 peppercorns; strain it. An hour before dinner put in the bouillon ¼ of a head of cabbage, boil and add the brine from pickled beetroot to taste. At the same time take 2–3 red beetroots, wash them well without using a knife, that is do not peel them, and boil them separately in water. When they are soft, take them out, pare them with a knife, slice finely, sprinkle on half a spoonful of flour, mix that together, add to the bouillon, salt it and bring to a boil twice. Place in the soup bowl one shredded raw beetroot with its juice, cooked and finely chopped beef, pork, or smoked pork fat, pour over the hot borscht, add sour cream or whey, sprinkle with herbs; serve buckwheat porridge separately. It is possible to make it without beef, and in that case take 4–6 dried mushrooms, boil them, chop them finely, sauté with onion in a spoonful of vegetable oil, add that to the borscht, bring it to a boil once and sprinkle with herbs.[9]

Natasha's Borscht
[Narrated to me in Kazan, May 1998]

Take 3 beetroots, diced. Cover with bouillon or water and add 1 tablespoon vinegar, 1 teaspoon sugar. Cook over low flame until tender (about 30 minutes). At the same time, sauté 1 smallish onion in oil, add 1 carrot, finely diced, 1 spoonful tomato paste. Cook for 10 minutes. Add 2 small potatoes, diced, and ⅓ to ½ head cabbage finely sliced. Cover with water, cook for about 15 minutes. Combine with the cooked beetroots, add 1 bay leaf, several whole allspice, several stems of fresh dill. Cook for about 7 minutes. At the very end, add 1 clove garlic, minced, and turn off heat. Serve with chopped dill, sour cream and a thin lemon slice.

Botvinia *with Cucumbers* (1862)

Thinly slice the necessary quantity of cleaned cucumbers into squares, put in a pot and place over ice. Clean, wash and boil sorrel in salted water, drain through a fine sieve and put in a cold place. Clean a little young spinach and the same amount of young beet greens, wash, blanch until soft in boiling water and when it is ready, put in cold water, squeeze out the water and chop finely. Fifteen minutes before serving put everything in one pot, add strained *kislye shchi* or *kvas*, add salt and sugar to taste and add finely chopped herbs, like tarragon, chervil, dill, shallots, grated horseradish, and add several pieces of clean ice. Boil a piece of salmon (according to the number of people) in salted water, chill it on ice and then put on a plate and cover with the sliced fresh cucumbers, crabmeat, grated horseradish and chopped herbs and onion.[10]

Lapsha *(Noodle Soup)* (1891)

Make a bouillon from 2 *funty* of beef and root vegetables. Stir together and knead well a thick dough of 1 egg, an eggshell of salted water and 1½ cups, that is ½ *funt*, of flour; roll it out thinly, sprinkle the rolled-out circle with flour on both sides. Cut it into strips, place the strips one on top of each other, slice finely, with a sharp knife, spread them out on the table to dry out, shaking the flour off the noodles. Just before dinner sprinkle the *lapsha* in the boiling bouillon, salt it with a teaspoon of salt and bring to a boil. When the *lapsha* is done, serve with chopped herbs. If you cook it without beef, then make the bouillon of root vegetables, potato, onion and 4 dried mushrooms; when they have been boiled, chop finely, sauté with onion and a spoonful of oil, add to the *lapsha*, bring to a boil, sprinkle with chopped herbs.[11]

Rassolnik (1891)

Make a bouillon from 1–2 *funty* beef, one baked onion, carrots and 1 bay leaf. An hour before, add ⅛ cup pearl barley or farina, let it cook; a half hour before, add a small dish of cleaned, raw potato, 2 salted, cleaned and diced cucumbers, add pickle brine to taste, so that it has a pleasant taste, thicken with another half spoonful of flour dissolved in ¼ cup cold water, bring to a boil, whiten it with ¼ cup sour cream or ½–1 cup of whey, add the boiled beef, cubed. Serve sprinkled with chopped herbs. This *rassolnik* can be cooked without beef; and instead cook 2 dried mushrooms.[12]

Shchi, *Lazy* (1834)

Having cut a head of cabbage into pieces, add beef, mutton, chicken and ham in a pan and let it boil; first blanch the cabbage and together with it put in carrots, turnips and onion; add something sour and thicken with flour and butter, let it boil. When it's done, serve with chopped parsley and a dollop of sour cream.[13]

Shchi, *Real Russian* (1835)

Take cabbage, beef, ham, a handful of oatmeal and onion; pour water over all this and cook until done; then, having mixed a bit of flour and butter in a separate dish, add it to the *shchi* and afterwards add sour cream. When serving, sprinkle with pepper and add finely chopped onion and breadcrumbs.[14]

Shchi, Sbornye (1835)

Take pork, beef, ham, a goose and two chickens cut up into pieces, sour white cabbage and onion cut into circles. Boil all this together; add flour with butter, as described above, and afterwards add sour cream.[15]

Shchi, *Lazy* (1835)

Take a fresh head of cabbage, cut it into quarters and boil it with only beef; then season and whiten it [with flour/butter and sour cream] as stated above.[16]

Shchi, *French-style* (1835)

Take cabbage, as much as is needed for *shchi* that is neither thin nor very thick; put it for half an hour in cold water so it is soaked; then having taken it out, squeeze the water from it. Put several pieces of the best speck, cut up finely, into the bottom of a pot, and mix it with fat skimmed from some sort of meat bouillon; cook it on a low flame, and when the cabbage is cooked enough, put it in a meat decoction prepared in advance, to which add depending on taste, the liquid in which the cabbage was cooked; skim off the fat and serve.[17]

Shchi, *Lazy, Lenten* (1851)

Having boiled a quarter *funt* of dried white (or whatever kind you have) mushrooms, drain the bouillon into a cup. Then, having cut up a head of Russian white cabbage, put it in a pot, add fish bouillon, salt, cover with a lid and let it boil on the stove for about an hour. Then, having chopped two onions and fried them with a cup of walnut or poppy seed oil, sprinkle in a handful of flour, add two bottles of *kislye shchi*, pour that into the *shchi*, adding carrots cut into pieces and mashed potato, cover with a lid and cook until done. Finally, having cleaned the reconstituted mushrooms, dip them in batter and breadcrumbs, fry in oil and put in the *shchi* and, having finished it with a teacup of almond milk, serve with chopped parsley.[18]

Potage tchy à la russe (Shchi, *Lazy*) (1862)

Clean and cut into eight pieces a head of fresh cabbage and some root vegetables, such as celery, leeks, carrots and parsley. Blanch, and when

it has come to a boil drain and pour over cold water and put back in the
pot. At the same time put a piece of beef with top fat into a pot, add water
and blanch; when it has come to a boil, put the beef in cold water, wash,
cut it into pieces, put it into the pot with the cabbage, pour over strained
bouillon, add salt to taste, spices, and cook until done. Fifteen minutes
before it is ready cook a little flour in butter, add bouillon, whisk it into
the *shchi*, bring to a boil, skim off the fat, thicken with a liaison and add a
little chopped green parsley and pepper.[19]

Solianka *with Cucumbers* (1848)

Take three *funts* of good beef for bouillon, 10 salted cucumbers and an
onion, clean them, cut up everything finely and put in the bouillon. When
it's done, thicken with flour and butter.[20]

Selianka, *Meat* (1891) [alternative spelling of *solianka*]

Make a bouillon from a *funt* of bones cut into pieces . . . an onion, 1–2
bay leaves and 3–6 peppercorns; strain it. Add ½ dish of various meats cut
up into small pieces, like boiled or roast beef, veal, ham, salt beef, goose,
duck, sausage, just a little of everything. Finely chop an onion, sauté in
½ spoonful of oil, add ½ spoonful of flour, lightly brown it, add it to the
bouillon. Add 2 salted cucumbers cut into pieces, 4–8 marinated saffron
milk caps [*ryzhiki*], 4–8 milk caps [*gruzdy*], having dunked them once
in boiling water, or fresh white, boletus or milk cap mushrooms, which
first must be cleaned, washed, boiled separately and squeezed dry. Add
around ½ cup of pickle brine, and add also fresh or sour cabbage blanched
in boiling water. Mix it all together with the bouillon, bring to a boil, serve
with ½ cup of sour cream or thick cream, dill and a handful of chopped
green onion.[21]

Monastery Ukha (1835)

Having cleaned and gutted ten carp, ten perch, ten ruff and ten gudgeon,
cut the perch and carp in half and having taken a pan in proportion to the
fish, fill it with water, cleaned and chopped root vegetables, two whole
onions, and bring to a boil once; skim off the foam; then add the perch
and carp, bring to a boil two times; then add the ruff and gudgeon, a little
bay leaf, and cook until done; add salt, dill, herbs, pour in white wine and
add fresh lemon, in proportion, and serve.[22]

Potage de morilles à la russe *(Morel Soup, Russian-style)* (1862)
Pick over and clean the necessary quantity of morels, choose a part of them
to stuff, remove the middles (stems) from them, wash a second time, and
put them on a strainer to let the water completely drain. Take the remaining morels, cut them in half and wash. Chop them finely, and put them in
a pot with melted butter and let them sweat. Then add a little flour, mix it
up, pour on bouillon, bring to a boil and, leaving it over a low flame, add
a piece of cleaned ham, a bouquet garni of green dill, onion, parsley, and
simmer covered until soft. Meanwhile prepare a forcemeat as for quenelles,
from veal mixed with chopped eggs, ham and herbs; stuff the [reserved]
morels with it. Put them in a sauté pan, pour over a little bouillon, add
butter and salt and cook on a low flame, covered, until soft and until the
bouillon has boiled off. Before serving, remove the herbs and ham, thicken
with sour cream, pour into a soup tureen and add the stuffed morels. Into
this soup one may add small braised chickens, cut up into pieces.[23]

Russian Soup in a Pumpkin (1834)

Cut out a good-sized circle from the top of a ripe pumpkin so that afterwards it is possible to cover the pumpkin with the circle. Clean out the
seeds and everything that is in it. Clean two pairs of young chickens and a
pair of fresh grouse; cut them into pieces. Having saved the trimmings and
having cut into small circles parsley root, parsnip, celery root, leek and a
little carrot, sauté in sour butter; sprinkle on a little flour, pour over some
good bouillon, add the chicken and grouse, let it come to a boil once and
taking it off the fire, put it in the pumpkin. Having chopped up veal with
butter, add pepper, herbs, white bread and eggs and form it into quenelles,
blanch them in boiling water and put them in [the pumpkin] with the
chicken and sausages. Lard two onions with cinnamon and cloves, put
them all together with nutmegs and bay leaves. Having cleaned a fresh
lemon, cut it into circles, take out the seeds, and put all of it into the
pumpkin, also the pumpkin flesh and a bottle of good Médoc, layering it
all so that the pumpkin isn't too full. Make a dough of wheat flour mixed
with water and roll it out. Cover the pumpkin with its top and cover the
whole with dough so that no pumpkin is visible and so that steam can't
escape. Having chopped parsley and dill, sprinkle the pumpkin with them
and mark the lid with a knife so that it can be removed at the table. Then
put the pumpkin in the oven on a pan, and when it's done, serve it at table
in the dough. Note: Pumpkin prepared in this way can be taken on the
road, noting only that then add less liquid and when you take it out of

the oven, take off the lid, let the soup cool, add a good gelatine and cover it to freeze.[24]

Ukrainian Soup (1834)

Having beforehand cleaned and washed tripe in a change of water, so that it doesn't smell, boil it in salted water until it is halfway cooked, then chop it not very finely and sauté with root vegetables in a pan with sour butter; add flour and bouillon, let it boil, then put in chicken and veal, and when it's done, add chopped green parsley. Before serving, add a dollop of fresh sour cream.[25]

SECOND COURSES: ENTRÉES

Braised Beef with Kvas (1891)

Take 2–3 *funty* of soft beef shank or chuck, cut it into big pieces, hit them with a wooden mallet, salt, coat with flour. Put a piece of butter in the bottom [of a pan], then the beef, sprinkle it with finely chopped onion, 1–2 bay leaves, 3–6 peppercorns and small pieces of butter, put it on the stove or in a hot oven so that it just browns, then pour in simple *kvas* so that it is just covered. When it comes to a boil, cover with a lid and stew the beef for an hour. You can add raw potatoes or serve with fried ones. As a variation, you can coat the meat not with flour but sprinkle it with rye breadcrumbs, 2–3 handfuls. This proportion is for four people, for one meal, but to cook 2 *funty* of beef in pieces is not economical you should cook at least 4 *funty* for two days.[26]

Roast Chicken (1848)

After cleaning the chicken, being sure not to break it, carefully separate the skin from the meat. Take 9 or more hard-boiled eggs depending on the size of the chicken; chop them finely, mix with raw egg, season with salt, add a little finely chopped parsley. Sew the opening closed, pour the egg mixture between the skin and the meat and tie it off at the neck. The chicken so prepared should be put in boiling water for half an hour; after taking it out place it on a pan, rub it with oil/butter, put it in the oven and watch out that the chicken browns, turning and basting with oil/butter if needed.[27]

Roast Mutton (1848)

After washing it, salt it a little, pour over water, put it in the oven and let it cook well. Under roast mutton there is usually a lot of fat and juices; therefore, when it is roasting, leave some of the drippings under it and use the remainder to fry thick buckwheat or millet *kasha*. *Kasha* prepared in this way is very tasty.[28]

Roast Pumpkin (1848)

Take a ripe pumpkin, cut it into pieces the width of a finger, melt butter in a frying pan, put the pumpkin in it, salt, sprinkle with flour and put in the oven. When it browns, turn it over and again put in the oven. Then take five or six eggs, beat them, add two cups of milk, pour it over the pumpkin and put it in the oven to cook. Serve hot.[29]

Kotlety (1891)
[Note: Molokhovets lists this as a food for breakfast, but it turned into a common second dish in the Soviet era]

Take 1 *funt* soft beef shank or chuck, chop it very finely, removing the veins, which you can put in soup. Salt it, add 5 ground peppercorns, the crumbs from a 3-kopek roll soaked in water and squeezed dry, a half spoonful of butter/oil sautéed with half an onion, a little water or bouillon, and mix. Make round cutlets, coat them in breadcrumbs, put in a frying pan in hot oil, fry on both sides. To serve, pour over the same oil, in which you can add a spoonful or two of water, cream or a spoonful of sour cream, let it come to a boil and sprinkle in green onion. Serve with boiled or fried potatoes, with potato *kasha*, with carrots, mashed Swede/rutabaga, with green peas, stewed crabs and so on.[30]

Potato Kotlety with Mushroom Sauce (1891)
[Note: Molokhovets classifies these as a 'second' dish]

Wash [about a litre and a half] of potatoes, peel them, boil in salted water, pour off the water, then right away mash them, adding a spoonful of butter, 1 or 2 eggs, ¼ cup of flour and salt. Make *kotlety* in the shape of a flat patty, coat with flour or dried breadcrumbs. Fry in oil. Serve them with mushroom sauce, which is prepared in the following manner: put ⅛ *funt* butter (sour) or ⅛ cup Lenten oil in a pan or a clay pot, add a spoonful of grade 2 wheat flour, fry it while stirring, add 2 cups of mushroom bouillon, made from 4–8 dry mushrooms with salt and 2 whole onions, boil well, add the finely chopped boiled mushrooms, sprinkle with chopped herbs, serve. These *kotlety* can be made for Lent, in which case do not add eggs to the *kotlety* but a little more flour and use some sort of Lenten oil to fry them: mustard seed oil is best of all.[31]

Meat Selianka *in a Frying Pan* (1891)
[Note: Molokhovets gives recipes for *selianka/solianka* as both a soup and here as a second course]

Finely chop ½ onion, sauté in ⅛ *funt* oil/butter, add ½ *funt* – that is, a cup – of rinsed and drained sour cabbage, mix it, cover with a lid and let it steam until it is just about soft, stirring so that it does not burn. Sprinkle with a half spoonful of flour and mix well. Then move the cabbage into the frying pan, putting in a layer of cabbage, a layer of small pieces of boiled beef, ham, sausage, [or] roast wild fowl, and cover with a layer of cabbage. On top put 1–2 salted cucumbers, saffron milk caps, milk caps, all cut into pieces, pour over oil or drained fat, with ½ cup of water or bouillon, pour on a spoonful of sour cream, sprinkle with dried breadcrumbs and put in the oven until it browns.[32]

KASHA, KISEL, BREAD, PIROGI, DUMPLINGS

Buckwheat Kasha *in a Pot* (1862)
Prepare buckwheat groats and use a sieve to shake out the fine bits, pour out onto a sheet and toast over a low flame until it gets some colour. At the same time prepare in a clay pot of appropriate size boiling water, a little more than halfway up, add a little butter or olive oil, salt to taste, ground spices and, having put it on the fire, bring to a boil; then add in the buckwheat groats, mix, and cover the pot tightly with a lid, and when the *kasha* thickens, put it in a hot oven for half an hour; when it's done take it out, clean off the pot, wrap the pot in a napkin and serve. Toast the buckwheat according to the size of the pot and put in enough so that the pot is full.[33]

Kisel (1945)
For one cup of berries, [use] ½ cup sugar, 2 tablespoons potato flour. Sort berries – strawberries, currants, cherries, raspberries, blackberries – rinse with hot water and smash them well with a pestle, add ½ cup of boiled cold water, mix, strain through a sieve or press out the juice through cheesecloth. Take the pressed-out berries, add 2 cups of boiling water, boil for five minutes, then strain. Add sugar to the strained concoction, bring

to a boil, add in the potato flour dissolved in cold water and, while stirring, bring to a boil another time. Pour the pressed-out juice into the hot *kisel* and mix well.[34]

Rye Bread (1945)

Dough for rye bread should be kneaded in a special wooden rising bowl [*kvashnia*]. The first time, dough should be mixed with yeast (15 g yeast per 1 kg flour); in the future leave a little piece of dough [a *zakvaska*, or starter] in the rising bowl for the next bake.

Dissolve the starter in warm water, add in ⅓ of the flour, mix, let the dough rise, knead it again and let it sour for 7–8 hours. After this add salt, the remaining flour, knead the dough well with your hands, let it rise another time and then divide it up and shape into forms or on a tray, pour in some boiling water (so there are no cracks), let it rise first and put in the oven.[35]

Pirog *of Fresh Cabbage* (1891)

In the morning make a rich dough of 1⅔ cups water together with 3 *zolotniki* [about 12 g] of dry yeast and a teaspoon of salt, 1 egg, ⅛ or ¼ *funt* butter/oil and about 2 *funts* of flour. Mix well, cover with a napkin, let rise. When it has risen, make an elongated pie, filling it with cabbage: shred half a medium-sized head of cabbage, salt it, press it out after ten minutes, put it in a pan with ⅛ or ¼ *funt* of butter/oil, fry while stirring, until it is soft but has not burned nor browned. When it has cooled, add 2 chopped hard-boiled eggs, salt, add a little simple pepper. Having filled the dough with the cabbage, turn up all four edges, so the *pirog* has a correct, elongated rectangular shape, place it on a baking sheet, sprinkle with flour and let rise for half an hour. Then smear it with a glaze of beaten egg with a spoonful of water, but don't glaze the back of the *pirog*, sprinkle with breadcrumbs, put it right away into a hot oven for half an hour. This gives 8 big portions.[36]

Kulebiaka *(Non-Lenten)* (1848)

Take a rich, sour dough, roll it out to the size you want to make your *kulebiaka* and let it sit and spread a bit. The filling you can make in various ways, whatever you like. 1. Boil *viziga*, chop it finely, mix with finely chopped hard-boiled eggs, add melted butter and a little salt in proportion, and mix it all together. 2. Boil rice in water and drain it; chop hard-boiled eggs and mix with the rice, add melted butter and salt. 3. Take fillets of fish, fry them in a pan, chop, and mix with eggs, adding butter. You can put any fish you like in a *kulebiaka*, or whatever you have, osetra, salmon, trout, whitefish, carp, eel, but best of all is fresh or lightly salted osetra or salmon. Having taken the fish, if it is osetra, clean it, skin it and cut it into small pieces. Roll the dough prepared for the *kulebiaka* to the thickness of a finger, put it on an iron sheet, cover with the filling, whichever of the ones described above you want, to the thickness of a finger, and then place on it the fish; if the fish is fresh, then sprinkle on salt, pepper, nutmeg, and when the filling is made of *viziga* or fillets, then put it on top of the fish to the thickness of a finger, then pinch the *kulebiaka* closed, brush it with egg, sprinkle with breadcrumbs and put in the oven.[37]

Kulebiaka *(Lenten)* (1848)

You can make a filling out of fish fillets, pan-fried in Lenten oil, adding finely chopped onion, pepper, salt, nutmeg, *viziga*, chopped finely, and oil. The fish, as described above, cut into pieces, if it is osetra or salmon, and if it is whitefish or perch, then cut off the head and tail, pull out the bones, but leave on the skin. If you make it out of eel, then you have to boil it in salted water and take off the skin first. Then take the fish, cover with the filling, pinch the *kulebiaka* closed and put it in the oven.[38]

Siberian Pelmeni (1848)

Take three *funty* of good soft beef, chop finely, add onion, pepper, nutmeg, salt, and mix together well. Having prepared the filling in that way, take two eggs and a teacup of cold water, mix the eggs with the water, add a bit of salt and mix a thick dough, so that it can be rolled out. Then divide the dough into several parts and roll out with a rolling pin into thin sheets, like you would do for noodles, only a little thicker; from the prepared sheets cut out circles with a glass, or cut into squares. Having put on each some of the beef filling, pinch them shut and put them on a rack. When the *pelmeni* are ready, strain bouillon that has already been prepared from beef; once it has come to a boil, put in a few *pelmeni*; when they have come to a boil twice, they are ready. *Pelmeni* are usually cooked before dinner; they do not need to be cooked for long, like other soups, and having come to a boil on the stove or hearth twice, they are ready. Squares should be pinched shut in the following way: having cut the dough, put some filling on each square; fold on the diagonal and pinch shut; then pinch the two ends together, like Lenten or fish dumplings. You can simply boil *pelmeni* in water, but they are tastier in bouillon. In Siberia, they are one of the favourite foods. In winter, having prepared them, [people] freeze them and take them along on the road. Where there is no good prepared food, they just boil some water, put the *pelmeni* in, and in half an hour have a filling, tasty dish.[39]

Vareniki *with Cherries* (1891)

Make a dough [of 2 eggs or 1 egg and the same amount of water, measured in its shell, and about 1½ cups, which is half a *funt*, of flour, and salt], roll it out. Earlier prepare the cherries: pit them, sprinkle with sugar – to 2 cups of pitted cherries, 1 cup of sugar – [and] put them in the sunshine. In 3–4 hours, put them into a strainer; put the juice that comes out of the cherries into a pan; fill the *vareniki* with the cherries, boil. Serve with the juice from the cherries either brought to a boil or uncooked, together with the very freshest sour cream.[40]

Holidays

Buckwheat Blini (1848)

This favourite Russian dish is made in various manners, but here is the real way to prepare them: take good buckwheat flour, boil water and having let it sit for an hour, mix the boiled water in the necessary proportion; when this dough has cooled to the temperature of new milk, add yeast. In the morning, having kneaded the dough, take away part of it, and when the blini rise, mix in the remaining dough, salt, let it rise and bake.

Another version of blini is prepared in the following way: take good wheat flour, make a sponge with warm water, in the morning mix in buckwheat flour and let it rise two or three times; then take boiling water and having added it, mix so there are no lumps, and having added boiled water to the dough so that it is of the thickness as if to make biscuits, let it rise, salt it and bake.[41]

Buckwheat Blini (1891)

[Molokhovets lists this as a 'breakfast for *Maslenitsa*']

Five or six hours before breakfast make a dough of four cups of buckwheat flour, three cups of warm milk or water, 1 tablespoon of melted butter, two egg yolks and 2 *zolotniki* [about 8 g] of dry, or 2–4 spoonfuls of fresh yeast. Mix it all together and beat with a beater, the more the better. When it has risen, beat it again, seasoning thoroughly with a spoonful of salt.

Scald 1½ or 2 cups of hot milk or water, bringing it just to the boil but not letting it boil; mix that in, let it rise, and once it has risen bring it carefully to the stove, not bothering the dough so it does not fall. Bake/fry it by the spoonful in little pans, which to prepare to cook the blini you must first sprinkle with fine salt, heat, wipe out with a towel, wipe with oil with a feather or a rag and then pour in enough dough to cover the pan. Cook blini on the stovetop or better on hot coals in a Russian oven in which the heat must be kept constant. When the blini begin to rise and brown, you must brush the top with oil/butter. If they are cooked on the stovetop, then turn them over, fry, and then put to the side and keep them in a warm place so they do not cool. In general, begin to cook them just before you eat them. When you add fresh dough to the pan, each time you must wipe it with oil with a feather; do not skimp on oil. For blini you use the same number of cups of water or milk as cups of flour, along with yeast. Russian blini should be taller than *blinchiki*; they should be fluffy, airy, light.[42]

Yeast Blini (1945)

For 1 kg wheat flour, 6 cups of milk or water, 2 eggs (or 1 tablespoon of powdered eggs), 2 tablespoons of sugar, 1½ teaspoons of salt, 40 g yeast.

Make a starter: dissolve the yeast in 2 cups of warm water, gradually add 500 g of wheat flour, mix it so that there are no lumps, cover with a towel and put in a warm place to rise. When the starter has risen, add salt, sugar and raw eggs or reconstituted powdered eggs; mix all of this well and add the remaining flour and, while continuing to mix it, add the 4 cups of milk or water in two portions. After this again put the dough in a warm place to rise. When it has risen, mix it again, so that it falls, and then let it rise again, and then turn to cooking the blini.

The dough may be prepared with an addition of buckwheat flour, then the blini will turn out drier. In this case half of the wheat flour can be replaced with buckwheat flour. Make the sponge with wheat flour, and add the buckwheat flour after it has risen, together with the fats.

[An additional note on cooking: Before you cook blini, heat the frying pan very hot, smear with vegetable oil or schmaltz [chicken fat] and right away pour in the blini batter. Use a spoon and pour in enough so the blin is thin and even. When cooked on a stovetop, after one side has browned, turn it onto its other side with a thin knife. In a Russian oven it is not necessary to turn the blini, because there they brown on both sides.][43]

Blinchiki (1891)

1 egg, 1 cup flour and 1½ cups milk or water: mix together, season with salt. Heat the frying pan sprinkled with salt, wipe with a towel, smear with butter or a piece of fatback (*salo*), heat again, pour in a spoonful of batter so that it covers the entire bottom of the frying pan, put on the stovetop. When the blinchik begins to rise and separate from the pan and when it has cooked on one side, take it out and put on a clean table. Grease the pan again with butter or speck, pour in batter and so on until the end. Before dinner, fold every blinchik into a triangle, white side out, put them in the greased pan, fry on both sides, serve with sugar and jam.[44]

Kulich (Pain pour la fête de Pâcques) *(Easter Bread)* (1862)

For a *kulich* of average size, take the following proportions: 5 *funty* of flour, 10 eggs, ½ *funt* of butter, ¼ *funt* sugar, ½ *funt* of cleaned raisins and as much milk and yeast as it turns out you need. Prepare it in the following way: place half the flour, sifted, in a bowl for dough, pour in a little warm milk, mix a dough that is neither thick nor watery and add in enough yeast for the dough to rise in an hour (½ a teacup of good brewer's yeast should be enough). Then mix, sprinkle flour on top and put in a warm place for half an hour. When the dough has risen, gradually add egg yolks, butter, sugar, add flour and mix, until the dough does not stick to the bowl. Then add the egg whites beaten into a foam and the raisins, mix again, add the last part of the flour, as much as turns out to be necessary for a thick dough, put the dough in a warm place, covered, and let it rise. When it has risen, turn it out onto the table, knead it a little, divide into four parts and shape the biggest part into a disc the size a *kulich* should be, put it on a greased baking sheet and brush with egg. Do the same with the other pieces of dough: shape each into a circle a little smaller than the last and decorate the fourth part of dough on the top of the *kulich* with a cross as you like, and put it in a warm place. When it has risen as it should, brush with egg, put in an oven at moderate heat, and bake until done. It should be done in an hour and a half.[45]

Paskha, *Usual* (1891)

For an average-sized mould, take 7–8 *funty* of fresh *tvorog*, put it in a press for a day and then push through a sieve. Add 1 cup of the freshest sour cream, ½ f. of the freshest sweet butter, 2 teaspoons of salt, with ½ cup or more, to taste, of sugar. Mix it all together well so that there are no lumps, put it in a wooden form lined with a clean, thin napkin, cover with the top and a heavy stone. After a day turn it out carefully onto a plate.

Many people put raisins in a *paskha* and decorate it. For that, instead of sugar you can add ¼ c. or more of cherry, strawberry or raspberry syrup. Or, having used sugar, add in lemon or orange rind for aroma and taste. Keep it in a cold place, because after 3–5 days it begins to spoil.[46]

Sharlotka, *Apple with Rusks* (1891)

Take French white bread, cut off the crust, cut the loaf into strips, put in a frying pan, grease every strip with oil with a feather, put in the oven, so that they brown slightly. Then line the bottom and sides of a greased ceramic baking dish with them, put in the middle 4–8 peeled and thinly sliced apples, sprinkle them with sugar, pieces of butter, and bake. To serve turn out onto a plate, pour over a cup of water boiled with a spoon of sugar, honey or treacle and either a piece of lemon peel or cinnamon.[47]

Glossary

barshchina	labour obligations owed by serfs to their owners
berezovitsa	lightly alcoholic drink brewed from birch sap
blinchiki (s. *blinchik*)	crêpes (thin pancakes)
blini (s. *blin*)	small, yeast-raised pancakes, usually made from buckwheat flour
borscht	soup made with beetroot
botvinia	cold summer soup with *kvas* as its base
boyar	pre-Petrine Russian nobleman
boyarina	pre-Petrine Russian noblewoman
buzhenina	baked ham/pork
chakhokhbili	Georgian chicken stew
chernozem	black earth
chukhonskoe maslo	butter made from sour cream
Domostroi	sixteenth-century household manual
funt (pl. *funty*)	unit of weight equivalent to 1/40 of a *pud*, or 0.41 kg (14½ oz)
golubtsy	cabbage rolls stuffed with meat and rice
grenki	croutons – small pieces of toasted or fried bread
grivna	Old Russian unit of currency
izba	peasant cottage
kabak	tavern or pub
kalach	wheaten bread, often associated with Moscow
karavai	celebratory bread, often made from wheat flour and enriched, highly decorated
kasha	porridge, often made with buckwheat groats but possibly with other grains
kefir	cultured/fermented milk
khachapuri	Georgian cheese bread
kharchevnia (pl. *kharchevni*)	eating establishment for non-elite consumers
kharcho	Georgian soup
khlebosolstvo	hospitality, from the words for bread and salt

kisel	fruit juice or other liquid thickened with starch (now usually potato starch), either thin enough to drink or slightly thicker to eat with a spoon
kislye shchi	effervescent *kvas*
kolbasy	cured sausage
kompot	fruit drink made from boiling fruit, dried or fresh, in plenty of water; the fruit-infused water is then cooled and served with some of the cooked fruit in the bottom of the glass
kopek	unit of money, now standardized at 100 kopeks: 1 rouble; in the early nineteenth century there were different kinds of roubles and kopeks (silver, copper, paper) circulating at the same time; the silver monies were valued at 3½ times their copper or paper equivalents
kotlet	usually pan-fried patty of minced meat or vegetables held together with egg and breadcrumbs
krupchatka	a kind of wheat flour ground slightly coarsely, particular to Russian milling practices
kulebiaka	also known as *coulibiac*; an extravagant fish-filled pie, usually highly decorated
kulich	enriched yeasted cake associated with Easter
kumys	fermented mare's milk
kundiumy	baked and then steamed dumplings
kvas	lightly fermented beverage usually brewed from rusks or ends of rye bread
kvashennaia kapusta	fermented cabbage
lapsha	noodles
lenivye golubtsy	'lazy' cabbage rolls, in which the normal filling of cabbage rolls (meat and rice) is simply mixed with chopped cabbage and baked
Maslenitsa	Carnival, the pre-Lent festival; the word derives from *maslo*, meaning butter or oil, and blini are the food most associated with the festival
mors	berry juice
nalivki	fruit cordials
obrok	quitrent – dues paid by serfs to their owners in lieu of labour
obshchepit	short form of *obshchestvennoe pitanie*
obshchestvennoe pitanie	'social nutrition' – the Soviet-era term for public catering
okroshka	cold soup
paskha	dessert based on *tvorog* (fresh cheese) and associated with Easter
pech	stove/oven
pelmeni	small meat-filled dumplings associated with Siberia
pirog (pl. *pirogi*)	filled pie or pasty, usually made with a yeasted dough; either savoury or sweet, baked or fried

pirozhok (pl. *pirozhki*)	small *pirogi*, often more like a filled bun
plov	rice, meat and vegetable dish associated with Central Asia
pokhlebka (pl. *pokhlebki*)	generic term for soup
ponchiki	doughnuts
postila	fruit cooked and pureed, sweetened (originally with honey) and possibly lightened with beaten egg whites, then dried (var. *pastila*)
postnyi (pl. *postnye*)	Lenten (adj.); used for days on which no animal products were allowed according to the Orthodox fasting calendar
prianik (pl. *prianiki*)	spice cakes
prostokvasha	cultured or soured milk
pud (pl. *pudy*)	unit of weight equivalent to 40 *funty*, or 16.3 kg (36 lb)
pyshki	doughnut
rassolnik	soup involving pickled cucumbers and their brine (*rassol*)
rouble	standard unit of money, equivalent to 100 kopeks
salnik (pl. *salniki*)	organ-meat dumplings wrapped in caul fat
salo	cured fatback
samogon	home-distilled vodka
samovar	literally 'self-boiler', the large metal urn used to heat water for tea
sbiten	hot, spiced drink
shashlik	meat placed on a skewer and usually cooked over an open flame
shchi	cabbage soup
shtof	unit of volume, equivalent to 1.2 litres (over 2 pints)
skoromnyi (pl. *skoromnye*)	the opposite of *postnyi*, or Lenten; the days on which animal foods are allowed according to the Orthodox fasting calendar
smetana	sour cream
solianka	thick, sour soup (var. *selianka*)
solonina	dried/cured salted beef
stolovaia (pl. *stolovye*)	canteen/cafeteria
studen	aspic
sukhari	dried bread/rusks
syr	cheese; originally synonymous with *tvorog*, later used for ripened cheeses, initially imported
syrnik (pl. *syrniki*)	small patties of *tvorog* with egg and flour and possibly raisins, pan-fried
syvorotka	whey
terem	seclusion of elite women in pre-Petrine Muscovy
tiaglo	work unit in serf Russia, consisting of one man and one woman
tiuria	bread doused with *kvas* to a soup-like consistency

tolokno	oats soaked in water, dried and pounded to a flour; eaten by mixing with *kvas*
traktir (pl. *traktiry*)	tavern with food
tvorog	unripened, fresh cheese; slightly sour
ukha	fish soup
varenets	cooked milk
vareniki	boiled dumplings filled with savoury or sweet fillings, associated initially with Ukraine
varenye	fruit jam or preserves of a thin consistency
vatrushki	yeasted dough with an open filling, often of *tvorog*
verst	unit of length equivalent to 1.1 km (⅔ mi.)
vetchina	boiled or smoked ham
vinegret	salad, now usually of beetroot, potato, canned peas, carrot, pickles
vino	either wine or, particularly in early texts, vodka
viziga	dried spinal cord usually from sturgeon or similar fish
zakuski	pre-dinner practice of serving small bites of savoury foods along with vodka or other drinks

References

INTRODUCTION: Let Us Begin with Soup

1 Viktor Bur'ianov [Vladimir Burnashev], *Besedy s det'mi o khoziaistve: domashnem, sel'skom, manufakturnom i o tovarov* (St Petersburg, 1837), pp. 76–7.
2 Ibid., pp. 88–9.
3 M. M., *Prakticheskii khoziain, ili kniga vsekh sostoianii, izlagaiushchaia polnoe sobranie noveishikh opytov i otkrytii, sdelannykh izvestnymi v Evrope Agronomami po vsem otrasliam estestvennykh nauk, tekhnogii, zemledel'cheskoi promyshlennosti, sel'skogo khoziaistva, iskustv i proch.* (Moscow, 1838), vol. I, p. I.
4 Bur'ianov [Burnashev], *Besedy s det'mi*, pp. 79–80.
5 Ibid., p. 81.
6 Ibid., pp. 72–3.
7 Viktor Bur'ianov [Vladimir Burnashev], *Progulka s det'mi po Rossii* (St Petersburg, 1837), vol. I, p. 120.
8 Ibid., pp. 120–22.
9 August von Haxthausen, *The Russian Empire: Its People, Institutions, and Resources*, trans. Robert Farie (London, 1856), vol. I, p. 106.
10 Ibid., p. 163.
11 Edward Tracy Turnerelli, *Russia on the Borders of Asia. Kazan, the Ancient Capital of the Tartar Khans; with an Account of the Province to Which It Belongs, the Tribes and Races Which Form Its Population, Etc.* (London, 1854), vol. I, p. 212.
12 Edward P. Thompson, *Life in Russia; or, The Discipline of Despotism* (London, 1848), p. 279.
13 J.-B. May, *Saint-Petersbourg et la Russie en 1829* (Paris, 1830), vol. I, pp. 244–6.
14 Robert Robinson, *Black on Red: My 44 Years Inside the Soviet Union* (Washington, DC, 1988), pp. 48, 90; see also Jukka Gronow, *Caviar with Champagne: Common Luxury and the Ideals of the Good Life in Stalin's Russia* (Oxford, 2003).
15 Robert Ker Porter, *Travelling Sketches in Russia and Sweden, during the Years 1805, 1806, 1807, 1808* (Philadelphia, PA, 1809), p. 94.
16 Captain Jesse, *Notes of a Half-pay in Search of Health; or, Russia, Circassia, and the Crimea, in 1839–40* (London, 1841), vol. II, p. 272.
17 K. I. Arsen'ev, *Nachertanie statistiki Rossiiskogo gosudarstva* (St Petersburg, 1818), p. 65.

18 Sharon Hudgins, 'Raw Liver, Singed Sheep's Head, and Boiled Stomach Pudding: Encounters with Traditional Buriat Cuisine', *Sibirica*, III/2 (2003), pp. 132–4.

19 Maya Peterson, 'The Power of Belief: Food as Medicine in the Kumys Cure from Samara to San Francisco', paper presented at ASEEES, November 2019; *Otchet meditsinkogo departamenta za 1886 god. Chast' meditsinskaia* (St Petersburg, 1888), p. 217; Vasilii Grigor'evich P'iankov, *Edushchim v Krym* (Evpatoriia, 1888), p. 128.

20 Gerasim Stepanov, *Noveishii dopolnenie k opytnomu povaru, o prisovokupleniem Aziatskogo stola, ili vostochnogo gastronoma* (Moscow, 1837), pp. 38–71.

21 A. I. Nikishova, *Povarennaia kniga: rukovodstvo domashnego stola* (Tver, 1928), pp. 68–9.

22 Erik R. Scott, 'Edible Ethnicity: How Georgian Cuisine Conquered the Soviet Table', *Kritika*, XIII/4 (2012), pp. 831–58. On the rich variety of Georgian cuisine, see Darra Goldstein, *The Georgian Feast: The Vibrant Culture and Savory Food of the Republic of Georgia* (New York, 1993).

23 For some stories, see Jeff Sahadeo, *Voices from the Soviet Edge: Southern Migrants in Leningrad and Moscow* (Ithaca, NY, 2019), pp. 121–2.

24 Julia Ioffe, 'The Borscht Belt: Annals of Gastronomy', *New Yorker*, LXXXVIII/9 (2012).

25 Reginald E. Zelnik, 'Wie es Eigentlich Gegessen: Some Curious Thoughts on the Role of Borsch in Russian History', in *For Want of a Horse: Choice and Chance in History*, ed. John M. Merriman (Lexington, MA, 1985), pp. 77–90; Terence Lau, 'How Russian Borscht Became a Hong Kong Staple', www.goldthread2.com, accessed 15 January 2020.

ONE: The Elements of Russian Cuisine

1 'Prosheniia, raporty i otnosheniia na imia Glavnoupravliaiushchego Obol'ianinova', RGIA f. 491, op. 1, d. 93, l. 175 (1797).

2 Henry Sutherland Edwards, *The Russians at Home* (London, 1861), p. 335.

3 John Carr, *A Northern Summer; or, Travels round the Baltic, through Denmark, Sweden, Russia, Prussia, and Part of Germany, in the Year 1804* (London, 1805), pp. 269–70.

4 V. A. Levshin, *Slovar' povarennyi, prispeshnichii, kanditorskii i distillatorskii, soderzhashchii po azbuchnomu poriadku podrobnoe i vernoe nastavlenie k podrobnoe i vernoe nastavlenie k prigotovleniiu vsiakogo roda kushan'ia iz Frantsuzskoi, Nemetskoi, Gollandskoi, Ispanskoi i Angliskoi povarni, pirozhnogo, dessertov, varenii, salatov, vod, essentsii, ratafii, likerov, dvoviiu vodok, i pr.; takzhe k uchrezhdeniiu stola s planami, podach, uslugi i proch. i s prisovokupleniem v osoblivykh paragrafakh polnoi Meshchanskoi povarni i Novoi; ravnym obrazom povaren Avstriiskoi, Berlinskoi, Bogemskoi, Saksonskoi i Ruskoi* (Moscow, 1795–7).

5 Ivan Boltin, *Primechaniia na istoriiu drevniia i nynyshniia Rossii G. Leklerka* (St Petersburg, 1788), vol. II, pp. 403, 410.

6 Edwards, *Russians at Home*, p. 341.

7 Henry Moor, *A Visit to Russia in the Autumn of 1862* (London, 1863), p. 12 [emphasis in original].

8 Charles W. Thayer, *Bears in the Caviar* (Philadelphia, PA, 1950), p. 57.

9 Marquis of Londonderry, *Recollections of a Tour in the North of Europe in 1836–1837* (London, 1838), vol. II, pp. 5–6.

10 'Oplachennye scheta', RGADA f. 1264, op. 1, d. 195, ll. 30–31; nearly the same purchases were repeated, often with a note that they were for '*zakuski* and dessert'.

11 George Augustus Sala, *A Journey Due North; Being Notes of a Residence in Russia* (Boston, MA, 1858), p. 332.

12 Kemp Tolley, *Caviar and Commissars: The Experiences of a U.S. Naval Officer in Stalin's Russia* (Annapolis, MD, 1983); Betty Roland, *Caviar for Breakfast* (Melbourne, 1979); Charles Wheeler Thayer, *Bears in the Caviar* (Philadelphia, PA, 1951).

13 On the history of caviar see Inga Saffron, *Caviar: The Strange History and Uncertain Future of the World's Most Coveted Delicacy* (New York, 2002), and Nichola Fletcher, *Caviar: A Global History* (London, 2010).

14 K. A. Avdeeva, *Ruchnaia kniga russkoi opytnoi khoziaiki*, 6th edn (St Petersburg, 1848), vol. I, pp. 9–11.

15 Ibid., pp. 55–60.

16 *Kniga o vkusnoi i zdorovoi pishche* (Moscow, 1945), pp. 134–41.

17 Nikita Aronov, 'Ot sala do "Mimozy"', *Ogonek*, 49 (2018), p. 40; Adrianne K. Jacobs, 'The Many Flavors of Socialism: Modernity and Tradition in Late Soviet Food Culture, 1965–1985' (PhD diss., University of North Carolina, Chapel Hill, 2015), pp. 55–71.

18 Boltin, *Primechaniia*, vol. II, p. 410.

19 Edwards, *Russians at Home*, p. 337.

20 G. Reinbeck, *Travels from St Petersburgh through Moscow, Grodno, Warsaw, Breslaw &c to Germany in the Year 1805* (London, 1807), p. 25.

21 I. M. Snegirev, *Ruskie v svoikh poslovitsakh. Razsuzhdeniia i issledovaniia ob otechestvennykh poslovitsakh i pogovorkakh* (Moscow, 1831), vol. II, pp. 8–9.

22 Alison K. Smith, *Recipes for Russia: Food and Nationhood under the Tsars* (DeKalb, IL, 2008), p. 79.

23 A. P., *Ruchnaia ekonomicheskaia entsiklopediia* (Moscow, 1835), p. 24.

24 Doktor Puf [V. F. Odoevskii], 'Lektsiia IV', *Zapiski dlia Khoziaev*, 4 (1844), pp. 30–31.

25 'Prizhival'shchiki i prizhivalki', *Russkii arkhiv*, 3 (1883), p. 73.

26 Sergei Drukovtsov, *Povarennye zapiski* (St Petersburg, 1779), pp. 12–13.

27 'Zapisnye knizhki po denezhnym raskhodam na pokupku stolovykh produktov', RGADA f. 1261, op. 2, d. 918, ll. 1–110b.

28 V. N. Semenev, *Obshchestvennoe pitanie na perelome* (Moscow, 1932), p. 43.

29 E. Molokhovets, *Prostaia, obshchedostupnaia kukhnia*, 2nd edn (St Petersburg, 1891), p. 48.

30 See J. G. Kohl, *Russia* (London, 1844), p. 136, for a discussion of the radically different summer and winter cuisines.

31 'O morozhenom, sherbete; Neschastnye sluchai ot upotrebleniia slivok', *Zhurnal obshchepoleznykh svedenii (supplement)*, 23–4 (1838), p. 130.

32 Richard Southwell Bourke, *St Petersburg and Moscow: A Visit to the Court of the Czar* (London, 1846), vol. I, p. 245.

33 A. B. Granville, *St Petersburgh: A Journal of Travels to and from That Capital* (London, 1828), vol. II, p. 365.

34 Samuel Robert Graves, *A Yachting Cruise in the Baltic* (London, 1863), p. 212.
35 Doktor Puf [V. F. Odoevskii], 'Lektsiia VI', *Zapiski dlia khoziaev*, 6 (1844), pp. 46–7.
36 [Jacques] Boucher de Perthes, *Voyage en Russie, retour par la Lithuanie, la Pologne, la Silèsie, la Saxe et le Duche, de Nassau; séjour a Wisebade en 1856* (Paris, 1859), p. 301.
37 'Iz istorii bor'by za farsh', *Obshchestvennoe pitanie*, I (1933), p. 27; *Kniga o vkusnoi i zdorovoi pishche* (Moscow, 1954), p. 167.
38 T. V. Privalova, *Byt Rossiiskoi derevni 60-e gody XIX-20-e gody XX v.* (Moscow, 2000), p. 44.
39 Snegirev, *Ruskie v svoikh poslovitsakh*, vol. II, p. 7.
40 *Polnoe prakticheskoe nastavlenie kak pech' khleb obyknovennyi (nasushnyi)* (St Petersburg, 1851), p. 3.
41 Robert D. Pinkerton, *Russia; or, Miscellaneous Observations on the Past and Present State of That Country and Its Inhabitants* (London, 1833), p. 70.
42 Paul of Aleppo, *The Travels of Macarius, Patriarch of Antioch*, trans. F. C. Belfour (London, 1836), vol. II, pp. 40–41.
43 Viktor Bur'ianov [Vladimir Burnashev], *Besedy s det'mi o khoziaistve: domashnem, sel'skom, manufakturnom i o tovarov* (St Petersburg, 1837), p. 89.
44 V. Anichkov, *Voennoe khoziaistvo* (St Petersburg, 1860), p. 70.
45 'Pis'ma k doktoru Pufu', *Zapiski dlia khoziaev*, 27 (1845), p. 215.
46 Snegirev, *Ruskie v svoikh poslovitsakh*, vol. II, p. 8.
47 Adrianne K. Jacobs, 'V. V. Pokhlëbkin and the Search for Culinary Roots in Late Soviet Russia', *Cahiers du monde russe*, LII/1–2 (2013), p. 174(n.).
48 Moor, *A Visit to Russia*, pp. 110–11.
49 Leitch Ritchie, *A Journey to St Petersburg and Moscow through Courland and Livonia* (London, 1836), p. 209.
50 Alexander Michie, *The Siberian Overland Route from Peking to Petersburg, through the Deserts and Steppes of Mongolia, Tartary, &c.* (London, 1864), p. 249.
51 Snegirev, *Ruskie v svoikh poslovitsakh*, vol. II, p. 9.
52 Ernst Rudol'f, *Zemledel'cheskii kalendar'* (St Petersburg, 1849), p. 55.
53 Doktor Puf, 'Lektsiia XXXV', *Zapiski dlia khoziaev*, 35 (1844), p. 279.
54 Avdeeva, *Ruchnaia kniga*, vol. I, p. 23.
55 V. B., 'Tolokno', *Ekonom*, 84 (1842), p. 252.
56 Snegirev, *Ruskie v svoikh poslovitsakh*, vol. II, p. 11.
57 Ibid., pp. 10–11.
58 'O vozmozhnosti uluchshit' sostoianie zemledeliia i zemledel'tsa v Rossii', RGIA f. 398, op. 8, d. 2537, ll. 90b–10.
59 Avdeeva, *Ruchnaia kniga*, vol. I, p. 221.
60 On the sayings, Snegirev, *Ruskie v svoikh poslovitsakh*, vol. II, p. 11.
61 Maks Fasmer, *Etimologicheskii slovar' russkogo iazyka* (St Petersburg, 1996), vol. III, p. 230.
62 'Priem gostei u Tatar', *Kazanskie izvestiia* (7 October 1814), pp. 563–4.
63 I. M. Radetskii, *S.-Peterburgskaia kukhnia, zakliuchaiushchaia v sebe okolo 2,000 razlichnykh kushan'ev i prigotovlenii, s podrobnym ob''iasneniem i risunkami kak prigotovliat' i nakladyvat' na bliuda* (St Petersburg, 1862), pp. 169–70.

64 'Kukhnoistoricheskie i fililogicheskie iz"iskaniia doktora Pufa, professora vsekh nauk i mnogikh drugikh', *Zapiski dlia khoziaev*, 25 (1845), pp. 198–9.

65 Avdeeva, *Ruchnaia kniga*, vol. I, p. 152.

66 Craig Claiborne, 'To My Mind, the World's Greatest Dish', *New York Times* (27 December 1976), p. 41.

67 Nikolai Novikov, *Drevniaia rossiiskaia vivliofika, ili sobranie drevnostei rossiiskikh, do rossiiskie istoriia, geografii i genealogii kasaiushchikhsia* (St Petersburg, 1775), vol. VII, pp. 3–21, 39–40, 124, 127.

68 *The Englishwoman in Russia: Impressions of the Society and Manners of the Russians at Home. By a lady, ten years resident in that country* (New York, 1855), p. 199.

69 Algernon Mitford, *Memories* (London, 1915), p. 272.

70 Doktor Puf, 'Lektsiia v', *Zapiski dlia khoziaev*, 5 (1844), p. 58.

71 'Kukhnia', *Ekonom*, 76 (1842), p. 191.

72 Thomas Michell, *Russian Pictures, Drawn with Pen and Pencil* (London, 1889), p. 130.

73 'Zapisnye knizhki', l. 114.

74 Snegirev, *Ruskie v svoikh poslovitsakh*, vol. II, p. 13.

75 Giles Fletcher, *Of the Russe Common Wealth; or, Maner of Gouerment of the Russe Emperour (Commonly Called the Emperour of Moskouia)* (London, 1591), p. 1120b.

76 John Foster Fraser, *Russia of To-day* (New York, 1915), p. 29.

77 'Kvas', *Zhurnal obshchepoleznykh svedenii*, 1 (1847), p. 65.

78 Captain Jesse, *Notes of a Half-pay in Search of Health; or, Russia, Circassia, and the Crimea, in 1839–40* (London, 1841), vol. II, p. 240.

79 *Deiatel'nost' komissii pitaniia russkogo obshchestva okhraneniia narodnogo zdraviia v 1892–1893 gody* (St Petersburg, 1893), p. 56.

80 The literature is huge, but one popular account is Sandor Ellix Katz, *The Art of Fermentation* (White River Junction, VT, 2012).

81 N. I. Polevitskii, *Domashnee prigotovlenie fruktovykh prokhladitel'nykh napitkov: prigotovlenie meda, bragi, buzy, kvasa, fruktovykh vodichek, gazirovannykh vod, shipovok, siropov, sokov i proch* (Leningrad, 1927), pp. 26–7.

82 *Kartina Rossii izobrazhaiushchaia istoriiu i geografiiu, khronologicheski, genealogicheski i statisticheski so vkliucheiem obozreniia o dukhovnoi, voennoi i grazhdanskoi ei chastiam, kak v pervobytnom ei sostoianii, tak i v Tsarstvovanie gosudaria imperatora Aleksandra I* (Moscow, 1807), vol. II, p. 312.

83 Snegirev, *Ruskie v svoikh poslovitsakh*, vol. II, p. 12.

84 Robert Jones, *Bread upon the Water: The St Petersburg Grain Trade and the Russian Economy, 1703–1811* (Pittsburgh, PA, 2013), p. 152.

85 Boris Rodionov, *Istoriia russkoi vodki: Ot polugara do nashikh dnei* (Moscow, 2012), p. 14; David Christian, *'Living Water': Vodka and Russian Society on the Eve of Emancipation* (Oxford, 1990), p. 26. On the challenges of words for vodka, see Christian, pp. 53–6.

86 Christian, *'Living Water'*, pp. 80–85.

87 B. A. Kolchin and T. I. Makarova, eds., *Drevniaia Rus': Byt i kultura* (Moscow, 1997), p. 14; M. Monk and P. Johnston, 'Perspectives on Non-wood Plants in the Sampled Assemblage from the Troitsky Excavations of Medieval Novgorod', in *The Archaeology of Medieval Novgorod in Context*, eds Mark A. Brisbane, Nikolaj A. Makarov and Evgenij N. Nosov (Oxford, 2012), p. 306.

88 Snegirev, *Ruskie v svoikh poslovitsakh*, vol. II, pp. 101–2.

89 *Kartina Rossii*, vol. II, p. 310.

90 I. M. Snegirev, 'Vospominaniia I. M. Snegireva', *Russkii arkhiv*, 4 (1866), pp. 525–6.

91 On the early appearance of mead, see V. V. Pokhlëbkin, *Istoriia vodki* (Moscow, 1997), pp. 38–9.

92 Adam Olearius, *The Voyages and Travels of the Ambassadors from the Duke of Holstein, to the Great Duke of Muscovy, and the King of Persia*, trans. John Davies (London, 1662), pp. 87–8.

93 Pinkerton, *Russia*, p. 73.

94 *Kartina Rossii*, vol. II, p. 311.

95 Paul of Aleppo, *The Travels of Macarius*, Patriarch of Antioch, trans. F. C. Belfour (London, 1836), vol. II, p. 138.

96 'Uluchshenie samovarov', *Zhurnal obshchepoleznykh svedenii*, 31 (1837), p. 281.

97 Raida Varlamova, *Semeinyi magazin sovremennykh usovershenstvovanii k rasprostraneniiu mezhdu vsemi klassami liudei iziashchnego vkusa, poriadka i udobstva v domashnei i obshchestvennoi zhizni* (Moscow, 1856), vol. III, p. 149.

98 S. M., 'Novyi chainyi magazin', *Kazanskie gubernskie vedomosti (neoffitsialnye)* (25 January 1860), p. 31.

99 'Sukhari – Krendeli – khlebi', *Zhurnal obshchepoleznykh svedenii* (1837), p. 218.

TWO: Environment, Agriculture and Technology

 1 Michael Bitter, 'George Forbes's "Account of Russia", 1733–1734', *Slavonic and East European Review*, LXXXIV/4 (2004), p. 907.

 2 On Novgorod, Heli Huhtamaa, 'Climatic Anomalies, Food Systems, and Subsistence Crises in Medieval Novgorod and Ladoga', *Scandinavian Journal of History*, XL/4 (2015), p. 565.

 3 William Tooke, *View of the Russian Empire during the Reign of Catharine the Second, and to the Close of the Present Century* (London, 1799), vol. III, p. 333.

 4 K. A. Avdeeva, *Rukovodstvo k ustroistvu ferm i vedeniiu na nikh khoziaistva* (St Petersburg, 1863), p. 188.

 5 Paul of Aleppo, *The Travels of Macarius, Patriarch of Antioch*, trans. F. C. Belfour (London, 1836), vol. II, p. 152.

 6 Tooke, *View of the Russian Empire*, vol. III, p. 333.

 7 *Bagatelles. Promenades d'un désœuvré dans la ville de St-Pétersbourg* (St Petersburg, 1811), vol. I, pp. 179–80.

 8 Robert Johnston, *Travels through Part of the Russian Empire and the Country of Poland along the Southern Shores of the Baltic* (New York, 1816), pp. 257–9.

 9 'Raporta v Mosk. dom. kont. iz votchinnykh pravlenii gr. S. R. Vorontsova', RGADA f. 1261, op. 7, d. 1172, ll. 73–730b.

10 'O razvedenii zemlianykh iablok', *Ezhemesiachnye sochineniia*, [1] (1758), pp. 378–9.

11 *Polnoe sobranie zakonov Rossiiskoi Imperii: Pervoe sobranie* (St Petersburg, 1830), XVII/12406 (3 May 1765).

12 V. O. Kliuchevskii, *Istoriia russkogo byta* (Moscow, 1995), p. 16(n.).

13 Léon Godard, *Pétersbourg et Moscou. Souvenirs du couronnement d'un tsar* (Paris, 1858), p. 358.

14 S. P. Tolstov, N. N. Cheboksarov and K. V. Chistov, eds, *Ocherki obshchei etnografiia. Evropeiskaia chast' SSSR* (Moscow, 1968), p. 121.

15 Melissa L. Caldwell, 'Feeding the Body and Nourishing the Soul', *Food, Culture and Society*, x/1 (2007), p. 61.

16 V. I. Tsalkin, *Materialy dlia istorii skotovodstva i okhoty v drevnei rusi* (Moscow, 1956), pp. 125–7.

17 *The Russian Primary Chronicle: Laurentian Text*, trans. and ed. Samuel Hazzard Cross and Olgerd P. Sherbowitz-Wetzor (Cambridge, MA, 1953), pp. 214–15.

18 Sheila Hamilton-Dyer, Mark Brisbane and Mark Maltby, 'Fish, Feather, Fur and Forest: Exploitation of Wild Animals in Novgorod and Its Territory', *Quaternary International*, 460 (2017), pp. 104–5.

19 *The Muscovite Law Code (Ulozhenie) of 1649*, trans. and ed. Richard Hellie (Irvine, CA, 1988), Chapter Ten, nos 216–17.

20 Viktor Bur'ianov [Vladimir Burnashev], *Besedy s det'mi o khoziaistve: domashnem, sel'skom, manufakturnom i o tovarov* (St Petersburg, 1837), pp. 113–14.

21 M. Monk and P. Johnston, 'Perspectives on Non-wood Plants in the Sampled Assemblage from the Troitsky Excavations of Medieval Novgorod', in *The Archaeology of Medieval Novgorod in Context*, ed. Mark A. Brisbane, Nikolaj A. Makarov and Evgenij N. Nosov (Oxford, 2012), pp. 299–301.

22 *The Englishwoman in Russia: Impressions of the Society and Manners of the Russians at Home. By a lady, ten years resident in that country* (New York, 1855), pp. 168–9.

23 Tooke, *View of the Russian Empire*, vol. III, p. 171.

24 Z. P. Gor'kovskaia and O. N. Kationov, 'Pishcha russkikh krest'ian Sibiri v povsednevnoi zhizni (period kapitalizma)', in *Kul'turnyi potential Sibiri v dosovetskii period* (Novosibirsk, 1992), p. 59.

25 E. Rego, 'Razvedenie shampinionov', *Zemledelcheskaia gazeta* (27 December 1855), p. 409.

26 William Coxe, *Travels into Poland, Russia, Sweden, and Denmark* (London, 1792), vol. II, pp. 205–6.

27 Charles Piazzi Smyth, *Three Cities in Russia* (London, 1862), vol. I, pp. 325–6.

28 Samuel Collins, *The Present State of Russia: In a Letter to a Friend at London* (London, 1671), pp. 138–40.

29 'Kukhnia', *Ekonom*, 79 (1842), p. 216.

30 'O proezdakh v g. Gatchine e.i.v. gosudaryni imperatritsy Marii Feodorovny i e. velichestva velikogo Kniazia Mikhaila Aleksandrovicha', GARF f. 97, op. 3, d. 16, l. 18.

31 Boris Mironov, 'Do Russians Need Cliotherapia?', *Bylye gody*, XLI-1/3-1 (2016), p. 1028.

32 Martha Lahana, 'The Usefulness of Bees in Muscovy', *Russian History*, XLV/1 (2018), p. 34.

33 *Muscovite Law Code*, Chapter Ten, nos 218–19.

34 Matthew P. Romaniello, *The Elusive Empire: Kazan and the Creation of Russia, 1552–1671* (Madison, WI, 2012), p. 98.

35 Lahana, 'Usefulness', pp. 36–7.

36 Adrianne K. Jacobs, 'V. V. Pokhlëbkin and the Search for Culinary Roots in Late Soviet Russia', *Cahiers du monde russe*, LII/1–2 (2013), p. 176.

37 Alexander Osipovich, 'At a Moscow Fair, Selling the Healing Powers of Honey', *International Herald Tribune* (13 September 2006); also at www.nytimes.com, 13 September 2006.

38 Paul of Aleppo, *The Travels of Macarius*, vol. I, p. 290.

39 Sigismund von Herberstein, *Zapiski o Moskovii* (Moscow, 2008), vol. 1, p. 291.

40 Carol B. Stevens, 'Shabo: Wine and Prosperity on the Russian Steppe', *Kritika*, XIX/2 (2018), pp. 273–304.

41 Stephen V. Bittner, *Whites and Reds: Wine in the Lands of Tsar and Commissar* (New York, 2021).

42 Susan Smith-Peter, 'Sweet Development: The Sugar Beet Industry, Agricultural Societies and Agrarian Transformations in the Russian Empire, 1818–1913', *Cahiers du monde russe*, LVII/1 (2016), p. 122; also Charles Steinwedel, 'Sugar as a "Basic Necessity": State Efforts to Supply the Russian Empire's Population in the Early Twentieth Century', in *The Life Cycle of Russian Things: From Fish Guts to Fabergé*, ed. Matthew P. Romaniello, Alison K. Smith and Tricia Starks (London, forthcoming).

43 Hamilton-Dyer, et al., 'Fish, Feather, Fur and Forest', pp. 99–100.

44 Henry Sutherland Edwards, *The Russians at Home* (London, 1861), p. 339.

45 P. S. Pallas, *Puteshestvie po raznym provintsiiam Rossiiskoi imperii* (St Petersburg, 1773), p. 199.

46 Edward Daniel Clarke, *Travels in Russia, Tartary and Turkey: A New Edition* (Aberdeen, 1848), p. 160.

47 Ibid., pp. 160–61.

48 L. N. Semenova, *Byt i naselenie Sankt-Peterburga (XVIII vek)* (St Petersburg, 1998), pp. 165–7; Robert Jones, *Bread upon the Water: The St Petersburg Grain Trade and the Russian Economy, 1703–1811* (Pittsburgh, PA, 2013).

49 James R. Gibson, *Feeding the Russian Fur Trade: Provisionment of the Okhotsk Seaboard and the Kamchatka Peninsula* (Madison, WI, 1969).

50 S. A. Kniaz'kov, *Golod v drevnei Rossii* (St Petersburg, 1913), p. 4.

51 Paul of Aleppo, *The Travels of Macarius*, vol. 1, p. 342.

52 Guy Miège, *La relation de trois ambassades de monseigneur le Comte de Carlisle, de la part du serenissime tres-puissant Prince Charles II, roy de la Grande Bretagne, vers leurs serenissimes Majestés Alexey Michailovitz Czar & Grand Duc de Moscovie, Charles roy de Suede, & Frederic III, roy de Dannemarc & de Norvege, commencées en l'an 1663 & finies sur la fin de l'an 1664* (Rouen, 1670), pp. 28–31.

53 Henry Moor, *A Visit to Russia in the Autumn of 1862* (London, 1863), p. 100.

54 Samuel Robert Graves, *A Yachting Cruise in the Baltic* (London, 1863), pp. 237–8.

55 John Foster Fraser, *The Real Siberia: Together with an Account of a Dash through Manchuria* (London, 1902), p. 13.

56 Graves, *A Yachting Cruise in the Baltic*, p. 265.

57 For more on the Russian stove, see Snejana Tempest, 'Stovelore in Russian Folklife', in *Food in Russian History and Culture*, ed. Musya Glants and Joyce Toomre (Bloomington, IN, 1997), pp. 1–14.

58 On the early history, see R.E.F. Smith and David Christian, *Bread and Salt: A Social and Economic History of Food and Drink in Russia* (Cambridge, 1984), pp. 13–16.

59 A. B. Granville, *St Petersburgh: A Journal of Travels to and from That Capital* (London, 1828), vol. 1, p. 504.

60 Genrikh Dikht, *Nastavlenie k uluchsheniiu russkoi pechi* (St Petersburg, 1838), pp. 3–4.

61 T. V. Privalova, *Byt Rossiiskoi derevni 60-e gody XIX-20-e gody XX v.* (Moscow, 2000), p. 22.

62 Dikht, *Nastavlenie*, p. 4.

63 K. A. Avdeeva, *Ruchnaia kniga russkoi opytnoi khoziaiki*, 6th edn (St Petersburg, 1848), vol. I, pp. 8–9.

64 M. M., *Prakticheskii khoziain, ili kniga vsekh sostoianii, izlagaiushchaia polnoe sobranie noveishikh opytov i otkrytii, sdelannykh izvestnymi v Evrope Agronomami po vsem otrasliam estestvennykh nauk, tekhnogii, zemledel'cheskoi promyshlennosti, sel'skogo khoziaistva, iskustv i proch*, vol. I (Moscow, 1838), pp. 1–2.

65 Jean Kathryn Berger, 'The Daily Life of the Household in Medieval Novgorod', PhD thesis, University of Minnesota, 1998, p. 103.

66 D. K. Zelenin, *Russkaia etnografiia* (Moscow, 2013), pp. 164–75.

67 'Muka', in *Entsiklopedicheskii slovar'* (St Petersburg, 1897), vol. XX, p. 147.

68 P. A., 'Krupchatka', in *Entsiklopedicheskii slovar'* (St Petersburg, 1895), vol. XVIa, p. 853.

69 Avdeeva, *Ruchnaia kniga*, vol. I, p. 25.

70 Ibid., p. 22.

71 Ivan Iakovlevich Vil'kins, *Sel'skii khoziain XIX veka, ili Polnoe sobranie noveishikh opytov i otkrytii, sdelannykh v Evrope i Severnoi Amerike kak po chasti zemledel'cheskoi promyshlennosti voobshche, tak i po vsem otrasliam estestvennykh nauk i tekhnologii, vkhodiashchim v sostav sel'skoi ekonomii, i vo osobennosti poleznym dlia russikh pomeshchikov i upravliaiushchikh votchinami* (Moscow, 1837), vol. III, p. 278.

72 Bitter, 'George Forbes's "Account of Russia"', p. 908.

73 Alison K. Smith, 'From Gruyère to Gatchina: The Meanings of Cheese in Modern Russia', unpublished paper.

74 V. B., 'O prigotovlenii soloniny', *Ekonom*, 86 (1842), p. 269.

75 Robert Ker Porter, *Travelling Sketches in Russia and Sweden, during the Years 1805, 1806, 1807, 1808* (Philadelphia, PA, 1809), p. 100.

76 Thomas Raikes, *A Visit to St Petersburg, in the Winter of 1829–30* (London, 1838), pp. 42–3.

77 Ibid., p. 289.

78 Doktor Puf [V. F. Odoevskii], 'Vzgliad na morozhenuiu zhivnost' voobshche i na indeek v osobennosti', *Zapiski dlia khoziaev*, I (1845), p. 7.

79 Stefan Abramovich, 'Rubka kapusta', *Ekonom*, 29 (1850), p. 225.

80 'Kapusta', *Trudy Imperatorskogo vol'nogo ekonomicheskogo obshchestva*, III/9 (1859), pp. 355–6.

81 'Poleznoe izobretenie dlia prodovol'stviia armii, flot i naroda', *Ekonom*, 20 (1849), p. 160.

THREE: Eating and Drinking in the Earliest Days of Russia

1 On the power of this origin story, see Serhii Plokhy, *Lost Kingdom: The Quest for Empire and the Making of the Russian Nation, from 1470 to the Present* (New York, 2017).

2 Valerie A. Kivelson and Ronald Grigor Suny, *Russia's Empires* (New York, 2017), pp. 17, 22.

3 B. A. Kolchin and T. I. Makarova, eds., *Drevniaia Rus': Byt i kultura* (Moscow, 1997), p. 8.

4 *Domostroi: russkii semeinyi ustav*, trans. V. V. Kolesov (Moscow, 2005), p. 182.

5 M. G. Rabinovich, *Ocherki material'noi kul'tury russkogo feodal'nogo goroda* (Moscow, 1988), p. 214.

6 E. A. Rybina, *Arkheologicheskie ocherki istorii novgorodskoi torgovli* (Moscow, 1978), p. 30.

7 A. V. Artsikhovskii, 'Pishcha i utvar', in *Ocherki russkoi kul'tury XIII–XV vekov, Chast' 1 Material'naia kul'tura* (Moscow 1968), p. 299.

8 M. A. Brisbane, N. A. Makarov and E. N. Nosov, 'Medieval Novgorod in Its Wider Context', in *The Archaeology of Medieval Novgorod in Context*, ed. Mark A. Brisbane, Nikolaj A. Makarov and Evgenij N. Nosov (Oxford, 2012), p. 7.

9 S. D. Zakharov, 'Buildings and Structures of the Minino Archaeological Complex', in *The Archaeology of Medieval Novgorod in Context*, pp. 58–75.

10 Mark Maltby, 'From *Alces* to *Zander*: A Summary of the Zooarchaeological Evidence from Novgorod, Gorodishche and Minino', in *The Archaeology of Medieval Novgorod in Context*, pp. 351–80.

11 Mark Maltby, 'From Bovid to Beaver: Mammal Exploitation in Medieval Northwest Russia', in *The Oxford Handbook of Zooarchaeology*, ed. Umberto Albarella et al. (Oxford, 2018), pp. 233–5.

12 Jean Kathryn Berger, 'The Daily Life of the Household in Medieval Novgorod' (PhD diss., University of Minnesota, 1998), pp. 102–3, 106, 119–20.

13 V. N. Shchepkin, 'Goloda v Rossii. Istoricheskii ocherk', *Istoricheskii vestnik*, VII/6 (1886), pp. 490–91.

14 S. A. Kniaz'kov, *Golod v drevnei Rossii* (St Petersburg, 1913), pp. 5–6.

15 A. S. Ermolov, *Nashi neurozhai i prodovol'stvennyi vopros* (St Petersburg, 1909), vol. I, p. 5.

16 Shchepkin, 'Goloda', p. 491.

17 Shchepkin counts fifteen, but also on average eight bad harvests a century during the era; Ermolov counts 25 famines, vol. I, p. 6; Kniaz'kov counts more: 43.

18 *The Laws of Rus': Tenth to Fifteenth Centuries*, trans. and ed. Daniel H. Kaiser (Salt Lake City, UT, 1992), pp. 15–19.

19 Ibid., pp. 20–34.

20 Ibid., pp. 20–34; some changes in the translation by me.

21 Ibid., pp. 15–19.

22 Serge A. Zenkovsky, ed., *Medieval Russia's Epics, Chronicles, and Tales* (New York, 1974), pp. 67–8.

23 Christian Raffensperger, *Reimagining Europe: Kievan Rus' in the Medieval World* (Cambridge, MA, 2012).

24 Natalia Zajac, 'Women between West and East: The Inter-rite Marriages of the Kyivan Rus' Dynasty, ca. 1000–1204' (PhD diss., University of Toronto, 2017), pp. 46–9.

25 R.E.F. Smith and David Christian, *Bread and Salt: A Social and Economic History of Food and Drink in Russia* (Cambridge, 1984), p. 12.

26 Gerasim Stepanov, *Polnyi kukhmister i konditer, ili Ruskii gastronom, sobrannyi i sostavlennyi iz sobstvennykh opytov i nabliudenii Gerasimom Stepanovym* (Moscow, 1834), pp. 9–12.

27 M. Shakhov, 'O poste', in *Monastyrskaia kukhnia* (Moscow, 1991), pp. 6–9.

28 Sigismund von Herberstein, *Zapiski o Moskovii* (Moscow, 2008), vol. I, p. 211.

29 Edward Daniel Clarke, *Travels in Russia, Tartary and Turkey: A New Edition* (Aberdeen, 1848), p. 37.

30 Iv[an Iakovlevich] Zatsepin, *O postnoi i skoromnoi pishche v meditsinskom otnoshenii* (Moscow, 1841).

31 Cited in Donald Ostrowski, *Muscovy and the Mongols: Cross-cultural Influences on the Steppe Frontier* (Cambridge, 1998), p. 67.

32 Zenkovsky, *Medieval Russia's Epics, Chronicles, and Tales*, p. 170.

33 Christopher Dawson, ed., *Mission to Asia: Narratives and Letters of the Franciscan Missionaries in Mongolia and China in the Thirteenth and Fourteenth Centuries Translated by a Nun of Stanbrook Abbey* (New York, 1966), pp. 29–30.

34 David Miller, 'Monumental Building as an Indicator of Economic Trends in Northern Rus´ in the Late Kievan and Mongol Periods, 1138–1462', *American Historical Review*, XCIV/2 (1989), pp. 360–90.

35 Artsikhovskii, 'Pishcha i utvar´', pp. 299, 304.

36 Stella Rock, 'Russian Piety and Orthodox Culture', in *The Cambridge History of Christianity*, vol. V, ed. Michael Angold (Cambridge, 2006), p. 266.

37 Carol Belkin Stevens, *Russia's Wars of Emergence, 1460–1730* (London, 2007), p. 13.

38 For example in the life of St Sergei of Radonezh, as explained in Artsikhovskii, 'Pishcha i utvar´', pp. 297–8.

39 Artsikhovskii, 'Pishcha i utvar´', p. 298.

40 Herberstein, *Zapiski*, vol. I, p. 289.

41 Ibid., p. 291, and for the doubt, Herberstein, *Zapiski*, vol. II, p. 404.

42 Herberstein, *Zapiski*, vol. I, p. 291.

43 Ibid., pp. 541–3.

44 Ibid., p. 543.

45 Ibid., pp. 543–61.

46 Ibid., p. 205.

47 On the origins of the *Domostroi*, see Carolyn Pouncy, *The Domostroi: Rules for Russian Households in the Time of Ivan the Terrible* (Ithaca, NY, 1994), p. 4. All descriptions below are my translations from *Domostroi. Russkii semeinyi ustav* (Moscow, 2005) unless otherwise noted.

48 Nikolaas Vitsen, *Puteshestvie v Moskoviiu, 1664–1665*, trans. V. G. Trisman (St Petersburg, 1996), p. 99.

49 *Domostroi*, pp. 92, 188.

50 Ibid., pp. 93–4.

51 Ibid., p. 140.

52 Ibid., p. 141.

53 Ibid., pp. 184–5.

54 Ann M. Kleimola, 'The Road to Beloozero: Ivan IV's Reconciliation with the "Devil in a Skirt"', *Russian History*, XLII/1 (2015), p. 69.

55 Ibid., p. 70.

56 Ibid., pp. 71–3, 77.

57 'Stolovaia kniga Patriarkha Filareta Nikiticha', *Starina i novizna*, XI (1906), pp. 67–163.

FOUR: Russia Becomes an Empire

1 Matthew P. Romaniello, *Enterprising Empires: Russia and Britain in Eighteenth-century Eurasia* (Cambridge, 2019).

2 Giles Fletcher, *Of the Russe Common Wealth; or, Maner of Gouerment of the Russe Emperour (Commonly Called the Emperour of Moskouia)* (London, 1591), p. 60b.

3 Ibid., pp. 7–12.

4 Ibid., p. 110b.

5 Ibid., p. 59.

6 On salt farming, see R.E.F. Smith and David Christian, *Bread and Salt: A Social and Economic History of Food and Drink in Russia* (Cambridge, 1984), Chapter Two.

7 Yuri Slezkine, *Arctic Mirrors: Russia and the Small Peoples of the North* (Ithaca, NY, 1994), p. 23.

8 On this problem in one region of Siberia, particularly in the eighteenth century, see James R. Gibson, *Feeding the Russian Fur Trade: Provisionment of the Okhotsk Seaboard and the Kamchatka Peninsula* (Madison, WI, 1969).

9 On numbers, see V. I. Shunkov, *Ocherki po historia kolonizatsii Sibiri v XVII–nachale XVIII vekov* (Moscow, 1946), p. 45.

10 F. G. Safronov, *Russkie na severo-vostoke azii v XVII–seredine XIX v. Upravlenie, sluzhilye liidi, krest'iane, gorodskoe naselenie* (Moscow, 1978), pp. 108–9.

11 Janet M. Hartley, *Siberia: A History of the People* (New Haven, CT, 2014), p. 59.

12 Ibid., pp. 63–4.

13 T. A. Voronina, 'The Diet of Siberian Peasants on Lenten Days (the 19th Century)', *Archaeology, Ethnology and Anthropology of Eurasia*, XXXIX/4 (2011) pp. 136–41.

14 Z. P. Gor'kovskaia and O. N. Kationov, 'Pishcha russkikh krest'ian Sibiri v povsednevnoi zhizni (period kapitalizma)', in *Kul'turnyi potentsial Sibiri v dosovetskii period* (Novosibirsk, 1992), p. 56.

15 Ibid., p. 58.

16 Harry de Windt, *Siberia as It Is* (London, 1892), p. 247.

17 Gor'kovskaia and Kationov, 'Pishcha russkikh krest'ian Sibiri', p. 58.

18 Augustus von Kotzebue, *The Most Remarkable Year in the Life of Augustus von Kotzebue; Containing an Account of His Exile into Siberia, and of the Other Extraordinary Events Which Happened to Him in Russia*, trans. Benjamin Beresford (London, 1802), vol. I, p. 211.

19 Kotzebue, *Most Remarkable Year*, vol. II, p. 17.

20 Ibid., pp. 58–61.

21 'The Life of Archpriest Avvakum by Himself', in *Medieval Russia's Epics, Chronicles, and Tales*, ed. Serge A. Zenkovsky (New York, 1974), pp. 416–17.

22 V. N. Shchepkin, 'Goloda v Rossii. Istoricheskii ocherk', *Istoricheskii vestnik*, VII/6 (1886), p. 491.

23 Fletcher, *Of the Russe*, p. 14.

24 Shchepkin, 'Goloda', p. 492.

25 *Istoricheskii obzor pravitel'stvennykh meropriiatii po narodonou prodovol'stviiu v Rossii*, vol. I (St Petersburg, 1892–3), p. 6; Shchepkin, 'Goloda', p. 493.

26 A. S. Ermolov, *Nashi neurozhai i prodovol'stvennyi vopros* (St Petersburg, 1909), vol. I, p. II.

27 The classic work on the Time of Troubles is S. F. Platonov, *The Time of Troubles: A Historical Study of the Internal Crisis and Social Struggle in Sixteenth- and Seventeenth-century Muscovy*, trans. John T. Alexander (Lawrence, KA, 1970). A more recent examination of the era is Chester S. L. Dunning, *Russia's First Civil War: The Time of Troubles and the Founding of the Romanov Dynasty* (University Park, PA, 2001).

28 Fletcher, *Of the Russe*, p. 44.

29 Samuel Collins, *The Present State of Russia: In a Letter to a Friend at London* (London, 1671), p. 59.

30 Fletcher, *Of the Russe*, p. 44.

31 David Christian, *'Living Water': Vodka and Russian Society on the Eve of Emancipation* (Oxford, 1990), pp. 28–9.

32 Adam Olearius, *The Voyages and Travels of the Ambassadors from the Duke of Holstein, to the Great Duke of Muscovy, and the King of Persia*, trans. John Davies (London, 1662), p. II.

33 Ibid., p. 82.

34 Paul of Aleppo, *The Travels of Macarius, Patriarch of Antioch*, trans. F. C. Belfour (London, 1836), vol. I, p. 400.

35 Collins, *The Present State*, p. 138.

36 Ibid., p. 61.

37 Olearius, *Voyages*, p. 87.

38 Fletcher, *Of the Russe*, p. 1080b.

39 Ibid., p. 112.

40 Olearius, *Voyages*, p. 52.

41 Ibid., pp. 14–15.

42 Ibid., p. 52.

43 Ibid., pp. 8–9.

44 Ibid., pp. 10–11.

45 Paul of Aleppo, *The Travels of Macarius*, vol. I, pp. 287, 303.

46 Olearius, *Voyages*, p. 26.

47 Ibid., p. 87.

48 Paul of Aleppo, *The Travels of Macarius*, vol. I, p. 392.

49 Paul of Aleppo, *The Travels of Macarius*, vol. II, pp. 83–4.

50 Guy Miège, *La relation de trois ambassades de monseigneur le Comte de Carlisle, de la part du serenissime tres-puissant Prince Charles II, roy de la Grande Bretagne, vers leurs serenissimes Majestés Alexey Michailovitz Czar & Grand Duc de Moscovie, Charles roy de Suede, & Frederic III, roy de Dannemarc & de Norvege, commencées en l'an 1663 & finies sur la fin de l'an 1664* (Rouen, 1670), pp. 34–5.

51 Olearius, *Voyages*, p. 64. This note, repeated from Herberstein, does suggest a degree of copying between the various travel accounts!

52 Olearius, *Voyages*, p. 65.

53 Lindsey Hughes, '"A Beard is an Unnecessary Burden": Peter I's Laws on Shaving and their Roots in Early Russia', in *Russian Society and Culture and the Long Eighteenth Century: Essays in Honour of Anthony G. Cross*, ed. Roger Bartlett and Lindsey Hughes (Münster, 2004), pp. 26–7.

54 Matthew P. Romaniello, 'Through the Filter of Tobacco: The Limits of Global Trade in the Early Modern World', *Comparative Studies in Society and History*, XLIX/4 (2007), pp. 914–37.

55 'The Life of Archpriest Avvakum', p. 407.

56 Evgenii V. Anisimov, *The Reforms of Peter the Great: Progress through Coercion in Russia*, trans. John T. Alexander (Armonk, NY, 1993), p. 23.

57 'Regulations for Holding Assemblies', in William Marshall, ed., *Peter the Great* (London, 1996), p. 124.

FIVE: Champagne and *Kvas*: Russia Divided

1 *Polnoe sobranie zakonov Rossiiskoi Imperii: Pervoe sobranie* [henceforth PSZ (St Petersburg, 1830), V/3338 (20 March 1719).

2 Evgenii V. Anisimov, *The Reforms of Peter the Great: Progress through Coercion in Russia*, trans. John T. Alexander (Armonk, NY, 1993), p. 145.

3 Ibid., p. 165.

4 Ibid.

5 On changes in dress, see Christine Ruane, *The Empire's New Clothes: A History of the Russian Fashion Industry, 1700–1917* (New Haven, CT, 2009).

6 'Peter III's Manifesto Freeing Nobles from Obligatory Service, 1762', *Documents in Russian History*, http://academic.shu.edu/russianhistory, accessed 24 July 2020.

7 Priscilla Roosevelt, *Life on the Russian Country Estate: A Social and Cultural History* (New Haven, CT, 1995).

8 John Randolph, *The House in the Garden: The Bakunin Family and the Romance of Russian Idealism* (Ithaca, NY, 2007); Katherine Pickering Antonova, *An Ordinary Marriage: The World of a Gentry Family in Provincial Russia* (New York, 2013).

9 W. Bruce Lincoln, *Nicholas I, Emperor and Autocrat of All the Russias* (London, 1978), p. 187.

10 Sheila Fitzpatrick, *Stalin's Peasants: Resistance and Survival in the Russian Village after Collectivization* (New York, 1994), p. 315.

11 David Moon, *The Russian Peasantry, 1600–1930: The World the Peasants Made* (London, 1999), p. 1.

12 Moon, *The Russian Peasantry*, p. 21.

13 Aleksandr Nikolaevich Radishchev, *A Journey from St Petersburg to Moscow*, trans. Leo Wiener, ed. Roderick Page Thaler (Cambridge, MA, 1958).

14 'Po otchetu o sostoianii Kazanskoi Gubernii za 1839 g.', RGIA f. 1281, op. 3, d. 105, l. 12.

15 Ivan Boltin, *Primechaniia na istoriiu drevniia i nynyshniia Rossii G. Leklerka* (St Petersburg, 1788), vol. II, pp. 179, 328–9.

16 I. M. Snegirev, *Ruskie v svoikh poslovitsakh. Razsuzhdeniia i issledovaniia ob otechestvennykh poslovitsakh i pogovorkakh* (Moscow, 1831), vol. II, p. 3.

17 Ibid., pp. 6–7.

18 Ibid., pp. 7–13.

19 Ibid., pp. 13–14.

20 *Bagatelles. Promenades d'un désœuvré dans la ville de St-Pétersbourg* (St Petersburg, 1811), vol. I, p. 95.

21 Samuel S. Cox, *Arctic Sunbeams; or, From Broadway to the Bosphorus by Way of the North Cape* (New York, 1882), p. 231.

22 Patricia Herlihy, *The Alcoholic Empire: Vodka and Politics in Late Imperial Russia* (New York, 2002), p. 6.

23 David Christian, '*Living Water*': Vodka and Russian Society on the Eve of Emancipation (Oxford, 1990), pp. 88–92.

24 D. Ch. Stremoukhov, 'Mysli o vozmozhnosti uluchsheniia Selskogo Khoziaistva v Rossii osnovannye na prirode chelovecheskoi i na drevnikh Rossiiskikh obychaiakh', *Zemledel'cheskii zhurnal*, IX/25 (1829), p. 72.

25 Boris Volzhin [Vladimir Burnashev], *Derevenskii starosta Miron Ivanov. Narodnaia byl' dlia Russkikh prostoliudinov* (St Petersburg, 1839), p. 2.

26 S. M., 'Novyi chainyi magazin', *Kazanskie gubernskie vedomosti (neoffitsialnye)* (25 January 1860), p. 31.

27 A. A., *O nastoiashchem sostoianii khoziaistva u krest'ian, s pokazaniem prichin, prepiatstvuiushchikh razvitiiu ego, s ukazaniem sredstv k otvrashcheniiu tekh prichin, i s prisovokupleniem kratkikh pravil zemledeliia, dlia srednei polosy Rossii* (Moscow, 1846), pp. 54–5.

28 Henry Sutherland Edwards, *The Russians at Home* (London, 1861), p. 352.

29 Thomas Hunt, *The Life of William H. Hunt* (Brattleboro, VT, 1922), p. 289.

30 Audra Jo Yoder, 'Tea Time in Romanov Russia: A Cultural History, 1616–1917', (PhD diss., University of North Carolina, Chapel Hill, 2016), Chapter Three.

31 E. Alipanov, *Khanskii chai. Sel. vodevil'* (St Petersburg, 1835).

32 Fridrich Vul'f, 'Prodolzhenie otvertov gospodina Barona fon Vul'fa na zadannye v pervoi chasti ekonomicheskie voprosy', *Trudy imperatorskogo vol'nogo ekonomicheskogo obshchestva*, X (1768), pp. 68–9.

33 Laksman, 'Ekonomicheskie otvety, kasaiushchiesia do khlebopashestva v lezhashchikh okolo reki Sviri i iuzhnoi chasti Olontsa mestakh', *Trudy imperatorskogo vol'nogo ekonomicheskogo obshchestva*, XIII (1769), p. 27.

34 Volzhin [Burnashev], *Derevenskii starosta*, p. 48.

35 O. G. Ageeva, *Evropeizatsiia russkogo dvora 1700–1796 gg.* (Moscow, 2006), and Paul Keenan, *St Petersburg and the Russian Court, 1703–1761* (Houndmills, Basingstoke, 2013).

36 Darra Goldstein, 'Gastronomic Reforms under Peter the Great', *Jahrbücher für Geschichte Osteuropas*, XLVIII/4 (2000), p. 495.

37 Shreter, 'Opyt domostroitel'stva i planov na ekonomicheskuiu zadachu 1770 i 1771 goda', *Trudy imperatorskogo vol'nogo ekonomicheskogo obshchestva*, XXII (1772), pp. 37–60.

38 Iosif Regensburger, 'O razdelenii izvestnoi summy na godovoi prozhitok', *Trudy imperatorskogo vol'nogo ekonomicheskogo obshchestva*, XXI (1772), pp. 117–327.

39 Ibid., p. 138.

40 Sergei Drukovtsov, *Povarennye zapiski* (St Petersburg, 1779), pp. 1–2.

41 Ibid., pp. [45–7].

42 V. A. Levshin, *Slovar' povarennyi, prispeshnichii, kanditorskii i distillatorskii, soderzhashchii po azbuchnomu poriadku podrobnoe i vernoe nastavlenie k podrobnoe i vernoe nastavlenie k prigotovleniiu vsiakogo roda kushan'ia iz Frantsuzskoi, Nemetskoi, Gollandskoi, Ispanskoi i Angliskoi povarni, pirozhnogo, dessertov, varenii, salatov, vod, essentsii, ratafii, likerov, dvoviiu vodok, i pr.; takzhe*

k uchrezhdeniiu stola s planami, podach, uslugi i proch. i s prisovokupleniem v
osoblivykh paragrafakh polnoi Meshchanskoi povarni i Novoi; ravnym obrazom
povaren Avstriiskoi, Berlinskoi, Bogemskoi, Saksonskoi i Ruskoi (Moscow, 1795–7).

43 Edward Daniel Clarke, *The Life and Remains of the Rev. Edward Daniel Clarke,*
L.L.D., Professor of Mineralogy in the University of Cambridge (London, 1824),
pp. 388–9.

44 They have been collected in Yuri Lotman and Jelena Pogosjan, *High Society*
Dinners: Dining in Tsarist Russia, trans. Marian Schwartz (Totnes, 2014).

45 'Oplachennye scheta', RGADA f. 1264, op. 1, d. 195, ll. 12, 38, 154.

46 E. R. Dashkova, *The Memoirs of Princess Dashkova*, trans. and ed. Kyril Fitzlyon
(Durham, NC, 1995).

47 'Nastavleniia grafa Aleksandra Romanovicha Vorontsova upravliaiushchemu
o vedenii domashnego khoziaistva i o sostavlenii meniu vo vremia prebyvaniia
kniagini v 1802-i godu', RGADA f. 1261, op. 7, d. 1203, ll. 3–30b.

48 'Vypiski o raskhode gospodskogo garderopa, o veshchakh, otpravlennykh
iz Peterburga v Andreevskoe i o khraniashchikhsia v Moskovskom dome, o
mel'nitsakh v slobode Vorontsovki, o sostoianii Istashenskogo doma o s"estnykh
pripasakh v kladovoi', RGADA f. 1261, op. 7, d. 900, ll. 12–120b.

49 'Raznye zapisi po khoziaistvu spiski posudy, materialov, produkhtov i dr.
predmetov iz sostava imushchestva Vorontsovykh', RGADA f. 1261, op. 2,
d. 668, l. 14.

50 'Usloviia i obiazatel'stva raznykh lits pri postuplenii ili prieme na rabotu po
khoziaistvu i v lichnye usluzhenie k Vorontsovym', RGADA f. 1261, op. 2, d. 605,
ll. 2–3, 21–4, 38–380b.

51 'Tetrad's zapisiami raskhoda stolovykh produktov i ezhednevnykh obedennykh
meniu', RGADA f. 1261, op. 2, d. 666, l. 1.

52 'Tetrad', l. 11.

53 Edward Daniel Clarke, *Travels in Russia, Tartary and Turkey: A New Edition*
(Aberdeen, 1848), pp. 27–8.

54 Arcadius Kahan, 'The Costs of "Westernization" in Russia: The Gentry and the
Economy in the Eighteenth Century', *Slavic Review*, XXV (1966), pp. 40–66.

55 A. A. Fet, *Moi vospominaniia, 1848–1889* (Moscow, 1890), vol. 1, p. 4.

56 O. P. Verkhovskaia, *Kartinki proshlogo. Iz vospominanii detstva* (Moscow, 1913),
pp. 89–90.

57 On Shcherbatov, see Isabel de Madariaga, *Politics and Culture in Eighteenth-*
century Russia (London, 1999), pp. 249–57; Gary M. Hamburg, *Russia's Path*
toward Enlightenment: Faith, Politics, and Reason, 1500–1801 (New Haven, CT,
2016), pp. 675–97.

58 M. M. Shcherbatov, *On the Corruption of Morals in Russia*, trans. A. Lentin
(Cambridge, 1969), pp. 120, 122; my translation.

59 Shcherbatov, *On the Corruption of Morals*, p. 140; on Peter the Great and cheese,
see Goldstein, 'Gastronomic Reforms', p. 499.

60 Shcherbatov, *On the Corruption of Morals*, pp. 239, 244.

61 Ibid., p. 222.

62 Ibid., p. 241.

63 M. M. Shcherbatov, 'O nyneshnem v 1787 godu pochti povsemestnom golode
v Rossii, o sposobakh onomu pomoch' i vpred predupredit' podobnoe zhe

neshchastie', *Chteniia v Imperatorskogo obshchestve istorii i drevnostei rossiiskikh pri moskovskom universitete*, 1 (Jan–Mar 1860), pp. 81–112, here 82.

SIX: Russia Becomes Modern

1 Richard Wortman, *Scenarios of Power: Myth and Ceremony in Russian Monarchy from Peter the Great to the Abdication of Nicholas II* (Princeton, NJ, 2006).

2 Léon Godard, *Pétersbourg et Moscou. Souvenirs du couronnement d'un tsar* (Paris, 1858), p. 60.

3 Helen Baker, 'Monarchy Discredited? Reactions to the Khodynka Coronation Catastrophe of 1896', *Revolutionary Russia*, XVI/1 (2003), p. 6.

4 David Moon, *The Abolition of Serfdom in Russia, 1762–1907* (Harlow, 2001).

5 'Sel'skokhoziaistvennye obshchestva', in *Entsiklopedicheskii slovar'* (St Petersburg, 1900), vol. XXIX, pp. 414–19.

6 Leonard G. Friesen, 'Toward a Market Economy: Fruit and Vegetable Production by the Peasants of New Russia, 1850–1900', *Canadian Slavonic Papers*, XL/1–2 (1998), pp. 27–42.

7 Cassius Marcellus Clay, *The Life of Cassius Marcellus Clay: Memoirs, Writings, and Speeches, Showing His Conduct in the Overthrow of American Slavery, the Salvation of the Union, and the Restoration of the Autonomy of the States* (Cincinnati, OH, 1886), vol. I, p. 419.

8 On this in the context of a longer history of migration, see Willard Sunderland, 'Catherine's Dilemma: Resettlement and Power in Russia, 1500s–1914', in *Globalising Migration History: The Eurasian Experience (16th–21st centuries)*, ed. Jan and Leo Lucassen (Leiden, 2014), p. 56.

9 John Foster Fraser, *Russia of To-day* (New York, 1915), p. 274.

10 Peter I. Lyashchenko, *History of the National Economy of Russia to the 1917 Revolution*, trans. L. M. Herman (New York, 1970), pp. 519–20.

11 Francis B. Reeves, *Russia Then and Now, 1892–1917: My Mission to Russia during the Famine of 1891–1892, with Data Bearing upon Russia of To-day* (New York, 1917), p. 61.

12 T. V. Privalova, *Byt Rossiiskoi derevni 60-e gody XIX-20-e gody XX v.* (Moscow, 2000), p. 44.

13 Augustus von Kotzebue, *The Most Remarkable Year in the Life of Augustus von Kotzebue; Containing an Account of His Exile into Siberia, and of the Other Extraordinary Events Which Happened to Him in Russia*, trans. Benjamin Beresford (London, 1802), vol. I, p. 171.

14 Robert D. Pinkerton, *Russia; or, Miscellaneous Observations on the Past and Present State of That Country and Its Inhabitants* (London, 1833), p. 295.

15 Harry de Windt, *Siberia as It Is* (London, 1892), pp. 83–4.

16 Iv. Ivaniukov, 'Ocherki provintsial'noi zhizni', *Russkaia mysl'* (August 1895), p. 172.

17 Patricia Herlihy, *The Alcoholic Empire: Vodka and Politics in Late Imperial Russia* (New York, 2002), pp. 6–7.

18 David Christian, *'Living Water': Vodka and Russian Society on the Eve of Emancipation* (Oxford, 1990), p. 6.

19 Raphael Pumpelly, *Across America and Asia: Notes of Five Years' Journey around the World and of Residence in Arizona, Japan, and China* (New York, 1870), p. 404.

20 Samuel Robert Graves, *A Yachting Cruise in the Baltic* (London, 1863), pp. 257–8.

21 Privalova, *Byt rossiiskoi derevni*, p. 61.

22 *Pervaia vseobshchaia perepis' naseleniia Rossiiskoi imperii 1897 goda*, vol. VIII (St Petersburg, 1905).

23 G. Reinbeck, *Travels from St Petersburgh through Moscow, Grodno, Warsaw, Breslau &c to Germany in the Year 1805* (London, 1807), p. 14.

24 Alison K. Smith, 'Provisioning Kazan´: Feeding the Provincial Russian Town', *Russian History*, XXX/4 (2003), p. 378n.

25 George Augustus Sala, *A Journey Due North; Being Notes of a Residence in Russia* (Boston, MA, 1858), pp. 452–4.

26 P. An – ov, 'Zamechanie provintsiala o S. Peterburge', *Zavolzhskii muravei,* no. 11 (June 1832), p. 618.

27 Ibid., p. 619.

28 Alison K. Smith, 'Eating Out in Imperial Russia: Class, Nationality, and Dining before the Great Reforms', *Slavic Review*, LXV/4 (2006), pp. 747–68.

29 I. Levitov, *Putevoditel'* (Moscow, 1881), p. 4.

30 F. V. Dombrovskii, *Polnyi putevoditel' po Peterburgu i vsem ego okrestnostiam* (St Petersburg, 1896), p. 43.

31 *Vsia torgovo-promyshlennaia Rossiia* (Kiev, 1913), columns 183–5, 502–3.

32 Pavel Sumarokov, *Progulka po 12-ti guberniiam s istoricheskimi i statisticheskimi zamechaniiami* (St Petersburg, 1839), pp. 75–6.

33 Godard, *Pétersbourg et Moscou*, p. 79.

34 [Jacques] Boucher de Perthes, *Voyage en Russie, retour par la Lithuanie, la Pologne, la Silèsie, la Saxe et le Duche, de Nassau; séjour a Wisebade en 1856* (Paris, 1859), pp. 307–8.

35 On its history, see Anya von Bremzen, *Mastering the Art of Soviet Cooking: A Memoir of Food and Longing* (New York, 2013), p. 316.

36 I. G., 'Moskva za stolom', *Moskvitianin*, II/8 (1856), p. 455.

37 Lee Meriwether, *A Tramp Trip: How to See Europe on 50 Cents a Day* (New York and London, 1886), p. 229.

38 Louise McReynolds, *Russia at Play: Leisure Activities at the End of the Tsarist Era* (Ithaca, NY, 2003), p. 204.

39 Advertisement in *Odesskaia pochta*, 1934 (1 May 1914), p. 4. Thanks to Felix Cowan for this and the following advertisements.

40 Advertisement in *Kievskaia pochta*, 2 (14 May 1909), p. 1.

41 Advertisement in *Odesskaia pochta*, 1931 (28 April 1914), p. 4; advertisement in *Saratovskaia kopeechka*, 414 (18 November 1911), p. 4; advertisement in *Kur'er-kopeika*, 183 (7 November 1910), p. 1.

42 Advertisement in *Saratovskaia kopeechka*, 1099 (18 October 1913), p. 1.

43 Advertisements in: *Kur'er-kopeika* (Tiflis), 113 (19 May 1911), p. 4; *Khersonskaia gazeta kopeika*, 140 (25 October 1909), p. 1.

44 *Povolzhskaia kopeika*, 20 (28 July 1910), p. 1.

45 Boucher de Perthes, *Voyage en Russie*, p. 307.

46 Advertisement for the Tiflis restaurant Versailles, *Kur'er-kopeika*, 46 (27 February 1911), p. 1.

47 *Kur'er-kopeika*, 46 (24 February 1913), p. 1.

48 Deirdre Ruscitti Harshman, 'A Space Called Home: Housing and the Management of the Everyday in Russia, 1890–1935' (PhD diss., University of Illinois at Urbana-Champaign, 2018), pp. 28–9.

49 August von Haxthausen, *The Russian Empire: Its People, Institutions, and Resources*, trans. Robert Farie (London, 1856), vol. II, pp. 141–2.

50 Thomas Michell, *Russian Pictures, Drawn with Pen and Pencil* (London, 1889), p. 103.

51 Henry Sutherland Edwards, *The Russians at Home* (London, 1861), pp. 385–6.

52 Ibid., p. 386.

53 S. A. Kniaz'kov, *Golod v drevnei Rossii* (St Petersburg, 1913), p. 4.

54 Alison K. Smith, *Recipes for Russia: Food and Nationhood under the Tsars* (DeKalb, IL, 2008), pp. 13–43.

55 A. S. Ermolov, *Nashi neurozhai i prodovol'stvennyi vopros* (St Petersburg, 1909), vol. I, pp. 98–101.

56 Ibid., pp. 100–101.

57 Ibid., pp. 102–3.

58 Ibid., p. 229.

59 Peter Gatrell, *A Whole Empire Walking: Refugees in Russia during World War I* (Bloomington, IN, 1999), p. 3.

60 Lars T. Lih, *Bread and Authority in Russia, 1914–1921* (Berkeley, CA, 1990), p. 8.

61 Sarah Badcock, *Politics and the People in Revolutionary Russia: A Provincial History* (Cambridge, 2009), p. 213.

62 Peter Gatrell, 'Poor Russia, Poor Show: Mobilising a Backward Economy for War, 1914–1917', in *The Economics of World War I*, ed. Stephen Broadberry and Mark Harrison (Cambridge, 2009), pp. 256–9.

63 Badcock, *Politics and the People*, pp. 213–18.

64 Sergei Nefedov, 'The Food Crisis in Petrograd on the Eve of the February Revolution', *Quaestio Rossica*, V/3 (2017), pp. 635–55.

65 For a detailed chronology of the events of February/March 1917, see Tsuyoshi Hasegawa, *The February Revolution, Petrograd, 1917* (Leiden, 2018).

SEVEN: Hunger and Plenty: The Soviet Experience

1 Alexander Vucinich, 'Soviet Ethnographic Studies of Cultural Change', *American Anthropologist*, LXII/5 (1960), p. 867.

2 S. P. Tolstov, N. N. Cheboksarov and K. V. Chistov, eds, *Ocherki obshchei etnografiia. Evropeiskaia Chast' SSSR* (Moscow, 1968), p. 120.

3 Ibid., p. 121.

4 Ibid., p. 123.

5 Ibid., p. 124.

6 A standard overview of this early phase is Sheila Fitzpatrick, *The Russian Revolution*, 4th edn (Oxford, 2017).

7 Vera S. Dunham, *In Stalin's Time: Middleclass Values in Soviet Fiction* (Cambridge, 1976).

8 Andrei Markevich, 'Russia in the Great War: Mobilisation, Grain, and Revolution', in *The Economics of the Great War: A Centennial Perspective*, ed. Stephen Broadberry and Mark Harrison (London, 2018), p. 104.

9 Mauricio Borrero, *Hungry Moscow: Scarcity and Urban Society in the Russian Civil War, 1917–1921* (New York, 2003).

10 Donald J. Raleigh, 'The Russian Civil War, 1917–1922', in *The Cambridge History of Russia*, ed. Ronald Grigor Suny (Cambridge, 2008), vol. III, pp. 140–67, and Hugh D. Hudson, *Peasants, Political Police, and the Early Soviet State: Surveillance and Accommodation under the New Economic Policy* (New York, 2012), pp. 25–45.

11 Sheila Fitzpatrick, *Stalin's Peasants: Resistance and Survival in the Russian Village after Collectivization* (New York, 1994), pp. 44–69, and Carole Leonard, *Agrarian Reform in Russia* (Cambridge, 2011), pp. 68–71.

12 Sarah Cameron, 'The Kazakh Famine of 1930–33: Current Research and New Directions', *East/West: Journal of Ukrainian Studies*, III/2 (2016), pp. 117–32, and *The Hungry Steppe: Famine, Violence, and the Making of Soviet Kazakhstan* (Ithaca, NY, 2018).

13 For a recent discussion of these issues, with comment from historians who argue both of these cases, see 'Soviet Famines', *Contemporary European History*, XXVII/3 (2018), pp. 432–81.

14 Donald Filtzer and Wendy Z. Goldman, 'Introduction: The Politics of Food and War', in *Hunger and War: Food Provisioning in the Soviet Union during World War II*, ed. Wendy Z. Goldman and Donald Filtzer (Bloomington, IN, 2015), pp. 1–2.

15 *Ob uvelichenii proizvodstva kartofelia* (Syktyvkar, 1942), p. 3.

16 Filtzer and Goldman, 'Introduction', pp. 14–20.

17 Alexis Peri, *The War Within: Diaries from the Siege of Leningrad* (Cambridge, MA, 2017), p. 6.

18 Peri, *The War Within*, p. 131, quoting the diary of Anna Likhacheva.

19 Rebecca Manley, 'Nutritional Dystrophy: The Science and Semantics of Starvation in World War II', in *Hunger and War*, ed. Goldman and Filtzer, pp. 602–64.

20 Peri, *The War Within*, p. 57, quoting the diary of Natalia Uskova.

21 Alexander Solzhenitsyn, *One Day in the Life of Ivan Denisovich*, trans. Ralph Parker (New York, 1998), p. 14. I have slightly altered the translation.

22 Golfo Alexopoulos, *Illness and Inhumanity in Stalin's Gulag* (New Haven, CT, 2017), p. 10. The following paragraph draws from her account, esp. pp. 19–43.

23 E. Kabo, *Pitanie russkogo rabochego do i posle voiny* (Moscow, 1926).

24 Alison K. Smith, *Recipes for Russia: Food and Nationhood under the Tsars* (DeKalb, IL, 2008), pp. 61–2.

25 Anton Masterovoy, 'Eating Soviet: Food and Culture in the USSR, 1917–1991' (PhD diss., CUNY, 2013), p. 44.

26 Basile Kerblay, L'Évolution de l'alimentation rurale en Russie (1896–1960)', *Annales*, XVII/5 (1962), p. 898.

27 Fitzpatrick, *Stalin's Peasants*, pp. 130–31.

28 Il'ia E. Zelenin, 'N. S. Khrushchev's Agrarian Policy and Agriculture in the USSR', *Russian Studies in History*, L/3 (2011), pp. 53–4.

29 Zelenin, ' N. S. Khrushchev's Agrarian Policy', pp. 55–7, and Anatolii Strelianyi, 'Khrushchev and the Countryside', in *Nikita Khrushchev*, ed. William Taubman, Sergei Khrushchev and Abbott Gleason (New Haven, CT, 2000), pp. 113–37.

30 On this point, I. V. Glushchenko, *Obshchepit: Mikoian i sovetskaia kukhnia* (Moscow, 2010), p. 10.

31 Glushchenko, *Obshchepit*, p. 118.

32 Masterovoy, 'Eating Soviet', p. 55.

33 Sheila Fitzpatrick, *Everyday Stalinism: Ordinary Life in Extraordinary Times. Soviet Russia in the 1930s* (New York, 1999), pp. 79–106.

34 Masterovoy, 'Eating Soviet', pp. 35–45.

35 Glushchenko, *Obshchepit*, pp. 120–21.

36 Jenny Leigh Smith, 'Empire of Ice Cream: How Life Became Sweeter in the Postwar Soviet Union', in *Food Chains: From Farmyard to Shopping Cart*, ed. Warren Belasco and Roger Horowitz (Philadelphia, PA, 2009), pp. 142–57.

37 Leigh, 'Empire of Ice Cream', and Nataliia Lebina, *Sovetskaia povsednevnost′: Normy i anomalii ot voennogo kommunizma k bol′shomu stiliu* (Moscow, 2015), pp. 39–40.

38 Glushchenko, *Obshchepit*, p. 137.

39 Ibid., p. 143.

40 Diane P. Koenker, 'The Taste of Others: Soviet Adventures in Cosmopolitan Cuisines', *Kritika*, XIX/2 (2018), pp. 243–72.

41 'Pitanie', *Bol′shaia sovetskaia entsiklopediia* (Moscow, 1940), vol. XLV, pp. 453–4.

42 Nataliia Lebina, *Passazhiry kolbasnogo poezda. Etiudy k kartine byta rossiiskogo goroda: 1917–1991* (Moscow, 2019), p. 368.

43 Postanovlenie TSK VKP(b), 19 August 1931.

44 Lebina, *Passazhiry*.

45 A. I. Mikoyan, 'Za vysoko kul′turnuiu stolovuiu', *Obshchestvennoe pitanie*, 1 (1933), p. 2.

46 *Obshchestvennoe pitanie v Moskve* (Moscow, 1962).

47 Iu. Appak, E. Danchevskaia, and Norkina, 'Luchshaia stolovaia v gorode', *Obshchestvennitsa*, 3 (September 1936), p. 12.

48 On the restaurants, *Obshchestvennoe pitanie v Moskve*, pp. 24–5, and Lynn and Wesley Fisher, *The Moscow Gourmet: Dining Out in the Capital of the USSR* (Ann Arbor, MI, 1974), p. 61.

49 Adrianne K. Jacobs, 'The Many Flavors of Socialism: Modernity and Tradition in Late Soviet Food Culture, 1965–1985' (PhD diss., University of North Carolina, Chapel Hill, 2015), p. 110.

50 Ibid., pp. 121–2.

51 Erik R. Scott, 'Edible Ethnicity: How Georgian Cuisine Conquered the Soviet Table', *Kritika*, XIII/4 (2012).

52 Masterovoy, 'Eating Soviet', p. 148.

53 T. V. Privalova, *Byt Rossiiskoi derevni 60-e gody XIX-20-e gody XX v.* (Moscow, 2000), pp. 63–4; also David Christian, 'Prohibition in Russia, 1914–1925', *Australian Slavonic and East European Studies*, IX/2 (1995), pp. 89–118.

54 A. Bezrodnyi, *Samogonka i golod* (Moscow, 1919), p. 3.

55 Patricia Herlihy, *The Alcoholic Empire: Vodka and Politics in Late Imperial Russia* (New York, 2002), p. 152.

56 Ibid., p. 154.

57 Anna L. Bailey, *Politics under the Influence: Vodka and Public Policy in Putin's Russia* (Ithaca, NY, 2018), pp. 19–22; Stephen V. Bittner, *Whites and Reds: A History of Wine in the Lands of Tsar and Commissar* (New York, 2021).

58 Venedikt Erofeev, *Moscow to the End of the Line*, trans. H. William Tjalsma (New York, 1980).

59 Herlihy, *The Alcoholic Empire*, pp. 154–6.

60 Anya von Bremzen, *Mastering the Art of Soviet Cooking: A Memoir of Food and Longing* (New York, 2013), p. 226.

61 E. A. Osokina, *Ierarkhiia potrebleniia. O zhizni liudei v usloviiakh stalinskogo snabzheniia. 1928–1935 gg.* (Moscow, 1993), and *Our Daily Bread: Socialist Distribution and the Art of Survival in Stalin's Russia, 1927–1941*, trans. Kate Transchel and Greta Bucher (London, 2001).

62 William Taubman, *Khrushchev: The Man and His Era* (New York, 2003), pp. 606–8.

63 Chris Miller, 'Gorbachev's Agriculture Agenda: Decollectivization and the Politics of Perestroika', *Kritika*, XVII/1 (2016), p. 113.

64 Susan E. Reid, 'Cold War in the Kitchen: Gender and the De-Stalinization of Consumer Taste in the Soviet Union under Khrushchev', *Slavic Review*, LXI/2 (2002), p. 211.

65 Anastasia Lakhtikova and Angela Brintlinger, 'Introduction: Food, Gender, and the Everyday through the Looking Glass of Socialist Experience', in *Seasoned Socialism: Gender and Food in Late Soviet Everyday Life*, ed. Anastasia Lakhtikova, Angela Brintlinger and Irina Glushchenko (Bloomington, IN, 2019), p. 9.

66 'Govoriat rabotnitsy Rostova: POCHEMU DOMA GOTOVIAT VKUSNEE, CHEM V STOLOVOI?', *Obshchestvennoe pitanie*, 2 (1933), pp. 10–11.

67 Masterovoy, 'Eating Soviet', p. 63.

68 Ibid., p. 64.

69 Ibid., p. 67, quoting Donald J. Raleigh, *Soviet Baby Boomers: An Oral History of Russia's Cold War Generation* (New York, 2012), p. 224.

70 Bremzen, *Mastering the Art*, p. 250.

71 Reid, 'Cold War in the Kitchen'.

EPILOGUE: Russia Again

1 Anthony Ramirez, 'Pepsi Will Be Bartered for Ships and Vodka in Deal With Soviets', *New York Times* (9 April 1990), section A, p. 1.

2 Francis X. Clines, 'Upheaval in the East; Moscow McDonald's Opens: Milkshakes and Human Kindness', *New York Times* (1 February 1990).

3 Theodore P. Gerber and Michael Hout, 'More Shock Than Therapy: Market Transition, Employment, and Income in Russia, 1991–1995', *American Journal of Sociology*, CIV/1 (1998), pp. 21–3.

4 David Sedik and Doris Wiesmann, 'Globalization and Food and Nutrition Security in the Russian Federation, Ukraine and Belarus', ESA Working Paper No. 03–04 (May 2003), pp. 1–2.

5 Gerber and Hout, 'More Shock Than Therapy', pp. 21–3.

6 J. Patrick Lewis, 'Down and Out in Russia: The Pain of Emerging Capitalism', *Business and Society Review*, 87 (1993), p. 20.

7 Konstantin E. Axenov, Isolde Brade and Alex G. Papadopoulos, 'Restructuring the Kiosk Trade in St Petersburg: A New Retail Trade Model for the Post-Soviet Period', *GeoJournal*, XLII/4 (1997), p. 419.

8 Margaret Shapiro, 'Perils of Kiosk Capitalism: Russia's New Entrepreneurs Pay for Permits and Protection', *Washington Post* (28 August 1993).

9 Sedik and Wiesmann, 'Globalization and Food and Nutrition Security', pp. 3–4.

10 Andrea Chandler, 'Democratization, Social Welfare and Individual Rights in Russia: The Case of Old-age Pensions', *Canadian Slavonic Papers/Revue canadienne des slavistes*, XLIII/4 (2001), pp. 409–35.

11 James Meek, 'Winter Survival Down to Toil of Villagers', *The Guardian* (19 September 1998), p. 19. See also Melissa L. Caldwell, *Not by Bread Alone: Social Support in the New Russia* (Berkeley, CA, 2004).

12 Louiza M. Boukhareva and Marcel Marloie, *Family Urban Agriculture in Russia: Lessons and Prospects* (Cham, 2015), p. 22.

13 Melissa L. Caldwell, 'Feeding the Body and Nourishing the Soul', *Food, Culture and Society*, X/1 (2007), pp. 48–50.

14 Danielle Berman, 'When Global Value Chains Are Not Global: Case Studies from the Russian Fast-food Industry', *Competition and Change*, XV/4 (2011), p. 281.

15 Andrew E. Kramer, 'Russia's Evolution, as Seen through the Golden Arches', *New York Times* (2 February 2010), p. B3.

16 Stephen K. Wegren, Frode Nilssen and Christel Elvestad, 'The Impact of Russian Food Security Policy on the Performance of the Food System', *Eurasian Geography and Economics*, LVII/6 (2016), p. 682.

17 Stephen K. Wegren and Christel Elvestad, 'Russia's Food Self-sufficiency and Food Security: An Assessment', *Post-Communist Economies*, XXX/5 (2018), pp. 565–87.

18 Zvi Lerman and David Sedik, 'Russian Agriculture and Transition', in *The Oxford Handbook of the Russian Economy*, ed. Michael Alexeev and Shlomo Weber (Oxford, 2013), pp. 514–40.

19 USDA GAIN Report, Number RS1819 (July 2018).

20 Julia Ioffe, 'The Borscht Belt: Annals of Gastronomy', *New Yorker*, LXXXVIII/9 (2012).

21 Anastasia Lakhtikova, 'Professional Women Cooking: Soviet Manuscript Cookbooks, Social Networks, and Identity Building', in *Seasoned Socialism: Gender and Food in Late Soviet Everyday Life*, ed. Anastasia Lakhtikova, Angela Brintlinger and Irina Glushchenko (Bloomington, IN, 2019), pp. 80–109.

22 Ivan Gutterman, et al., 'A Timeline of All Russia-related Sanctions', Radio Free Europe/Radio Liberty, www.rferl.org, accessed 28 July 2020.

23 Alec Luhn, 'Shoppers React: Crimea or Cheese?', *The Guardian* (8 August 2014), p. 21.

24 'Putin vs Parmesan', *The New York Times* (21 August 2015).

25 Tom Parfitt, 'Russians Find Whey around Sanctions by Copying Cheese', *The Times* (London) (6 March 2018), p. 31.

26 Bayard Taylor, *Travels in Greece and Russia, with an Excursion to Crete* (New York, 1859), pp. 325–6.

Recipes

1 Gerasim Stepanov, *Prodolzhenie k knige: polnyi kukhmister i konditer, ili russkii gastronom* (Moscow, 1835), pp. 8–9.

2 K. A. Avdeeva, *Ruchnaia kniga russkoi opytnoi khoziaiki*, 6th edn (St Petersburg, 1848), vol. I, p. II.

3 E. Molokhovets, *Prostaia, obshchedostupnaia kukhnia*, 2nd edn (St Petersburg, 1891), p. 58.

4 Ibid., p. 12.

5 *Kniga o vkusnoi i zdorovoi pishche* (Moscow, 1945), p. 139.

6 Avdeeva, *Ruchnaia kniga*, vol. I, pp. 59–60.

7 *Kniga o vkusnoi i zdorovoi pishche* (1945), p. 138.

8 Stepanov, *Prodolzhenie k knige*, pp. 55–6.

9 Molokhovets, *Prostaia, obshchedostupnaia kukhnia*, pp. 38–9.

10 I. M. Radetskii, *S.-Peterburgskaia kukhnia, zakliuchaiushchaia v sebe okolo 2,000 razlichnykh kushan'ev i prigotovlenii, s podrobnym ob''iasneniem i risunkami kak prigotovliat' i nakladyvat' na bliuda* (St Petersburg, 1862), p. 115.

11 Molokhovets, *Prostaia, obshchedostupnaia kukhnia*, p. 36.

12 Ibid., p. 38.

13 Gerasim Stepanov, *Polnyi kukhmister i konditer, ili Ruskii gastronom, sobrannyi i sostavlennyi iz sobstvennykh opytov i nabliudenii Gerasimom Stepanovym* (Moscow, 1834), p. 53.

14 A. P., *Ruchnaia ekonomicheskaia entsiklopediia* (Moscow, 1835), p. 23.

15 Ibid., p. 24.

16 Ibid.

17 Ibid., pp. 24–5.

18 *Russkaia postnaia povarikha, zakliuchaiushchaia v sebe 121 pravilo dlia postnogo stola, sostavlennaia iz mnogoletnikh opytov i nabliudenii russkoi khoziaikoi* (Moscow, 1851), p. 24.

19 Radetskii, *S.-Peterburgskaia kukhnia*, p. 110.

20 Avdeeva, *Ruchnaia kniga*, vol. I, pp. 4–5.

21 Ibid., p. 43.

22 Stepanov, *Prodolzhenie k knige*, pp. 8–9.

23 Radetskii, *S.-Peterburgskaia kukhnia*, pp. 76–7.

24 Stepanov, *Polnyi kukhmister i konditer*, pp. 42–5.

25 Ibid., p. 37.

26 Molokhovets, *Prostaia, obshchedostupnaia kukhnia*, pp. 64–5.

27 Avdeeva, *Ruchnaia kniga*, vol. I, pp. 12–13.

28 Ibid., p. 14.

29 Ibid., pp. 15–16.

30 Molokhovets, *Prostaia, obshchedostupnaia kukhnia*, p. 23.

31 Ibid., pp. 86–7.

32 Ibid., pp. 87–8.

33 Radetskii, *S.-Peterburgskaia kukhnia*, p. 171.

34 *Kniga o vkusnoi i zdorovoi pishche* (1945), pp. 146–7.

35 Ibid., pp. 119–20.

36 Molokhovets, *Prostaia, obshchedostupnaia kukhnia*, p. 16.

37 Avdeeva, *Ruchnaia kniga*, vol. I, pp. 152–3.

38 Ibid., pp. 153–4.

39 Ibid., pp. 5–6.

40 Molokhovets, *Prostaia, obshchedostupnaia kukhnia*, p. 94.

41 Avdeeva, *Ruchnaia kniga*, pp. 30–31.

42 Molokhovets, *Prostaia, obshchedostupnaia kukhnia*, pp. 24–5.

43 *Kniga o vkusnoi i zdorovoi pishche* (1945), pp. 115–16.

44 Molokhovets, *Prostaia, obshchedostupnaia kukhnia*, pp. 107–8.

45 Radetskii, *S.-Peterburgskaia kukhnia*, p. 478.

46 Molokhovets, *Prostaia, obshchedostupnaia kukhnia*, pp. 128–9.

47 Ibid., p. 113.

Bibliography

Archival Materials

'Nastavleniia grafa Aleksandra Romanovicha Vorontsova upravliaiushchemu o vedenii domashnego khoziaistva i o sostavlenii meniu vo vremia prebyvaniia kniagini v 1802-i godu', Rossiiskii gosudarstvennyi arkhiv drevnykh aktov [Russian State Archive of Ancient Acts, henceforth RGADA] f. 1261, op. 7, d. 1203

'O proezdakh v g. Gatchine e.i.v. gosudaryni imperatritsy Marii Feodorovny i e. velichestva velikogo Kniazia Mikhaila Aleksandrovicha', Gosudarstvennyi arkhiv Rossiiskoi Federatsii [State Archive of the Russian Federation, henceforth GARF] f. 97, op. 3, d. 16

'O vozmozhnosti uluchshit' sostoianie zemledeliia i zemledel'tsa v Rossii', R ossiisskii gosudarstvennyi istoricheskii arkhiv [Russian State Historical Ardhive, henceforth RGIA] f. 398, op. 8, d. 2537

'Oplachennye scheta', RGADA f. 1264, op. 1, d. 195

'Po otchetu o sostoianii Kazanskoi Gubernii za 1839 g.', RGIA f. 1281, op. 3, d. 105

'Prosheniia, raporty i otnosheniia na imia Glavnoupravliaiushchego Obol'ianinova', RGIA f. 491, op. 1, d. 93

'Raporta v Mosk. dom. kont. iz votchinnykh pravlenii gr. S. R. Vorontsova', RGADA f. 1261, op. 7, d. 1172

'Raznye zapisi po khoziaistvu spiski posudy, materialov, produkhtov i dr. predmetov iz sostava imushchestva Vorontsovykh', RGADA f. 1261, op. 2, d. 668

'Tetrad' s zapisiami raskhoda stolovykh produktov i ezhednevnykh obedennykh meniu', RGADA f. 1261, op. 2, d. 666

'Usloviia i obiazatel'stva raznykh lits pri postuplenii ili prieme na rabotu po khoziaistvu i v lichnye usluzhenie k Vorontsovym', RGADA f. 1261, op. 2, d. 605

'Vypiski o raskhode gospodskogo garderopa, o veshchakh, otpravlennykh iz Peterburga v Andreevskoe i o khraniashchikhsia v Moskovskom dome, o mel'nitsakh v slobode Vorontsovki, o sostoianii Istashenskogo doma o s"estnykh pripasakh v kladovoi', RGADA f. 1261, op. 7, d. 900

'Zapisnye knizhki po denezhnym raskhodam na pokupku stolovykh produktov', RGADA f. 1261, op. 2, d. 918

Printed Primary Materials

A., A., *O nastoiashchem sostoianii khoziaistva u krest'ian, s pokazaniem prichin, prepiatstvuiushchikh razvitiiu ego, s ukazaniem sredstv k otvrashcheniiu tekh prichin, i s prisovokupleniem kratkikh pravil zemledeliia, dlia srednei polosy Rossii* (Moscow, 1846)

Abramovich, Stefan, 'Rubka kapusta', *Ekonom*, 29 (1850), p. 225

Alipanov, E., *Khanskii chai. Sel. vodevil'* (St Petersburg, 1835)

An—ov, P., 'Zamechanie provintsiala o S. Peterburge', *Zavolzhskii muravei* no. 11 (June 1832), pp. 614–22

Anichkov, V., *Voennoe khoziaistvo* (St Petersburg, 1860)

Appak, Iu., E. Danchevskaia, and Norkina, 'Luchshaia stolovaia v gorode', *Obshchestvennitsa*, 3 (September 1936), p. 12

Arsen'ev, K. I., *Nachertanie statistiki Rossiiskogo gosudarstva* (St Petersburg, 1818)

Avdeeva, K. [A.], *Ruchnaia kniga russkoi opytnoi khoziaiki*, 6th edn (St Petersburg, 1848)

——, *Rukovodstvo k ustroistvu ferm i vedeniiu na nikh khoziaistva* (St Petersburg, 1863)

B., V., 'O prigotovlenii soloniny', *Ekonom*, 86 (1842), p. 269

——, 'Tolokno', *Ekonom*, 84 (1842), p. 252

Bagatelles. Promenades d'un désœuvré dans la ville de St-Pétersbourg (St Petersburg, 1811)

Bezrodnyi, A., *Samogonka i golod* (Moscow, 1919)

Bitter, Michael, 'George Forbes's "Account of Russia", 1733–1734', *The Slavonic and East European Review*, LXXXIV/4 (2004), pp. 886–920

Boltin, Ivan, *Primechaniia na istoriiu drevniia i nynyshniia Rossii G. Leklerka* (St Petersburg, 1788)

Boucher de Perthes, [Jacques], *Voyage en Russie, retour par la Lithuanie, la Pologne, la Silèsie, la Saxe et le Duche, de Nassau; séjour a Wisebade en 1856* (Paris, 1859)

Bur'ianov, Viktor [Burnashev, Vladimir], *Besedy s det'mi o khoziaistve: domashnem, sel'skom, manufakturnom i o tovarov* (St Petersburg, 1837)

——, *Progulka s det'mi po Rossii* (St Petersburg, 1837)

Burke, Richard Southwell, *St Petersburg and Moscow: A Visit to the Court of the Czar* (London, 1846)

Carr, John, *A Northern Summer; or, Travels round the Baltic, through Denmark, Sweden, Russia, Prussia, and Part of Germany, in the Year 1805* (London, 1805)

Clarke, Edward Daniel, *The Life and Remains of the Rev. Edward Daniel Clarke, L.L.D., Professor of Mineralogy in the University of Cambridge* (London, 1824)

——, *Travels in Russia, Tartary and Turkey: A New Edition* (Aberdeen, 1848)

Clay, Cassius Marcellus, *The Life of Cassius Marcellus Clay: Memoirs, Writings, and Speeches, Showing His Conduct in the Overthrow of American Slavery, the Salvation of the Union, and the Restoration of the Autonomy of the States* (Cincinnati, OH, 1886)

Collins, Samuel, *The Present State of Russia: In a Letter to a Friend at London* (London, 1671)

Cox, Samuel S., *Arctic Sunbeams; or, From Broadway to the Bosphorus by Way of the North Cape* (New York, 1882)

Coxe, William, *Travels into Poland, Russia, Sweden, and Denmark* (London, 1792)

Dashkova, E. R., *The Memoirs of Princess Dashkova*, trans. and ed. Kyril Fitzlyon
(Durham, NC, 1995)

Dawson, Christopher, ed., *Mission to Asia: Narratives and Letters of the Franciscan
Missionaries in Mongolia and China in the Thirteenth and Fourteenth Centuries
Translated by a Nun of Stanbrook Abbey* (New York, 1966)

*Deiatel'nost' komissii pitaniia russkogo obshchestva okhraneniia narodnogo zdraviia v
1892–1893 gody* (St Petersburg, 1893)

Dikht, Genrikh, *Nastavlenie k uluchsheniiu russkoi pechi* (St Petersburg, 1838)

Dombrovskii, F. V., *Polnyi putevoditel' po Peterburgu i vsem ego okrestnostiam*
(St Petersburg, 1896)

Domostroi: russkii semeinyi ustav, trans. V. V. Kolesov (Moscow, 2005)

Drukovtsov, Sergei, *Povarennye zapiski* (St Petersburg, 1779)

Edwards, Henry Sutherland, *The Russians at Home* (London, 1861)

*The Englishwoman in Russia: Impressions of the Society and Manners of the Russians at
Home. By a lady, ten years resident in that country* (New York, 1855)

Ermolov, A. S., *Nashi neurozhai i prodovol'stvennyi vopros* (St Petersburg, 1909)

Erofeev, Venedikt, *Moscow to the End of the Line*, trans. H. William Tjalsma
(New York, 1980)

Fet, A. A., *Moi vospominaniia, 1848–1889* (Moscow, 1890)

Fletcher, Giles, *Of the Russe Common Wealth; or, Maner of Gouerment of the Russe
Emperour (Commonly Called the Emperour of Moskouia)* (London, 1591)

Fraser, John Foster, *Russia of To-day* (New York, 1915)

G., I., 'Moskva za stolom', *Moskvitianin*, II/8 (1856), pp. 417–58

Godard, Léon, *Pétersbourg et Moscou. Souvenirs du couronnement d'un tsar* (Paris, 1858)

'Govoriat rabotnitsy Rostova: POCHEMU DOMA GOTOVIAT VKUSNEE, CHEM V
STOLOVOI?', *Obshchestvennoe pitanie*, 2 (1933), pp. 10–11

Granville, A. B., *St Petersburgh: A Journal of Travels to and from That Capital*
(London, 1828)

Graves, Samuel Robert, *A Yachting Cruise in the Baltic* (London, 1863)

Haxthausen, August von, *The Russian Empire: Its People, Institutions, and Resources*,
trans. Robert Farie (London, 1856)

Herberstein, Sigismund von, *Zapiski o Moskovii* (Moscow, 2008)

Hunt, Thomas, *The Life of William H. Hunt* (Brattleboro, VT, 1922)

Istoricheskii obzor pravitel'stvennykh meropriiatii po narodonou prodovol'stviiu v Rossii
(St Petersburg, 1892–3)

Ivaniukov, Iv., 'Ocherki provintsial'noi zhizni', *Russkaia mysl'* (August 1895),
pp. 160–77

'Iz istorii bor'by za farsh', *Obshchestvennoe pitanie*, 1 (1933), p. 27

Jesse, Captain, *Notes of a Half-pay in Search of Health; or, Russia, Circassia, and the
Crimea, in 1839–40* (London, 1841)

Johnston, Robert, *Travels through Part of the Russian Empire and the Country of
Poland along the Southern Shores of the Baltic* (New York, 1816)

Kabo, E. *Pitanie russkogo rabochego do i posle voiny* (Moscow, 1926)

'Kapusta', *Trudy Imperatorskogo vol'nogo ekonomicheskogo obshchestva*, III/9 (1859), pp.
347–56

*Kartina Rossii izobrazhaiushchaia istoriiu i geografiiu, khronologicheski, genealogicheski
i statisticheski so vkliucheiem obozreniia o dukhovnoi, voennoi i grazhdanskoi*

ei chastiam, kak v pervobytnom ei sostoianii, tak i v Tsarstvovanie gosudaria imperatora Aleksandra I (Moscow, 1807)

Kniga o vkusnoi i zdorovoi pishche (Moscow, 1945)

Kniga o vkusnoi i zdorovoi pishche (Moscow, 1954)

Kohl, J. G., *Russia* (London, 1844)

Kotzebue, Augustus von, *The Most Remarkable Year in the Life of Augustus von Kotzebue; Containing an Account of His Exile into Siberia, and of the Other Extraordinary Events Which Happened to Him in Russia*, trans. Benjamin Beresford (London, 1802)

'Kukhnoistoricheskie i fililogicheskie iz"iskaniia doktora Pufa, professora vsekh nauk i mnogikh drugikh', *Zapiski dlia khoziaev*, 23–26 (1845), pp. 182–3, 190–91, 198–9, 205–7

'Kvas', *Zhurnal obshchepoleznykh svedenii*, 1 (1847), p. 65

Laksman, 'Ekonomicheskie otvety, kasaiushchiesia do khlebopashestva v lezhashchikh okolo reki Sviri i iuzhnoi chasti Olontsa mestakh', *Trudy imperatorskogo vol'nogo ekonomicheskogo obshchestva*, XIII (1769), pp. 7–43

The Laws of Rus': Tenth to Fifteenth Centuries, trans. and ed. Daniel H. Kaiser (Salt Lake City, UT, 1992)

Levitov, I., *Putevoditel'* (Moscow, 1881)

Levshin, V. A., *Slovar' povarennyi, prispeshnichii, kanditorskii i distillatorskii, soderzhashchii po azbuchnomu poriadku podrobnoe i vernoe nastavlenie k podrobnoe i vernoe nastavlenie k prigotovleniiu vsiakogo roda kushan'ia iz Frantsuzskoi, Nemetskoi, Gollandskoi, Ispanskoi i Angliskoi povarni, pirozhnogo, dessertov, varenii, salatov, vod, essentsii, ratafii, likerov, dvoviiu vodok, i pr.; takzhe k uchrezhdeniiu stola s planami, podach, uslugi i proch. i s prisovokupleniem v osoblivykh paragrafakh polnoi Meshchanskoi povarni i Novoi; ravnym obrazom povaren Avstriiskoi, Berlinskoi, Bogemskoi, Saksonskoi i Ruskoi* (Moscow, 1795–7)

'The Life of Archpriest Avvakum by Himself', in *Medieval Russia's Epics, Chronicles, and Tales*, ed. Serge A. Zenkovsky (New York, 1974)

Londonderry, Marquis of, *Recollections of a Tour in the North of Europe in 1836–1837* (London, 1838)

M., M., *Prakticheskii khoziain, ili kniga vsekh sostoianii, izlagaiushchaia polnoe sobranie noveishikh opytov i otkrytii, sdelannykh izvestnymi v Evrope Agronomami po vsem otrasliam estestvennykh nauk, tekhnogii, zemledel'cheskoi promyshlennosti, sel'skogo khoziaistva, iskustv i proch* (Moscow, 1838)

M., S., 'Novyi chainyi magazin', *Kazanskie gubernskie vedomosti (neoffitsialnye)* (25 January 1860), p. 31

May, J.-B., *Saint-Petersbourg et la Russie en 1829* (Paris, 1830)

Meriwether, Lee, *A Tramp Trip: How to See Europe on 50 Cents a Day* (New York and London, 1886)

Michell, Thomas, *Russian Pictures, Drawn with Pen and Pencil* (London, 1889)

Michie, Alexander, *The Siberian Overland Route from Peking to Petersburg, through the Deserts and Steppes of Mongolia, Tartary, &c.* (London, 1864)

Miège, Guy, *La relation de trois ambassades de monseigneur le Comte de Carlisle, de la part du serenissime tres-puissant Prince Charles II, roy de la Grande Bretagne, vers leurs serenissimes Majestés Alexey Michailovitz Czar & Grand Duc de*

Moscovie, Charles roy de Suede, & Frederic III, Roy de Dannemarc & de Norvege, commencées en l'an 1663 & finies sur la fin de l'an 1664 (Rouen, 1670)

Mikoyan, A. I., 'Za vysoko kul'turnuiu stolovuiu', 1 *Obshchestvennoe pitanie* (1933), p. 2

Mitford, Algernon, *Memories* (London, 1915)

Molokhovets, E[lena], *Prostaia, obshchedostupnaia kukhnia*, 2nd edn (St Petersburg, 1891)

Moor, Henry, *A Visit to Russia in the Autumn of 1862* (London, 1863)

The Muscovite Law Code (Ulozhenie) of 1649, trans. and ed. Richard Hellie (Irvine, CA, 1988)

Nikishova, A. I., *Povarennaia kniga: rukovodstvo domashnego stola* (Tver, 1928)

Novikov, Nikolai, *Drevniaia rossiiskaia vivliofika, ili sobranie drevnostei rossiiskikh, do rossiiskie istoriia, geografii i genealogii kasaiushchikhsia* (St Petersburg, 1775)

'O morozhenom, sherbete; Neschastnye sluchai ot upotrebleniia slivok', *Zhurnal obshchepoleznykh svedenii* (supplement), 21–22, 23–4 (1838), pp. 127–8, 130–31

'O razvedenii zemlianykh iablok', *Ezhemesiachnye sochineniia*, [1] (1758), pp. 378–9

Ob uvelichenii proizvodstva kartofelia (Syktyvkar, 1942)

Obshchestvennoe pitanie v Moskve (Moscow, 1962)

Olearius, Adam, *The Voyages and Travels of the Ambassadors from the Duke of Holstein, to the Great Duke of Muscovy, and the King of Persia*, trans. John Davies (London, 1662)

P., A., *Ruchnaia ekonomicheskaia entsiklopediia* (Moscow, 1835)

Pallas, P. S., *Puteshestvie po raznym provintsiiam Rossiiskoi imperii* (St Petersburg, 1773)

Paul of Aleppo, *The Travels of Macarius, Patriarch of Antioch*, trans. F. C. Belfour (London, 1836)

Pavil'on 'kartofel' i ovoshchi'. Putevoditel' (Moscow, 1939)

Pervaia vseobshchaia perepis' naseleniia Rossiiskoi imperii 1897 goda, vol. VIII (St Petersburg, 1905)

'Peter III's Manifesto Freeing Nobles from Obligatory Service, 1762', *Documents in Russian History*, http://academic.shu.edu/russianhistory, accessed 24 July 2020

Pinkerton, Robert D., *Russia; or, Miscellaneous Observations on the Past and Present State of That Country and Its Inhabitants* (London, 1833)

'Pis'ma k doktoru Pufu', *Zapiski dlia khoziaev*, 27 (1845), pp. 214–15

Polevitskii, N. I., *Domashnee prigotovlenie fruktovykh prokhladitel'nykh napitkov: prigotovlenie meda, bragi, buzy, kvasa, fruktovykh vodichek, gazirovannykh vod, shipovok, siropov, sokov i proch* (Leningrad, 1927)

'Poleznoe izobretenie dlia prodovol'stviia armii, flot i naroda', *Ekonom*, 20 (1849), p. 160

Polnoe prakticheskoe nastavlenie kak pech' khleb obyknovennyi (nasushnyi) (St Petersburg, 1851)

Polnoe sobranie zakonov Rossiiskoi Imperii: Pervoe sobranie, 45 vols (St Petersburg, 1830)

Porter, Robert Ker, *Travelling Sketches in Russia and Sweden, during the Years 1805, 1806, 1807, 1808* (Philadelphia, PA, 1809)

'Priem gostei u Tatar', *Kazanskie Izvestiia* (7 October 1814), pp. 563–4

'Prizhival'shchiki i prizhivalki', *Russkii arkhiv*, 3 (1883), pp. 70–79

Puf, Doktor, [Odoevskii, V. F.,] 'Lektsiia IV', *Zapiski dlia khoziaev*, 4 (1844), pp. 30–31

——, 'Lektsiia V', *Zapiski dlia khoziaev*, 5 (1844), pp. 58–9

——, 'Lektsiia XXXV', *Zapiski dlia khoziaev*, 35 (1844), pp. 278–9

——, 'Vzgliad na morozhenuiu zhivnost' voobshche i na indeek v osobennosti', *Zapiski dlia khoziaev*, 1 (1845), p. 7

Pumpelly, Raphael, *Across America and Asia: Notes of Five Years' Journey around the World and of Residence in Arizona, Japan, and China* (New York, 1870)

Radetskii, I. M., *S.-Peterburgskaia kukhnia, zakliuchaiushchaia v sebe okolo 2,000 razlichnykh kushan'ev i prigotovlenii, s podrobnym ob"iasneniem i risunkami kak prigotovliat' i nakladyvat' na bliuda* (St Petersburg, 1862)

Radishchev, Aleksandr Nikolaevich, *A Journey from St Petersburg to Moscow*, trans. Leo Wiener, ed. Roderick Page Thaler (Cambridge, MA, 1958)

Raikes, Thomas, *A Visit to St Petersburg, in the Winter of 1829–30* (London, 1838)

Reeves, Francis B., *Russia Then and Now, 1892–1917: My Mission to Russia during the Famine of 1891–1892, with Data Bearing upon Russia of To-day* (New York, 1917)

Regensburger, Iosif, 'O razdelenii izvestnoi summy na godovoi prozhitok', *Trudy imperatorskogo vol'nogo ekonomicheskogo obshchestva*, XXI (1772), pp. 117–327

Rego, E., 'Razvedenie shampinionov', *Zemledelcheskaia gazeta* (27 December 1855), p. 409

'Regulations for Holding Assemblies', in *Peter the Great*, ed. William Marshall (London, 1996)

Reinbeck, G., *Travels from St Petersburgh through Moscow, Grodno, Warsaw, Breslaw &c to Germany in the Year 1805* (London, 1807)

Ritchie, Leitch, *A Journey to St Petersburg and Moscow through Courland and Livonia* (London, 1836)

Robinson, Robert, *Black on Red: My 44 Years Inside the Soviet Union* (Washington, DC, 1988)

Roland, Betty, *Caviar for Breakfast* (Melbourne, 1979)

Rudol'f, Ernst, *Zemledel'cheskii kalendar'* (St Petersburg, 1849)

The Russian Primary Chronicle: Laurentian Text, trans. and ed. Samuel Hazzard Cross and Olgerd P. Sherbowitz-Wetzor (Cambridge, MA, 1953)

Russkaia postnaia povarikha, zakliuchaiushchaia v sebe 121 pravilo dlia postnogo stola, sostavlennaia iz mnogoletnikh opytov i nabliudenii russkoi khoziaikoi (Moscow, 1851)

Sala, George Augustus, *A Journey Due North; Being Notes of a Residence in Russia* (Boston, MA, 1858)

Semenev, V. N., *Obshchestvennoe pitanie na perelome* (Moscow, 1932)

Shcherbatov, M. M., 'O nyneshnem v 1787 godu pochti povsemestnom golode v Rossii, o sposobakh onomu pomoch' i vpred predupredit' podobnoe zhe neshchastie', *Chteniia v Imperatorskogo obshchestve istorii i drevnostei rossiiskikh pri moskovskom universitete*, 1 (Jan–Mar 1860), pp. 81–112

——, *On the Corruption of Morals in Russia*, trans. A. Lentin (Cambridge, 1969)

Shreter, 'Opyt domostroitel'stva i planov na ekonomicheskuiu zadachu 1770 i 1771 goda', *Trudy imperatorskogo vol'nogo ekonomicheskogo obshchestva*, XXII (1772), pp. 1–240

Smyth, Charles Piazzi, *Three Cities in Russia* (London, 1862)

Snegirev, I. M., *Ruskie v svoikh poslovitsakh. Razsuzhdeniia i issledovaniia ob otechestvennykh poslovitsakh i pogovorkakh* (Moscow, 1831)

——, 'Vospominaniia I. M. Snegireva', *Russkii arkhiv*, 4 (1866), pp. 513–62

Solzhenitsyn, Alexander, *One Day in the Life of Ivan Denisovich*, trans. Ralph Parker (New York, 1998)

Stepanov, Gerasim, *Noveishii dopolnenie k opytnomu povaru, o prisovokupleniem Aziatskogo stola, ili vostochnogo gastronoma* (Moscow, 1837)

——, *Polnyi kukhmister i konditer, ili Ruskii gastronom, sobrannyi i sostavlennyi iz sobstvennykh opytov i nabliudenii Gerasimom Stepanovym* (Moscow, 1834)

——, *Prodolzhenie k knige: polnyi kukhmister i konditer, ili russkii gastronom* (Moscow, 1835)

'Stolovaia kniga Patriarkha Filareta Nikiticha', *Starina i novizna*, XI (1906), pp. 67–163

Stremoukhov, D. Ch., 'Mysli o vozmozhnosti uluchsheniia Selskogo Khoziaistva v Rossii osnovannye na prirode chelovecheskoi i na drevnikh Rossiiskikh obychaiakh', *Zemledel'cheskii zhurnal*, IX/25 (1829), pp. 3–27

'Sukhari – Krendeli – khlebi', *Zhurnal obshchepoleznykh svedenii*, 23–4 (1837), pp. 218–19

Sumarokov, Pavel, *Progulka po 12-ti guberniiam s istoricheskimi i statisticheskimi zamechaniiami* (St Petersburg, 1839)

Taylor, Bayard, *Travels in Greece and Russia, with an Excursion to Crete* (New York, 1859)

Thayer, Charles W., *Bears in the Caviar* (Philadelphia, PA, 1950)

Thompson, Edward P., *Life in Russia; or, The Discipline of Despotism* (London, 1848)

Tolley, Kemp, *Caviar and Commissars: The Experiences of a U.S. Naval Officer in Stalin's Russia* (Annapolis, MD, 1983)

Tooke, William, *View of the Russian Empire during the Reign of Catharine the Second, and to the Close of the Present Century* (London, 1799)

Turnerelli, Edward Tracy, *Russia on the Borders of Asia. Kazan, the Ancient Capital of the Tartar Khans; with an Account of the Province to Which It Belongs, the Tribes and Races Which Form Its Population, Etc.* (London, 1854)

'Uluchshenie samovarov', *Zhurnal obshchepoleznykh svedenii*, 31 (1837), pp. 281–2

Varlamova, Raida, *Semeinyi magazin sovremennykh usovershenstvovanii k rasprostraneniiu mezhdu vsemi klassami liudei iziashchnego vkusa, poriadka i udobstva v domashnei i obshchestvennoi zhizni* (Moscow, 1856)

Verkhovskaia, O. P., *Kartinki proshlogo. Iz vospominanii detstva* (Moscow, 1913)

Vil'kins, Ivan Iakovlevich, *Sel'skii khoziain XIX veka, ili Polnoe sobranie noveishikh opytov i otkrytii, sdelannykh v Evrope i Severnoi Amerike kak po chasti zemledel'cheskoi promyshlennosti voobshche, tak i po vsem otrasliam estestvennykh nauk i tekhnologii, vkhodiashchim v sostav sel'skoi ekonomii, i vo osobennosti poleznym dlia russikh pomeshchikov i upravliaiushchikh votchinami* (Moscow, 1837)

Vitsen, Nikolaas, *Puteshestvie v Moskoviiu, 1664–1665*, trans. V. G. Trisman (St Petersburg, 1996)

Volzhin, Boris, [Burnashev, Vladimir,] *Derevenskii starosta Miron Ivanov. Narodnaia byl' dlia Russkikh prostoliudinov* (St Petersburg, 1839)

Vsia torgovo-promyshlennaia Rossiia (Kiev, 1913)

Vul'f, Fridrich, 'Prodolzhenie otvertov gospodina Barona fon Vul'fa na zadannye v pervoi chasti ekonomicheskie voprosy', *Trudy imperatorskogo vol'nogo ekonomicheskogo obshchestva*, X (1768), pp. 59–78

Windt, Harry de, *Siberia as It Is* (London, 1892)

Zatsepin, Iv[an Iakovlevich], *O postnoi i skoromnoi pishche v meditsinskom otnoshenii* (Moscow, 1841)

Zenkovsky, Serge A. ed., *Medieval Russia's Epics, Chronicles, and Tales* (New York, 1974)

Secondary Materials

Ageeva, O. G., *Evropeizatsiia russkogo dvora 1700–1796 gg.* (Moscow, 2006)

Alexopoulos, Golfo, *Illness and Inhumanity in Stalin's Gulag* (New Haven, CT, 2017)

Anisimov, Evgenii V., *The Reforms of Peter the Great: Progress through Coercion in Russia*, trans. John T. Alexander (Armonk, NY, 1993)

Antonova, Katherine Pickering, *An Ordinary Marriage: The World of a Gentry Family in Provincial Russia* (New York, 2013)

Artsikhovskii, A. V., 'Pishcha i utvar'', in *Ocherki russkoi kul'tury XIII–XV vekov, Chast' I Material'naia kul'tura* (Moscow, 1968), pp. 297–306

Axenov, Konstantin E., Isolde Brade and Alex G. Papadopoulos, 'Restructuring the Kiosk Trade in St Petersburg: A New Retail Trade Model for the Post-Soviet Period', *GeoJournal*, XLII/4 (1997), pp. 419–32

Badcock, Sarah, *Politics and the People in Revolutionary Russia: A Provincial History* (Cambridge, 2009)

Bailey, Anna L., *Politics under the Influence: Vodka and Public Policy in Putin's Russia* (Ithaca, NY, 2018)

Baker, Helen, 'Monarchy Discredited? Reactions to the Khodynka Coronation Catastrophe of 1896', *Revolutionary Russia*, XVI/1 (2003), pp. 1–46

Berg, Auri C., 'Reform in the Time of Stalin: Nikita Khrushchev and the Fate of the Russian Peasantry' (PhD diss., University of Toronto, 2012)

Berger, Jean Kathryn, 'The Daily Life of the Household in Medieval Novgorod' (PhD diss., University of Minnesota, 1998)

Berman, Danielle, 'When Global Value Chains are Not Global: Case Studies from the Russian Fast-food Industry', *Competition and Change*, XV/4 (2011), pp. 274–95

Bittner, Stephen V., *Whites and Reds: Wine in the Lands of Tsar and Commissar* (New York, 2021)

Borrero, Mauricio, *Hungry Moscow: Scarcity and Urban Society in the Russian Civil War, 1917–1921* (New York, 2003)

Boukhareva, Louiza M., and Marcel Marloie, *Family Urban Agriculture in Russia: Lessons and Prospects* (Cham, 2015)

Bremzen, Anya von, *Mastering the Art of Soviet Cooking: A Memoir of Food and Longing* (New York, 2013)

Brisbane, M. A., N. A. Makarov and E. N. Nosov, eds, *The Archaeology of Medieval Novgorod in Context* (Oxford, 2012)

Caldwell, Melissa L., 'Feeding the Body and Nourishing the Soul', *Food, Culture and Society*, X/1 (2007), pp. 43–71

——, *Not by Bread Alone: Social Support in the New Russia* (Berkeley, CA, 2004)

Cameron, Sarah, *The Hungry Steppe: Famine, Violence, and the Making of Soviet Kazakhstan* (Ithaca, NY, 2018)

——, 'The Kazakh Famine of 1930–33: Current Research and New Directions', *East/West: Journal of Ukrainian Studies*, III/2 (2016), pp. 117–32

Chandler, Andrea, 'Democratization, Social Welfare and Individual Rights in Russia: The Case of Old-age Pensions', *Canadian Slavonic Papers/Revue canadienne des slavistes*, XLIII/4 (2001), pp. 409–35

Christian, David, *'Living Water': Vodka and Russian Society on the Eve of Emancipation* (Oxford, 1990)

——, 'Prohibition in Russia, 1914–1925', *Australian Slavonic and East European Studies*, IX/2 (1995), pp. 89–118

Claiborne, Craig, 'To My Mind, The World's Greatest Dish', *New York Times* (27 December 1976), p. 41

Dunham, Vera S., *In Stalin's Time: Middleclass Values in Soviet Fiction* (Cambridge, 1976)

Dunning, Chester S. L., *Russia's First Civil War: The Time of Troubles and the Founding of the Romanov Dynasty* (University Park, PA, 2001)

Fasmer, Maks, *Etimologicheskii slovar russkogo iazyka* (St Petersburg, 1996)

Filtzer, Donald, and Wendy Z. Goldman, 'Introduction: The Politics of Food and War', in *Hunger and War: Food Provisioning in the Soviet Union during World War II*, eds Wendy Z. Goldman and Donald Filtzer (Bloomington, IN, 2015), pp. 1–43

Fisher, Lynn and Wesley, *The Moscow Gourmet: Dining Out in the Capital of the USSR* (Ann Arbor, MI, 1974)

Fitzpatrick, Sheila, *Everyday Stalinism: Ordinary Life in Extraordinary Times. Soviet Russia in the 1930s* (New York, 1999)

——, *The Russian Revolution*, 4th edn (Oxford, 2017)

——, *Stalin's Peasants: Resistance and Survival in the Russian Village after Collectivization* (New York, 1994)

Fletcher, Nichola, *Caviar: A Global History* (London, 2010)

Fraser, John Foster, *The Real Siberia: Together with an Account of a Dash through Manchuria* (London, 1902)

Friesen, Leonard G., 'Toward a Market Economy: Fruit and Vegetable Production by the Peasants of New Russia, 1850–1900', *Canadian Slavonic Papers*, XL/1–2 (1998), pp. 27–42

Gatrell, Peter, 'Poor Russia, Poor Show: Mobilising a Backward Economy for War, 1914–1917', in *The Economics of World War I*, ed. Stephen Broadberry and Mark Harrison (Cambridge, 2009), pp. 256–9

——, *A Whole Empire Walking: Refugees in Russia during World War I* (Bloomington, IN, 1999)

Gerber, Theodore P., and Michael Hout, 'More Shock Than Therapy: Market Transition, Employment, and Income in Russia, 1991–1995', *American Journal of Sociology*, CIV/1 (1998), pp. 1–50

Gibson, James R., *Feeding the Russian Fur Trade: Provisionment of the Okhotsk Seaboard and the Kamchatka Peninsula* (Madison, WI, 1969)

Glushchenko, I. V., *Obshchepit: Mikoian i sovetskaia kukhnia* (Moscow, 2010)

Goldstein, Darra, 'Gastronomic Reforms under Peter the Great', *Jahrbücher für Geschichte Osteuropas*, XLVIII/4 (2000), pp. 481–510

——, *The Georgian Feast: The Vibrant Culture and Savory Food of the Republic of Georgia* (New York, 1993)

Gor'kovskaia, Z. P., and O. N. Kationov, 'Pishcha russkikh krest'ian Sibiri v povsednevnoi zhizni (period kapitalizma)', in *Kul'turnyi potential Sibiri v dosovetskii period* (Novosibirsk, 1992), pp. 55–67

Gronow, Jukka, *Caviar with Champagne: Common Luxury and the Ideals of the Good Life in Stalin's Russia* (Oxford, 2003)

Hamburg, Gary M., *Russia's Path toward Enlightenment: Faith, Politics, and Reason, 1500–1801* (New Haven, CT, 2016)

Hamilton-Dyer, Sheila, Mark Brisbane and Mark Maltby, 'Fish, Feather, Fur and Forest: Exploitation of Wild Animals in Novgorod and Its Territory', *Quaternary International*, 460 (2017), pp. 97–107

Harshman, Deirdre Ruscitti, 'A Space Called Home: Housing and the Management of the Everyday in Russia, 1890–1935' (PhD diss., University of Illinois at Urbana-Champaign, 2018)

Hartley, Janet M., *Siberia: A History of the People* (New Haven, CT, 2014)

Hasegawa, Tsuyoshi, *The February Revolution, Petrograd, 1917* (Leiden, 2018)

Herlihy, Patricia, *The Alcoholic Empire: Vodka and Politics in Late Imperial Russia* (New York, 2002)

Hudgins, Sharon, 'Raw Liver, Singed Sheep's Head, and Boiled Stomach Pudding: Encounters with Traditional Buriat Cuisine', *Sibirica*, III/2 (2003), pp. 131–52

Hudson, Hugh D., *Peasants, Political Police, and the Early Soviet State: Surveillance and Accommodation under the New Economic Policy* (New York, 2012)

Hughes, Lindsey, '"A Beard is an Unnecessary Burden": Peter I's Laws on Shaving and their Roots in Early Russia', in *Russian Society and Culture and the Long Eighteenth Century: Essays in Honour of Anthony G. Cross*, ed. Roger Bartlett and Lindsey Hughes (Münster, 2004), pp. 21–34

Huhtamaa, Heli, 'Climatic Anomalies, Food Systems, and Subsistence Crises in Medieval Novgorod and Ladoga', *Scandinavian Journal of History*, XL/4 (2015), pp. 562–90

Ioffe, Julia, 'The Borscht Belt: Annals of Gastronomy', *New Yorker*, LXXXVIII/9 (2012)

Jacobs, Adrianne K., 'The Many Flavors of Socialism: Modernity and Tradition in Late Soviet Food Culture, 1965–1985' (PhD diss., University of North Carolina, Chapel Hill, 2015)

——, 'V. V. Pokhlëbkin and the Search for Culinary Roots in Late Soviet Russia', *Cahiers du monde russe*, LII/1–2 (2013), pp. 165–86

Jones, Robert, *Bread upon the Water: The St Petersburg Grain Trade and the Russian Economy, 1703–1811* (Pittsburgh, PA, 2013)

Joravsky, David, *The Lysenko Affair* (Chicago, IL, 1986)

Kahan, Arcadius, 'The Costs of "Westernization" in Russia: The Gentry and the Economy in the Eighteenth Century', *Slavic Review*, XXV (1966), pp. 40–66

Keenan, Paul, *St Petersburg and the Russian Court, 1703–1761* (Houndmills, Basingstoke, 2013)

Kerblay, Basile, L'Évolution de l'alimentation rurale en Russie (1896–1960)', *Annales*, XVII/5 (1962), pp. 885–922

Kivelson, Valerie A., and Ronald Grigor Suny, *Russia's Empires* (New York, 2017)

Kleimola, Ann M., 'The Road to Beloozero: Ivan IV's Reconciliation with the "Devil in a Skirt"', *Russian History*, XLII/1 (2015), pp. 64–81

Kliuchevskii, V. O., *Istoriia russkogo byta* (Moscow, 1995)

Kniaz'kov, S. A., *Golod v drevnei Rossii* (St Petersburg, 1913)

Koenker, Diane P., 'The Taste of Others: Soviet Adventures in Cosmopolitan Cuisines', *Kritika*, XIX/2 (2018), pp. 243–72

Kolchin, B. A., and T. I. Makarova, eds, *Drevniaia Rus': Byt i kultura* (Moscow, 1997)

Kramer, Andrew E., 'Russia's Evolution, as Seen through the Golden Arches', *New York Times* (2 February 2010), p. B3

Lahana, Martha, 'The Usefulness of Bees in Muscovy', *Russian History*, XLV/1 (2018), pp. 29–51

Lakhtikova, Anastasia, 'Professional Women Cooking: Soviet Manuscript Cookbooks, Social Networks, and Identity Building', in *Seasoned Socialism: Gender and Food in Late Soviet Everyday Life*, ed. Anastasia Lakhtikova, Angela Brintlinger and Irina Glushchenko (Bloomington, IN, 2019), pp. 80–109

——, and Angela Brintlinger, 'Introduction: Food, Gender, and the Everyday through the Looking Glass of Socialist Experience', in *Seasoned Socialism: Gender and Food in Late Soviet Everyday Life*, ed. Anastasia Lakhtikova, Angela Brintlinger, and Irina Glushchenko (Bloomington, IN, 2019), pp. 1–30

Lebina, Nataliia, *Passazhiry kolbasnogo poezda. Etiudy k kartine byta rossiiskogo goroda: 1917–1991* (Moscow, 2019)

——, *Sovetskaia povsednevnost': Normy i anomalii ot voennogo kommunizma k bol'shomu stiliu* (Moscow, 2015)

Leonard, Carole, *Agrarian Reform in Russia* (Cambridge, 2011)

Lerman, Zvi, and David Sedik, 'Russian Agriculture and Transition', in *The Oxford Handbook of the Russian Economy*, ed. Michael Alexeev and Shlomo Weber (Oxford, 2013), pp. 514–40

Lewis, J. Patrick, 'Down and Out in Russia: The Pain of Emerging Capitalism', *Business and Society Review*, 87 (1993), pp. 18–22

Lih, Lars T., *Bread and Authority in Russia, 1914–1921* (Berkeley, CA, 1990)

Lincoln, W. Bruce, *Nicholas I, Emperor and Autocrat of All the Russias* (London, 1978)

Lotman, Yuri, and Jelena Pogosjan, *High Society Dinners: Dining in Tsarist Russia*, trans. Marian Schwartz (Totnes, 2014)

Luhn, Alec, 'Shoppers React: Crimea or Cheese?', *The Guardian* (8 August 2014), p. 21

Lyashchenko, Peter I., *History of the National Economy of Russia to the 1917 Revolution*, trans. L. M. Herman (New York, 1970)

McReynolds, Louise, *Russia at Play: Leisure Activities at the End of the Tsarist Era* (Ithaca, NY, 2003)

Madariaga, Isabel de, *Politics and Culture in Eighteenth-century Russia* (London, 1999)

Maltby, Mark, 'From Bovid to Beaver: Mammal Exploitation in Medieval Northwest Russia', in *The Oxford Handbook of Zooarchaeology*, ed. Umberto Albarella et al. (Oxford, 2018), pp. 230–44

Manley, Rebecca, 'Nutritional Dystrophy: The Science and Semantics of Starvation in World War II', in *Hunger and War: Food Provisioning in the Soviet Union during World War II*, eds Wendy Z. Goldman and Donald Filtzer (Bloomington, IN, 2015), pp. 206–64

Markevich, Andrei, 'Russia in the Great War: Mobilisation, Grain, and Revolution', in *The Economics of the Great War: A Centennial Perspective*, ed. Stephen Broadberry and Mark Harrison (London, 2018), pp. 103–8

Masterovoy, Anton, 'Eating Soviet: Food and Culture in the USSR, 1917–1991' (PhD diss., CUNY, 2013)

Meek, James, 'Winter Survival Down to Toil of Villagers', *The Guardian* (19
     September 1998), p. 19
Miller, Chris, 'Gorbachev's Agriculture Agenda: Decollectivization and the Politics
     of Perestroika', *Kritika*, XVII/1 (2016), pp. 95–118
Miller, David, 'Monumental Building as an Indicator of Economic Trends in
     Northern Rus′ in the Late Kievan and Mongol Periods, 1138–1462', *American
     Historical Review*, XCIV/2 (1989), pp. 360–90
Mironov, Boris, 'Do Russians Need Cliotherapia?' *Bylye gody*, XLI-1/3-1 (2016),
     pp. 1003–52
Moon, David, *The Abolition of Serfdom in Russia, 1762–1907* (Harlow, 2001)
——, *The Russian Peasantry, 1600–1930: The World the Peasants Made* (London, 1999)
Nefedov, Sergei, 'The Food Crisis in Petrograd on the Eve of the February Revolution',
     Quaestio Rossica, V/3 (2017), pp. 635–55
Osipovich, Alexander, 'At a Moscow Fair, Selling the Healing Powers of Honey',
     International Herald Tribune (13 September 2006)
Osokina, E. A., *Ierarkhiia potrebleniia. O zhizni liudei v usloviiakh stalinskogo
     snabzheniia. 1928–1935 gg.* (Moscow, 1993)
——, *Our Daily Bread: Socialist Distribution and the Art of Survival in Stalin's Russia,
     1927–1941*, trans. Kate Transchel and Greta Bucher (London, 2001)
Ostrowski, Donald, *Muscovy and the Mongols: Cross-cultural Influences on the Steppe
     Frontier* (Cambridge, 1998)
Parfitt, Tom, 'Russians Find Whey around Sanctions by Copying Cheese', *The Times*
     (London) (6 March 2018), p. 31
Peri, Alexis, *The War Within: Diaries from the Siege of Leningrad* (Cambridge,
     MA, 2017)
Platonov, S. F., *The Time of Troubles: A Historical Study of the Internal Crisis and
     Social Struggle in Sixteenth- and Seventeenth-century Muscovy*, trans. John T.
     Alexander (Lawrence, KA, 1970)
Plokhy, Serhii, *Lost Kingdom: The Quest for Empire and the Making of the Russian
     Nation, from 1470 to the Present* (New York, 2017)
Pokhlebkin, V. V., *Istoriia vodki* (Moscow, 1997)
Pouncy, Carolyn, trans. and ed., *The Domostroi: Rules for Russian Households in the
     Time of Ivan the Terrible* (Ithaca, NY, 1994)
Privalova, T. V., *Byt Rossiiskoi derevni 60-e gody XIX-20-e gody XX v.* (Moscow, 2000)
Rabinovich, M. G., *Ocherki material′noi kul′tury russkogo feodal′nogo goroda*
     (Moscow, 1988)
Raffensperger, Christian, *Reimagining Europe: Kievan Rus′ in the Medieval World*
     (Cambridge, MA, 2012)
Raleigh, Donald J., 'The Russian Civil War, 1917–1922', in *The Cambridge History of
     Russia*, vol. III, ed. Ronald Grigor Suny (Cambridge, 2008), pp. 140–67
Ramirez, Anthony, 'Pepsi Will Be Bartered for Ships and Vodka in Deal with Soviets',
     New York Times (9 April 1990), section A, p. 1
Randolph, John, *The House in the Garden: The Bakunin Family and the Romance of
     Russian Idealism* (Ithaca, NY, 2007)
Reid, Susan E., 'Cold War in the Kitchen: Gender and the De-Stalinization of
     Consumer Taste in the Soviet Union under Khrushchev', *Slavic Review*, LXI/2
     (2002), pp. 211–52

Rock, Stella, 'Russian Piety and Orthodox Culture', in *The Cambridge History of Christianity*, vol. V, ed. Michael Angold (Cambridge, 2006), pp. 251–75

Rodionov, Boris, *Istoriia russkoi vodki: Ot polugara do nashikh dnei* (Moscow, 2012)

Romaniello, Matthew P., *The Elusive Empire: Kazan and the Creation of Russia, 1552–1671* (Madison, WI, 2012)

——, *Enterprising Empires: Russia and Britain in Eighteenth-century Eurasia* (Cambridge, 2019)

——, 'Through the Filter of Tobacco: The Limits of Global Trade in the Early Modern World', *Comparative Studies in Society and History*, XLIX/4 (2007), pp. 914–37

Roosevelt, Priscilla, *Life on the Russian Country Estate: A Social and Cultural History* (New Haven, CT, 1995)

Ruane, Christine, *The Empire's New Clothes: A History of the Russian Fashion Industry, 1700–1917* (New Haven, CT, 2009)

Rybina, E. A., *Arkheologicheskie ocherki istorii novgorodskoi torgovli* (Moscow, 1978)

Saffron, Inga, *Caviar: The Strange History and Uncertain Future of the World's Most Coveted Delicacy* (New York, 2002)

Safronov, F. G., *Russkie na severo-vostoke azii v XVII–seredine XIX v. Upravlenie, sluzhilye liidi, krest'iane, gorodskoe naselenie* (Moscow, 1978)

Scott, Erik R., 'Edible Ethnicity: How Georgian Cuisine Conquered the Soviet Table', *Kritika*, XIII/4 (2012), pp. 831–58

Sedik, David, and Doris Wiesmann, 'Globalization and Food and Nutrition Security in the Russian Federation, Ukraine and Belarus', ESA Working Paper No. 03–04 (May 2003)

Semenova, L. N., *Byt i naselenie Sankt-Peterburga (XVIII vek)* (St Petersburg, 1998)

Shakhov, M., 'O poste', in *Monastyrskaia kukhnia* (Moscow, 1991), pp. 6–9

Shapiro, Margaret, 'Perils of Kiosk Capitalism: Russia's New Entrepreneurs Pay for Permits and Protection', *Washington Post* (28 August 1993)

Shchepkin, V. N., 'Goloda v Rossii. Istoricheskii ocherk', *Istoricheskii vestnik*, VII/6 (1886), pp. 489–521

Shunkov, V. I., *Ocherki po historia kolonizatsii Sibiri v XVII–nachale XVIII vekov* (Moscow, 1946)

Slezkine, Yuri, *Arctic Mirrors: Russia and the Small Peoples of the North* (Ithaca, NY, 1994)

Smith, Alison K., 'Eating Out in Imperial Russia: Class, Nationality, and Dining before the Great Reforms', *Slavic Review*, LXV/4 (2006), pp. 747–68

——, 'From Gruyère to Gatchina: The Meanings of Cheese in Modern Russia', unpublished paper

——, 'Provisioning Kazan': Feeding the Provincial Russian Town', *Russian History*, XXX/4 (2003), pp. 373–401

——, *Recipes for Russia: Food and Nationhood under the Tsars* (DeKalb, IL, 2008)

Smith, Jenny Leigh, 'Empire of Ice Cream: How Life Became Sweeter in the Postwar Soviet Union', in *Food Chains: From Farmyard to Shopping Cart*, ed. Warren Belasco and Roger Horowitz (Philadelphia, PA, 2009), pp. 142–57

Smith, R.E.F., and David Christian, *Bread and Salt: A Social and Economic History of Food and Drink in Russia* (Cambridge, 1984)

Smith-Peter, Susan, 'Sweet Development: The Sugar Beet Industry, Agricultural Societies and Agrarian Transformations in the Russian Empire, 1818–1913', *Cahiers du monde russe*, LVII/1 (2016), pp. 101–24

'Soviet Famines', *Contemporary European History*, XXVII/3 (2018), pp. 432–81

Steinwedel, Charles, 'Sugar as a "Basic Necessity": State Efforts to Supply the Russian Empire's Population in the Early Twentieth Century', in *The Life Cycle of Russian Things: From Fish Guts to Fabergé*, ed. Matthew P. Romaniello, Alison K. Smith and Tricia Starks (London, forthcoming)

Stevens, Carol Belkin, *Russia's Wars of Emergence, 1460–1730* (London, 2007)

——, 'Shabo: Wine and Prosperity on the Russian Steppe', *Kritika*, XIX/2 (2018), pp. 273–304

Sunderland, Willard, 'Catherine's Dilemma: Resettlement and Power in Russia, 1500s–1914', in *Globalising Migration History: The Eurasian Experience (16th–21st centuries)*, ed. Jan and Leo Lucassen (Leiden, 2014), pp. 55–70

Taubman, William, *Khrushchev: The Man and His Era* (New York, 2003)

Tempest, Snejana, 'Stovelore in Russian Folklife', in *Food in Russian History and Culture*, ed. Musya Glants and Joyce Toomre (Bloomington, IN, 1997), pp. 1–14

Thayer, Charles Wheeler, *Bears in the Caviar* (Philadelphia, PA, 1951)

Tolstov, S. P., N. N. Cheboksarov and K. V. Chistov, eds, *Ocherki obshchei etnografiia. Evropeiskaia Chast' SSSR* (Moscow, 1968)

Tsalkin, V. I., *Materialy dlia istorii skotovodstva i okhoty v drevnei rusi* (Moscow, 1956)

Voronina, T. A., 'The Diet of Siberian Peasants on Lenten Days (the 19th Century)', *Archaeology, Ethnology and Anthropology of Eurasia*, XXXIX/4 (2011) pp. 136–41

Vucinich, Alexander, 'Soviet Ethnographic Studies of Cultural Change', *American Anthropologist*, LXII/5 (1960), pp. 867–77

Wegren, Stephen K., and Christel Elvestad, 'Russia's Food Self-sufficiency and Food Security: An Assessment', *Post-Communist Economies*, XXX/5 (2018), pp. 565–87

Wegren, Stephen K., Frode Nilssen and Christel Elvestad, 'The Impact of Russian Food Security Policy on the Performance of the Food System', *Eurasian Geography and Economics*, LVII/6 (2016), pp. 671–99

Wortman, Richard, *Scenarios of Power: Myth and Ceremony in Russian Monarchy from Peter the Great to the Abdication of Nicholas II* (Princeton, NJ, 2006)

Yoder, Audra Jo, 'Tea Time in Romanov Russia: A Cultural History, 1616–1917' (PhD diss., University of North Carolina, Chapel Hill, 2016)

Zajac, Natalia, 'Women between West and East: The Inter-rite Marriages of the Kyivan Rus' Dynasty, ca. 1000–1204' (PhD diss., University of Toronto, 2017)

Zelenin, D. K., *Russkaia etnografiia* (Moscow, 2013)

Zelenin, Il'ia E., 'N. S. Khrushchev's Agrarian Policy and Agriculture in the USSR', *Russian Studies in History*, L/3 (2011), pp. 44–70

Zelnik, Reginald E., 'Wie es Eigentlich Gegessen: Some Curious Thoughts on the Role of Borsch in Russian History', in *For Want of a Horse: Choice and Chance in History*, ed. John M. Merriman (Lexington, MA, 1985)

Acknowledgements

After thinking about it for possibly too long, I really started writing this book sitting in the reading room of the Russian State Library – commonly known as the Leninka after its Soviet-era full name – in the centre of Moscow. I spent my mornings working there, took a lunch break in its fantastic canteen (described in the opening of Chapter One), then walked across Red Square to visit Moscow's other great library, the State Public Historical Library of Russia. After several weeks in Moscow, I moved on to St Petersburg, where I worked at the Russian National Library, again enjoying the mix of easy access to materials and an excellent canteen (someone there is a soup genius). This book would not have been possible without these three libraries. Not only do they have vast collections to access on site but also they have done remarkable work digitizing their materials and making them available more widely.

I am also grateful to a faculty research fellowship from the Jackman Humanities Institute at the University of Toronto. It allowed me a solid six months to work on this book. I must also thank three research assistants who went through dozens of travel accounts looking for references to food: thank you to Maria Dawson, Alex Judge and Sevda Sparks. Thanks also to Felix Cowan for sending me dozens of scans of advertisements from kopek newspapers after a conversation in St Petersburg, and especially to Matt Romaniello and Trish Starks, who read through the entire manuscript looking for errors and making suggestions, and perhaps above all to Emma Davydovna Antselevich, who has been my host and friend in Moscow for the last thirteen years.

Photo Acknowledgements

The author and publishers wish to express their thanks to the below sources of illustrative material and/or permission to reproduce it. Some locations of artworks are also given below, in the interest of brevity:

From K. K. Arsen'ev and F. F. Petrushevskiĭ, eds, *Entsiklopedicheskii slovar*, vol. XXVII (St Petersburg, 1899): pp. 40, 94, 141; from Piotre Artamof, *La Russie historique, monumentale et pittoresque*, vol. I (Paris, 1862): p. 10; from Katerina Avdeeva, *Ruchnaia kniga Russkoi opytnoi khoziaiki, sostavlennaia iz sorokaletnikh opytov i nabliudenii dobroi khoziaiki russkii*, 10th edn (St Petersburg, 1865): pp. 58, 59, 191; from Platon Petrovich Beketov, *Opisanie v litsakh torzhestva* (Moscow, 1810), photos courtesy Getty Research Institute, Los Angeles: p. 154; from George G. Chisholm, *Handbook of Commercial Geography* (London, 1889): p. 75; collection of the author: pp. 63, 261, 266, 272; from Samuel Collins, *The Present State of Russia, in a Letter to a Friend at London* (London, 1671): p. 13; from *Contes de L'isba* (Paris, 1931): p. 111; Davis Center for Russian and Eurasian Studies, Harvard University, Cambridge, MA: p. 146; photo David Fedulov/Unsplash: p. 67; from John Foster Fraser, *Russia of To-day* (New York, 1915): p. 236; Hoover Institution Library & Archives, Stanford, CA: p. 26; Houghton Library, Harvard University, Cambridge, MA: p. 144; from *Illustrated London News*, 30 January 1892: p. 229; iStock.com: pp. 42 (Ihor Smishko), 46 (JackF), 47 (bondarillia), 57 (maxsol7), 106 (Nikolaeva Elena); from E. O. Kabo, *Pitanie russkogo rabochego do i posle voiny* (Moscow, 1926): p. 254; from *Kur'er-kopeika*: pp. 223 (27 February 1911), 224 (*left*, 23 October 1911), 224 (*right*, 24 February 1913); Library of Congress, Prints and Photographs Division, Washington, DC: pp. 25, 27, 55, 86 (Prokudin-Gorskiĭ Collection), 95 (Photochrom Print Collection), 114 (Brumfield Photograph Collection), 166, 185, 211, 212 (Prokudin-Gorskiĭ Collection), 232 (Winokur-Munblit Collection of Russian Empire Postcards), 277 (Brumfield Photograph Collection); McHenry Library, University of California, Santa Cruz: p. 68; from Anastas Mikoian and I. K. Sivolap, eds, *Kniga o vkusnoi i zdorovoi pishche* (Moscow, 1952): pp. 15, 237; National Galleries of Scotland, Edinburgh: p. 8; The New York Public Library: pp. 22, 35, 61, 82, 118, 127, 129, 132, 149, 171, 173, 180, 181, 183, 204, 205, 214; from *Niva*, XXI/44 (1890): p. 18; from Edmund Ollier, *Cassell's Illustrated History of the Russo-Turkish War*, vol. I (London, 1890): p. 16; from Robert Pinkerton, *Russia: Or, Miscellaneous*

Index

Page numbers in *italics* indicate illustrations